KEEPING GOOD COMPANY

KEEPING GOOD COMPANY

A Study of Corporate Governance in Five Countries

Jonathan P. Charkham

CLARENDON PRESS · OXFORD
1994

Oxford University Press, Walton Street, Oxford OX2 6DP

Oxford New York Toronto
Delhi Bombay Calcutta Madras Karachi
Kuala Lumpur Singapore Hong Kong Tokyo
Nairobi Dar es Salaam Cape Town
Melbourne Auckland Madrid

and associated companies in
Berlin Ibadan

Oxford is a trade mark of Oxford University Press

Published in the United States
by Oxford University Press Inc., New York

British Library Cataloguing in Publication Data
Data available

Library of Congress Cataloging in Publication Data
Charkham, Jonathan P.
Keeping good company: a study of corporate governance in five
countries / Jonathan P. Charkham.
p. cm.
Includes bibliographical references.
1. Corporate governance—Case studies. I. Title.
HD2741.C457 1994 93–30539
658.4—dc20
ISBN 0 19 828828 X

1 3 5 7 9 10 8 6 4 2

Typeset by Datix International Limited, Bungay, Suffolk

Printed in Great Britain
on acid-free paper by
Bookcraft (Bath) Ltd., Midsomer Norton, Avon

Preface

THE Bank of England maintains extensive liaison with industrial and commercial companies and is deeply aware of the challenges that confront them. Meeting these challenges is a continual and often daunting task for a company's leadership, and it is essential that they should operate within a framework of corporate governance that is conducive to long-term effectiveness and profitability.

The board of directors is obviously the single most important element in the UK system and the one which most stood in need of attention when my predecessor as Governor, Lord Richardson of Duntisborne, lent his support to the creation of PRO NED (Promotion of Non-Executive Directors). His colleagues, Sir David Walker and Lord Benson, were able to secure the active involvement of the banking and investment communities as well as the Confederation of British Industries and the Institute of Management. The first director of PRO NED, Jonathan Charkham, was a member of the Bank's staff—brought in specially; he gave it a firm foundation and I am glad to see that it flourishes to the present day.

More recently the Bank played a part in the establishment of the Cadbury Committee, whose report has received widespread interest. I am glad to see that the Cadbury Code is reproduced in this book.

During Jonathan Charkham's years with me at the Bank (1985–93), I encouraged him to study various elements of corporate governance. In 1989 the Bank published two of his papers on aspects of the shareholders' role and these reached a wide audience. He also produced for consumption within the Bank a series of papers on the corporate governance systems in other countries, as a means both of understanding more clearly how they really work and also of shedding light on our own practices and assumptions. I encouraged him to expand these papers, as I thought they contained much that would be of value to a wider audience. He used them as the foundation for further studies on which this book is based. I warmly commend it to those who trade with Germany, Japan, France, the USA, and the UK; to those who study or are responsible for the legal framework within which the modern company operates; and to all who care about the success of their national industries in the twenty-first century.

ROBIN KINGSDOWN

Acknowledgements

THE five studies on which this book is based were made in the period 1986–90 and updated in the second half of 1992. Each is based on a wide-ranging series of discussions in each country with members of the industrial, financial, and governmental sectors, undertaken after I had studied relevant literature. So many experts from various walks of life—industry; academia; the professions; the financial world; and government—have helped in the research for this book and its subsequent preparation that it would be impossible to list them all, grateful as I am to them. During my years at PRO NED and the Bank of England I had the advantage of numerous informal discussions with colleagues and with industrialists, lawyers, and academics in many countries; and I have been privileged to serve on both sides of the Atlantic on other committees besides Cadbury. Below I mention only a fraction of my interlocutors, many of whom have given me particular assistance in considering drafts, correcting inaccuracies, and supplying data. I list them by country in the order in which the studies were undertaken and the chapters of the book written. In all cases the position of the interlocutor is the one held at the time the discussion took place.

In regard to *Germany* especial thanks go to Sir Christopher Mallaby KCMG, HM Ambassador to Germany (1988–93), and his colleagues C. A. Munro, D. S. Broucher, and D. J. Peate, and also to Professor Dr Theodor Baums (Universität Osnabrück), Herr Gottfried Bruder (Commerzbank, London), and Frau Ellen Schneider-Lenné (Deutsche Bank). I am also particularly grateful to:

Dr Michael Auge (Bank für Gemeinwirtschaft AG)
Dr Hartmut Bechtold (DGB Düsseldorf)
Herr Borucki (Economics Ministry, Bonn)
Mr John Craven (Deutsche Bank, Frankfurt, and Morgan Grenfell, London)
Dr Walter Damm (Sal. Oppenheim jr & Cie KGaA, Cologne)
Herr Rolf Derikartz (JCB, Cologne)
Dr Hanns Arnulf Engels (Bundesaufsichtsamt für das Kreditwesen, Berlin)
H.-G. Grunewild and Dr W. W. Muller (Henkel)
Dr Gurgens (German Trade Union Headquarters)
Dr Hermann H. Hollmann (Ford, Cologne)
Herr Kurt Kasch (Deutsche Bank AG, Berlin)
Dr Knauss (Finance Ministry, Bonn)

Herr Norbert Kühne (Ford, Cologne)

Herr Frightjof Leufen (SMS)

Professor Dr Heinz Markmann (Geschaftsführer des Wirtschafts und Sozialwissenschaftlichen Instituts des Deutschen Gerwerkschaftsbundes GmbH)

Herr Rudolf Panowitz (Landeszentralbank in Hessen, Frankfurt)

Dr Detler Rahmsdorff (Landeszentralbank in Hessen, Frankfurt)

Dietrich Ruh (E. Merck, Darmstadt)

Dr Reudiger von Rosen (Federation of German Stock Exchanges AG, Frankfurt)

Herr Peter Weisner (BDI, Cologne)

Herr M. Weltmeyer (Bundeskartellamt, Berlin)

In *Japan* especial thanks go to the UK Ambassadors to Tokyo—Sir Hugh Cortazzi GCMG (1980–4), Sir John Whitehead GCMG (1986–92), and Sir John Boyd KCMG (1992–)—and to the many members of their staff who helped me, especially David Raikes and John Kirby, both colleagues from the Bank of England on secondment. I am also particularly grateful to:

Dr James Abegglen (President, Asia Advisory Service)

Professor Ronald Dore (Imperial College School of Management, London)

Miss Haruko Fukuda (Director of Nikko Europe plc, London)

Mr Iwane Furuya (Senior Executive Managing Director, Mitsukoshi Ltd.)

Mr Akira Harada (Senior Adviser, Matsushita Electric Industrial Company Ltd.)

Mr Eiichi Hasegawa (Deputy Director, Business Behaviour Division, Ministry of International Trade and Industry)

Mr Anthony G. W. Hodge (Chief Manager for Japan, National Westminster Bank, Tokyo)

Mr Hideo Ishihara (President, IBJ Leasing)

Mr Asahiko Isobe (Board Director and General Manager of Hitachi)

Mr Kevin F. Jones (Principal, McKinsey & Company, Inc.)

Mr Ken Kakurai (Hitachi Maxell Ltd.)

Mr Yogo Kimura (Hamada and Matsumoto)

Mr Shinobu Kobayashi (Bank of Japan, Kyoto)

Mr Yukiharu Kodama (former MITI Vice-Minister)

Mr Toru Kusukawa (Chairman, Fuji Research Institute)

Mr Rei Masunaga (Head of Foreign Department, Bank of Japan, Tokyo)

Mr Jiro Mayekawa (President of Teijin Seiki Company Ltd.)

Mr Akio Mikuni (President, Mikuni & Co. Ltd.)

Mr Yuzaburo Mogi (Managing Director, Kikkoman Corporation)

Mr Shigenobu Nagamori (President and Chairman of the Board, Nippon Densan Corporation, Kyoto)

Mr Kazuo Nukazawa (Managing Director, Keidanren)

Mr Shijuro Ogata (Deputy Governor, Japan Development Bank, Tokyo)

Mr Takeshi Ohta (Vice-Chairman, Daiwa Bank)

Mr Sadao Okano (Vice-President, Toshiba Corporation Principal Office)

Mr Mitsuya Okubo (Active Auditor, Long-Term Credit Bank)

Mr Ariyoshi Okumura (Managing Director and Chief Financial Economist, The Industrial Bank of Japan)

Mr Paul J. Penrose (Managing Director, KPMG Marwick Minato)
Mr Shoichi Saba (Adviser to the Board, Toshiba Corporation)
Mr Kuneo Seiki (Managing Director, Industrial Bank of Japan)
Mr Hideo Suetsugu (President, International Digital Communications)
Mr Aki Sugawara (Auditor, NYK Line)
Mr Shigeo Takayama (President, Hakuto Company Ltd.)
Mr Osamu Toba (President, Morgan Trust Bank Ltd.)
Viscount Trenchard (Kleinwort Benson International Inc.)
Mr Kosaku Ujihara (Chief Representative in Japan, Baring Brothers)
Mr Shigeru Umeda (Managing Director, Fujisawa Pharmaceutical Co.)
Mr Shigeru Watanabe and Mr Isao Yamamoto (Nomura Research Institute)
Dr K. Yamazaki (Deputy Chairman, Board of Counsellors) and Miss Y. Okina
(Senior Economist, Japan Research Institute)
Mr Shiro Yoshikawa (Chairman, Fujitsu General Ltd.)

In regard to *France* especial thanks go to Mme Hélène Ploix (Directeur Général
Adjoint, Caisse des Dépots et Consignations). I am also particularly grateful to:

Dominique Bazy (Département des Investissements Sécrétariat Générale, UAP)
Alain Benlezar (Secrétaire Confédéral de Confédération Française Démocratique du
Travail)
François Boucher (Direction Générale, Carrefour)
Barnard Cambournac and M. de Lestang (Chambre de Commerce et d'Industrie de
Paris)
Herve de Carmoy (Société Générale de Belgique)
Dominique Chatillon (Président Directeur Général, Campagnie La Henin)
Christopher Crabbie (Economic Counsellor at the British Embassy in Paris) and his
colleagues
François Didier (Senior Vice-President, corporate strategy of Elf Aquitaine)
Dupont-Fauville (Président du Directoire Banque de Neuflize)
Jean Huet (UK General Manager, Société Générale London branch)
Georges-Yves Kervern (Executive Vice-President of UAP)
Pierre Lacanière and M. Bonjet (James Capel)
Yann de Lestang (Directeur Adjoint, Chambre de Commerce et D'Industrie de Paris)
M. Leveque (a former PDG of Crédit Lyonnais)
Philippe de Margerie (Pompes Funebres Générale)
Gérard de la Martinière (AXA)
Christian Ménard (Chief Executive, Crédit Lyonnais Securities)
Paul Mentre (Chairman of Analyse des Strategies Industrielles et Energetiques
(ASIE))
André Mercier (President Directeur Général de la Société La Radiotechnique)
Alain Minc (Compagnie Européennes Réunies)
Alain Monod-Broca (Directeur Général Adjoint of SICOVAM)
Sir Peter Petrie (Adviser to the Governor, Bank of England)
Ambroise Roux (On the board of many companies)
Christian Stoffaes (Deputy Administrator ASIE and Executive Managing Director,
Strategy EDF)

Sir Anthony Tennant (Chairman of Guinness plc)

My involvement in committees in the *USA* has meant that I have enjoyed enormous help and guidance generously given. Of the very many concerned I am particularly indebted to:

Mr H. Brewster Atwater, jun. (Chairman and chief Executive Officer of the Board of General Mills and Chairman of the Business Roundtable)

Professor Bernard Black (Professor of Law, Columbia University)

Dr Carolyn Brancato (Director, Riverside Economic Research and Executive Director, Columbia Institutional Investor Project)

Mr John Charlton (Vice-President, Chase Manhattan Bank, New York)

Mr E. C. Courtney (Minister for Public Affairs, US Embassy, London)

Mr Stephen M. Davis (Director of Investor Responsibility Research Center, Inc.)

Mr Michael Jacobs (Director of Corporate Finance at the US Treasury Department in the first two years of the Bush Administration, 1989–90, then Director of Corporate Finance, Kurt Salmon Associates)

Mr Garnett Keith (Vice-Chairman, Prudential Insurance Company of America)

Mr Martin Lipton (Wachtell, Lipton, Rosen, and Katz)

Mr Bevis Longstreth (Debevoise and Plimpton)

Professor Louis Lowenstein (Columbia University School of Law)

Mrs Patricia A. MacLagan (Chief Executive of McLagan International)

Mr Ira Millstein (Senior Partner of Weil, Gotshal, and Manges and Chairman of the Board of Advisers, Columbia University Center for Law)

Mr R. A. G. Monks (President, Institutional Shareholder Partners, Inc.)

Mr John M. Nash (President, National Association of Corporate Directors)

Ms Linda Quinn (Director of Corporate Finance, Securities and Exchange Commission)

Mr A. A. Sommer, jun. (Attorney-at-Law, Morgan Lewis and Bockius)

Ms Sarah A. B. Teslik (Executive Director, Council of Institutional Investors)

Many leaders of *UK* industry helped in the preparation of this section by advice, comment, and information. Many experts also gave invaluable assistance with various drafts, especially:

Sir Adrian Cadbury (Chairman, Cadbury Committee)

Professor Julian Franks (London Business School)

Mr Michael Goold (Ashridge Strategic Management Centre)

Sir David Walker (Vice-Chairman, Lloyds Bank)

I am similarly indebted to many colleagues from the Bank of England, particularly Ian Plenderleith, Brian Quinn, and Michael Smith.

To my old friend, Percy R. Levy MBE, go grateful thanks for the title.

List of Contents

List of Figures

List of Tables

List of Abbreviations

AG	Aktiengesellschaft
AGM	Annual General Meeting
AMEX	American Stock Exchange
BDI	Federation of German Industries
CB	Conference Board
CBI	Confederation of British Industry
CBV	Conseil des Bourses de Valeurs
CEO	Chief Executive Officer
COB	Commission des Opirations de Bourse
COCOM	The International Organization that supervises certain types of Western Trade with Communist countries
CSO	Central Statistical Office
DGU	Directeur Général Unique
DSVR	Deposited Shares Voting Rights
EGM	Extraordinary General Meeting
ERISA	Employee Retirement Income Security Act
FIBV	Fédération Internationale des Bourses de Valeurs
FMDA	Fauchier-Magnan-Durant des Aulnois
GM	Geregelter Markt
GmbH	Gesellschaft mit beschrankter Haftung
IBIS	Integrated Stock Exchange Trading and Information System (a trading system for securities in Germany)
JSAA	Japanese Statutory Auditors Association
KPMG	KPMG Peat Marwick (Chartered Accountants)
LBO	Leveraged Buy-Out
MBI	Management Buy-In
MBO	Management Buy-Out
MITI	Ministry of International Trade and Industry
MoF	Ministry of Finance
NASDAQ	National Association of Securities Dealers Automated Quotations (a screen based trading system)
NYSE	New York Stock Exchange
PDG	Président Directeur Général
PE	Price Earnings
PLC	Public Limited Company

PRO NED	Promotion of Non-Executive Directors (a not-for-profit organization set up to encourage industry to appoint non-executive directors)
RINGI	A process for decision making in which the originating document starts at lower levels in an organization and moves upwards through the hierarchy gathering improvements on the way.
RSA	Royal Society of Arts
SA	Sociétés anonymes
SAR (in UK)	Substantial Acquisitions Rule(s)
SAR (in USA)	Stock Appreciation Rights
SARL	Société à responsibilité limiteé
SEC	Securities and Exchange Commission
SICOVAM	Société Interprofessionelle pour la Compensation des Valeurs Mobilières
TOP	Takeover Panel
TPI	Titre au Porteur Identifiable (indentifiable bearer shares)

1

INTRODUCTION

The way business is run matters to us all, wherever we live. We need the goods and services it produces, the employment it provides. The wealth it creates is the source of help for the sick and needy, of education for youth, and dignity for old age. Its prosperity nourishes the spirit of mankind. This book is about the system by which companies are directed and controlled that operate in five countries, Germany, Japan, France, the USA, and the UK; the ugly but popular name for these systems is corporate governance. The book's aim is to shed light on the underlying principles and the way in which each system conforms to them.

The subject of corporate governance has attracted increasing attention on both sides of the Atlantic in recent years—for good reasons. Every country wants the firms that operate within its borders to flourish and grow in such a way as to provide employment, wealth, and satisfaction, not only to improve standards of living materially but also to enhance social cohesion. These aspirations cannot be met unless those firms are competitive internationally in a sustained way, and it is this medium- and long-term perspective that makes good corporate governance so vital.

The careful study of systems of corporate governance is important at the present time because the world of the next century will be even more competitive than it is now as the economies of the Far East gather speed and the former Communist states enter the fray. Countries will need to take a long hard look at the way other systems work and keep their own under review; to tolerate a poor system is to impose upon oneself an unnecessary competitive handicap. No nation be it ever so powerful can afford to luxuriate in the evanescent success of its own system, without regard to the progress of others. No system, however, can be understood without looking first at the salient features of the particular society in which it developed. Everyone is to some extent imprisoned by their history, social, political, and economic. The way we think and the assumptions we bring to bear are not the product of an emotional spasm but the consequence of a long historical development which touches us throughout our lives without our understanding it. Only when we strike our shins on some iron protrusion of another system does the pain make us realize why we were so blind to it and why our imagination did not even contemplate the possibility of its existence. So each of the five studies begins with an account of the historical assumptions and features which bear most on the particular system of corporate governance, that is to say, on the exercise of power within it.

Of course, systems of governance are not all that matters, but two factors one might have thought vital—the size of the home market and natural resources—prove not to be so: many of the world's biggest companies—Nestlé, Glaxo, Shell, Unilever, Toyota, Volkswagen—do not have large home markets (in international terms). Japan, Singapore, and Hong Kong have no natural resources but their people. For market economies to function effectively, however, government must provide what government alone can do in regard to education, the infrastructure, and macro-economic management. These may individually or collectively be more important than systems of corporate governance. It is nevertheless observable that in all circumstances the effectiveness of corporate governance is a factor in the tendency of companies to survive and prosper or falter and fail.

We cannot escape the conclusion that government has an important role, because in corporate governance, as in other spheres, it is the only power in any land which can strike a balance between the conflicting wishes of competing interests. Furthermore, the framework within which these interests compete is one of governments' own making. Everywhere the company or corporation is a creature of statute not nature, designed to encourage the agglomeration and continuity of power that the sophistication of modern economies requires. Such a concentration of resources, however beneficial in intention, inevitably leads to effects on those inside and outside an individual corporation. It is not government's duty to double-guess individual commercial decisions—but to ensure as best it can that the structure it creates for companies contains checks and balances that are effective in resolving the tensions between differing legitimate claims.

The development of the modern corporation has placed enormous power in the hands of the leadership: some great multinational groups like Exxon or Mitsui are richer than some sovereign states. Some are run by self-perpetuating oligarchies, others by dictators. The best are accountable and responsible, but the corrupting effect of power is as manifest in the economic sphere as in the political. Across the bleak economic landscape have straggled in recent years the tattered remnants of once proud companies led towards defeat by a charismatic chairman cum chief executive with a weak board.

Prosperity is sometimes said to rest wholly on people, in the sense that businesses are competently led and that the system of governance is of secondary importance. But the main point of a good system is to give power to those best able to use it, and to remove it if they use it poorly or evilly. There are numerous examples of firms failing under leaders left too long in power—however agreeable they were. There are also numerous examples of companies being saved by a change of leadership: a good system of governance is one which produces timely though not precipitate action. A system of government and a system of corporate governance have this in common, that they are concerned with checks and balances on the exercise of power and with its peaceful transfer. To require a take-over to change a CEO is like needing a revolution or foreign conquest to change a government.

We shall encounter, for instance, CEO dominance in some countries, non-functioning boards in others. We shall meet the might of the markets and the self-interest of those who profit from them as well as the immodesty of some executive pay. Systems of corporate governance touch on all these issues, and we shall find that beneath the cool and sometimes abstruse language of corporate governance lurks the reality of power. Those who discuss the subject invariably 'talk their own book', whether they be CEOs, investment analysts, stockbrokers, institutional shareholders, government officials, or even academics. Academics come closer to being disinterested observers than anyone else, but even they have livings to earn and names to make for themselves. There are few altruists around the business world, however high minded or public spirited commentators may seem.

Even so, modern business is the heir not only to the piratical merchant adventurers and the self-protecting guilds of craftsmen of the Middle Ages, but also to the constructors of the great cathedrals, who began what they knew they would not live to see completed. In their time they were able to harness a greater proportion of the available resources than we can in ours (except perhaps to wage war). There is no short-termism about the spire of Salisbury or the nave of Notre-Dame.

As we look at corporate governance systems today we shall see plenty of evidence that the men and women in business are not dedicated just to getting the most for the least personal effort. Many are by nature and instinct builders who invest themselves in their enterprises and may well in some cases continue to do so long after their economic needs have been satisfied. The better the system of corporate governance the better chance there is of all employees of the corporation being able and inspired to give of their best—which is what they, their firm, and their country want and need.

Even so, when people reach high places the borderline between dedication and power-lust may over time become blurred. To wield authority well and wisely in any sphere requires a balance between confidence and humility. Too much of the one produces dictatorship; too much of the other vacillation. It is the aim of good systems of corporate governance to help company leadership maintain this balance.

Many who read this book in the United Kingdom will be familiar with the report produced in 1992 by the Committee on the Financial Aspects of Corporate Governance (the Cadbury Committee, of which I was a member). The committee stated succinctly the two basic principles which underlie corporate governance in the UK: 'They [i.e. the managers] must be free to drive their companies forward but exercise that freedom within a framework of effective accountability.' These fundamental principles are common to all countries. The following chapters show the various ways in which they are applied (or not) in each country. In doing so they traverse Cadbury country—and go beyond it to consider broader issues of corporate govern- ance which lay outside the committee's terms of reference.

The book is laid out in seven chapters. Chapter 1 is this Introduction. Chapters 2, 3, 4, 5, and 6 describe successively Germany, Japan, France, the USA, and the UK. Chapter 7 considers which system is best. The chapters on each country start with a brief account of the salient features of the society in which each corporate governance system is based and of which it forms an important part. There follows in each a description of the formal framework and the way the system works; each concludes with a statement of current issues and tendencies, where these can be discerned.

Special points of interest are:

- The 'networking' nature of the German and Japanese systems in their different ways and the important role of the banks in both.
- The co-determination system in Germany.
- The limited role of Japanese boards.
- The unique choice of system in France.
- The 'adversarial' nature of the US and UK systems and the importance of the CEO (in contrast to more collegiate systems).
- The role of take-overs in corporate governance and the present and potential role of shareholders in the UK and USA.

My intention is to give readers a clear understanding of the broad issues, not to burden them with masses of detail—which would require a book of such great length and complexity that the real issues might be obscured. Footnotes have been kept to a minimum and references limited for the sake of simplicity. The books I considered during the studies and which contain much valuable material for the specialist are listed at the end. There is now such a great stream of material on every aspect of corporate governance that it is difficult not to be swept away by it: by the time this book is published some developments will have occurred to render some detail obsolete. The two principles identified by the Cadbury Committee endure, and provide a framework to which all the main aspects of corporate governance relate.

2 GERMANY

i. Introduction

To understand the system—corporate governance—by which companies are run in Germany as in any country means studying both its structure and its dynamics, that is to say, not just the legal framework and institutions but also personal relationships. Looking at the formal framework tells only a fraction of the story: the attitudes people have and their patterns of behaviour are just as important. To attempt to describe these, however, means leaving behind the comfortable clarity of the law and making an excursion into the misty world of unmeasurable generalizations. The people of Germany are as varied and diverse in character as those of any other nation, so any generalization is bound to be more true of some than others. The reason why it is worth risking generalizations at all is to show that the transplanting of formal structures will not necessarily produce identical patterns of behaviour. German institutions work the way they do because their composition itself reflects a certain mode of thought—which is also reflected in the way people work within them. Generalized observations are by definition imprecise, but they may nevertheless be true enough to matter.[1]

ii. Background

Conflict & Co-operation

If there were a spectrum with 'confrontation' at one end and 'co-operation' at the other, we would confidently place German attitudes and behaviour far closer to the 'co-operation' end than, say, those of the British or

[1] They are often made (which does not of course justify their content)—and not just by British authors. Yoshimichi Yamashita, for instance, in writing about Japanese management in 1992, said, among other interesting remarks: 'The Japanese executive approaches management intuitively rather than rationally, while the Western executive is too rational' (*Directors and Boards*, 17:1 (Fall 1992), 25). He is President of Arthur D. Little, Inc.

Americans. In the economic sphere the Germans have never been obsessed by the idea that their economy will work best if unrestricted competition is studiously enforced: cartels existed in the nineteenth century. There is competition between companies, of course, but very often co-operation between them at the same time (not in price-fixing but in, say, jointly producing certain common components). The adversarial approach does not commend itself as the best way of reaching conclusions—even though Germans are doughty fighters. A more co-operative approach facilitates taking a long perspective in thinking about things and people and lowers concern about potential conflicts of interest by trusting people to use sensitive information in an appropriate way and not improperly. If one cherishes a relationship one does not betray it.

It is worth considering for a moment why there should be so marked an emphasis on co-operation and long-term thinking. Does it reflect in some way Germany's geographical position? The land mass of Central Europe occupied for centuries by German-speaking people has no clearly defined natural boundaries in the West and East other than rivers, and the consequential restlessness goes back beyond and through Roman times up to our own day. The first draft of this paper was written when the current German state was still divided into the Federal German Republic and the Democratic German Republic: by the time it was revised old Yugoslavia was in bitter turmoil and Czechoslovakia splitting asunder. This political restlessness with its varying inward and outward pressures and the contrasting tendencies of centralization and fragmentation mean that in everyone's mind there are echoes of changing political boundaries and war. There are those who believe that Louis XIV's seizure of Strasburg and devastation of the Palatinate left scars as yet unhealed.

Was it a reaction to this history of central Europe so punctuated by invasion and destruction that caused the Germans to attach much importance to co-operation and to good order? Certain attitudes have clear historical causes. Hyper-inflation so disrupted this order in every aspect of life that the fear of it has been a dominant feature of the German consensus since 1945. It has given the Bundesbank, which enjoys a high degree of independence from the state by virtue of its constitutional position, a firm base of moral unity in pursuing a consistent anti-inflationary policy.

Much of the modern German business framework has clearly discernible historical origins. Compulsory schooling had been introduced in Prussia by Frederick the Great. The importance of the banking system as a source of finance for industry relative to the stockmarket reflects the later development of a centralized German state. Welfare legislation, which others developed, started in Bismarck's day and contained a streak of idealism which some might label 'Socialist' except that it owes nothing to Marxist economics. The 1991 Annual Report of the Federation of German Stock Exchanges refers to the 'Social market economy model', which is a direct descendant of those early days. Another title might be co-operative managerial capitalism. Whatever the name, it is certainly a special type of market economy.

It would be interesting to know how much attitudes and behaviour are affected by having a written constitution and legal code. I found the law mentioned more often than it is in the UK and in a different way than in the USA. There did not seem to be evidence of as much recourse to litigation in contract and tort as there might be in the latter, but there were many applications to the courts in administrative matters. To take an example: employees can take an employer to court for breaches of the laws which cover works councils. Many, perhaps most, civil servants are trained as lawyers; lawyers often switch into industry. Recourse to the courts or other kinds of administrative tribunal appears to be increasing in industrial and administrative contexts.

Social Obligation

The sense of co-operation is also evident in the social sphere. Although individual Germans or their organizations are as adept at pursuing self-interest as anyone else, this pursuit may be constrained by a genuine sense of obligation to the community. The assumption behind co-operation, for example, is that it will produce a general benefit for the community as a whole. The grounds on which a commercial decision is taken may not relate narrowly to the company's immediate interests: there was, for instance, a case where the board would not permit management to use the insurance money from a burnt-down plant to enhance production elsewhere. They argued successfully that economic criteria came second to social duty and the company was obligated to the community in which the factory had stood. Again, firms often train too many people not simply to cover potential wastage but as a conscious attempt to produce more well-trained people for the country.

This sense of co-operation and social obligation sits well with an approach both to planning and education which seems generally geared to the longer term. German industrial managers, members of management boards and of the supervisory tier, are alike in this respect. Bankers also seem to think in the long term and not to expect too much too soon. It would be tempting to describe such attitudes as either the cause or the effect of the limited influence the capital markets have on German industrial behaviour:

certainly no one wants quarterly accounts, which are felt to emphasize the short term far too much. Even annual reports and accounts are as much concerned with the narrative as the figures: as the interest is in the longer term, figures (which are only a snapshot of the past) are by themselves an inadequate indication of the future. The relative unimportance of the capital market may have quite separate economic causes, but the attitude of the banks, through which a high proportion of savings was and is channelled, does directly reflect the prevailing ethos: companies and their shareholders think likewise.

Education

This emphasis on social obligation and a long time scale is also consistent with the Germans setting great store by education and devoting much time to it (and starting working careers later). Formal qualifications are much valued as marks of earned distinction by which people can be classified. They have helped to take much of the importance away from the class system by strengthening the meritocracy—a process assisted by Germany only having a single school system. Germans do not feel that this investment of time and money in acquiring a sound education and first-rate professional and technical knowledge automatically implies a career in banking or the civil service; on the contrary, many of the most talented go into commerce and industry. German industry enjoys the benefit of large numbers of well-trained recruits at various levels and spends heavily on improving, completing, and updating their training. Every year about 700,000 young people start their apprenticeship, which is a combination of on the job training and theoretical instruction at school lasting for about three years, thus producing skilled workers for trade and industry (*Facharbeiter*).

The German educational system works closely with industry and has never undervalued—much less despised—it. In this it reflects the prevalent attitude of esteem towards industry. It is socially not just acceptable but really well considered: the children of successful entrepreneurs are often proud to follow their fathers and keep the business in the family.

The Status of Industry

The following table reflects how a number of German and British managers themselves ranked the status of twenty-five activities. It is drawn from research and quoted by Shell UK Ltd. in a paper called 'Management Matters' published in 1992. (The UK is used for the purposes of comparison; it would be interesting to know whether the USA, Japan, or France would be closer to the German view.)

German ranking	British ranking

TOP FIVE

Health-related professions	Banking and brokerage
Manufacturing management	Journalism and interpretation
Mechanical engineering	Marketing and promotion
Legal and finance	Health-related professions
Civil engineering	Entertainment and leisure

BOTTOM FIVE

Entertainment and leisure	Civil engineering
Forestry, fisheries, and farming	Manufacturing management
Journalism and interpretation	Teaching and education
Real estate and property	Mechanical engineering
Mining and quarrying	Local government

The Purpose of Companies

These attitudes are underlined in Article 14(2) of the German constitution, which states 'Property imposes duties. Its use should also serve the public weal.' This should not be read as an echo of Socialism but as a background to the legislation, serving much the same purpose as the preamble to a British statute. Against such a background it is not surprising to find a consensus in Germany that the purpose of companies is to deliver to the community the goods and services it needs on a continuing basis. This is significant in two ways. First, that there is no divergence between sectors of society about the purpose of companies, and secondly, that profit, whilst important, is not the be all and end all (which it is, for instance, to the financial sector in some other countries). Shareholders' immediate values are not important—though of course, consistently poor profits and a depressed share price would reflect on the competence of management. Shareholders are one set of stakeholders among several, and German management thinks of its customers and employees first. This orientation and consensus matter, for they underline so much of the German approach to corporate governance.

Ellen Schneider-Lenné, a member of the management board of Deutsche Bank, made the point as follows in an article in the *Oxford Review of Economic Policy* (Autumn 1992): 'The objectives of German companies however do not stop at maximisation of the return on investment. Their philosophy is based on "The concept of the interest of the company as a whole", a key concept of German corporate culture.' She enlarged on this theme in her 1992 Stockton Lecture, quoting H. Abs, whom she described as 'The grand old man of Deutsche Bank': 'Profit is as necessary as the air we breathe but it would be terrible if we worked only to make a profit, just as it would be terrible if we lived only to breathe.'

Reunification

After reunification the Eastern Länder were brought within the scope of the existing West German laws on corporate governance. By 1992, despite the best efforts of the Treuhand, it had appeared that there were not many enterprises left there to which to apply them, as most of the old companies were no longer viable and even the best had lost their markets in the East. Companies already operating in the former West German Länder, both domestic and foreign, were buying various enterprises, but the cost of doing so (because of redundancy obligations in very overmanned businesses and the uncertainty of legal title to the premises) often made it easier to start from scratch. There were many start-ups, a high proportion of which will probably fail, as the spirit of the market economy had been choked to death and people found it hard to adapt to it after a lifetime under Communism 'working the system'. Medium-size businesses—so crucial in the Western Länder—had nearly all been absorbed in 1972 into state conglomerates, and it was proving difficult to dismember them.

The cost of rebuilding the infrastructure and industry in the Eastern Länder, plus the transfer payments needed to keep the population up to a reasonable standard of living during a period of high unemployment, not only imposed political strains (what we call the Eastern Länder were once the central provinces), but also economic ones, which were being felt by all Germans in one way or another, and which had repercussions across Europe. The corporate governance system was finding itself under pressure as a consequence (from wage claims, resistance to shortening of hours, etc.). Even the unions were in a dilemma. They wanted parity of pay to stop the drift of the ablest to the West, but if this were to precede improvements in productivity, it would price people out of the market, especially as Czech competition was severe because wages were lower there.

Although much of the money pouring into the Eastern Länder (said to be DM 150–200 billion per annum), went through the state in one way or another, the banking system was playing a key role, particularly in helping to get small businesses off the ground. The big banks expanded their network eastwards rapidly (sometimes reoccupying premises they had owned years ago). Their task was immense. German banks have always had good contacts with young businesses—perhaps three discussions in depth annually as well as normal meetings. But the Eastern businesses needed far more help than that—often lengthy monthly sessions. It was costly for the banks, and it says much for their long-term vision and their staff resources that they were willing and able to do it. When prosperity returns to the Eastern Länder in due course, as it assuredly will, and comments are made about the influence of the banks, it will be as well to remember their contribution at a crucial time, which is wholly consistent with the part German banks have long played.

iii. Corporate Governance at Work

Industrial Relations

Although of course good industrial relations are essential for the long-term well-being of a company and of all the employees in it, paragraphs on this subject would not be prominent in works on corporate governance systems in most countries, or at best would be regarded as peripheral. In Germany, however, good industrial relations are much nearer centre stage and it is appropriate to start with them, taking in sequence unions, works councils, and company boards.

Unions

Germany has a simple union structure, introduced by the UK after the War and based on industry not craft. The consultative arrangements operate harmoniously—though some unions, notably metalworkers and printers, are more militant than others. At one time some unionists were inspired by political rather than economic motives, but the collapse of Communism has discredited the overt pursuit of political objectives by industrial means.

Works councils

The Works Constitution Act of 15 January 1972 lays down the rights of the body representing workers' interests at plant level in private (i.e. non-state) companies. In practice the Act covers virtually all German businesses except the miniscule. In the case of bigger businesses there will be a main works council to which the others are joined. The size of a council is relative to the size of the establishment. Its members are chosen—for a period of four years—by election from the workforce, whether an individual worker belongs to a union or not. The council has to meet quarterly at least; its members continue receiving pay for the time they spend on their duties, and woe betide any management that tries to bully them or discriminate against them.

The business of the councils is, broadly speaking, all matters appertaining to conditions of employment: hours, flexible working, overtime, payment, leave, safety at work, incentives, suggestion schemes. Councils negotiate agreements with their employers, and there is a conciliation procedure if they fail—a committee with a neutral chairman which can make a binding settlement. The works council also has rights of co-determination in the case of dismissals, in the field of employees' vocational training, and in the case of grievances.

In bigger companies (those with more than 100 employees), there must also be a small economic committee. This does *not* have rights of co-determination but rights to *information*—and these are extensive, including information on:

the economic and financial situation of the company
the production and sales situation
the investment programme
rationalization projects and closures
organizational changes, including mergers
proposed changes in method.

The idea behind the works councils is that co-determination, that is the right to participate in decisions (about matters that affect them, plus getting crucial background information about the enterprise) should promote trust, co-operation, and harmony. What actually seems to happen is that this helps improve the whole network of relationships between employer and employee, because the mere existence of a formal right to be consulted ensures that informal discussions occur. And the supply of information forms the background for participation at board level.

It must not be imagined that employers regard works councils as superfluous structures, inflicted on them by a socialistic state. They are an embodiment of the attitude of co-operation rather than confrontation. Employers believe that informed and trusted employees are more likely to have the welfare of the business at heart, to be sympathetic to its aims and understanding of its problems—and it would seem they are. The price employers pay is that action is slowed and any promised change can be turned into a bargaining counter: 'If you want A, we demand B.' Co-operation comes at a price.

The relationship of works councils to trade unions is particularly interesting. The unions have sole bargaining rights on basic pay and conditions, backed by a right to strike; agreements are on a regional basis (roughly but not precisely corresponding to the Länder boundaries). Works councils do not have the right to strike and must deal with disagreements through the conciliation procedures and ultimately, if necessary, through the labour courts. The councils do not formally have bargaining rights, but in practice enjoy them for all matters outside the unions' domain. They will negotiate, for instance, on terms and conditions, above those agreed nationally. The more heavily unionized a firm is, the more likely it is that union officials will be elected as members of the works councils. There may even be tension between unions and works councils, with the former worrying that the latter are muscling in on their territory; if union members see councils negotiating deals above the nationally agreed minima, for instance, the unions may find themselves being criticized. Some unionists as a consequence would prefer a shop steward system, which would keep the power more firmly in their hands. If, however, a firm is not unionized, management is in a better position to impose its will on a works council unless the employee representatives have strong characters.

Employees on the Board

We shall examine the German board system in detail later. Suffice it to say here that all big companies have a supervisory tier (Aufsichtsrat), as well as a management board (Vorstand). As far back as 1920/2 legislation provided for two members of the works council to sit on the Aufsichtsrat, but the Nazis abolished this provision in January 1934. In March 1947, the British military government accepted the German trade unions' request for seats on the Aufsichtsrat and the employers agreed for fear of getting something worse. There were intense discussions in the following years and threatened strikes. A series of laws followed, the last one of which was the Co-determination Act of May 1976. The law not only sets out the proportions of employee and shareholder representatives but also requires that one of the directors on the management board shall have special responsibility for labour matters.

At one time the unions and management struggled about the limits of employees' rights and in particular about the casting vote of a shareholder chairman of the supervisory tier. Nowadays (1992), everyone seems more or less content with the present arrangements.

For the most part shareholders and employee representatives on the Aufsichtsrat share management's concern about the prosperity of the enterprise and would much rather proceed by co-operation than confrontation. They therefore respond best when treated well and trusted—but can get spiky when they are not. The existence of a formal obligation to inform and consult often means that there are extensive prior consultations to run over the ground, for example, on complex accounts (which as members of the supervisory board the employee representatives must approve). The employees take a long-term view of the business and are relatively unconcerned about dividends; their general view is quite close to that of the banks (though of course they have their particular interests like pay and conditions to pursue). They would, for instance, be wholly supportive of a company being prudent in its accounting by tucking 'profits' away for a rainy day.

Although employees routinely see confidential information, there is no recorded case of their having released it (though others, such as directors' wives and disaffected secretaries, have).

Trade unions value the system highly, even though it can cause awkward conflicts of interest for their members. There is common ground that it results in employees' representatives being better informed and in their taking a more rational approach to problems: and it is seen to have a political benefit. As one industrialist put it to me, 'No employee has ever walked off an Aufsichtsrat even though there was a strike on and near rioting in the streets.' The system seems to stand strain. In 1992, for instance, Lufthansa faced several problems and these were discussed jointly by employees, unions, Vorstand, and Aufsichtsrat, although all parties knew that painless solutions were impossible and in the event involved job losses and a pay freeze as well as a concession by management on the proposed structure. More generally, my interlocutors preferred a two-tier system on grounds both of principle and of pragmatism. In principle they like the clarity of having a clear division of function. Pragmatically they felt that the principle of co-determination would be unworkable on a unitary board.

Types of Company

General

German law provides for various types of framework for business ranging from partnerships to PLCs, but most of German industry is carried out by two types of incorporated company, namely:

- GmbH (Gesellschaft mit beschränkte Haftung; lit.'company with limited liability');
- AG (Aktiengelleschaft; lit. 'share company').

There are some significant German companies which do not fall into either of these categories, and are hybrids. The background to these is often that the family has retained and wishes to maintain control. An example is the

KGaA company (Kommanditgesellschaft auf Aktien), in which one group of shareholders have limited liability and the other group, who run the business, are personally liable with all of their assets.

Unlimited Partnerships

One structure to be found among even major German companies is the unlimited partnership. (The Monopolkommission in 1984/5 noted that ten of the top 100 companies were not joint stock companies (p. 446), and were therefore presumably partnerships.) The partners between them own the business and if it failed would be personally liable for its debts. The partnership as such does not pay tax but each partner does, depending on his or her emoluments and personal tax position. Such a partnership may have a limited liability company (GmbH or AG) as a subsidiary. The laws governing works councils apply to the partnership, but not the laws about boards. There is formally no supervisory tier, so there are no employee representatives, though the partners may if they choose appoint an advisory committee. If they do there is nothing to prevent someone serving on both management and advisory committees. The advantages of such a structure are its total freedom from market pressure and the threat of take-over; its disadvantages include the impossibility of tapping the capital markets and, of course, personal liability. It works best when partners are content to see profits ploughed back (the main source of new money), and are not in a hurry to realize their investment. Some big businesses have run like this for years— Merck of Darmstadt is more than 200 years old, turnover amounted to nearly DM 3.8 billion in 1991 (DM 4.6 billion if the Lipha group is included), and it employs over 25,000 people in 42 countries. The partners' equity in 1991 stood at DM 1,344.9 million.

Nationalized Industries

Germany still has a number of nationalized industries (leaving aside the companies from the Eastern Länder which are in a state of transition), and they have the AG structure. The main difference is in the composition of the Aufsichtsrat, to which the state, as controlling shareholder, makes the nominations. It frequently chooses officials and junior ministers. If a left-wing minister is appointed he may vote with the employee representatives and thus give them a majority. Denationalization of the Postal and Telecommunications industries and the Railways would require an amendment to the Federal constitution and therefore a two-thirds majority in Parliament.

Number of Companies

Considering the size of the economy few German companies are quoted—only 665 out of the 2,806 AGs in Germany at the end of 1991 (of these, ninety-eight are quoted on the second-tier market and account for only DM 12 billion of the market's capitalization of DM 600 billion). A large proportion of industry is in the hands of unquoted AGs and GmbHs: small businesses (with less than 500 employees or a turnover of less than DM 100 million), usually family-owned, account for two-thirds of the work-force, take 86 per cent of the apprentices, and produce nearly half of the GNP. There are about 433,731 private limited liability companies. On the other hand some of the quoted AGs, such as Siemens, Daimler Benz, and Volkswagen, are big by any standards. (In 1990 their turnovers would have put them above all UK companies except BP and Shell.)

Board Structure

The Two-Tier Principle

From the early days of German industrialization small or medium businesses were managed by their owners. As time went on and shareholdings split and many shareholders were no longer in the business, the general meetings of such companies became too big and the idea was developed of putting control, or at least supervision, into the hands of a committee of the shareholders. Joint stock companies were supervised by the state; state supervision was abolished in 1870. What this means is that since the last century Germany has had a governance system for all sizes of company but the smallest, based on the premiss that the function of supervising management, which is implied in some other systems, should be made explicit and should be separated. The line between 'direction' or 'management' is always difficult to draw with absolute clarity, and the German system does not attempt it. It simply identifies one particular function—supervision—sets bounds to it and places it in the hands of a separate body of people (the Aufsichtsrat). One of the reasons underlying this division is that the stronger management is (and arguably needs to be) the less safe it is to assume that its interests coincide with those of the owners of the business. The application of this principle is to place all the functions of direction and management in the hands of the management board—the Vorstand—except appointment to the Vorstand itself, which is the responsibility of the supervisory tier—the Aufsichtsrat. All AGs must have a Vorstand; GmbH companies have a managing director (Geschäftsführer).

In small GmbH companies—those with fewer than 500 employees, the structure is simple:

Shareholders

Geschäftsführer

But in the bigger GmbH companies the principle of co-determination applies and they must have a supervisory tier—and this is true even where the shares are in one man's hands. The determining factor is the number of employees:

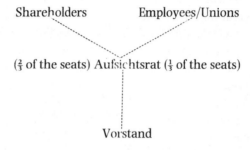

Shareholders   Employees/Unions

($\frac{2}{3}$ of the seats) Aufsichtsrat ($\frac{1}{3}$ of the seats)

Vorstand

The same arrangements and proportions apply to AG companies with fewer than 2,000 employees.

The AG companies with more than 2,000 employees have a similar structure, but the composition of the Aufsichtsrat is different. The total number of seats relates to the number of employees in the company, but the proportion is 50:50. In a company with 2,000–10,000 employees, for instance, the board is twelve strong. Typically two of the six employee representatives will be external trade unioinists.

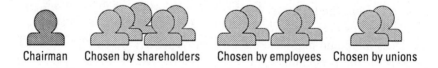

Chairman   Chosen by shareholders   Chosen by employees   Chosen by unions

But there are more subtleties. Of the employee representatives one must come from the salaried and one from the executive staff. The chairman is always drawn from the shareholders' representatives. If a vote is deadlocked a second vote is taken and he has two votes, a right he cannot delegate. Coal, iron, and steel companies form a separate category, in that the chairman is not drawn from the shareholders, but is neutral.

The Vorstand

The German system has a different starting-point from most others in that the law confers power on the Vorstand as an organ. It *is* the board—with a massive concentration of power. It is envisaged as a collectivity and is expected to operate collegiately. In contrast to Japanese boards it is a real decision-making body; in contrast to the UK/USA board it is not seen as an adjunct to the CEO.

What the Vorstand actually does depends on the size and structure of the business. In a very large company, for instance, the main subsidiaries may have Vorstands (and Aufsichtsräte) of their own and the main board will in effect be a holding company: the Vorstand may be running the German subsidiary of a great multinational like Ford or IBM. But whatever the size, the fundamental fact remains—it is by law the engine of management and no one may instruct it (for reasons which may appear valid in a wider context) to act in a way that is injurious to the business. If, for instance, a foreign owner wished to instruct its German subsidiary to market products that failed in some way to meet German standards, the members of the German Vorstand would have to refuse under threat of personal liability. Again the members of a German Vorstand must satisfy themselves that if they depend on a parent company for finance, it will be forthcoming, or they may risk personal liability.

Of course all groups tend to want good leaders and the Vorstand is no different. What the leader is called—and how his role is conceived—depends formally on the Aufsichtsrat. The Companies Act lays it down that the Vorstand may elect a chairman from their midst. This is not mandatory, and in some companies the leadership varies with the role. In law no specific powers are ascribed to the leader. The word 'speaker' or 'spokesman' (Sprecher) is not in fact used in the Act, though it is the one most commonly found in German companies, the idea being to give the clear impression that the leader of the Vorstand is a *primus inter pares*. In many companies, however, the Sprecher becomes more than a *primus inter pares* and looks more and more like his American counterpart—a CEO. So much depends on the personalities. In some cases the leader of the Vorstand is indeed called 'chairman', which may indicate a more powerful role. The members of the Vorstand generally feel more accountable to the body as a whole than to the Sprecher or chairman alone. One exception to the general rule is where the founder (or a powerful member of the founding family) remains head of the Vorstand. In such cases there may be no doubt who is 'boss' and this casts a quite different light on the collegiality of the board.

As the Sprecher or chairman's role varies so much in accordance with his personality or power, the relative power of his fellow members on the Vorstand must vary also. They often have clearly defined spheres of executive responsibility within the business, but even so, are expected to think and act collegiately rather than as a series of warring barons each trying to defend his own patch. This is also reflected in law. Members of the Vorstand have—to a certain extent—to have an eye on what is going on in their colleagues' departments and can be held liable if they fail to do so. The consensual approach is emphasized. On the Vorstand, when it comes to the crunch—which it seldom does—it is 'one person one vote'. Lack of consensus on the Vorstand *never* implies reference to the Aufsichtsrat. The Vorstand usually meets once a week. Meetings are far from perfunctory and may well last all day. In Appendix 2A there is an extract from the rules of procedure of a major company which gives some flavour of the general approach one might expect to find.

Commentators on the comparative merits of the supervisory system have been inclined to overlook the important issue of patronage. The power of appointment to the Vorstand lies formally with the supervisory board and requires a two-thirds majority. If a decision is not reached in the first round of voting a simple majority will suffice. This means the employees' representatives can register their feelings but not prevent a nomination going through. The source of nominations is usually the Vorstand itself and the Aufsichtsrat. There have been cases when the Aufsichtsrat has brought in candidates from outside; this is rare, not least because it implies a far higher degree of responsibility for the person's performance than if they had agreed on the internal nominee. And if the Aufsichtsrat does decide to appoint its own nominee the Vorstand has no right of veto. The idea that the Aufsichtsrat is a mere rubber stamp in patronage matters is not borne out by reports—especially in difficult times. The succession at Volkswagen, for instance, has attracted much comment (see the *Financial Times* (30 March 1992)) and was the task of a special committee of the Aufsichtsrat. In that company at that time it sounded far more like the selection of a CEO (from whom especially positive leadership was expected) than the choice of a committee chairman. The position of the Vorstand (in the nominating process) in the big firms, like Volkswagen, is completely different from that in smaller firms (subsidiaries; family-owned AGs).

Indeed, the shareholding structure may affect profoundly the way the process works. If the founding family or a major shareholder is represented on the Aufsichtsrat (or sometimes even if they are not), they are nevertheless in a position to exert influence, and the balance of power may shift substantially away from the Vorstand.

Members of the Vorstand enjoy reasonable security—a deliberate stratagem to prevent boards being 'packed' or over-dominated even after a take-over. They are usually appointed by the Aufsichtsrat for five years (the maximum permitted by law), and can only be dismissed for very good reasons such as gross breach of duty, inability to exercise proper management, or after the passing of a vote of no confidence by the general meeting—provided this is not done arbitrarily. Even in this case the Aufsichtsrat is free to decide whether to dismiss the respective member of the Vorstand or not. A contract may be renewed, but not more than six months before it is due to expire. A Geschäftsführer may however be dismissed at any time regardless of the contractual rights (unless the articles say otherwise), though he remains entitled to his contractual payments.

The Vorstand itself monitors the individual competence of its own members. If a member's performance declines, the treatment he gets will depend on his age and the gravity of the situation. Whenever possible he will be allowed to serve out his contract, though his position may be made clear to all by the appointment of a deputy. If he is asked to retire early it will be done discreetly and generously: the Aufsichtsrat alone has the power to compel a member of a Vorstand to stand down. Neither the Vorstand itself nor the shareholders in general meetings can do so.

Board remuneration in Germany is not the hot issue it has become in the USA (and to some extent in the UK). There are virtually no stock options for tax reasons and no great disposition to tie pay to profits—even less to share price. Although profit is important, it is not seen as the be-all and end-all; there are other issues on which Germans want their managers to concentrate besides this year's profits or today's share price. Directors would expect to get around 65 per cent of their remuneration in the form of basic salary; the rest is divided about equally between annual bonuses and perquisites/benefits. As to relativities and absolute levels, the accounts of German companies provide only a total for the Vorstand. It is generally thought, however, that the Sprecher (or chairman) receives 30–50 per cent more than his colleagues. As for the Aufsichtsrat, the usual provision in company articles is for the chairman to get 200 per cent and the vice-chairman 150 per cent of their colleagues' remuneration.

The Aufsichtsrat

Functions: The area of the Aufsichtsrat's authority is prescribed by law and covers:

The company's accounts for a specified period (usually quarterly);
Major capital expenditure and strategic acquisitions; closures;
Appointments to the Vorstand;
Approving the dividend.

This list is often extended by a company's articles, but even so the function of the Aufsichtsrat is limited to approval or disapproval. The Vorstand proposes, the Aufsichtsrat disposes. Properly speaking, therefore, Germany does not have two-tier boards and much misunderstanding flows from so describing them.

The primary function of the Aufsichtsrat is to ensure the competence of the Vorstand. To act effectively it needs to be able to operate collegiately itself—which imposes a considerable burden of leadership upon the chairman, who has to build a consensus. He must also establish an adequate relationship with the Vorstand: he needs to know what is happening.

A second important function is the approval of the annual profit-and-loss statement and balance sheet. Both are audited by independent public accountants who report to the Aufsichtsrat and can be questioned by it. The Aufsichtsrat must also approve the dividend.

The formal time commitment of members of an Aufsichtsrat is considerably less than that of a non-executive director in the UK, reflecting the smaller number of meetings—three or four a year. There will, however, be other informal meetings, and preparatory work. Bankers are particularly well placed to cope because of the support they get—or they could not assume the loads they bear. Ornamental directors and 'Frühstück' directors (so called because of their partiality for late lunches) are going out of fashion. It seems that as the role of the Aufsichtsrat is taken ever more seriously, the queue of candidates for them has shrunk. The new technology companies pose problems. The judgements to be made on propositions put by the Vorstand require a technical understanding that few members of an 'average' Aufsichtsrat would normally possess, though they may set up special committees to deal with particular problems. The Aufsichtsrat may, moreover, appoint inspectors on matters of concern to it, who will have to report back direct, not through the Vorstand.

The importance of the presence of employee representatives should not be overlooked. It is true that their absolute power is limited by the chairman's casting vote and ultimately by the general meeting, but Germans hate such conflicts and strain to avoid them. (Sometimes the employee members actually push for a vote knowing it will be adverse, just to show colleagues they did their utmost, or to create an impasse which it would be appropriate to settle in the courts.) The employee members can use their position to bargain for other advantages, for example, by threatening to vote down an appointment to the Vorstand they may secure some concessions elsewhere; in fact, however, if they feel strongly that a person should not be appointed to the Vorstand, he is unlikely to go forward. On the other hand they have been known to acquiesce peaceably in the appointment of a hard man when the circumstances clearly required one.

The employee representatives sometimes bring an otherwise comatose Aufsichtsrat to life, typically in enterprises dominated by the family or a parent company. In such cases there is often a danger of the Aufsichtsrat being purely nominal, as the family or parent company will control the Vorstand directly and bypass it. The fact that the Aufsichtsrat does have legal duties and that the employees have rights can stop this happening; management must at the very least prepare its case and justify its proposals (and the accounts).

When looking at the German system it is the supervisory tier and union representation on it that tends to attract much of the attention. It is easy to overlook the important part played by the works councils. Through them flows a stream of information which enables the employee representatives on the Aufsichtsrat to play a fuller, proper part in its deliberations. Many major proposals for change will necessarily have been discussed in the works councils, so that by the time the matter reaches the Aufsichtsrat some difficulties will have been eased; many companies have special committees to help in this predigesting process. All this consultation may help but it does not necessarily produce agreement; Aufsichtsrat debates do go to genuinely contested votes. In describing the system the outside commentator has to guard against making it sound as if best practice is universally followed. The Germans themselves are clear it is not (see below).

The Aufsichtsrat may delegate important topics to committees. Although it is largely dependent for its information on what the Vorstand provides, it can investigate subjects directly which it wishes to consider more deeply. There are three main incentives for members of the Aufsichtsrat to take a keen interest in what is going on. The first is their personal reputation, which would suffer from association with failure. The second is that they (particularly banks' representatives) are often 'interested' in the technical sense through shareholdings or loans or in some other way, any of which mean that the prosperity and survival of the business would be of great importance to them or their employees. The third is the law—if they neglect their duties they may be personally liable.

In practice, they ratify proposals put before them by the chairman, who within the company will normally have consulted other members of the board and the Sprecher of the Vorstand. He may also consult interested parties outside the company, particularly the banks. Indeed, a good chairman of the Aufsichtsrat would regard it as a danger signal if a candidate looked too 'comfortable' to the management. In some companies, however, the boot is on the other foot. The Vorstand effectively selects the members of the Aufsichtsrat.

The members of the Aufsichtsrat other than the employee representatives are appointed by the general meeting of shareholders for a period of four years (but *de facto*, five). In some companies the founding family still effectively have a power of appointment—even one as big as Siemens, where the family have 1 per cent of the shares but 10 per cent of the votes; as no one else has anything like as many they are able still to exercise a substantial power of patronage. Shareholders may have a statutory right to a board seat (which is not a rare case for founders, even though they may be minority shareholders) (Section 101, Stock Corporation Act). As to security of tenure, it takes a 75 per cent vote of those cast to remove prematurely a member of the Aufsichtsrat.

An analysis of the 100 largest companies by turnover in *Die Welt* (19 July 1988), shows that eighty-seven had Aufsichtsräte and that in 1988 the incumbents' backgrounds were as follows:

542 were employee representatives
187 were representatives of trade unions
385 were industrialists
152 were other shareholder representatives, e.g. lawyers
104 were bankers
57 were from other financial institutions, including insurance companies.

The importance of the bankers is greater than their numbers suggest (see 'Bankers on Boards', below).

It is appropriate to draw attention at this point to the personnel link-ups in 1990 between the 100 biggest companies as set out by the Monopolies Commission's 9th Official Report. For the sake of brevity I list only the first eight (Table 2.1).

The Aufsichtsrat on smaller or family businesses: As we have seen, German law requires all AGs, irrespective of size, to have an Aufsichtsrat, though co-determination is not required if there are fewer than fifty employees. There

TABLE 2.1. *Personnel link-ups in 1990 between the 100 biggest companies in Germany*

Ranking in 1990	Company	No. of companies among top 100 …		
		to whose Aufsichtsrat the company has sent members of its Vorstand	which have sent members of their Vorstand to the company's Aufsichtsrat	with which the company has personnel links through other office-holders on the Aufsichtsräte
1	Daimler Benz AG	5	5	26
2	Siemens AG	8	3	23
3	Volkswagen AG	3	3	21
4	Hoechst AG	3	3	16
5	BASF AG	2	4	22
6	Robert Bosch GmbH	7	0	6
7	Bayer AG	5	3	20
8	Thyssen AG	7	4	24

are different provisions for companies with 500–2,000 and over 2,000 employees. A GmbH with fewer than 500 employees is not required to have an Aufsichtsrat. Many companies that are bigger than that are still run by the founding families, who may well comprise much of both Vorstand and Aufsichtsrat, with the older members tending to gravitate to the latter. Power often goes with them, and although German law expressly forbids an Aufsichtsrat to run a company, it often does, giving orders either to the Vorstand or the Geschäftsführer, despite the fact that in law the Vorstand is obliged to act independently. Nevertheless, power is power, and if it could— ultimately—be exercised legitimately at the shareholders' meeting, independence may not in practice be absolute. With such a power hanging over them the members of the Vorstand are in a weak position—not that *conflict à l'outrance* is inherently likely, given the situation.

Other Organs of Management

Besides the Aufsichtsrat and Vorstand themselves there are subsidiary parts of the structure which help create a series of interlocking relationships and assist the effective working of the system. The Aufsichtsrat may well set up small committees (Praesidium or Praesidial committees), which may well include employees' representatives (though they do not always do so). The composition is often the chairman and vice-chairman of the Aufsichtsrat (the vice-chairman always comes from the employees' side) and two or three others, including perhaps the chairman of the works council. This is a convenient forum for handling awkward issues before they reach the whole Aufsichtsrat. The Aufsichtsrat may also create other committees to report to it on certain aspects of the business, for instance, on matters of high technology. A Praesidial committee has the authority to summon members of the Vorstand before it; such a command is taken with the utmost seriousness and careful preparation. Banks in particular may have credit committees to sanction major loans recommended by the Vorstand: this type of committee meets almost every month. As has already been noted there are formal links between the works council and the Aufsichtsrat and the Praesidium.

Shareholders

The Type of Shares

It is only too easy to underestimate the importance of the formal arrangements under German law in respect of the German system of shareholdings. In GmbHs transfers are by contracts in notarial form, a formal and cumbersome procedure: share certificates are unnecessary and therefore uncommon. Shares in AG companies are nearly all in bearer form. This affects the physical aspects of custody and transfer (in which the Central Depositories, Kassenvereine, play an important part), but these technicalities are outside the scope of this paper. There is, however, an important consequence for the exercise of voting rights (see below).

Who Owns What?

Private shareholders are not major shareholders in Germany; the cult of the equity has few worshippers. The Bundesbank monthly report in May 1990 showed that only 6.6 per cent of the financial assets of households were in shares, compared with 48.3 per cent in banks and 15.7 per cent in bonds. Some commentators link this to a low rate of inflation which makes it unnecessary to seek nominal growth in values to counter the depreciation of real value of the currency. Be that as it may, private shareholders only hold about 16 per cent and the trend is downwards; around 7 per cent of German households own shares directly.

The Bundesbank in June 1991 gave the following figures for 1990 showing that shares in German companies were held as follows:

Private individuals	15.94%
Companies	40.19%
Insurance companies	11.28%
Banks	9.98%
The Federal and Länder governments	6.38%
External	16.22%

Other sources give a rather different breakdown, which is understandable, given that shares are in bearer form. Even so, all the series I have seen, including the Bundesbank numbers, present a different picture from other countries. Foreign holdings tend to be concentrated in the major companies. The average of 16.22 per cent conceals the fact that in many companies 35–40 per cent of the equity is held abroad. In the case of VEBA, for instance, it has reached 49 per cent.

The pension funds and insurance companies are relatively insignificant—with only about 12 per cent between them. This is because German companies hold their pension funds on the liability side of the balance sheet of the company as accrued pensions and can use them as working capital.[2] They are not obliged to create a separate trust (or equivalent) in which to house them, but pay a premium to the Pension Guarantee Association to insure these funds. In the public sector, pensions are unfunded. About DM 300 billion of pension assets are now held within companies as working capital, of which DM 181 billion or 60 per cent is in the form of pension provisions. The annual report of the Federation of German Stock Exchanges suggested in 1988 that German companies should fund more of their pension-related assets so as to reduce risk (which would have the incidental effect of enhancing the efficiency of Germany's securities markets). Companies do not appear to have made major moves in that direction, but new tax-efficient devices such as 'spezial Fonds' have been created—though so far they have had a limited impact. These were used by insurance companies and corporations setting up funded pension schemes, but their growth diminished in 1990 and 1991. (The Wyatt Company EIS has published a good account of German pension arrangements.)

The investments of pension funds ('Pensions Kassen') are subject to the same rules and regulations as insurance funds, including a limit of 20 per cent of assets held against current obligations being in securities and not more than a 10 per cent stake being held in the share capital of any one company.

[2] This was at first a consequence of the German Pension Insurance system.

The law on the Supervision of Insurance Companies requires that the majority of assets (the so called 'cover stock', i.e. assets held against current obligations) is subject to a limit of 20 per cent in equity holdings. All assets have to be located in Germany—and there has to be 100 per cent currency matching. Small wonder then that in 1989 German life insurers only had 9.3 per cent of their assets in equities. That said, Allianz is in fact the biggest single shareholder in Germany: if it takes more than 10 per cent of a company's equity it usually wants a seat on the Aufsichtsrat. The shareholdings and therefore the potential influence of the insurance companies are growing rapidly. Taking all things together, however, it seems that German institutional shareholders are not generally in a position to play a leading role in corporate governance matters, though they may have an important role in particular companies. Even the investment funds have relatively small equity holdings (about 12.8 per cent in 1990, including 2.8 per cent in foreign equities).

General Meetings

General meetings are mandatory for AG companies. Individual shareholders seldom attend but a high proportion of the total voting power will be present in the hall—about 70 per cent would be normal for an unexceptional meeting. The high attendance is largely due to the bearer share system. It is the banks as custodians of deposited shares who are notified about GMs and they in turn notify the owners: conversely, a shareholder cannot attend and vote unless he has lodged his certificate with certain specified banks. Some decisions require 75 per cent of the votes so a 25 per cent shareholder has a power of veto. Because of the importance of the banks (see below) and the complexity of their relationship with the company, there is ample opportunity for them to make contact with management during the year. A *démarche* at a general meeting is therefore rare: meetings are seldom controversial, but may be protracted, with a wide range of general questions. A tendency has grown for special interest groups to use them for propaganda, for instance—in former days on South Africa—or on environmental issues. Such groups often purchase a minimal holding just to have the right to attend. They sometimes make use of a provision in German law which entitles them to introduce a counter-proposal' which the company must distribute with its proxy materials before the meeting. In fact counter-proposals seldom reach a vote because the management's own proposals must first be rejected and this is extremely rare. There is, however, absolutely no record of shareholders at a general meeting doing anything positive about a company going downhill even in cases in which it is clear that both Vorstand and Aufsichtsrat are ineffective. The percentage of voting power present at AGMs has been steadily declining in recent years, especially in 'blue chip companies' because of foreign institutional investments.

There are shareholder associations of which the two most prominent are:

DSW (Deutsche Schutzvereinigung für Westpapierbesitz);
SdK (Schutzgemeinschaft der Kleinaktionäre e.V.).

DSW's aim is 'to protect, maintain and strengthen private property, in particular, savings capital'. It claims about 10,000 members. According to *Börsenzeitung* (11 August 1987), all the shareholder associations together do not on average represent more than 1 per cent of listed share capital.

There is no obligation on a GmbH to have an annual general meeting. It is up to the directors to call a general meeting of shareholders when they wish, but a member's resolution is required in certain circumstances (e.g. to raise more capital), or if more than half the capital has been lost in a given year. Members holding one-tenth of the share capital can require a meeting to be held. There is an interesting provision that where otherwise a meeting would have been necessary by law, a unanimous vote in writing of the shareholders may instead declare themselves agreed on the decision to be made.

The Market

General

The German public's agnosticism to the cult of the equity reflects German management's lack of enthusiasm for the stock market. With unquestionably the most powerful economy in Europe and one of the strongest in the world, only 665 German companies were quoted at the end of 1991 (Annual Report of the Federation of German Stock Exchanges: cf. 6,309 in the USA on NYSE, AMEX, and NASDAQ; 2,343 in London; and 839 in Paris, including investment funds). Important as these companies are, their market capitalization was only DM 596 billion compared with 6,222 in the USA and 1,507 in the UK. 1991 was not an easy year for most economies but even so thirty-eight new companies were listed in the USA, 118 in the UK and only nineteen in Germany, of which only nine were in the first segment (Geregelter Markt: GM). (In the two previous years the total had been 25 and 26.) The total market capitalization of quoted companies was DM 596,476 million at the end of 1991; savings accounts exceeded DM

1,000,000 million. Germany has a high savings ratio—12.2 per cent of disposable household income in 1989—but the money does not seem to find its way into equities. In that year only 10 billion out of 150 billion of private sector savings reached the equity market directly or indirectly.

In this context, and later when we consider the role of the banks, it is worth looking at industry's sources of finance. Table 2.2 is drawn from an OECD Financial Statement. The double column for Germany reflects the provisions for pensions carried in the balance sheet.

The eight German stock markets are quite active; Frankfurt does more than two-thirds of the business. Total turnover (double counted) was DM 1,259 billion in 1991, but most of this was accounted for by 50 companies. Siemens alone accounted for 12.18 per cent. Indeed, the top five companies together accounted for 42.47 per cent, and the top thirty for 65 per cent.[3] Taking the market as a whole, the average turnover rate was about 1.1 in 1991. Turnover in some major companies was as follows:

Siemens	2.5
Daimler Benz	2.0
VEBA	1.7
Allianz	0.5
Hoesch	5.5
Schering	1.7
VW	4.0
BASF	1.2
Mannesmann	2.0
Deutsche Bank	2.2
Commerzbank	1.8

Trading is indeed active. Single-counted turnover in 1992 was £253.3 billion compared with London's £216.9, even though the relative end of 1991 market capitalizations were £209.8 billion and £541.1 billion respectively. The difference between the velocity ratios (121 per cent to 40 per cent) is so marked that there may be some technical reason why the comparisons are inappropriate. Whatever the volume, it is still a market for shares not companies. Though there are many mergers, there are virtually no take-overs against the wishes of the incumbent management (i.e. 'hostile' bids, see below).

[3]   1991 *Annual Report of the Federation of German Stock Exchanges*, p. 137.

TABLE 2.2. *Debt/equity ratio of non-financial enterprises (gross liabilities less equity as a proportion of equity)*

Year	Japan	USA	UK	Germany	
				Provisions classified as debt	Provisions classified as equity
1977	5.49	0.51	1.06	2.60	1.82
1980	5.16	0.48	1.06	3.02	1.92
1985	4.40	0.61	1.04	2.99	1.72
1988	4.19	0.76	1.03	4.25	1.52
1989		0.82	1.14	4.33	1.53

Accounting

In contrast with the UK convention that accounts should show a 'true and fair view', in Germany the auditors' philosophy is the principle of commercial prudence—and this is authorized in legislation. Heinrich Weiss, then President of the Federation of German Industries BDI, speaking in London on 23 June 1992 to the Royal Society of Arts, said 'This means that whenever you see a risk you have a right to make a reserve in the balance sheet or make a deduction on the assets side, creating some reserve for risks, which of course means that at the time you reduce your profits but you get a reserve in case you have some problems with the company.' German companies do in fact tuck substantial reserves away, and their employees through their membership of works councils and Aufsichtsräte know perfectly well what is going on and approve, as it strengthens the company's power to survive and enhances their own prospect of continuity of employment. Paul Rutterman of accountants Ernst & Young, speaking in Oxford in September 1992, said that one analysis suggested that, by using the accounting treatment appropriate to each country, the same figures would produce profits of:

  88 in Spain
  89 in Germany
  94 in Holland
100 in France
117 in Italy
129 in the UK.

Underlying this view of best accounting practice is the German evaluation of the importance of stakeholders, particularly employees, customers, and community relative to shareholders. It is the continuity of the business that has top priority, so prudence takes precedence over profits. And although this is not tax-driven it doubtless has tax advantages too. At the time I was drafting this paper, Terry Smith's book appeared called *Accounting for Growth*. In it he discusses various ways in which UK companies present the data in the ways best calculated to enhance profits. A book on accounting practice in Germany would need to be called *Accounting for Survival* and would show the various ways in which profits are concealed for a rainy day.

Mergers

The number of mergers has grown in recent years. Paper 12/847 produced by the Bundestag (12th term) shows there were 445 in 1975, 635 in 1980, 709 in 1985, and 1,548 in 1990. About 1,100 of the companies acquired were quite small, with a turnover of less than DM 50 million, but fifty-five had turnovers in excess of DM 1 billion and four had turnovers in excess of DM 12 billion. Figures from the Federal Cartel Office have a rather different classification but show a similar growth pattern—from 287 partial or full acquisitions in 1980 to 616 in 1988.

Friendly mergers often occur for normal commercial reasons such as lack of succession or synergy. Mergers also take place in circumstances in which one of the parties is troubled. If so they will be quietly negotiated. Companies go downhill as they do anywhere else in the world. The stock market itself is not the scene of remedial action when an Aufsichtsrat fails to arrest a company's decline. Germany has no long-stop mechanism of this sort, though it comes quite close to it when certain types of marriage are arranged (e.g. AEG–Daimler Benz). The banks play a leading part in such arrangements, as well they might, for they have much at stake.

The 1,548 mergers in 1990 were followed by over 2,000 in 1991, partly as a result of reunification. There is some concern that this process is causing the disappearance of highly effective medium and small businesses to the detriment of their productivity. The issue of greater concentration is worth a closer look.

Concentration

One of the developments of the German economy which has attracted attention there is the tendency for major companies to gain a substantially larger share of it by merger and by organic growth (see for instance an article in *Wirtschaftswoche* (10 July 1992), from which many of the following facts are drawn). Daimler Benz had a turnover of nearly DM 100 billion in 1991—ten times more than the biggest group twenty-five years ago, Volkswagenwerk. Indeed, of the 100 largest companies in 1966 only fifty-five are in the 1991 list. One-third have been taken over. Furthermore, the top ten companies in 1991 had 46 per cent of the turnover and 49 per cent of the staff of all companies in the top 100. The importance of family-owned firms has declined; in 1991 they accounted for a turnover which amounted to 12 per cent of those in the top 100. The comparable figure for 1966 was 19 per cent. In steel, energy, and mechanical engineering, there is a marked move to concentration, with seventeen leading firms having disappeared in the last twenty-five years. The top ten firms in 1991 were, in order of size of turnover, Daimler Benz; Siemens; Volkswagen; VEBA; Hoechst; BASF; RWE; Bayer; Thyssen; Robert Bosch. The biggest five firms in 1966 to have been absorbed are: AEG by Daimler Benz; Rheinstahl by Thyssen; Salzgitter by Preussag; Gensenk by Veba; and DEA by RWE. The question arises for the Germans how far to let this process go without feeling concern.

Mergers are scrutinized by the Cartel Office, whose main criterion is market domination—that is, they will interfere if a proposed merger so weakens competition as to allow a company to dominate the market. In reaching their judgement they may take financial strength and vertical integration into account, as well as the structure of the market, that is, the size and number of competitors as well as other factors. Between 1973 and 1988 they scrutinized 9,500 mergers, of which rather less than 200 were prohibited. Such a policy by its very nature favours conglomerates since the purchase of a company in an unrelated business is least likely to offend the basic criterion.

The significant feature of the German system is that virtually none of the very large number of mergers would be classified as 'hostile' in the USA or UK, that is, none was preceded by an open market bid over the heads of the management of the target company: they were all negotiated. There are however 'hostile' take-overs, very often with the support of one or several banks which may have built up a controlling block of shares secretly—for years if necessary. Secret purchases, if big enough, do move the market by the sheer pressure they exert. The bid for Hoesch by Krupp was an example of this kind. With virtually no 'hostile' bids of the 'open market' variety and few of the others, the Germans have seen little need for any regime to control them and have not yet implemented the EC directive (which should have been adopted in national law at the beginning of 1991, but was not). It is still not necessary to disclose a significant stake before reaching 25 per cent and even then it is not necessary to give precise figures or make a further registration before reaching 50 per cent. (The EC directive foresees registration at 10, 20, 33⅓, 50, and 66⅔ per cent, or lower thresholds, and includes shares held or controlled directly or indirectly.) The state of German law technically leaves German companies exposed to foreign purchasers who may themselves be protected by stringent disclosure rules, as in the UK. In the meantime, the take-over of Hoesch by Krupp shows how the German rules currently favour a bidder, because the target cannot marshal defences and the bidder can buy in the market secretly without the bid premium factor coming into play.

The examples of hostile take-overs are so rare that everyone quotes the same cases. A major battle took place between 1990 and 1992 over Pirelli's unwelcome bid for Continental, and this involved:

- mobilization of support by both parties;
- court action to remove the 5 per cent cap on shareholders' voting rights;
- court action by shareholders about violation of minority interests;
- the removal of the Sprecher of the Continental Vorstand because of his implacable hostility to the bid.

This kind of struggle with or without the building of clandestine stakes is counter to the prevailing ethos, which remains strongly opposed to open market hostile bids. There are many other reasons why they are difficult to mount, for example:

- The founding family still has a strong position in many companies; or there may be a sizeable but supportive shareholder. Hoppenstedt Franks and Mayer looked at 171 quoted companies and concluded that 85.4 per cent of them had a shareholder with 25 percent of its voting capital (this would include a family group).
- The accounts of German companies tend to be relatively opaque so that unfriendly bidders would be taking great risks even though the general tendency is for balance sheets to be conservative.
- The banks often hold shares, which they would generally not offer an unwanted bidder even if it meant foregoing a premium over the market price, because it would impair their relationship with the target company.
- The banks effectively control a large proportion of outstanding shares through deposited share voting rights.
- The shareholders' representatives on the Aufsichtsrat can only be dismissed before the expiry of their term of office (usually five years) by a 75 per cent majority of the votes cast.

- There are voting limitations in companies' by-laws which provide that however many shares a shareholder may own, not more than *n* per cent may be voted. According to Baums, twenty-three of the large AG companies with widely distributed shares had a cap on voting rights;
- There is concentrated ownership other than that through the banks.

As an example of this last factor, a list compiled by Commerzbank (*A Guide to Capital Links in West German Companies* (1988)), shows, for instance that:

25% of Allianz was held by Münchener Rückversicherungs Gesellschaft;

28% of Daimler Benz was held by Deutsche Bank;

10% of Siemens was held by Familie Siemens;

20% of Volkswagen was held by Land Niedersachsen and 20% by Bundesrepublik Deutschand;

over 25% of MAN AG was held by Regina Verwaltungsgesellschaft;

and there are many others.

The whole atmosphere, however, is one in which the stock market is far less at the centre of the stage. The Germans find it odd that the evening BBC broadcast to Germany at peak time includes a long financial report, identical or similar to the one London receives as part of the national 6 o'clock news.

The Banks

General

It is significant that by this point in the description of the German system it has already been necessary to mention the banks in so many different contexts. In other countries it would not have been important to single them out for their shareholdings and board membership as well as for their key role in providing working capital and other services. To understand corporate governance in Germany it is essential to examine each aspect of the banks' relationship with industrial companies, but never to lose sight of the fact that whole is much greater than the sum of its parts.

The Germans have 4,500 banks of various sorts, many of them relatively small and local—3,000 are regional or co-operative or people's banks, and there are many public sector savings banks.[4] The big three are clearly in the lead but they have plenty of competition, and relatively small shares of the total credit market. Deutsche Bank, easily the leaders, have an estimated 5–8 per cent, and Dresdner 3–4 per cent; Commerzbank and Bayerische Vereinsbank are not far behind. It is their association with bigger business that creates such an impression of overwhelming domination: when it

[4] See 'Die 500 grössten deutschen Kreditinstitute', *Kreditwirtschaft* (Jan. 1992).

comes to private persons, the joint stock banks have only 30 per cent of the market.

As an interesting footnote, the voting system means that the banks virtually control themselves. At general meetings in recent years, Deutsche held voting rights for 47.2 per cent of its own shares, Dresdner 59–25 per cent, and Commerzbank 30.29 per cent.

The Banks as Lenders

As has been the case from the early days of industrialization, Germans starting business have no choice but to look to the banks for long-term money. The banks for their part approach their lending from the inception on the basis that it will be long term. This approach means that both parties realize that they are in together for the long term: in modern parlance it implies 'relationship' not 'transaction' banking, which in turn requires the bankers to understand their customers and the industries in which they are engaged. The consequence of this is the need not only for a good flow of information from company to bank, but for a good cadre of well-trained personnel within the banks to understand and evaluate the intelligence they receive.

Universalbanken

With a customer base securely tied to them on long-term arrangements, the banks set about developing a wider range of services as a means of improving profits (for relationship banking is expensive), and for cementing relationships by broadening the opportunities for contacts. Entrepreneurs are lonely men and the banks were able to provide valuable counsel when needed; and they were trusted. (This will remain especially significant in the Eastern Länder where young companies run by people quite unused to a market system need intense care and nursing. What the banks provide is a cross between counselling and management consultancy.) Much of the structure and dynamics of this relationship between the banking system and industry still applies across a wide swathe of German industry. The major banks have developed into what the Germans describe as Universalbanken—a term applying to the range of services they provide rather than their geographical spread. (Deposits; lending; all aspects of investment; foreign exchange.)

The Banks as Shareholders

The German banking system has not set out as a matter of policy to acquire shares in its customers' companies. Even so, in 1975 the banks had become substantial shareholders, owning 9 per cent of AGs (14 per cent if financial companies are excluded). Many of their holdings were acquired *faute de mieux* from impecunious companies which could not repay their debt and had nothing else to offer.[5] Sometimes the companies failed and the shares became worthless; sometimes, however, they prospered mightily and the banks found themselves holding shares which could not be sold without incurring a serious tax charge.

There are some cases on record of the government using the banks to acquire a significant shareholding in the national interest: the government got the Deutsche Bank and Dresdner Bank to save Hapag Lloyd by acquiring a majority of the shares. There are still cases of banks taking shares in private companies, though this is generally done (in the case of the big banks) through a separate venture capital arm.

The banks' shareholdings have been criticized, for instance by the Monopolkommission and the Kartellamt. The provisions of the Second Banking Co-ordination Directive (adopted in December 1989) limited banks' shareholdings in individual companies to 15 per cent of banks' capital and the total of such holdings to 60 per cent of banks' capital. This will not have much impact on the German banks. The FDP has proposed a limit on banks' holdings of 15 per cent of the company's capital, and the Kartellamt and Monopolkommission both proposed a 5 per cent limit, but it seems unlikely the idea will be pressed.

The banks' direct holdings do seem to be diminishing, though it is difficult to be certain. The 1978 Monopolkommission report gave a figure of 5 per cent for the top companies, and in 1990 the Bundesverband Deutsche Banken reported that the banks owned 2.8 per cent of the capital of all non-bank companies. Wherever the truth lies there was at one time a reduction—perhaps because fewer rescues have been necessary, though major ones still occur, such as Deutsche Bank's purchase of Klöckner in 1988. Recently, however, the trend has been reversed; the proportion of quoted shares in the hands of the banks at the end of 1990 was 10.8 per cent according to the Bundesbank. (Other sources put the figure as high as $12\frac{1}{2}$ per cent.)

The Banks as Proxies

As German shares are predominantly in bearer form they are negotiable and valuable; receipt of the dividend requires production of a coupon. For

---

[5] A published analysis of the acquisition of shareholdings by the ten top banks between 1 Jan. 1987 and 1 Sept. 1989 shows that fourteen were made for rescue or financial support, nine for placement purposes, five for investment, and one to stop a take-over.

these reasons, and other reasons connected with the ability to deal in shares at the best prices, German shareholders generally lodge the instruments with banks authorized to do all the necessary work. The banks are obliged by law to consult the owners about voting instructions and give them advice. They do this by means of a fifteen months' proxy form covering all a shareholder's holdings. Shareholders are then sent the agendas for companies as they are issued, together with a bank's views on how to vote. In the absence of a contrary instruction the bank will then exercise the proxy in the way indicated. Very few shareholders bother to respond (as might be expected, since few issues are controversial). This is the system which gives rise to deposited share voting rights (DSVR). An example some years ago was Deutsche's advice to abstain from voting on motions arising from Volkswagen's currency tribulations. A bank may go further and inform owners that it will not, on a controversial issue, exercise votes on their behalf; in that case the owners themselves must cast their votes if they wish an opinion to be registered. Banks would easily be put into an invidious position were this not so; for instance, if one of their clients were in negotiation with another. Institutional shareholders, like insurance companies, generally leave it to their depository bankers to vote (though this is illegal for investment companies). Business is usually uncontentious; if, however, they wish to register opposition the banks will generally require them to do it themselves.

Except in the relatively few cases where a bank has a major holding it is doubtful whether the bank's own shareholdings are a significant factor in corporate governance. What they do have is effective control of a very large number of shares they do not own through DSVR. The proportion of shares in the banks' care under DSVR is far higher than the banks' own holdings: 36 per cent of the votes of the 100 largest companies according to the 1978 Monopolkommission report, if their own holdings are added in; for the ten largest companies it rose to 50 per cent—a commanding position.

The DSVR system facilitates the effective mobilization of shareholdings because it adds a banks' own holdings (a subsidiary factor) to its deposited shares (DSVR). There is a third factor: inter-bank co-operation. Some figures taken from a 1986 survey illustrate the importance of the banks' position (Table 2.3).

Differences in Corporate Governance

The German banks' direct holdings in some of the top 100 companies are substantial (Table 2.4). Competition between banks does not preclude

TABLE 2.3. *Voting holdings of the major German banks, 1986*

Rank of Company	% of shares voted at meeting	Voting holdings of:			
		Deutsche Bank	Dresdner Bank	Commerz-bank	All big banks
1. Siemens	60.64	17.64	10.74	4.14	32.52
2. Daimler Benz	81.02	41.80	18.78	1.07	61.66
Mercedes Hold	67.20	11.85	13.66	12.24	37.75
3. Volkswagen	50.13	2.94	3.70	1.33	7.98
4. Bayer	53.18	30.82	16.91	6.77	54.50
5. BASF	55.40	28.07	17.43	6.18	51.68
6. Hoechst	57.73	14.97	16.92	31.60	63.48
9. VEBA	50.24	19.99	23.08	5.85	47.92
11. Thyssen	68.48	9.24	11.45	11.93	32.62
12. Deutsche Bank	55.10	47.17	9.15	4.04	60.36
13. Mannesmann	50.63	20.49	20.33	9.71	50.53
18. MAN (GHH)	64.10	6.97	9.48	13.72	30.17
21. Dresdner Bank	56.79	13.39	47.08	3.57	64.04
27. Allianz-Holding	66.20	9.91	11.14	2.35	23.41
28. Karstadt	77.60	37.03	8.81	33.02	78.86
29. Hoesch	45.39	15.31	15.63	16.73	47.67
34. Commerzbank	50.50	16.30	9.92	34.58	60.81
35. Kaufhof	66.70	6.29	13.33	37.18	56.80
36. Kloeckner-Werke	69.13	17.30	3.78	3.55	24.63
37. KHD	72.40	44.22	3.82	1.50	49.54
41. Metallgesellschaft	90.55	16.42	48.85	0.35	65.62
44. Preussag	69.58	11.5	5.60	2.59	19.34
51. Degussa	70.94	6.86	33.03	1.89	41.79
52. Bayr. Vereinsbank	62.40	11.42	2.71	3.59	17.72
56. Continental	35.29	22.77	9.99	6.04	38.81
57. Bayr. Hypobank	67.90	5.86	7.05	1.20	14.11
59. Deutsche Babcock	67.13	7.58	9.67	5.29	22.54
67. Schering	46.60	23.86	17.46	10.17	51.50
68. Linde	52.99	22.76	15.73	21.36	59.87
73. Ph. Holzmann	82.18	55.42	0.91	6.49	62.82
94. Strabag	83.02	6.80	19.15	1.37	27.32
96. Bergmann	99.12	36.89	—	—	36.89
98. Hapag-Lloyd	84.50	48.15	47.82	0.39	96.36
Average	64.49	21.09	15.30	9.05	45.44

Source: Arno Gottschalk, 'Der Stimmrechtseinfluss der Banken in den Aktionarsversammlungen der Grossunternehmen', 5 *WSI-Mitteilungen*, 5 (1988), 294–404.

TABLE 2.4. *Holdings in German corporations held directly by German banks, 1988*

Company rank	Company	Bank	% of stock
1	Daimler Benz	Deutsche Bank	28.2
		Dresdner Bank	1.6
		Commerzbank	1.6
		DG Bank	.3
		Bayerische Landesbank	1.6
10	Thyssen AG	Commerzbank	4.94
14	BMW	Dresdner Bank	5
16	Deutsche Lufthansa	Bayerische Landesbank	5
21	MAN AG	Commerzbank	4.94
23	Messerschmitt Boelkow-Blohm	Dresdner Bank	5
	GmbH	Bayerische Vereinsbank	5
25	Karlstadt AG	Deutsche Bank	over 25
		Commerzbank	over 25
35	Kaufhof	Dresdner Bank	9 (1986)
		Commerzbank	3 (1986)
40	Vereinigte Elektrizitaets-werke	Deutsche Bank	6.3
	Westfalen	Westdeutsche Landesbank	over 7.2
42	Metallgesellschaft AG	Deutsche Bank	10.72
		Dresdner Bank	23.1
		Westdeutsche Landesbank	48.8
57	Linde AG	Deutsche Bank	10
		Commerzbank	10
58	Kloechner Werke	Deutsche Bank	19.6
67	Hochtief AG	Commerzbank	12.5
71	Klockner-Humboldt Deutz AG	Deutsche Bank	41.4
75	Philipp Holzmann AG	Deutsche Bank	35.4
		Commerzbank	5.0
90	PWA Papierwerke Waldhof Aschaffenburg	Bayerische Hypotheken und Wechselbank	25.0
92	Bergmann-Elektricitats-Werke AG	Deutsche Bank	36.5
		Bayerische Vereinsbank	25.4

Source: 'Hauptgutachten der Monopolkommission', 11 Deutsche Bundestag, Drucksache 7582, at 203–6 ff.

collusion. The concentration of voting power mentioned above may become intense if the banks choose to act in concert. A 1988 study by Gottschalk selects thirty-two of the 100 largest quoted firms accounting for about a quarter of the market's nominal capital: he found that banks collectively represented 82.67 per cent of all votes present at the meetings. The big three banks accounted for 45 per cent of the votes present. Though the veil was only slightly lifted on co-operation, I had an impression that the banks would indeed act together on and off supervisory boards and in regard to other issues (like take-overs—see below) where they felt it right. Sometimes, however, the banks do disagree—and publicly, for example, when the research arm of Deutsche Bank (DB Research) downgraded Commerzbank because of the exposure to Hafnia, Commerzbank reacted angrily. Deutsche Bank's defence was that DB Research operated independently and their own Vorstand did not vet its recommendations.

Bankers on Boards

As we have seen, the banks' pre-eminence as suppliers of capital and the range of their services gave them the opportunity to establish strong personal links with companies at working levels. These links, which themselves ensure influence and information, are reinforced more formally by the bank taking seats on the Aufsichtsrat of industrial companies. As we have seen, the value to a company of these links is enhanced by the company's being able to draw on its bank's logistic support in the form of research and analysis.

The Monopolkommission report of 1978 showed that at that time banks had 9.8 per cent of the seats on Aufsichtsräte—but this bare figure disguised the prominent role of Deutsche Bank, the interlocking role of these director-ships, and the fact that many of the total number of seats available were by law reserved for employee representatives. (Also that there are legal restric-tions on the number of directorships an individual might hold.) A further 1.2 per cent of available seats were held by representatives of insurance companies. At that time the big banks were represented on forty-nine Aufsichtsräte, private bankers on thirty-one, and savings banks on eleven. The 1984 report shows that among the top 100 companies, Deutsche had thirty-nine seats on Aufsichtsräte, Dresdner twenty-two, and Commerzbank fifteen. Some examples of boards of major companies are given in Appendix 2B, reproduced from recent annual reports.

The Bundesverband Deutscher Banken report of 1989 notes that while in the mid-1970s the banks held 10 per cent of the total seats on the boards of the top 100 companies, by 1988 the figure had fallen. Böhm noted that in 1986 the big three banks had more than 61 per cent of all bank seats. Deutsche Bank held fifty-four seats on the boards of forty-four of the 100 largest firms and, significantly, a banker was chairman of the Aufsichtsrat in twenty. The BHF bank report of September 1990 said that banks then held 8 per cent of all seats on the boards of Germany's 100 largest companies. There seems to have been a decline, but the banks' presence is still impressive and significant.

The position is more complex still. The big banks have advisory boards on which industrialists sit. These industrialists also sit on the boards of other industrial companies. There is a whole range of secondary links which commentators have attempted to measure. The figures suggest linkages of one sort or another between the big banks and perhaps 3,000 thousand enterprises.

To be more specific, a study of some major companies reveals the following numbers of bankers on their boards:

BASF	4 bankers out of 22
Bayer	3 bankers out of 20
BMW	1 banker out of 21
Daimler Benz	4 bankers out of 21
Hoechst	2 bankers out of 20
Siemens	4 bankers out of 22
Volkswagen	2 bankers out of 20

(The total number in all cases includes the chairman and the employee representatives. Some examples are given in Appendix 2A.)

It should not be supposed from this, however, that representatives of the banks force themselves on the boards of unwilling or even reluctant companies. Companies are glad to have them and they are generally glad to serve. The company benefits from their considerable personal skills and experience, the intelligence network they can tap, and their contacts. The banks gain by cementing the relationship with the company, by adding to their sources of information, and by the kudos board positions give them—not to mention the money, which generally they keep. 'We have day to day involvement in a functioning network of information. We are necessarily well informed and owing to our swift access to information are in a position to give management boards proper advice. That is why we are so often asked to serve on supervisory boards' (F. W. Christians, Deutsche Bank, (writing in *Die Zeit* 1987)).

With such an interwoven series of relationships the banks are in a position, if they choose, to act as monitors of companies, not in any formal, methodical sense, but informally when they judge that their influence is needed to nudge a company back on track, or in extreme cases to put it under some other company's wing. Banks do act in this way and many a company's survival and many a merger have depended on a bank's quiet initiative: it is a role which banks accept and in which, in important cases, their own board may be involved.

Summary

What this combination of direct ownership, DSVR, length of lending, and breadth of services together imply is:

- Deep firm relationships between company and banks, not lightly put aside. At best banks become counsel and guide to proprietors and the relationship lasts for decades.
- A massive flow of information into the banks.
- Deep knowledge by the banks about sectors of industry which can be used to customers' advantage.
- The development by the banks of well trained staff capable of sustaining the relationships described above.
- The banks very often have the knowledge, motivation and authority to exert influence on company management.

iv. The Basic Principles

Entrepreneurial Drive

The driving power in many small and medium German enterprises comes from the people who founded them and their successors. Many highly successful companies—even in international terms—have payrolls of a few hundred, but their niche products, sold by the proprietor personally, have a valued place in world markets.

In bigger companies, as we have seen, the Vorstand is entrusted with the task of driving the business forward. We know that its members are not inhibited by fear of hostile take-over; or by concern about government interference. As far as the law is concerned, they do not stand in fear of private lawsuit, but nevertheless have regard to the duties that are placed upon them; the state could take them to task if they did not. Their employees too would take them to court were they to disregard the proper processes in which the works councils are entitled to participate.

Within the Vorstand the drive may come largely from the Sprecher or chairman or general membership, according to the relative strength of the personalities and the company's tradition. Some Vorstands operate in a more collegiate way than others, and of course some companies have more drive than others, as they do the world over. The main point is that there is nothing within the German system to constrain this drive harmfully and there is a great deal to encourage it. The ethos and culture within which my interlocutors work seemed to encourage long-term thinking, planning, and investment with a conspicuous interest in quality and technical excellence.

Accountability

We have already seen that in a formal sense the Vorstand is accountable to the Aufsichtsrat; that its effectiveness is affected in some ways for the better by having employee representatives on it; that bankers have a key role on and off the Aufsichtsrat; and that as there are no hostile take-overs the role of the stockmarket is minimal. The question is, does the system really work? Is the Vorstand's accountability nominal or real?

One thing we can say from the start: that there can be no real accountability without a flow of information. In the UK and USA information to the outside directors flows through chairman/CEO. In the German system the employee representatives have a flow of information through works councils—to the point where they may well be the best- informed people on the Aufsichtsrat. On the shareholders' side, bankers will have external flows of information from their own contacts with the company, from colleagues, and often from their research departments, both about the company and its sector. It is these supplementary flows which make many Aufsichtsrat meetings important. Where they do not exist, because works councils are weak or there are no bankers, an Aufsichtsrat will depend almost exclusively on the power and personality of its members, particularly the chairman. And sometimes it is not up to the mark, a mere rubber stamp. The better the flow the better the dynamics, as it is reasonable to assume that the Germans are like everyone else—they prepare the ground better if they have to explain and argue the reasons for a proposed course of action. The mere fact of having to present figures quarterly and justify them is a discipline in itself—and they go far beyond the information presented to shareholders quarterly or half-yearly.

The bankers on the Aufsichtsrat are often not alone in reading the runes and asking the penetrating question. Many experienced senior industrialists serve on them, and even if they hesitate to embarrass managers in front of their employees at joint meetings, they may very well take up the cudgels informally on other occasions. As a matter of fact, companies are divided about having bankers on their Aufsichtsrat. Some like the connection (not to mention the information flow and contacts), but others feel they can get all they need from their bankers anyway without having to have them on their supervisory tier—they might, for instance, put them on an Advisory Committee.

In fact, even when a company's main banker is not on the Aufsichtsrat, he has every chance to assess management both from personal contacts and from the figures, and he is in a position to exercise influence on a day-to-day basis if necessary. It is impossible to assess precisely how important the influence of the German banks is on companies, for evidence only breaks surface in troubled times. It must, of course, depend on a company's relative strength. If it is cash rich and prospering its hausbank will have neither the cause nor the power to intervene. But if a company is troubled the banks' combination of information and voting power—plus perhaps a place on the supervisory board—strengthens the authority their position as lenders would normally provide.

Critics of the Aufsichtsrat contend that a group which meets quarterly at most cannot really understand a business, particularly if it is big and complex. A good Vorstand will in fact make sure its Aufsichtsrat is properly informed, and a strongly led Aufsichtsrat will ensure this is so (appointing special committees for the purpose if necessary). As noted above, many Aufsichtsrats are very well informed from various sources. Besides, the chairman of the Aufsichtsrat and some members of special subcommittees usually have much closer contact with the firm. He may even have an office in the company; in some cases he will come in often, even daily. The potential authority of the Aufsichtsrat should not be underestimated. The shareholders' representatives will generally be experienced industrialists or bankers. Members of the company's Vorstand will themselves serve on the Aufsichtsrat of other companies. The practical effects are to provide companies with an excellent flow of intelligence and guidance and to create a significant personal network.

Although the role of the Aufsichtsrat is formally limited, its members' experience is tapped by the Vorstand either at formal meetings or outside them, in a way which a US/UK non-executive director would find familiar: it is not true therefore to say that they are only supervisors and do not contribute. In smaller companies the articles may prescribe a wider range of subjects in which the Aufsichtsrat must be consulted.

On boards of companies of all sizes, personalities count as they always do. The balance of power in the Vorstand will be influenced by the strength of its chairman, just as the effectiveness of the Aufsichtsrat will depend heavily on its chairman. If there is a poor Vorstand and a weak Aufsichtsrat a company will flounder. Sometimes an Aufsichtsrat can see what needs to be done and be slow about doing it. (There is a striking similarity here to the UK and USA, where exactly the same is true if there is a poor CEO and weak outside directors.) Significant companies with strong Vorstands often seek strong and experienced Aufsichtsräte which can make a positive contribution to the company.

Some German critics of their own system regard Aufsichtsräte as otiose. It is true that some meetings are short and perfunctory ('two hours followed by lunch and a pleasant afternoon' as one man said), but this is not necessarily because they are neglecting their duties (though of course they may). If a company is palpably going really well there may be no cause to intervene. There are however signs that Aufsichtsräte are getting tougher—quicker to act when things go radically wrong. The Volkswagen currency scandal was a spur in this direction.

Although my impression is that most Germans would not wish to change the principle of employee representation on the Aufsichtsrat (or risk the turmoil of engineering such a change), and do in fact see many advantages, they are not slow to point out the faults. Heinrich Weiss, President of the Federation of German Industries (BDI), in the speech mentioned earlier, drew attention to the fact that there are trade-offs and compromises between management and employees which may disadvantage shareholders (not least in regard to management's own service contracts, which the Aufsichtsrat must approve), and that the whole process of decision-making can be slowed down. The chairman of the Aufsichtsrat needs to be strong. He said:

Another problem is that, for political reasons, the supervisory board sometimes has no real control over the managing board. If you sit on the supervisory board of a large company and have labour representatives at the same table, you do not dare to put a critical question to members of the management board because you would be blaming them in the presence of the works councillors, when the managers need to keep their full authority. It is not written in any by-laws, but my experience of different companies is that it has come to be considered impolite for a member of a supervisory board to ask a question that is critical of management.

This has led to a situation, especially in very large companies, where control over the management board has diminished to the point where management-board members invite their friends and colleagues from other companies to join the supervisory board, rather than have the situation where the supervisory board is set up by the shareholders and then controls the managers. So from time to time we have a reverse hierarchy.

The supervisory element in the two-tier system should not be regarded as the invigilation of a regular series of examinations. It is concerned with establishing and maintaining standards, and to the extent that it succeeds remedial action is unnecessary. Sometimes however it fails. What if things really do start to go wrong? If the Vorstand as a whole is competent, inadequate individuals will be dealt with quietly; poor performers will be tolerated temporarily or eased out, depending on age and the degree of incompetence. The Aufsichtsrat will only intervene if it thinks the Vorstand is being slow or wet—and even then it will try to avoid a public fracas in front of the unions. One element, though not a major one, is that the degree to which the Aufsichtsrat is ready to take drastic action will depend to some extent on the degree of its involvement in the original appointment of the manager concerned. It will in all cases have had to approve the appointment, but if the name had been originally proposed by the management board the Aufsichtsrat may feel rather less committed to it than if it had been directly suggested by them. To sack their own candidate would be an admission of failure—though it does happen. Banks incidentally do not claim any special knowledge in this area except for the company's financial management. Their own credibility might come into question were they to presume to exercise special judgement on people from spheres like design or engineering where they have no special knowledge.

A far more difficult circumstance arises when the Vorstand as a whole appears to be performing poorly. My general impression is that the Aufsichtsrat can be slow to take remedial action. This partly reflects the general attitudes mentioned earlier: management is often given the benefit of the doubt—and a further chance to redeem itself. Reciprocal appointments are prohibited by Section 100 of the Stock Corporation Law, that is, A serving on B's board and vice versa. Other cross appointments are permitted and frequently exist, for example, A on B's board, B on C's and C on A's. This is not an act of deliberate policy but simply the result of the fact that there is a coterie of suitable people who are natural candidates and are therefore chosen. Between such people there may be an instructive and unspoken non-aggression pact on the principle 'There but for the Grace of God go I.' Even in cases when an Aufsichtsrat has steeled itself to act, it may choose to ride out the storm, particularly if the media are involved, and then move quietly but effectively when it has abated. It can only make matters worse if the Vorstand was slow in producing the information—and this happens too. Even when the information is timely and the Aufsichtsrat skilled, keen, and determined, it can make mistakes. The Aufsichtsrat of Karstadt did not veto the disastrous purchase of Neckermann, nor did the Volkswagen Aufsichtsrat stop the purchase of Triumph-Adler which lost them DM 1 billion. No system is or ever could be perfect.

The major weapon in the hands of the Aufsichtsrat is its power to appoint or dismiss. In this as in other matters, the chairman has to build a consensus for action; the company and indeed the country looks to him to play his part when circumstances require it. Sometimes he fails. Action in regard to the Vorstand of AEG is commonly regarded as having been dilatory to say the least: the management had their appointments renewed several times when (in the view of commentators) some might well have been replaced. The Aufsichtsrat's role is bound to be less important in times of prosperity, especially as it is not in German nature to try to buy short-term prosperity without proper consideration for the longer term. If a German company looks prosperous today, there is a reasonable inference that there is little to be served by interfering. If, however, the evidence of decline is accumulating, the influence of the Aufsichtsrat becomes potentially greater, so that ultimately it can steel itself for action. But 'ultimately' is the crucial word. Germans are like their competitors elsewhere in being reluctant to remove those who have served a company well until the evidence of their diminished capacity has become irresistible.

There is another factor which may come into play. It is a not unusual sequence for the chairman or Sprecher of the Vorstand to join the Aufsichtsrat when he retires, often as its chairman. Meanwhile, he will have had a major part in picking his own successor. The complications can be imagined. If his successor fails he will feel responsible, and in any event his propensity to intervene will, at least to begin with, be considerable. The German system may look as if relationships and responsibilities are clear cut, but the reality is often more blurred.

A recent (1991), and as yet unresolved, take-over case illustrates the system at work. The Aufsichtsrat of Continental, chaired by Horst Urban, disagreed with its Vorstand about the appropriate response to a bid by Pirelli. But as the contest progressed trading conditions worsened and the Aufsichtsrat ditched Urban in order to open serious negotiations. What was interesting about this case, apart from the light it shed on German take-over laws, was the role of the Aufsichtsrat—clearly playing a major part in determining a strategic issue.

Summing up the balance on accountability, the judgement of most of my interlocutors was that it was reasonably effective and consistent—with banks and employees/unions playing an important part in making the supervisory tier function adequately. It is undoubtedly a system that depends heavily upon networks and they in turn only function effectively (even with abundant interlocking directorates) because co-operation is seen as the proper mode. There were fewer examples than in some other economies of power-hungry industrial moguls running amok in an excess of megalomania: given the success of German industry over the last forty years, the absence of such characters is rather remarkable. Perhaps account-ability is mainly about how one feels; my impression is that the German system does induce this feeling to a considerable degree in major public companies. In private businesses where the boss is still very much the boss, accountability in a formal or narrow sense is probably not so much in evidence, but even then the influence of the banks may be considerable and a sense of social obligation general.

v. The Developing Scene

An Economic Sea Change?

Up till the present time, the combination of factors noted earlier, in particular, the availability of a well-motivated and trained workforce, technical competence, stable macro-economic climate, and effective governance system, have together enabled German industry to prosper even though its currency has firmed and the hours worked by its labour force have declined (37-hour week). (It is easier to reach a British or American executive on a Friday afternoon than it is a German.)

Now, however, largely because the 'social on-costs' have risen and amount to 82 per cent, unit labour costs are rising too. The increases in productivity are no longer big enough to absorb them. It is true that unemployment at around 7 per cent in the former West and 15.5 per cent and rising in the former Eastern Länder keep inflationary pressures in check to some extent (as do currently high interest rates—in August 1992 around $9\frac{1}{2}$ per cent). Even so, the basis from which German industry views the world—'make everything at home'—is not as solid as it was, and there are signs of more plants being established and more components being sourced abroad. The strains on the corporate governance system are perhaps greater now than for some time, so it is worth considering its main components one by one.

The Two-Tier System Changing?

There is a trade-off between the clear definition of function that a two-tier system provides and the specialization of the supervisory function among board members of the unitary system where everyone has the same legal duties. Actually both systems fudge the issue. The members of a German Aufsichtsrat do not have a stand-off from management, but all sorts of informal ways and some machinery to get close enough to them to make sense of the business: both systems have their conflicts of interest. The Germans continue to prefer their arrangements, and given the role of the banks believe on the whole they work adequately. The Aufsichtsrat can be attacked from either flank—as too distant and out of touch, or, rarely, as too intrusive and interfering. The test of any system is how good it is at accommodating individual idiosyncrasies: does it, despite all the variations, broadly get the balance right between entrepreneurial thrust and account-ability? Perhaps because of the basic German approach referred to earlier the answer to this question is generally positive. No Germans I encountered foresaw radical change. What some see is a gradual evolution in the role of the Aufsichtsrat. In her Stockton Lecture Schneider Lenné said 'In the course of the years, the focus of the supervisory board's work has begun to shift more and more towards advising and counselling the board of manag-ing directors. The rationale of monitoring companies' management is no longer perceived to be a question of detecting past mistakes but rather of preventing them from being made in the first place.'

For similar reasons there seemed little pressure to change the basic rules of co-determination. Perhaps the unions have advanced as far as they are going to, but they are not in retreat. A position of some stability has been reached, though doubtless there will be nibbling away at the edges by both sides.

German industry for many years did not wish to expand its manufacturing base abroad very widely, preferring wherever possible to manufacture at home and export finished products. This has now changed and will continue to do so under the pressure of rising wage costs and social costs and a hard currency. Even Germany's legendary productivity may not be enough to stop some products becoming uncompetitive. This may well lead to more plants being based abroad, which has a number of important repercussions. In the field of corporate governance an obvious one is representation on the Aufsichtsrat. Does co-determination only apply to the German employees of German multinationals? After all, the Vorstand or Aufsichtsrat may take decisions which affect plants abroad. This is one of the many matters which are of interest in the context of the proposed European company statute.

More Market Influence?

At the present moment the stock market is not particularly important to German savers. The German stock exchanges regret this (they would, wouldn't they), but there is little sign of a change in sentiment or behaviour.[6]

---

[6] There are, however, important changes in structure. After many months of negotiation, the eight German stock exchanges have finally agreed to centralize their operations (with effect from 1 Jan. 1993), in a bid to make Germany's financial services more competitive internation-ally. The Frankfurt exchange will be transformed into a holding company, Deutsche Börse AG, which will acquire both the Deutsche Terminbörse (futures and options exchange) and the Deutsche Kassenverein (clearing and settlement house) as well as the other regional stock exchanges. Trading, clearing, and settlement are to be linked electronically, while regulation and management will also be centralized. However, in deference to the regional exchanges, which fear that electronic trading will undermine their *raison d'être*, floor trading is to be maintained in parallel with the IBIS screen trading system, at least until the mid-1990s.

The private investor seems content with less risky investments than equities, and whilst the Bundesbank fights so fiercely to contain inflation, may well continue to be risk-averse. A major change could come if more pensions were funded, and there are some signs of a drift in that direction through *Spezial Fonds* etc. but it is a very gradual one. Thinking more broadly, however, it would be surprising if over time such a powerful economy as Germany's (and the integration and rehabilitation of the East will in a decade strengthen its already strong position) were not to be reflected somehow in a wider and deeper stock market. As a source of capital the stock market is not of particular significance to companies. Even in modern times, the bulk of funds is channelled through the banks and they dominate the organized capital markets (see above and Friedmann, 1984) though there are some recent signs that big German companies may turn more to the capital markets than in the past. At the end of 1981 UK equity/debt was 49/51 per cent, German equity/debt 19/81 per cent of liabilities. In the decade to 1985 companies in both countries raised negligible amounts by bond issues.

As we have seen the German view of the purpose of companies gives shareholders an interest and a role, but not such a pronounced one as in the UK and USA. They are important, but further down the pecking order. Private shareholders, other than proprietors, do not constitute a large proportion of the market anyway; companies and banks, which between them hold a large proportion of equity, tend to take an understanding and essentially long-term view. They already have the means at their disposal to exert influence and seem to do it more or less effectively. There is no suggestion as far as one can tell that their role should change or that they should become more active.

Take-overs

Perhaps a more interesting area is take-overs. It used always to be assumed that contested bids would be a waste of time and money, but one or two recent cases have suggested that the obstacles may not be as unsurmountable as supposed. Even so, this assumption is so strongly held that it has seldom been thought worthwhile to test it. Where the banks themselves have a significant holding they would not contemplate taking a profit if an unwanted bid appeared, as it would not only ruin their relationship with the company concerned but also expose them to criticism in the media— especially if the bidder were foreign. Besides, German accounts tend to be opaque, so an unfriendly bidder would be shooting in the dark—though there may be some consolation in knowing that the target company is likely to have hidden reserves of one sort or another. As noted above, the bidder has the advantage of being able to stalk his target unseen. He only has to declare his stake when it reaches 25 per cent, and as the shares are in bearer form a company cannot keep track of them.

It may therefore be conjectured that if shares in a company are widely held, and the banks' own stakes relatively small, and if at the same time the bid price were well above the current market price, the banks might be in a difficult position in advising their DSVR clients and might be faced with a sharp conflict of interest. If therefore the bidder were serious, and no cartel implications arose, it is by no means clear that the current assumption is correct, even though at the moment almost everyone acts upon it.

The 'Discipline' of the Market

There does not seem to be any great concern within Germany that the perceived immunity from stock market pressures, or the absence of threat of take-over is harmful. Companies that do consistently badly come under pressure from some shareholders and from their bankers. Vorstands are not wholly insensitive to a declining share price when it is clear that it signals specific market disapproval: nor are Aufsichtsräte. It is not clear, however, that the absence of greater pressure has done much damage. The country has so far managed to live with a rising currency—though not to keep intact without subsidies the heavy industries, like coal, iron/steel, and shipbuilding, which are in general decline in the West. What the absence of general stock market pressures has undoubtedly assisted is the Germans' natural tendency to think in the long term and invest accordingly. A substantial part of the German economy is in the hands of private companies, but even where shares are quoted, German shareholders are said to take a long-term view—slow steady increases in real earnings, and heavy reinvestment leading to an increase in real assets employed, rather than a high level of distribution. Perhaps the picture may be changing with dividend payments becoming a more important measure of a company's health. In any event, low inflation has made it easier for Germans to see what the real picture is.

It is easy to over-simplify as regards investment and the timescale of returns, but it does seem highly probable that the absence of pressure from the German stock market reinforces the natural tendency German manage-ment would have anyway to set the balance at the point they feel right to equal the best foreign competition. If this is true one would expect the German system to show good advantage internationally in areas where the balance needed to be set long-term—like engineering. Observations suggest this is so. In industries where the timescale is naturally shorter the comparative advantages are likely to be less marked—and so it seems. But this balance seems on the whole satisfactory to the Germans and there is little urge to change it.

Co-operation or Confrontation?

The prevailing ethos is still one of co-operation rather than confrontation. It is demonstrated in the relationships between sections of the German economy—proprietors, professional management, employees generally, the financial sector, government, and academia. The dangers of exploitation inherent in co-operation are held in check partly by German institutional arrangements, partly by a sense of duty to the community. The question is whether a lack of 'constructive tension' will lead to inefficient cosiness. There are those who believe that there is a distinct possibility that the German system could lead to inefficiency and structural over-rigidity. Such critics have been less in evidence in the light of the sharpness of German reaction to reunification, which was anything but dilatory or sclerotic.

Reunification has, however, imposed severe pressures on Germany, economic and political. The resurgence of extremism with overtones of violence and racism has so far (late 1992) affected only a small fragment of the population. It is, moreover, exactly the kind of confrontation most Germans abhor and struggle to avoid. It remains to be seen how far it will spread and whether economic pressures will corrode the corporate governance systems. One leading banker said to me, 'The obituaries for consultation and consensus are premature.' I am sure most Germans fervently hope he is right.

The Law

I could detect no change in the basic attitude to the law described earlier, but there is a cloud on the horizon. Law has become a popular subject for study. There are now as many law students in training as there are lawyers. If they stay in the profession (which of course many may not), how will they all make a living, except by greater general litigiousness?

A Change in the Role for the Banks?

The banks are vitally important to the system, but as we have seen it is a great over-simplification to say that 'their power depends on their shareholdings'. In many cases they have influence rather than power—companies often have more than one bank and can change bankers if they choose. Banks' shareholdings have usually been acquired as a side-effect of their operations and not as part of any scheme to gain influence or leverage. If they sold every share they held it would arguably make little difference except in the handful of companies (some of which are very important) where their holdings are really big. The reason for this is the DSVR system described above, which in effect mobilizes shareholdings. So the *influence* of the banks rests primarily on their relationship with individual companies, and partly on the interlocking relationships across the whole industrial financial spectrum which, taken together, produce a massive flow of intelligence. The *power* of banks rests on DSVR and only secondarily on their shareholdings. And because of the attitudes described earlier, influence is more important than power—which shows up when tough action is taken more slowly than appears warranted. Is their power and influence declining? The answer at the moment is surely no. One of the most remarkable phenomena of reunification was the speed with which the big three swung into action, establishing networks so that the lifeblood of finance could flow through the new arteries to every part of the body politic.

From time to time there have been comments on and criticisms of the banks' influence and power; from the opposite flank comes concern that the banks' closeness to and investment in industry may be a danger to the banks themselves. Commentators observed that a shiver ran through the Japanese economy when the Nikkei plunged. In 1992, however, the impression was that all these comments, criticisms, and concerns were dormant. Competition among the banks was easily sufficient to allay fears of any particular one being unduly dominant; the banks' balance sheets were thought to be sound enough easily to accommodate their industrial investments; their influence owed much to industry's desire to have it and was generally regarded as benign. And their contribution was regarded as indispensable. The close relationship of a company with its hausbank had often proved especially useful in times of trouble; banks did not interfere unless they had to—never prematurely. They were regarded as the keystone of the whole system. The arch could not exist without them and there was no desire to replace it with any other kind of structure.

There has been a tendency for major German companies, often cash rich, to do in house many of the operations previously carried out by the banks for them—highly sophisticated treasury operations, in fact. Sometimes in house 'banks' have been created for the purpose, though very few, one gathers, take external deposits. (These institutions are unsupervised, which does not please the authorities.) The question arises whether these developments will weaken bank–industry links for the companies concerned. Opinion seems to be that this is possible to a limited extent, but that companies still see advantage in traditional relationship banking, though an exclusive relationship with one bank is now uncommon for big companies. Indeed, they may well have half a dozen main banks and use others for particular purposes. It is felt that the principle of relationship banking will survive, but with a new generation of chairmen relationships may perhaps be less close.

Reports suggest that the German market for commercial paper has grown rapidly since its establishment in February 1991. A market report by LZB in Hessen in late 1992 said that forty-seven programmes with a total value of DM 35 billion had been undertaken to date. It is too early to say what effect, if any, this will have on the relationship between banks and their commercial customers.

Dual Relationships

There may be a certain tension within a dual or multiple relationship. A lender, for instance, is primarily interested in safety; an investor in equity shares is also concerned about safety, but will tend to be less risk-averse. Banks or other credit institutions which are major shareholders may have to ride both horses at once. Perhaps this is not as uncomfortable as it sounds because the banks are happy to see companies retain earnings rather than distribute them as it helps protect their borrowings—but only up to a point, since ultimately such a policy can lead to companies becoming cash rich and therefore more independent. All these tensions are there potentially, but there is little sign on the surface, at any rate, of their being actually troublesome. There are many subtleties—taxation among them—but concern does not seem to have reached a point when action is likely to inhibit multiple relationships and the potential conflicts of interest they sometimes occasion.

The European Dimension

The Germans have long been supporters of the EC Fifth Directive which seeks to harmonize company structure in Europe and in particular to introduce the principle of co-determination. This support rests partly on a genuine belief that co-determination is socially desirable and economically beneficial; partly on a fear that German industry would become uncompetitive if less responsible systems remained in place; and partly because of concern lest German companies move their bases to countries that did not require co-determination.

vi. Envoi

An Interesting Comparison

It is always difficult to obtain an objective comparison of systems. Herr Gottfried Bruder, who has served as the London General Manager of the Commerzbank for many years, made some interesting observations in the course of an address to the Royal Society of Arts on 24 March 1992. On the role of the stock market in the UK he said:

The Stock Exchange in London has developed over something like 150 years into the most sophisticated equity market on this side of the Atlantic, possibly the world. Its very efficiency and excellence have propelled it into a monopoly position; one however operated not in the interest of its users, but in the interest of its members. By no stretch of the imagination could it be demonstrated that these interests could be anything other than in long term conflict with each other. In addition, there are the opposing interests of the two user groups, investors and listed companies. It is a pious sham to claim that their interests are complementary in that investors provide the long term funding which the companies need. That is the theoretical model, but it is rendered largely illusory by the fact that the share designed as an instrument of long term investment is today treated by the financial markets in the Anglo Saxon environment like a short term money market instrument.

Totally unpredictable stock market fluctuations, often unrelated to overall economic performance or to that of individual companies, but frequently affected by fairly capricious investment behaviour of institutional investors, make that claim that the stock market is a reliable provider of long term capital to British industry a bit of a fairy tale.

The proponents of a stock exchange dominated culture, who with stars in their eyes point to the liquid London Stock Exchange and its vastly larger turnover than that of its continental rivals, normally answer with the most platitudinal clichés when one asks them who the beneficiaries of these impressive turnovers are. Whatever their answer is, it is certainly not British industry.

He commented on the greater German dependence on bank finance and their lesser use of the capital market by inverting the point (which does not of course impair its validity):

The obsessive preoccupation of the British capital market with the gearing of companies—shockingly often unmatched by a true understanding of different gearing requirements for different types of companies—is quite different from the more relaxed views on gearing in Germany. As a result, we regard British companies as historically over-capitalised.

The expectations of institutional investors in Britain regarding short term earnings force dividend policies on companies which are incompatible with the latter's long term health, a point clearly demonstrated by companies paying dividends even out of reserves in the present and previous recessions. By comparison, institutional investors are in Germany insignificant, equity investment plays not nearly as great a role generally, and therefore in the absence of equivalent shareholder pressure I could not conceive of a German company committing the folly of voluntarily depleting its reserves to pay dividends.

Britain has traditionally been a high interest rate country with a resulting greater penalty on borrowing, something which was reinforced by the lowering of corporate tax rates in the 80s and thus lower tax offset value of the cost of borrowing. On the other hand, Germany is traditionally a low interest rate country with higher corporation tax rates which taken together make borrowing more attractive than capital and thus adds to the weaker influence of the capital markets.

These conclusions lead to his stressing the importance of the relationships between German banks and their customers (reflected above in this paper):

The larger importance of debt, however, in German companies, the mutual exchange of supervisory board members between banks and industry and the absence of stock exchange imposed limitations on information flowing from companies to banks, make for greater mutual confidence and thus a more successful symbiosis, all of which together allow for better informed lending practices, not greater risk happiness.

A German company would jeopardise its relationship with its bankers if it paid dividends out of retained earnings because it felt it had to mollify the stock market. At the same time, however, companies are safeguarded against bankers in their turn acquiring a monopoly position over them by the much greater number and variety of indigenous banks than exist in this country.

He followed with a sharp attack on take-overs in the UK and concluded that its system was inherently antipathetic to long-term development expenditure of any kind, including R&D and training. The unspoken contrast with German attitudes confirms all that has been written above. He ends with a requiem which could apply to industry in the USA just as much (and perhaps even more) as it does to the UK. To understand what he feels is good about Germany one must hear his comment on what he perceives in the UK:

You can always provide a very plausible or even virtuous sounding reason for axing anything which has a long term intent. The entire financial culture in Britain and its effects on industry are such that taken together they constitute a strong disincentive for investment in any form which cannot almost instantly provide returns pleasing to the stock market. The invidious feature of this is that it is a creeping process without dramatic highs and lows which can only be demonstrated over the long term. The plotting of the fortunes of British industry over past decades would indeed demonstrate this.

The important question is whether the financial services sector has already successfully crowded out the industrial one to such an extent that even objective analysis may be perceived to be offensive because it arrives at inconvenient answers.

British industry will have to decide once and for all whether it will continue to be used as a vehicle, a pretext only, by an extremely highly developed and, in its own right, immensely successful stock market culture, or whether it wishes to assert itself and relegate the stock market if not to the role of servant, then at least that of a truly equal partner.

Many people will disagree with Bruder totally, or accuse him of hyperbole, or both. This is to miss the point. I have deliberately included his comments in the section on German corporate governance, not on the UK, because it shows quite clearly what he regards as virtuous about his own country's system, namely, that the financial sector serves industry and not vice versa. What this paper has shown is how German industry has continued to prosper without the constraints the markets impose in the UK and USA. It is because there are few impediments to dynamism and a reasonably effective (though far from perfect) system of accountability. It appears—in 1992— that Germany may be heading for one of its toughest periods for some years. Company management may find itself contending with external factors that impair its international competitiveness—an overvalued currency and high social on-costs among them, together with high real and nominal interest rates. If Bruder is right its system of corporate governance will stand the strain because its balance between dynamism and accountability is fundamentally sound, and—critically—because dynamism is not fettered by market pressures, and accountability works reasonably well.

Appendix 2A. *Vorstand Rules of Procedure*
An example

The Vorstand shall direct the affairs of the company in accordance with the law, the articles of association, and these rules of procedure. It shall work together in a spirit of trust with the other executive bodies of the company and staff representatives for the good of the company.

The Vorstand shall allocate areas of responsibility to its individual members; in this respect the Vorstand's spokesman shall have the right of veto. The Aufsichtsrat must be advised immediately of how the responsibilities have been allocated and of any subsequent amendments.

The members of the Vorstand shall be jointly responsible for all aspects of management. They shall work together as a body and shall advise one another on a regular basis of all important business transactions.

Each individual member of the Vorstand shall be solely responsible for the area of responsibility assigned to him within the scope of Vorstand's decisions. Where measures and transactions in one area of responsibility will significantly affect one or more other areas of responsibility at the same time, the Vorstand member must come to an agreement beforehand with the other members concerned. Vorstand members can insist that measures of transactions to be carried out by another area which will significantly affect their own areas must be formally approved by the full Vorstand.

It is the duty of the speaker of the Vorstand to co-ordinate all the areas of responsibility. It is his task to ensure standard management procedures designed to secure the objectives laid down by Vorstand decisions. He may at any time demand information from the Vorstand members concerning particular matters falling within their areas of responsibility and decide that he should be notified in advance of specific types of transactions.

The Vorstand's speaker shall represent the Vorstand and the company in their dealings with the public, in particular with the authorities, associations, economic organizations, and the press, in matters concerning the company as a whole or several areas of management. He shall represent the Vorstand in dealings with the Aufsichtsrat, with particular reference to meeting the legal obligation to report to it. All members must support the speaker in carrying out this task.

The speaker shall chair Vorstand meetings. He shall decide the order in which the items on the agenda are dealt with and the procedure and order for voting. In the event of the speaker being unable to attend, he shall be represented by the longest-serving managing board member present.

The Vorstand must strive to the best of its ability to reach unanimity in its decision-taking; if unanimity cannot be reached, decisions shall be taken on the basis of a simple majority of the members taking the decisions, unless other majorities are provided for by law, the articles of association or these rules of procedure. If the votes are equal, the speaker shall have the casting vote.

The Vorstand shall be quorate if all members have been invited and at least half of the members take part in adopting resolutions.

Absent members shall be informed immediately of the resolutions adopted.

[Typically at this point the statement will cover in some detail the matters which had to be brought to the Vorstand, e.g. investments over a certain size.]

Where the Aufsichtsrat does not approve a transaction that has already been concluded, the Vorstand must unwind the transaction immediately.

If members of the Vorstand wish to become members of the Aufsichtsrat of another company they must obtain approval from their own Aufsichtsrat. The holders of any such offices are entitled to any earnings arising from those offices. Holders of such offices shall have sole liability.

Appendix 2B. *Aufsichtsräte of Selected Companies*

Bayer A G
Ehrenvorsitzender:
Professor Dr.-Ing. Kurt Hansen,
Leverkusen

Professor Dr. Herbert Grünewald,
ehemaliger Vorstands-vorsitzender der
    Gesellschaft,
Leverkusen,
Vorsitzender

Paul Lax,
technischer Angestellter,
Leverkusen,
stellvertretender Vorsitzender

Werner Bischoff,
Bezirksleiter und Vorsitzender der IG
    Chemie Nordrhein-Westfalen,
Düsseldorf

Adolf Busbach,
Elektroinstallateur,
Leverkusen

Hans Drathen,
Chemielaborant,
Krefeld

Dr. Gerhard Fritz,
ehemaliges Mitglied des Vorstands der
    Gesellschaft,
Bergisch Gladbach

Rechtsanwalt
Dr. Heinz Gester,
Justitiar des Deutschen
    Gewerkschaftsbundes,
Düsseldorf

Constantin Freiherr Heereman von
    Zuydtwyck,
Präsident des Deutschen
    Bauernverbandes e.V.,
Bonn-Bad Godesberg

Robert A. Jeker,
Präsident der Generaldirektion der
    Schweizerischen Kreditanstalt,
Zürich, Schweiz

Dr.-Ing. Karlheinz Kaske,
Vorsitzender des Vorstands der Siemens
    Aktiengesellschaft,
München

Peter Klug,
kaufmännischer, Angestellter,
Leverkusen

Hilmar Kopper,
Sprecher des Vorstands der Deutsche
    Bank Aktiengesellschaft,
Frankfurt (Main)

Dr.-Ing. Manfred Lennings,
Industrieberater,
Essen-Kettwig

Dr. h.c. André Leysen,
Vorsitzender des Verwaltungsrats der
    Gevaert NV,
Mortsel,
Belgien

Dr. h.c. Hermann Rappe, MdB,
Vorsitzender der IG Chemie,
Hannover

Karl-Willi Schellscheidt,
Horizontalbohrer,
Leverkusen

Dr. Walter Seipp,
Vorsitzender des Aufsichtsrats der
    Commerzbank Aktiengesellschaft,
Frankfurt (Main)

Professor Dr. Walter Simmler,
Chemiker,

Odenthal-Glöbusch

Professor Dr. Dr. Heinz A. Staab,
Direktor der Abteilung Organische
    Chemie am Max-Planck-Institut für
    medizinische Forschung,
Heidelberg

Hans Unger,
Maschinenschlosser,
Dormagen

BMW AG

Hans Graf von der Goltz,
Bad Homburg v.d.H.,
Vorsitzender
Kaufmann

Manfred Schoch,*
München,
stellv. Vorsitzender,
Vorsitzender des Gesamtbetriebsrats

Eberhard von Heusinger,
Bad Homburg v.d.H.,
stellv. Vorsitzender
Rechtsanwalt

Johann Vilsmeier,*
Dingolfing
stellv. Vorsitzender,
Vositzender des Betriebsrats,
Werk Dingolfing

Johanna Quandt,
Bad Homburg v.d.H.,
stellv. Vorsitzende,
Mitglied des Aufsichtsrats der Altana
    Industrie-Aktien und Anlagen AG

Dr.-Ing. E.h. Klaus Barthelt,
Erlangen,
ehem. Mitglied des Vorstands der
    Siemens AG

Reinhold Bauer,*
Landshut,
Vorsitzender des Betriebsrats,
Werk Landshut

Helmuth Baumgärtner,*
Dingolfing,
Mitglied des Betriebsrats,

Werk Dingolfing

Klaus Bernhardt,*
Frankfurt/Main,
Gewerkschaftssekretär

Nikolaus Held,*
Regensburg,
Mitglied des Betriebsrats,
Werk Regensburg

Dr. Hartmut Kämpfer,*
Berlin,
Leiter Sparte Motorrad

Cornelis J. van der Klugt,
Eindhoven,
Niederlande,
ehem. Vorsitzender des Vorstands der
    NV Philips' Gloeilampenfabrieken

Dr. Wolfgang Leeb,
München,
Mitglied des Aufsichtsrats der Dresdner
    Bank AG

Dr. h.c. André Leysen,
Mortsel,
Belgien,
Vorsitzender des Verwaltungsrats der
    Gevaert NV

Rudolf Lukes,*
München,
Gewerkschaftssekretär

Alois Mathe,*
München,
stellv. Vorsitzender des Betriebsrats,
Werk München

Dr. Hans Meinhardt,
Wiesbaden,
Vorsitzender des Vorstands der Linde AG

Dr. Dr.-Ing. E.h. Dr. phil. h.c. Kurt
    Werner,
Darmstadt,
Vorsitzender des Aufsichtsrats der
    Maschinenfabrik Goebel GmbH

* Arbeitnehmervertreter

Dr. Kurt Wessing,
Düsseldorf,
Rechtsanwalt

Klaus Zwickel,*
Frankfurt/Main,
2. Vorsitzender des Vorstands der IG
    Metall

Daimler Benz A G

Hermann J. Abs,
Frankfurt am Main,
Ehrenvorsitzender der Deutsche Bank
    AG

Ehrenvorsitzender

Hilmar Kopper,
Frankfurt am Main,
Mitglied des Vorstands der Deutsche
    Bank AG

Vorsitzender

Karl Feuerstein,*
Mannheim,
Vorsitzender des Konzernbetriebsrats der
    Daimler-Benz AG,
Vorsitzender des Gesamtbetriebsrats der
    Mercedes-Benz AG

Stellvertretender Vorsitzender

Prof. Dr. rer. nat. Gerd Binnig,
München,
Leiter der IBM-Physikgruppe

Dipl.-Ing. Richard Bollmann,*
Mannheim,
Hauptabteilungsleiter,
Stellvertretender Vorsitzender des
    Gesamtsprecherausschusses der
    Mercedes-Benz AG

Prof. Dr.-Ing. E.h. Werner
    Breitschwerdt,
Stuttgart

Dr. rer. pol. Horst J. Burgard,
Frankfurt am Main,
Mitglied des Vorstands der Deutsche
    Bank AG

Helmut Funk,*
Stuttgart,
Vorsitzender des Betriebsrats des Werks
    Untertürkheim und der
    Hauptverwaltung der Mercedes-Benz
    AG

Erich Klemm,*
Calw,
Vorsitzender des Betriebsrats des Werks
    Sindelfingen der Mercedes-Benz AG

Martin Kohlhaussen,
Frankfurt am Main,
Sprecher des Vorstands der
    Commerzbank AG
(ab 26. Juni 1991)

Rudolf Kuda,*
Frankfurt am Main,
Abteilungsleiter im Vorstand der IG
    Metall

Hugo Lotze,*
Reinhardshagen,
Vorsitzender des Betriebsrats des Werks
    Kassel der Mercedes-Benz AG

Dipl.-Ing. Hans-George Pohl,
Hamburg,
Vorsitzender des Vorstands der Deutsche
    Shell AG

Dr. ref. pol. Wolfgang Röller,
Frankfurt am Main,
Sprecher des Vorstands der Dresdner
    Bank AG

Siegfried Sauter,*
Frankfurt am Main,
Stellvertretender Vorsitzender des

Konzernbetriebsrats der Daimler-Benz
AG, Vorsitzender des
Gesamtbetriebsrats der AEG
Aktiengesellschaft

Dr. jur. Roland Schelling,
Stuttgart,
Rechtsanwalt und Notar

Peter Schönfelder,*
Augsburg,
Mitglied des Betriebsrats der
Messerschmitt-Bölkow-Blohm GmbH

Prof. Dr. jur. Johannes Semler,
Kronberg/Taunus,
Mitglied des Vorstands der Mercedes
Aktiengesellschaft Holding

Franz Steinkühler,*

* Von den Arbeitnehmern gewählt

Frankfurt am Main,
1. Vorsitzender der IG Metall

Hermann-Josef Strenger,
Leverkusen,
Vorsitzender des Vorstands der Bayer
AG

Bernhard Wurl,*
Mainz,
Abteilungsleiter im Vorstand der IG
Metall

Aus dem Aufsichtsrat ausgeschieden

Dr. jur. Walter Seipp,
Frankfurt am Main,
Vorsitzender des Aufsichtsrats der
Commerzbank AG
(am 26. Juni 1991)

BASF AG

Dr. rer. nat. Hans Albers,
Bad Dürkheim

Vorsitzender

Professor Dr. rer. not. Matthias
Seefelder,
Heidelberg

Ehrenvorsitzender

Gerhard Blumenthal,
Schifferstadt,
Stellv. Vorsitzender,
Vorsitzender des Betriebsrats des Werkes
Ludwigshafen der BASF
Aktiengesellschaft, Verstorben am
20.4.1991

Volker Obenauer,
Ludwigshafen,
Stellv. Vorsitzender ab 27.6.1991,
Vorsitzender des Betriebsrats des Werkes
Ludwigshafen der BASF
Aktiengesellschaft

Dr. phil. Marcus Bierich,
Stuttgart,
Vorsitzender der Geschäftsführung der
Robert Bosch GmbH

Dieter Brand,
Dittelsheim-Heßloch,
Geschäftsführer der Verwaltungsstelle
der Industriegewerkschaft Chemie–
Papier–Keramik,
Ludwigshafen

Professor Dr. rer. nat. Manfred Eigen,
Göttingen,
Direktor am Max-Planck-Institut
für biophysikalische Chemie in
Göttingen

Heinz Götz,
Limburgerhof,
Mitglied des Betriebsrats des Werkes
Ludwigshafen der BASF
Aktiengesellschaft

Dr. rer. pol. Johan M. Goudswaard,
Wassenaar/Niederlande,
Ehem. stellv. Vorsitzender des
Verwaltungsrats der Unilever NV

Dr. rer. pol. Kurt Hohenemser,
Frankfurt am Main,
Ehrenmitglied der Deutschen
Schutzvereinigung für
Wertpapierbesitz e.V.

Dr. jur. Robert Holzach,
Zumikon/Schweiz,
Ehrenpräsident der Schweizerischen
   Bankgesellschaft

Roland Koch,
Ludwigshafen,
Mitglied des Betriebsrats des Werkes
   Ludwigshafen der BASF
   Aktiengesellschaft

Professor Dr. rer. nat. Hans Joachim
   Langmann,
Jugenheim/Bergstrasse,
Vorsitzender des Gesellschafterrats und
   der Geschäftsleitung der E. Merck

Ulrich Nickel,
Frankenthal,
Stellv. Vorsitzender des Betriebsrats des
   Werkes Ludwigshafen der BASF
   Aktiengesellschaft,
Ab. 21.4.1991

Dr. jur. Wolfgang Schieren,
München,
Vorsitzender des Aufsichtsrats der
   Allianz Aktiengesellschaft

Gerhard Söllner,
Philippsthal,
Vorsitzender des Betriebsrats des Werkes
   Hattorf der Kali und Salz AG

Hartmut Stahl,
Stuttgart,
Vorsitzender des Gesamtbetriebsrats der

BASF Lacke + Farben AG,
Ab 23.2.1992

Dr. Ing. Ferdinand Straub,
Weisenheim am Berg,
Mitglied des Sprecherausschusses der
   Leitenden Angestellten der BASF
   Aktiengesellschaft

Klaus Südhofer,
Bochum,
Zwieter Vorsitzender der
   Industriegewerkschaft Bergbau und
   Energie

Jürgen Walter,
Neustadt am Rübenberge,
Mitglied des geschäftsführenden
   Hauptvorstands der
   Industriegewerkschaft Chemi–Papier–
   Keramik

Dr. rer. pol. Ulrich Weiss,
Bad Soden,
Mitglied des Vorstands der Deutschen
   Bank AG

Horst Welskop,
Marl,
Mitglied des Betriebsrats der
   Gewerkschaft Auguste Victoria
   (Schacht 8),
Bis 18.12.1991

Professor Dr. rer. nat. Herbert
   Willersinn,
Ludwigshafen

Hoechst A G

Prof. Dr. rer. nat. Dr. h.c. mult. Rolf
   Sammet,
Vorsitzender,
früher Vorsitzender des Vorstands der
   Hoechst AG

Rolf Brand,
stellvertretender Vorsitzender,
Elektromechaniker,
Vorsitzender des Gesamtbetriebsrats der
   Hoechst AG

Oswald Bommel,
Chemie-Ingenieur,
stellvertretender Vorsitzender des
   Gesamtbetriebsrats der Hoechst AG

Erhard Bouillon,
früher Mitglied des Vorstands der
   Hoechst AG

Dr.-Ing. E.h. Werner H. Dieter,
Vorsitzender des Vorstands der
   Mannesmann AG

Willi Eßer,
Schlosser,
Mitglied des Gesamtbetreibsrats der
    Hoechst AG

Dietrich-Kurt Frowein,
Mitglied des Vorstands der
    Commerzbank AG

Dr. jur. Dr. h.c. mult. Kurt Furgler,
ehemals Bundesrat und Bundespräsident
    der Schweizerischen
    Eidgenossenschaft

Dr. jur. Robertus Hazelhoff,
    stellvertretender Vorsitzender des
    Vorstands der ABN AMRO Bank NV

George Heinz,
Diplom-Ingenieur, Vorsitzender des
    Wirtschaftsausschusses des
    Gesamtbetriebsrats der Hoechst AG

Dr. jur. h.c. Horst K. Jannott,
Vorsitzender des Vorstands der
    Münchener
    Rückversicherungs-Gesellschaft

Hermann-Heinz Konrad,
Diplom-Ingenieur,
Mitglied des Gesamtsprecherausschusses
    der Leitenden Angestellten der
    Hoechst AG

Volker Kraushaar,
Physiklaborant, Mitglied des
    Gesamtbetriebsrats der Hoechst AG

Prof. Dr. rer. nat. Hubert Markl,
Lehrstuhl für Biologie,
Universität Konstanz

Abdul Baqi Al-Nouri,
Petrochemical Industries Co. (KSC),
Kuwait

Peter-Michael Pruesker,
Diplom-Ökonom,
Leiter der Wirtschaftsabteilung beim
    Hauptvorstand der IG Chemie–
    Papier–Keramik

Dr. rer. pol. Wolfgang Röller,
Sprecher des Vorstands der Dresdner
    Bank AG

Egon Schäfer,
stellvertretender Vorsitzender der IG
    Chemie–Papier–Keramik

Konrad Starnecker,
Chemiefacharbeiter,
Mitglied des Gesamtbetriebsrats der
    Hoechst AG

Wolfgang Vetter,
Bauschlosser,
Mitglied des Gesamtbetriebsrats der
    Hoechst AG

Volkswagen A G

Dr. jur. Klaus Liesen (60),
Essen,
Vorsitzender,
Vorsitzender des Vorstands der Ruhrgas
    AG,
02.07.1987

Franz Steinkühler (54),
Frankfurt,
Stellvertretender,
Vorsitzender,
1. Vorsitzender der Industrie-
    gewerkeschaft Metall,
02.07.1987

Josef Bauer (52),

Ingolstadt,
Mitglied des Betriebsausschusses der
    AUDI AG,
02.07.1987

Rolf Diel (69),
Düsseldorf,
Vorsitzender des Aufsichtsrats der
    Dresdner Bank AG,
30.06.1988

Wilhelm Hemer (48),
Frankfurt,
Gewerkschaftssekretär beim Vorstand
    der Industriegewerkschaft Metall,
03.05.1989

Walter Hiller (59),
Hannover,
Niedersächsischer Minister für Soziales,
09.04.1986–20.06.1990 und seit
17.07.1990

Albert Hoffmeister (63),
Wolfsburg,
Prokurist der Volkswagen AG,
05.07.1977

Hans-Günter Hoppe (69),
Berlin,
Senator a. D.,
09.07.1974

Jann-Peter Janssen (47),
Norden, Vorsitzender des Betriebsrats,
Werk Emden der Volkswagen AG,
09.04.1986

Walther Leisler Kiep (66),
Frankfurt,
Persönlich haftender Gesellschafter,
Gradmann & Holler,
03.03.1976–01.07.1982 und seit
26.01.1983

Dr. jur. Otto Graf Lambsdorff (65),
Düsseldorf,
Präsident,
Deutsche Schutzvereinigung für
Wertpapierbesitz e.V.,
02.07.1987

Klaus-Peter Mander (49),
Wolfsburg,
Abteilungsleiter,
Volkswagen Finanz GmbH,
25.03.1985

Karl Heinrich Mihr (56),
Kassel,
Vorsitzender des Betriebsrats,
Werk Kassel der Volkswagen AG,
27.11.1972

Gerhard Mogwitz (58),
Hannover,
Vorsitzender des Betriebsrats,

Werk Hannover der Volkswagen AG,
05.07.1977

Dr.-Ing. E.h. Günther Saßmannshausen
(61),
Hannover,
Mitglied des Aufsichtsrats der Preussag
AG,
02.07.1987

Dr. rer. pol. Friedrich Schiefer (53),
München,
Geschäftsführer der Robert Bosch
GmbH,
04.07.1991

Gerhard Schröder (48),
Hannover,
Ministerpräsident des Landes
Niedersachsen,
17.07.1990

Dr. rer. pol. Albert Schunk (50),
Frankfurt,
Leiter der Abteilung Internationales
beim Vorstand der
Industriegewerkschaft Metall,
05.07.1977

Klaus Volkert (49),
Wolfsburg,
Konzern- und
Gesamtbetriebsratsvorsitzender der
Volkswagen AG,
02.07.1990

Dr. rer. pol. Ulrich Weiss (55),
Frankfurt,
Mitglied des Vorstands der Deutschen
Bank AG,
30.06.1988

Aus dem Aufsichtsrat ist ausgeschieden

Dr. jur. Wolfgang Schieren (64),
München,
Ehemaliger Vorsitzender des Vorstands
der Allianz Aktiengesellschaft
Holding,
30.06.1988–04.07.1991

Siemens AG

Dr.-Ing. E.h. Ernst von Siemens,
München,
Ehrenvorsitzender
(verstorben am 31.12.1990)

Dr. jur. Heribald Närger,
München,
Vorsitzender

Rudolf Mooshammer,
München,
stellv. Vorsitzender, Mechaniker

Dr. jur. Wolfgang Schieren
München,
stellv. Vorsitzender,
Vorsitzender des Vorstands der Allianz
   Aktiengesellschaft (bis 1.10.1991),
Vorsitzender des Aufsichtsrats der
   Allianz Aktiengesellschaft,
München

Alfred Bock,
Erlangen,
techn. Angestellter

Dr. jur. Ulrich Cartellieri,
Frankfurt a.M.,
Mitglied des Vorstands der Deutschen
   Bank AG,
Frankfurt a.M.

Rolf Diel,
Düsseldorf,
Vorsitzender des Aufsichtsrats der
   Dresdner Bank AG,
Düsseldorf

Eberhard Fehrmann
(bis 31.3.1991),
Bremen,
Geschäftsführer der Angestelltenkammer
   Bremen

Alfons Graf,
Amberg,
Werkzeugmachermeister

Prof. Dr. rer. nat. Herbert Grünewald,
Leverkusen,
Vorsitzender des Aufsichtsrats der Bayer
   AG, Leverkusen

Dr. jur. Maximilian Hackl,
München,
Vorsitzender des Aufsichtsrats der
   Bayerischen Vereinsbank AG,
München

Heinz Hawreliuk,
Frankfurt a.M.,
Leiter der Abteilung Vertrauensleute in
   der Vorstandsverwaltung der IG
   Metall

Ralf Heckmann,
München,
Fernmeldemonteur

Detlef Kreyenberg, München,
Dipl.-Ing.

Prof. Dr. rer. nat. Reimar Lüst,
Bonn,
Präsident der Alexander von Humboldt-
   Stiftung,
Bonn–Bad Godesberg

Werner Neugebauer,
München,
Bezirksleiter der IG Metall,
Bezirk München

Franz Rehm,
München,
Feinmechaniker

Helmut Reithmeier,
München,
Elektrotechniker

Alexander von Seidel,
Düsseldorf

Dr. jur. Nikolaus Senn,
Zürich,
Präsident des Verwaltungsrats der
   Schweizerischen Bankgesellschaft,
Zürich

Prof. Dr. jur. Dieter Spethmann,
Düsseldorf,
Vorsitzender des Vorstands (bis
   21.3.1991) der Thyssen AG vorm.
   August Thyssen-Hütte,
Düsseldorf

Horst Wagner
(ab 23.5.1991),
Berlin,
Bezirksleiter der IG Metall Berlin–
   Brandenburg

3 JAPAN

i. Introduction

There are marked differences in culture between Japan and all the four other nations studied and some of these have an important bearing on corporate governance. It is not a long list and some are more significant than others. We need to consider briefly what these are.

It is not necessary to delve too deeply into history or geography—not because either is unimportant—but because as time goes on it is impossible to ascribe precise causes and origins to what exists today. Suffice it to rehearse briefly the main factors that everyone knows. Geographically Japan has a large population on a series of extended islands without good natural resources and with much of its usable landmass subject to earthquakes. Spiritually it has tolerated many faiths and has woven into the fabric of thought and principle many threads of Confucianism and Buddhism: politically and economically its modern history starts with the convulsion of the Meiji restoration over 125 years ago.

Background: The Main Features . . .

The three main general features that affect Japanese attitudes towards corporate governance are their concepts of 'obligation', 'family', and 'consensus', and all are linked.

'Obligation' does not derive from broad general principles as it does in Judaeo-Christian cultures but from specific causes. This may be to return a service for one rendered or it may derive from a more general relationship, for example, to one's family or old alumni, or one's company (or Ministry), or the country. This sense of particular obligation is common elsewhere but it feels stronger in Japan.

So does the sense of 'family' which is part of the same approach. In the context of this study it certainly seems stronger in regard to the company than in other countries. It is not just a case of paternalism but of common membership of an enterprise which envelopes one's life to an unusual degree. It commands the allegiance and prime attention of everyone from top to bottom. They in turn expect to be treated as befits a member of the family. The type of group of companies known as Keiretsu, which are described later, is felt to be more than a simple economic concept (important as the economic aspects are); it is a family. The very word 'Kaisha' has this flavour—it is much nearer to 'company' than 'corporation'. Families are not all equal and companies are not, either. The big companies expect to provide more than smaller or weaker ones which can afford less. There are in this regard two Japans.

The third and most important element is that of consensus. The adversarial approach is uncommon. Immense efforts go into building a consensus in every walk of life, and this is particularly evident in corporate governance. Building a consensus does *not* mean that all parties to it are equal—often they are very unequal, but the Japanese feel it best (even at the cost of a slow and often cumbersome decision-making progress) to try to win the hearts and minds of people whenever possible rather than to proceed by diktat. Of course, there are exceptions, but consensus is the norm in a way most other countries would find strange, and it is not an obvious element, especially as the Japanese give seniors much deference.

. . . And Some of the Consequences

These concepts mean much mutual and reciprocal help for those within a 'family', but almost by definition much different treatment for those outside. It is not always difficult to get inside and many a foreigner has done so satisfactorily—and indeed, found it virtually imperative. Getting in deeply is, it appears, more difficult for all sorts of reasons of which perhaps individualism and language are the two best known. Language is obvious enough and real—but it can also be an excuse as well as a reason; given enough training and practice foreigners do become highly proficient. Individualism is very well illustrated in a book entitled 'You Gotta have Wa' by Robert Whiting, which describes how difficult US baseball stars, who were much wanted, found it to integrate into Japanese teams which had a more collegiate approach. It may be argued that to some extent all organizations have to work in a collegiate way: it is just that it is much more the norm in Japan, and much more heavily emphasized.

The emphasis on 'family' does have certain other effects. Although foreigners work happily in many Japanese companies (and vice versa), there seems to be a limit on how far they can go. Japanese companies are most assuredly not alone in this—the road to the top is not entirely open in many other countries, either. It will, I believe, present a growing problem generally as multinational companies account for an ever-increasing proportion of business, and it will therefore matter greatly to the Japanese who now have about 15 per cent of world trade. There may be few nationals of any country who are ambitious enough to make the changes to their lives necessary to qualify for the top places in a company, if it requires moving to a distant location, absorbing a strange culture, and learning a difficult language to a high degree of proficiency. But that road needs to be open to those who are brave enough to take it and competent enough to warrant advancement: one or two Japanese companies like Sony have shown the way.

The concept of family seems to have affected the way in which the market economy has developed. One interlocutor described the Japanese system as being based on 'community logic' against the US system which is based on 'market logic'. In the UK and US the tendency has been for the market to operate freely and in recent times for the state to pick up the social consequences, for example in unemployment pay and national assistance. In Japan, the tendency has been to regard it as preferable to prevent and delay potential tears in the social fabric and for government to act to mitigate the effects of any changes that cannot be avoided. This seems true at both company and national level. When an industry appears doomed, MITI moves in to achieve an orderly decline, as it did a few years ago in the case of aluminium-smelting (and helped push some of the companies from smelting into processing). When coal-mines at Hokkaido became hopelessly uneconomic, retraining and redeployment was organized. When a company in a group is beyond salvation it is dismembered or sold—and the redeployment of its staff quietly arranged. On a bigger scale, when a whole basic industry is threatened, like rice-growing or beef production, the Japanese will be as resolute as the French in protecting it rather than risk the social upheaval exposure to world competition would surely cause; of course, politics come into it in both countries, but in Japan the concept of 'family' is particularly significant.

There is, however, another side to it. The concept of 'family' is by definition a limited one; that is to say, those who are not members are excluded. So in a downturn small companies which have no 'family' protection may the more easily go to the wall.

The importance of the social fabric is reflected in the basic attitude to business. Whether we like it or not, the UK/US way of thinking about business has been conditioned by the importance of the stock market. The market has one common denominator—profit—which affects both investors' allocation of resources and managers' choice of investment. It gives the indications for (and in the long run achieves) switches of resource to where the best economic returns are to be had. What is more, competitive pressures tend to reduce the time-scale on which these judgements are made. Those working outside companies think in terms of profit not just as a yardstick for the allocation of resources but as the objective of business, and generally its sole objective. That is not how UK and US businessmen see it, so there is an uncomfortable tension between the industrial and financial sectors.

Although Japan has an important stock market, it does not appear to play much part in the allocative process. This is mainly because the post-war rebuilding of industry was financed by the banks and largely directed by the Ministry of International Trade and Industry (MITI). The banks' objective was, and is, not the maximization of profits, as is the stock market's, but safety and growth. First and foremost they want to be repaid (or at least, for their customers to maintain the capacity to repay), and they want their own profits to grow as their customers develop.

The UK/US system assumes the business family can be constantly broken up and redistributed in pursuit of the reallocation of resources by whatever means is available, including take-overs. The Japanese system accepts that the business family is not there simply to make a profit. Nevertheless the system also accepts that if the business family fails it may have to be disbanded.

Profit is important to Japanese companies, for without it they could not survive, invest, and grow. It is well known, however, that their goals are more often expressed in terms of market share rather than profit. There are various reasons for this. Size is regarded as the basic measure of success in relation to competitors and much importance is attached to ranking; power in other words may be more important than profit. Besides, a market can be exploited once it has been dominated. Furthermore the domestic market alone cannot maintain the level of economic activity necessary to maintain the Japanese social fabric, so international market share adds an additional dimension. The reasons for putting market share first may vary from case to case, but there is nothing in the general principle which is at variance with official policy, that is, to specify industries which it would suit Japan's social fabric and world markets to develop and to make cheap money available to do it with. In fact the official attitude to profitability is changing a little: profit is becoming more important.

There is a price to be paid for everything, and the virtual extinguishment of the market's allocative function means it has to be conducted elsewhere, if rigidity is not to set in. This is where MITI has in the past played such an important part. The point of mentioning it here is that the corporate governance process in any country is not a closed system—it is linked to the process of asset allocation. It would, however, be quite wrong to think in terms of Japan Inc. Competition at home can be ferocious, and it is this which has clearly driven the frenetic drive to shorten the development time for new products. (Anyone who doubts the ferocity should read the account of the Honda–Yamaha battle in Abegglen and Stalk 1985: 43 ff.) Fierce it may be but all-enveloping it is not; competitors unite for foreign projects and they happily (though discreetly) sell each other parts and sub-assemblies. But competition is the same the world over—it looks more attractive to an economist in an office who has never made or sold anything in his life, than it does to a businessman trying to get an order at a profit.

Summary

To understand how corporate governance works requires us to know what the participants perceive their objective to be. In Japan there appears to be a general consensus (which is lacking in some other countries) that although profit is important, the long-term preservation and prosperity of the family (which is how companies are viewed) are and should be primarily the aim of all concerned, and not profit maximization or shareholders' immediate values. The particular type of financial opportunism so evident in the 1980s in the UK and USA was and would be anathema in Japan: there was and appears still to be a consensus that it should be avoided, even if some people were enriched by it. The Japanese had their own kind of financial opportunism, using cheap money to buy shares and property—opportunism for which a high price is now being paid. But buying and selling companies— as distinct from shares—was not part of it.

Finally, the emphasis on 'family' and 'continuity' has led the Japanese to adopt what is in effect a policy of insurance for which they are prepared to pay a substantial premium. This is evident from banking relationships and from industrial groupings. Both points are dealt with in more detail below.

ii. The System at Work

Introduction

The Commercial Code governs the formulation and structure and conduct of companies in much the same way as the relevant laws in all the countries studied. The version referred to here is the translation in the EHS Law Bulletin Series, which includes amendments up to 29 June 1990.

Book II of the Code deals with companies, of which there are three types: commercial partnerships, limited partnerships, and limited companies. It is this third group, Kabushiki Kaisha with which the paper is concerned. In Japan it is generally considered advantageous to incorporate, not least for tax purposes, and at the end of June 1987 there were about two million companies including the financial sector; there were then 1,931 quoted companies and these (excluding the financial sector) accounted for 28.7 per cent of turnover—but in reality for much more because of all the unquoted companies associated with them.

Groups of Companies

Throughout the countries studied, many companies which are in law separate entities are bound to other companies by some sort of linkage, either formal or informal. Formal linkages include wholly owned subsidiaries, and associated companies in which another company has a minority shareholding. There are also companies which are in effect satellites because virtually all the goods or services they supply go to a single customer. Japan provides many examples of all these arrangements.

Some of these concepts have been gradually developed over a long period. One of the features of industrial reorganization after the Meiji restoration was the development of Zaibatsu—combines usually built round a bank. By 1941 they controlled 32 per cent of the national investment in heavy industry and nearly half of Japan's banking resources (Clark 1979: 43). Four of the most prominent were Mitsubishi, Yasuda, Sumitomo, and Mitsui. Their structure was a holding company controlled by the founding family which in turn controlled a dozen or so core companies including the bank, the trading company, the trust company, and the insurance company, and round them clustered other associates, affiliates, and subsidiaries.

After the war the Occupation authorities dismantled the Zaibatsu, and although nothing quite like them has emerged, they did leave one lasting legacy—that Japanese industry is in effect two nations, the big companies and the rest. It is possible—and indeed it has often happened since the War—for a small company to grow and make the transition; one of the most significant features of which are the capacity and resources to offer recruits a lifetime career with all the diversity and security that implies. At the moment this is being written (December 1992) the pressures on even the top companies are rising, but are being met by various means. These include passing on as much pressure as possible down the chain, cutting back on bonuses, outposting and 'gardening leave', reducing the hours for part-time workers, reducing recruitment, and natural wastage.

What has happened since the War is the development of two distinct types of group which foreigners often lump together, under the generic title 'Keiretsu' which means, broadly speaking, 'Association'. The more usual of these to UK/US eyes is the *vertical* Keiretsu, in which subcontractors and sub-subcontractors (unto the fourth generation) service a main manufacturer like Toyota. A variation of this theme occurs when, at the other end of the chain, a manufacturer controls retail outlets.

In such vertical Keiretsu there can be the whole range of linking arrangements. Hitachi, for instance, has four main divisions, 800 companies whose figures are consolidated for the purpose of the accounts, and so many associates or linked suppliers that no one knows precisely how many, but certainly well over a thousand. The organizational theory that lies behind this kind of arrangement is that entrepreneurial talent is more likely to flourish in independent subsidiaries (which may, if good enough, market their wares elsewhere), than in divisions. 'Partnership sourcing' is a convenient title for a common arrangement in which a big company develops a long-term relationship with a supplier; this involves deep contact at an early stage of the product cycle so that designs are developed together, and it implies that the purchaser nurtures the supplier (as well as squeezing him hard on quality, delivery, and price). Outsiders complain that such arrangements make it difficult to break in. Certainly they have to be good enough and to get in whilst the door is open, often some years before the order is finally placed.

It is in the *horizontal* Keiretsu groups that the memories of the pre-war Zaibatsu echo most loudly. These are a version of conglomerate in which companies in often dissimilar industries are grouped together, frequently with a bank at the centre: Fuyo (Fuji Bank), Sanwa, Dai-Ichi Kangyo, but sometimes more industrially centred: Mitsubishi, Mitsui, Sumitomo, though these groups include important banks too. This second trio are basically family groups with common trademarks and are the direct heirs of the pre-war Zaibatsu. Banks are said to have encouraged the formation and development of groups of this kind, as a source of mutual strength and reciprocal help. The Fair Trade Commission in 1992 reckoned that 188 companies were in these Keiretsu groups and that they accounted for 17 per cent of the capital, 19 per cent of the assets, and 16 per cent of the sales of all quoted companies (and their definition of a group was reckoned to be narrow). Companies in a horizontal Keiretsu group are often linked by cross-holdings. Here are some examples of the percentage holdings:

Mitsubishi Gas Chemical		Sumitomo Bank	4.3
Nippon Life Insurance	7.5	Sumitomo Cement	2.2
Mitsubishi Trust	5.8	Sumitomo Metal Mining	2.2
Meiji Life Insurance	5	Sumitomo Corporation	2.1
Mitsubishi Bank	4.4	Superior Home	1.9
Industrial Bank of Japan	3.0		
Norinchukin Bank	2.8	*Mitsui Petrochemical Industries*	
Bank of Yokohama	2.7	Toray Industries	11.5
Toyo Trust	2.3	Mitsui Trust	5.5
Sumitomo Life Insurance	1.9	MTKB	4.6
		Mitsui Life Insurance	4.2
Sumitomo Construction		Mitsui & Co.	4.1
Sumitomo Life Insurance	5.8	Koa Oil	3.4
Sumitomo Coal Mining	4.5	Mitsui Engineering	3.2
Sumitomo Trust	4.5	Mitsui Toatsu Chemicals	2.6

Some aggregate numbers for cross-shareholdings in the six main horizontal Keiretsu groups are given in Table 3.1.

The *vertical* Keiretsu are designed to produce a more efficent production–distribution chain for a particular range or ranges of products. The companies that comprise *horizontal* Keiretsu are often in quite different markets. Mitsubishi group companies are in gas, chemicals, plastics, steel, aluminium, cement, butter, brewing (Kirin), and paper—just to list a fraction of their enterprises. There tends in such groups to be a preference for products produced elsewhere in the Keiretsu, but it is not an absolute preference. If a better source of supply is available (in terms of quality, delivery, and price), it will not be excluded. How far Mitsubishi staff are expected to 'show solidarity' by drinking Kirin beer in preference to other brands is an interesting question.

There is no universal rule about the extent to which companies in a horizontal Keiretsu act in concert. There are certainly regular inter-company meetings at various levels. Much of the time the agenda will be general, for example, on economic prospects. Sometimes there will be ad hoc meetings of particular companies, for instance, in regard to launching jointly a new project or enterprise. One chairman told me that when he was the president of a leading Keiretsu he had difficulty in assembling all the other presidents for routine meetings; not a great deal of importance was attached to them.

One of the indicators about a Western company which shows whether it is integrated or a conglomerate is the extent of the central personnel function. In many conglomerates there is virtually no transfer of personnel

TABLE 3.1. *Cross-shareholdings of the six main company groupings* (%)

	1977	1981	1987	1989
Average shareholding *	2.19	1.78	1.52	1.42
Former Zaibatsu	2.16	2.05	1.70	1.57
Bank-related	2.22	1.51	1.33	1.27
Cross-shareholdings †	23.86	25.48	22.65	21.64
Former Zaibatsu	28.86	32.16	28.93	27.46
Bank-related	18.85	18.75	16.36	15.82

* Average shareholding: average shareholding of one company in any other one company belonging to a Keiretsu presidents' meeting-club.

† Cross-shareholdings: the percentage of shares in other club companies owned by member companies of a presidents' meeting-club.

Source: Fair Trade Commission, 'Company Groupings' (1992).

TABLE 3.2. *Numbers of placements of personnel by the big six groupings* (%)

	1977	1981	1987	1989
Companies taking placements *	64.15	69.79	67.69	62.26
Former Zaibatsu	69.12	71.94	64.13	62.74
Bank-related	59.17	67.63	71.25	61.78
Cross-shareholdings †	8.12	8.56	7.13	6.34
Former Zaibatsu	10.29	11.14	8.65	7.91
Bank-related	5.95	5.98	5.61	4.78

* Companies taking placements: the percentage of companies in a Keiretsu presidents' meeting-club with board members received from other companies in the grouping.

† Share of company board members: the percentage of all company board members of companies in a presidents' meeting-club accounted for by placements from other group companies.

Source: Fair Trade Commission, 'Company Groupings' (1992).

below board level. This seems to be the case in horizontal Keiretsu (see Table 3.2).

What the tables do not show is the extent of consultation on senior appointments. Does a group company, for instance, have to clear its proposal for a new president or board member with the group lead company or bank? The answer seems to vary. At the very least a courtesy call would be made; in some cases a more formal consultation would be required before the event. The extent to which other group companies will be informed will also vary.

It appears that the same variations apply at the other end of the spectrum—to displacement. Normally group companies do not interfere with each other and this goes for the lead company or bank too. If, however, a company gets into serious trouble the others will rally round to limit the damage, cure the problem, or save the employees. This may entail changes of management, negotiating mergers, and refinancing, and demonstrates the 'insurance' aspect of a Keiretsu group.

Banks may not by law hold more than 5 per cent of the capital of an industrial company, but there is no rule debarring an associated company from doing so. Industrial companies have no such restriction. It is not the purpose of this paper to argue for or against Keiretsu or comment on whether they are 'unfair'; in any event, there are parallel arguments for UK/US conglomerates, and for that matter big companies which choose to organize themselves in divisions rather than subsidiaries with separate access to the capital markets. Whether being within a Keiretsu group implies significant corporate governance features turns on the degree to which the centre of the group controls the boards of its associated companies. (An interesting discussion of some of the main issues is contained in Gibson and Roe 1992.)

The Kaisha at Work: The General Meeting of Shareholders

Part IV, Section 3 of the Commercial Code deals with the organs of the company and starts with the general meeting of shareholders. Articles 230–42 deal in detail with how meetings shall be called, when (at least once a year, art. 234), where (at or near the 'seat of the principal office'), and how they shall be conducted. The fact is that most AGMs are perfunctory (see Table 3.3).

In discussion with companies I found general agreement that AGMs were indeed for the most part perfunctory, but that they could indeed be long and troublesome. At one time gangs of professional trouble-makers, sometimes associated with 'gangsters'—the Sokaiya—used to make money by disrupting meetings so vigorously that management bought their silence. This practice has diminished, partly because all companies now have the same year end (31 March) and hold their AGMs on the same date, and partly because it has now been made illegal to buy off the agitators (as well as to receive such a bribe). At the time of writing, the practice had not been stopped altogether and proceedings were in train against one respected company (Ito Yokado) for breaking the law. The law is difficult to enforce anyway because the bribe can take various forms, such as expensive contributions to a publication. The Commercial and Legal Research Association in a white paper in December 1992 reported that of 1,638 respondents to a survey of 2,105 companies, 64 per cent thought that some companies

TABLE 3.3. *Japanese shareholder meetings*

(*a*) *Number of shareholder remarks at FY 1989 shareholder meetings*

No. of remarks	No. (and %) of companies
0	1,374 (88.0)
1	99 (6.3)
2	35 (2.2)
3	15 (1.0)
4	11 (0.7)
5	5 (0.3)
6	8 (0.5)
7	3 (0.2)
8	3 (0.2)
9	3 (0.2)
10	1 (0.1)
more than 10	5 (0.3)
TOTAL	1,562 (100.0)

(*b*) *Length of FY 1989 shareholder meetings*

Length	No. (and %) of companies
less than 10 minutes	3 (0.1)
20	612 (29.3)
30	1,133 (54.2)
40	207 (9.9)
50	34 (1.6)
60	20 (1.0)
90	31 (1.5)
120	1 (1.5)
150	8 (0.4)
180	3 (0.1)
more than 180	7 (0.3)
TOTAL	2,089 (100.0)

Source: Commercial Law Centre, 'Shareholder Meeting Fact Book 1990', quoted in Nomura Research Institute, Ltd., 'Japanese Corporate Finance' (1990).

continued to pay off greenmailers. They may of course be wrong, but the figures shed an interesting light on the atmosphere.

Who Owns What?

The reason why AGMs are 'ceremonial' is quite simple—management has the shares tied up through the system of 'stable' shareholdings (see Fig. 3.1). It may reasonably be assumed that most of the shares in the hands of the financial institutions and business corporations, that is, over 70 per cent, are firmly held; they are not for trading. If these shareholders want to convey a message to management the last place they would choose to do it is the AGM. The reason for this is that many of these shares are held on a reciprocal basis whether in a Keiretsu or not. Very often the cross-share-holding is part of an otherwise normal trading relationship, for example, banker : customer, supplier : customer. The shares are there partly 'to show sincerity'. The banking cross-holdings have more to them than that, as we shall see. In most cases neither party would sell without consulting the other. The exception to this is where shares are held for speculative purposes. In the 1980's, when the cost of equity was virtually nil, many companies accumulated otherwise unneeded capital to play the rising stock market. These were never stable shareholdings and the game—Zaitech—came to a sticky end at the end of the 1980's with the precipitous fall in share and property prices.

The size of institutional holdings is in itself unremarkable, bearing in mind that in the USA institutions own about half the outstanding equity, and about two-thirds in the UK. In Japan, however, individual holdings are bigger and—the crucial point—they are often regarded as 'stable', that is, not normally to be traded. (We shall meet a similar phenomenon when we look at France—in the form of the hard-core concept: 'noyau dur'.) The life insurance companies in Japan may become less stable because they need income, and because, being mutuals, they are not under the reciprocal obligations that cross-holdings impose. (See Table 3.4.)

Just to complete the picture by looking at it from the company's standpoint, here are some shareholdings taken at random from companies which are not part of a Keiretsu group (source: Japan Company Handbook, Spring 1992):

Honshu Paper

Japan Securities Clearing	7.3	DKB	3.0
Daiichi Life Insurance	5.7	Mitsui Trust	2.8
Nippon Life Insurance	5.7	LTCB	2.7
Mitsui Life Insurance	3.5		

Aica Kogyo (a manufacturer of melamine boards and adhesives)

Tokai Bank	4.8	Sumitomo Life Insurance	2.2
Fuji Bank	3.7	Bank of Yokohama	2.4
KSB	3.4	Asahi Life Insurance	2.5
MTKB	2.9	Chuo Trust	2.5
Tokyo M&F Insurance	2.6		

Toray Industries (textiles)

Daichi Life Insurance	5.4	Mitsubishi Trust	2.4
Nippon Life Insurance	5.2	Sumitomo Trust	2.2
Mitsui Life Insurance	4.5	Toyo Trust	2.1
MTKB	4.5	LTCB	1.9
Mitsui Trust	3.9	Daiwa Bank	1.8

Masaaki Kurokawa of Nomura (1988) summarized the position as follows:

Institutional investors became a strong factor in the Japanese stock market fairly recently. In 1960, individual investors held over 50 percent of Japanese equity, as a result of the post-war shareholder diversification. Banks and enterprises held only 23 percent and 18 percent respectively at that time. When the Japanese government loosened the restrictions on securities holdings by foreigners in 1965, however, Japanese banks and enterprises joined forces to prevent takeovers by foreign investors, especially enterprises. Then developed what became known as the 'interlock' stock system. According to this system Japanese companies would encourage banks and enterprises with common business interests to purchase a majority of shares of its stock. In return the company would promise to step up its loan and business relations with the shareholders. This virtually 'locks in' the stock from reaching the market place and potential foreign acquisition. I will refer to these banks and companies who participate in 'interlocking' as 'stable stockholders' since their investments represent more of a commitment than a profit-making strategy. By 1975 the share of banks' stockholdings to total issued stock increased by 10 percent to 35 percent. The share of corporate owned stock also increased by 10 percent to 26 percent. On the other hand, the share of individual investors' holdings, or 'non-interlocked' stock, fell by 20 percent to 30 percent.

There is nothing particularly odd in this kind of shareholding structure to UK eyes; the institutional shareholdings are more concentrated than is general in the UK, but the total pattern is similar. What is different is the attitude of the shareholders. Mr Kurokawa again:

Stable stockholders seek mainly to increase their business transactions and enhance their standings with their invested company. They have little interest in selling the stock for profit.... Japan's 'interlocked' stock system also dissuades takeover bids, as it forces the potential acquirer to negotiate with the 'stable

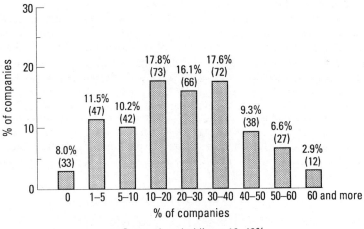

Stable shareholders ratio: 50–70% of total shares outstanding

Cross-shareholdings: 10–40%

Source: Commercial Law Centre, 'Shareholder Meeting Fact Book 1990' quoted in Nomura Research Institute, Ltd., 'Japanese Corporate Finance' (1990).

Fɪɢ. 3.1 **Shareholdings in the hands of long-term shareholders**

TABLE 3.4. *Equity investments of institutional investors, March 1991*

Rank	Institutions	No. of shares (million)	No. of companies invested in	Rank as shareholder			% of domestic issues
				1st	2nd	3rd	
1	Nippon Life Insurance	9,614	1,135	77	105	80	2.85
2	Mitsubisi Trust Bank	6,724	1,218	36	60	56	2.00
3	Dai-ichi Life Insurance	6.096	715	43	36	54	1.81
4	Sumitomo Trust Bank	5.876	1,173	33	76	63	1.74
5	Mitui Trust Bank	4,873	1,097	19	39	45	1.45
6	Sumitomo Life Insurance	4,336	738	22	31	17	1.29
7	Industrial Bank of Japan	4,151	647	15	46	60	1.23
8	Meiji Life Insurance	4,126	506	32	26	25	1.23
9	Toyo Trust Bank	4,119	1,019	10	23	45	1.22
10	Mitsui-Taishin Bank	3,912	905	21	60	74	1.16
11	Yasuda Trust Bank	3,684	928	13	33	36	1.09
12	Daiichi-Kangyou Bank	3,482	698	21	54	91	1.03
13	Fuji Bank	3,355	663	24	57	86	1.00
14	Sanwa Bank	3,035	667	18	52	64	0.90
15	Mitsubisi Bank	2,963	616	21	45	67	0.88
16	Sumitomo Bank	2,902	501	8	37	75	0.86
17	Asahi Life Insurance	2,748	367	16	15	19	0.82
18	Long-Term Credit Bank of Japan	2,726	437	5	14	30	0.81
19	Tokyo Marine Insurance	2,400	478	6	15	13	0.71
20	Daiwa Bank	2,024	470	12	25	22	0.60

Source: Toyo Keizai, quoted in Nomura Research Institute, Ltd., 'Japanese Corporate Finance'.

stockholders'. If the shareholder chose to sell, it would mean a renouncement of their agreement, and the termination of their business relationship. Takeover activity then is not highly productive in terms of overall profit-making. Rather, Japanese companies would prefer to diversify their market or enter a new market to see increased profits.

However 'ceremonial' or formal Japanese AGMs are, they do have two important functions: the appointment of directors (Code 254) and the approval of the dividend. If serious questions are raised they are usually in relation to the latter—and they can get personal, for example, the company's entertainment of directors at night clubs—no wonder that agitator groups are feared and bought off! There is, however, no case I can discover of shareholders simply using an AGM to oust a board or take other drastic action. If they have power they would exert it outside the AGM. If they do not they would be blocked. Formally power rests with the AGM: in reality it is exercised elsewhere. To this we now turn.

The Board of Directors

Subsection 2 of the Code deals with 'Directors and the Board of Directors' (arts. 254–72), laying down that they need not be shareholders (art. 254), cannot be incompetent or bankrupt, etc. (art. 254); that there shall be at least three (art. 255), and that they cannot be appointed for more than two years (art. 256). 'Directors shall be appointed at a general meeting of shareholders' (art. 254). Whatever the Articles say, directors need the support of a third of the shareholders to be elected (art. 256). Then follow the rules for dismissal; for summoning board meetings; and for representative directors. Article 260 defines the board's role: 'The board of directors shall decide the administration of affairs of the company and supervise execution of duties of directors.' Boards must meet quarterly, but usually meet monthly.

Within this basic legal framework company boards work in various ways, but they all have one thing in common—they are almost entirely composed of 'insiders', that is full-time employees of the business engaged in managing it. Part-time executives are sometimes directors. There are few non-executive or outside directors on the US/UK model. According to Toyo Keizai Shinposha (1992), 76.5 per cent of the directors of listed companies were internal appointments and 24.4 per cent external appointments. Of the latter more than four-fifths came from ordinary companies or banks.

In smaller companies the board may well be the decision-taking body. Its discussions will be real and substantive. It will in effect be both board and top management committee. In bigger companies this is seldom so. The company will be controlled by a top management committee (sometimes called the Jomukai), which is composed of the president and the top layers of directors—a hard core of 'proper people', that is, those who have come up through the ranks. The function of the board will be 'ceremonial'—like the AGM: substantive discussion will rarely occur, though questions may be raised if a director is worried about legal liability that may attach to a particular course of action. And in emergencies—very rarely indeed—the board can gird up its loins and take dramatic action, as in the famous case of firing the President of the Mitsukoshi store group in 1982. Apart from such occasions proposals go through on the nod, which is not as surprising as it may sound, as many members of the board will have been consulted about them at a much earlier stage.

TABLE 3.5. *The board composition of certain companies in 1993*

	The Daiwa Bank Ltd.	Mitsui & Co. Ltd.	Nikko Securities	Mitsukoshi
Chairman	1	1	1	1
Vice-chairman	1	1	1	—
President	1	1	1	1
Deputy or vice-president (executive)	2	4	5	—
Senior managing director (executive)	3	3	6	2
Managing directors	12	14	9	5
Directors	13	28	17	16

	Shiseido	East Japan Railway Co.	C Itoh	Sony
Chairman	1	1	1	1
Vice-chairman	1	1	1	1
President	1	1	1	1
(Senior) executive vice-president	2	2	3	4
Senior executive directors / Managing directors	2	7	6	6
Executive directors / Managing directors	4	—	15	6
Directors	17	20	23	19 *

* Includes three outside directors.

Although all directors as such are equal, their managerial rank is not, and it is the latter that counts. Table 3.5 shows the board composition of some companies in 1992, as indicated in company reports. This tells us two interesting things; first, that many members of the board are likely to be in a direct line relationship to various others and, second, that boards are quite big.

Given the respect for rank and authority that prevails, it is hardly the best recipe for constructive discussion to have so many people on a board with such line relationships, but as the board's role has atrophied, it may not matter much. Wholly executive boards are always likely to have this kind of problem, the more so if promotion to the board is seem primarily as the seal of approval, carrying with it status and benefits rather than onerous board obligations. But membership of the board is more than this. The president of a Japanese company is almost always promoted from inside, so membership of the board is a necessary step in the *cursus honorum*.

Election to the Board and to the Top Offices

In practice the president chooses directors, generally after nomination by or consultation with the man's superiors (who will be on the board already) and other colleagues, and his recommendations will be rubber-stamped, first by the board and then by the general meeting of shareholders. With such a well-structured system there will be few surprises (any more than there would be in promotion to the upper ranks of a civil service). People's track records and quality will be well known in the organization. Promotion thereafter largely depends on the president, who may seek advice from some company elders (who are perhaps advisers) and the chairman. The president also nominates his own successor, but generally consults no one about this, though he may tell the chosen man in order to give him time to prepare for office. The done thing is to receive preferment with surprise. 'This is a very sudden asking—most unexpected', as it was put to me. It is extremely rare for a nominee not to be appointed: in one case it took a combination of the unions and main bank to stop a nomination and work out a solution that avoided too much loss of face. If somehow the succession fails because a president is sacked or dies, the chairman will co-ordinate the search for his successor: if there is no chairman the board will organize itself to find the right man. The chairmanship is usually filled by a retiring president. Toyo Keizai Shinposha (1991) put some figures to the process. The decision in the choice of president was taken as follows:

by the president alone	48.3%
in consultation with the chairman and advisers	32.9%
in agreement with the board	22.1%
taking account of parent or related companies	11.1%
taking account of the company's bank(s)	1.4%
other	2.6%

In normal times the choice of people for the board and especially of the president are entirely internal matters. No one outside the company is consulted, though certain privileged people may be informed as a matter of courtesy, for instance, the presidents of the main banks, and shareholders, suppliers, and customers. In some Keiretsu-type groups some top appointments may require consultation with the lead company. In industrial companies which have built up a network of subsidiaries and divisions top appointments in them are generally made by head office. No company admitted to consulting a government department, though sometimes they too were informed as a matter of courtesy: it is rare but not unknown for an official very informally to give guidance about a particular person. The government does, however, retain formal powers in respect of appointments to the board of certain industries which once lay in the public domain.

Tenure and Dismissal

Finally there is the question of tenure. The code specifies a maximum period of appointment of two years for directors—and this means all of them, irrespective of level. Reappointment is normal up to the retiring age that companies specify for that particular class of director—generally the more senior one is, the later the retirement date. It used to be the case that there were no 'one term' appointments but this is so no longer.

What about directors who do not measure up? It is for the president (possibly with the advice of the chairman and advisers) to make sure that other senior executives are up to the mark. He has various remedies at his disposal if they are not, including non-reappointment or transfer to a subsidiary or associate company (which the receiving companies dislike as they increasingly have good people of their own). Outright dismissal would be rare: and it is always regarded as a very tough job to say to someone who expects reappointment, 'Thank you for your contribution ... '. Sometimes however—especially if their retirement is within sight—they are left in post but power is diverted from them.

There is often no set retiring age for president and chairman, and even if there is, it is nominal. Unless they are removed, presidents usually decide their own date of retirement, though this may be influenced by previous practice in the company. Table 3.6 gives the general picture (1975) of ages in the structure.

It is worth a small digression to consider the background of board members. In a big Japanese company the general rule is lifetime employment,

TABLE 3.6. *Average age in top management positions, 1975*

Position	Age
Kaicho (chairman)	68.0
Shacho (president)	64.9
Fuku-Shacho (vice-president)	61.0
Senmu (executive director)	59.5
Jomu (managing director)	57.9
Torishimariyaku (regular director)	53.8

Source: Kazuo Noda (1975), 'Big Business Organization' in E. Vogel (ed.), *Modern Japanese Organization and Decision Making*.

though there tends to be more mid-career recruiting than before. During their careers people will be switched about a great deal, turning them eventually into generalists, though many will have started with a specialist background and served in specialist posts. A technical background is said to be more common and a financial background less common than in the UK: engineers are much in evidence. This ties in well with the perceived strategy of so many major Japanese companies—to secure their markets through technological strength.

My discussions confirm the importance Japanese companies attach to the personnel function. One told me their slogan was 'Before we build products we build people.' Elevation to the board is part of this process (as it would be elsewhere in the case of executive directors). As noted above, consultation and consensus would have been particularly thorough. Consultation does not of course mean that all parties are equal, and this particularly applies to family influence which may survive long after its foundations in terms of shareholdings have crumbled.

The President

The top executive in a Japanese company is usually called the president. His main tasks are to ensure the machine runs well and that top personnel matters are properly handled. His is the most important voice in the determination of strategy, but how important will depend upon the man, the company, and the circumstances. If we were to place all companies on a spectrum on which dictatorship was at one end and collegiality at the other, most Japanese companies would appear to be at the latter end. Companies in trouble tend to want to hear the smack of firm governance from their presidents. And founding fathers tend to be more authoritarian.

There are several reasons for a collegial approach. It fits the principle of consensus. It is more practical, especially in a complex business where one man cannot possibly comprehend the technical aspects of all its main divisions. Presidents of such businesses may well be expert in a particular field but not the rest; if so he is likely to be at his most authoritarian in the field he knows best. There is a striking contrast here with many companies in the UK/USA in which the CEO has a financial background and technical aspects are subordinated to the financial.

In untroubled times a president generally follows his predecessor's policy for 12–18 months after taking office. As he has come up through the ranks he will generally know the background to policy well; he will be unlikely to approach the job with radical intent unless the circumstances require it. The Japanese sometimes talk of their decision-making system as being 'bottom up', which would imply that the president was a figurehead. It would be truer to say that the consultation process (including the upward-moving RINGI system) is deep and thorough but it is not just designed to tell the president to do what the factory floor wants. Its purpose is to marry in the decision-making process the strategic concepts of the leadership with the practicalities of execution.

One of the most difficult questions in corporate governance is how to deal with the top executive where performance has proved unsatisfactory. The Japanese response to my enquiry on this delicate issue produced the following sequence:

The selection process was so good that the question seldom arose. That if it did power could often be removed or transferred whilst leaving the incumbent in the top post to serve out his time; that if this were not possible the alternative was to grin and bear it—'Only God removes a president' as someone put it; that occasionally a putsch might be organized by the board. If a company were in dire trouble the bank might exert leverage as part of the price of support: so might other members of the company's group. But if a president chose to ignore the hints and decided to stand his ground he really is difficult to eject—a course of action which would in any event be felt to be most unattractive. There are cases, however, of a chairman being instrumental in persuading the president to stand down, and even instances of the chairman reverting to his former role whilst a more permanent solution was being organized: occasionally, to save a president's face, a chairman will stand down so that the president can be 'kicked upstairs'.

The more collegiate a system the less clear personal accountability becomes; the glory does not attach so clearly to success nor blame to disappointment. Some Japanese appreciate the virtues of the US system where the CEO is often much of a 'hero', complete with copious media coverage and the risk of dismissal if he fails. Indeed, in recent years there have been several Japanese company presidents whose public persona has seemed to indicate a stance much closer to that of an American CEO and much less close to the traditional Japanese *primus inter pares*.

Although a collegiate system makes it more difficult to personalize account-ability, the Japanese believe it to be the duty of seniors to look after and take responsibility for juniors. Taking responsibility publicly is regarded as the honourable course. The chairman of Japan Air Lines resigned after a disaster. Some years ago a subsidiary of Toshiba breached the COCOM rules and infuriated the Americans. Both the chairman and president of the main board resigned as a sacrificial gesture.

In one important way a Japanese company president does not resemble his US counterpart: remuneration. Graef S. Crystal illustrates the point graphically (1991: 204 ff.). He calculates that a typical president gets at most about sixteen times the pay of the average industrial worker, compared with a multiple of 125–160 for a typical US CEO. But the comparison is even more striking when one takes into account that Japanese directors do not get share options and that they bear heavy personal taxes—65 per cent at the top rate (1992). It always used to be reported that they enjoyed lavish 'perks', but the pressures in 1992/3 were said to have reined these in. In short, Japanese presidents live well but do not expect to retire rich. Entrepreneurs who found successful companies may well do so, but not those they employ.

When a president's term of office comes to an end he often moves to the chairmanship. The relative status of the two posts is indicated by the Japanese expression, 'Stepping down to the chairmanship'.

The Chairman

Many companies have a chairman as well as a president, though some combine the two roles either as a matter of deliberate company policy or as a matter of accident (because, for instance, a chairman has died and there is no convenient successor). Occasionally a company will combine the two roles and have as well the equivalent of a US chief operating officer (COO) to deal with day-to-day business. (The nomenclature may get confusing, for example, by calling the chairman–president 'executive chairman' and the Number 2 the 'president'.)

The post of chairman is generally filled by a retiring president. What his precise role will be will depend to some extent on his background. Typically it is that of elder statesman, the public face of the company, who represents it at official functions. He looks outward from the company towards the world. Sometimes, however, he exercises much more power than this, especially if he retains his representative function: some chairmen are slow to hand over the presidential reins and this causes trouble. The chairman always retains one critical function. The president is his nominee (whilst he was president himself), so his success reflects upon the choice he himself made. If the president proves inadequate, he must orchestrate his removal. (The Japanese talk about 'tapping the shoulder'.) That is perhaps why some presidents prefer to work without a chairman.

Representative Directors

Under Article 261 of the Code the company must by board resolution appoint at least one director as 'representative'. Certain transactions require the fiat of a representative director or someone acting under his authority (backed by a power of attorney which must exist but which it is regarded as bad manners to inspect). The president is usually a representative director, plus one or two of those closest to him in the hierarchy. If a chairman has this authority it says much about his real role: occasionally, too, an adviser may have the power of representation. To be a representative director implies seniority and the greater influence that accompanies it.

Advisers

Company reports show that they often appoint advisers. Advisers are of varying degrees of importance. Some are purely honorific: some may be appointed to give occasional advice on specific topics or markets (or for their contacts). Often however they are the seniors of the company, retired chairmen or presidents, who act as confidential advisers to the president and chairmen on sensitive issues such as the succession to the presidency or the dismissal of a president. Yet others may be important or valuable members of the company who for one reason or another have relinquished direct executive responsibility. One or two retain their representative role. As we shall see, companies are often persuaded to accept retirees from government or the banks. If they have nothing much to offer, providing them with an office, a stipend, and the honourable title of Adviser satisfies the *amour propre* of all parties: some start as advisers before moving to another role in the company.

Statutory Auditors (Kansayaku)

Statutory auditors should not be confused either with the external auditors, who are qualified accountants with much the same role as elsewhere, or with internal auditors, who are appointed by management. The statutory auditors are appointed by the shareholders. Articles 273–80 of the Code contain the relevant provisions, of which the following is a convenient précis:

The directors' functions are to decide policies and executive business. The Kansayaku's function is to audit the directors' activities to ensure that business is conducted in accordance with applicable laws and the company's regulations and in the best interest of the shareholders.

The Kansayaku must report at the shareholders' meeting whether or not company business was carried out properly and whether or not the agenda proposed by the directors is appropriate.

As such, the Kansayaku is expected to attend board meetings and other important meetings, obtain business reports and financial documents from company executives, inspect facilities, and check the operations of subsidiaries as deemed necessary.

Also, the Kansayaku accepts the audit report from the independent auditors, and may receive reports from the internal audit section.

If the Kansayaku finds any illegal or improper activities which may cause substantial damage to the company, he must advise, recommend, or request the directors to cease such activities or take actions appropriate under the circumstances.

The basic role of the Kansayaku is to monitor the entire scope of company operations, and if he finds any problems or wrongdoings, to advise the directors on a timely basis.

The Kansayaku's aim is to prevent any improper activities that would make the company liable to any third party.

I found, however, in discussion that the reality varies a great deal. Some interlocutors laughed at the question about the Kansayaku's role, regarding it as a mere formality without substance, a view confirmed by one person in regard to the company in which he himself was the statutory auditor. On the other hand, some companies take the role seriously, and even bring in outsiders to perform it, which they do assiduously, sitting at board meetings and visiting the company's operations. The normal tendency is to give the post to a retired employee or director, who with the best will in the world may not have the status or inclination to question superiors with the necessary penetration. Indeed, the Japanese are themselves unsure of the scope of the Kansayaku's functions. The précis above suggests he is concerned with propriety, but some feel that Article 274 of the Code, 'A Kansayaku shall audit the executive by the directors of their functions' takes them further—into questioning the substance of business decisions. As far as I could see, few companies act as if this were so and many just go through the motions. Perhaps, as was suggested to me, the role was taken more seriously when the company was so substantial that it cast its shadow wide; in short, significant companies are more likely to have statutory auditors with a real role. This view was apparently confirmed by research conducted by the Japan Statutory Auditors Association (JSAA) reported by the Asahi News Service on 27 November 1992. A survey revealed that 21 per cent of respondents said they had no opportunity to communicate with company presidents and 39 per cent did so only once or twice a year; 24 per cent said they could not attend board or other important meetings; 18 per cent said they received no information in advance about important decisions. JSAA is appealing to the Justice Ministry to strengthen the Kansayakus' position by making them more independent of management and extending their period of office beyond the present two-year term.

Summary: Dynamism

These then are all the elements—a powerful chief executive, very often a chairman, with varying degrees of influence and authority, several layers of executive management on a large board, and the rest of the company's executive management not on the board.

The process of decision-making does, of course, vary according to the subject-matter, structure of the company, and management system. Matters that are sufficiently important to warrant formal board approval will generally have been subject to wide consultation with all relevant parts of the business either through the RINGI system or less formally. This ensures that although direction and control unquestionably lie at the top, senior management is well in touch with the mood of the company and the boundaries of the possible. The total process of consultation does seem slow, and although in an emergency it can be much shortened, some Japanese are critical of it. Some consultative processes would be familiar in the West, for instance, the way in which budgets are presented, discussed (possibly amended), and agreed between the subsidiaries or divisions of a large company and head office (though the West usually lacks the theatricality of the final scene where the president meets all the divisional or subsidiary heads at a formal ceremony and personally hands them the agreed plan as evidence of their joint commitment to it). Not all companies have such a ritual.

We have been looking at the machinery by which Japanese companies are driven forward. We now turn to consider the context in which they are working and their effective accountability for their actions, remembering that neither the board nor the shareholders' meeting acting in a formal mode have any significant role. We shall consider in turn the roles of government, banks, other interested parties, and the market.

Government

When the government's role is mentioned it invariably refers to the civil service, not to politicians. Whatever scandals may have tarnished the reputation of Ministers or Members of Parliament, the civil service seems to have remained untainted and to continue to command general respect for its integrity and intelligence. Many of the ablest from the best universities are recruited into it.

Much has been written about the role of the Japanese civil service, particularly the Ministry of Finance (MoF) and MITI, so there is no need to give a historical account of their past actions. MoF and MITI are not the only 'sponsoring' Ministries: there are others like Transport and Agriculture, and the rationale for the division of responsibility is not always clear. Transport, for instance, is responsible for shipping, railways, airways, and shipbuilding.

The Ministries are not monolithic. Different bureaux in a ministry are powerful fiefdoms with considerable independence and a close relationship with their 'constituents'. They guard their independence jealously and will fight their corners with other Ministries or even different departments of the same Ministry (and this is admitted with a frankness which corresponding UK departments might find surprising).

The standards of the various Ministries appear to vary. I have heard allegations that politicians have put pressure on officials of the Transport Ministry to grant certain permits or licences, but there is no sure means of checking this and I have heard no such accusations about other Ministries. The civil service is generally held to be uncorrupt and dedicated to the national interest.

It is quite difficult to gauge the extent of Ministries' influence on corporate governance. In a direct sense there is virtually none. They do not try to interfere with appointments or dismissals. Senior civil servants coming to the end of their career may be helped by their Ministry to find a place in a company. In some cases they start second careers—and do very well in them. The practice is called *Amakudari* ('descent from heaven'); firms often find the connection useful, but in any case would be loath to risk exciting a Ministry's displeasure by spurning an offer. They take officials to secure their relationship with the department, but the department may turn its back on a colleague it has unshipped, having exhausted its obligation to him by finding him a niche. The officials may find themselves in proper jobs but are often shunted into agreeable sidings, perhaps in a specially created research centre, perhaps as the company's representative at international conferences. They may be able to contribute to the company by opening doors. With the onset of prosperity the charms of officials, although strong, are not perhaps quite what they used to be in the eyes of industrialists.

The scale of Amakudari is greater than outsiders might suppose. The figures given below are taken from the so-called Amakudari White Paper (Seiroren 1992).

Numbers of Amakudari Cases by Ministry

Cabinet	6
Board of Audit	3
Prime Minister's Office	45
Science and Technology Agency	8
Economic Planning Agency	7
National Policy Agency	4

National Land Agency	10
Environment Agency	4
PM's Office and other Agencies	12
Ministry of Foreign Affairs	7
Ministry of Finance	27
Ministry of Education	16
Ministry of Health and Welfare	10
Ministry of Agriculture, Forestry and Fisheries	41
Ministry of International Trade and Industry	36
Ministry of Transport	21
Ministry of Posts and Telecommunications	1
Ministry of Labour	12
Ministry of Construction	20
Ministry of Home Affairs	7
Local Authorities	18
Other	10

The destinations of most of the officials is as follows:

Government-related financial institutes	22
Major banks	23
Regional banks	49
Securities and investment trust companies	23
Insurance companies	26
Savings banks	14
Research institutions	13
Other business associates and exchanges	28
Other companies	50
Total	248

The Ministry of Finance's control of its sector is much tighter than any other Ministry's and need not concern us here. MITI's role has changed and diminished over the years as industry struggled, survived, and prospered. It still gives general indications of broad policy; in 1992 emphasis was being laid on developing trade with Japan's neighbours, including the former Soviet Union. Sometimes MITI gets more specific. It may, for instance, negotiate a trade agreement on, say, export limitation, which it then has to persuade an industry to accept. It operates by agreement not diktat and may spend a year or two getting one firm to forgo its short-term benefit for long-term rewards. Having secured the agreement of a leader in the industry it is then less difficult to corral the rest. This is an example of 'administrative guidance'—informal, negotiated, and private. Firms do not have to accept it, but MITI has a long memory and people remember the old Japanese adage, 'Attack in EDO, revenge in Nagasaki.'

In former days, MITI did not just rely on persuasion—it had weapons at its command like taxation and subsidy. Nowadays it does a careful job of *Nemawashi* ('preparing the ground') through an advisory body called the Industrial Structure Council which comprises bankers, unionists, industrialists, academics, officials, and journalists. The Council has a number of subcommittees and the whole machinery is used for defining, refining, promulgating, and getting acceptance for policy.

MITI comes under severe international pressure from time to time— which sometimes suits it, since it adds force to their requests to pursue a particular policy they quite probably wanted to follow anyway.

In considering whether Ministries interfere with the process of corporate governance we must remember that they are avid collectors of information which industry finds of value and that industry regards them as allies not antagonists. One source put it to me in these terms:

Japanese civil servants do not regard themselves as keepers of an open field on which a good game can be played; their interest is to ensure the Japanese win. To this end rules may be surreptitiously bent by officials at many levels.

An informed industrialist expressed the relationship between government and industry in this way: 'To make a successful voyage a ship needs motive power to drive it forward and a rudder to give it direction. The motive power must come from within the company: the state cannot provide it. What the state can do is to help the ship steer in the right direction.' But local opinion sometimes has doubts on the course MITI has set—for instance, in the oil industry.

The Banks

The important role Japanese banks have played in financing their industry is well understood and widely documented in quantitative terms. History repeated itself. Both in the establishment of industry in the second half of the nineteenth century and in its re-establishment after 1945, the banks were the most convenient way of channelling savings—and the most controllable by government in terms of direction, quantity (by fiscal incentives), and price (by interest rates). Even if the situation is now changing for bigger companies, it will be remembered that numerically more than 99 per cent of Japanese companies are unquoted and they look to the banking system as the only source of external capital.

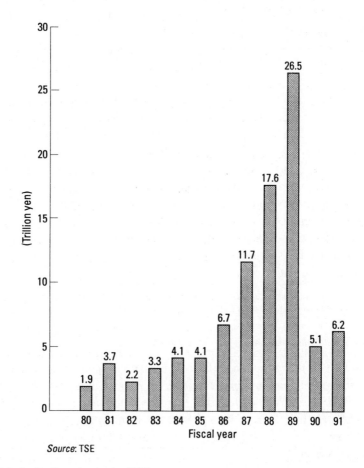

Source: TSE

FIG. 3.2 Equity financing in the 1980s

Although companies which cannot tap the capital markets depend mainly on the banks, those which can have done so increasingly over the last fifteen years. The figures for large manufacturing companies are given in Table 3.7 and Fig 3.2. Another set of figures, given in Table 3.8, suggests that the position is not so clear-cut and that the main banks' position has not changed much. Yet a further set of figures from the Bank of Japan's 1992 spring bulletin shows that small and medium-size firms have increased their share of total outstanding bank loans and now account for 51.2 per cent in the case of city banks and 62.7 per cent for regional banks.

There should, however, be no misapprehension that the role of the banks

TABLE 3.7. *Changes in capital structure of large manufacturing companies (book value)*

Fiscal year	Bank loan (%)	Bond (%)	Equity (%)
1977	63.0	7.4	29.6
1978	60.2	7.6	32.2
1979	58.2	7.4	34.4
1980	56.5	6.7	36.8
1981	55.2	6.4	38.4
1982	52.3	7.1	40.5
1983	47.8	8.3	43.9
1984	43.8	9.6	46.6
1985	41.4	10.8	47.7
1986	38.6	12.7	48.7
1987	34.5	14.0	51.6
1988	29.4	15.9	54.6
1989	22.7	20.9	56.4
1990	23.0	20.6	56.4

Source: Bank of Japan, quoted by Nomura Research Institute, Ltd.; Isao Yamamoto, 'Corporate Governance in Japan' (28 Oct. 1992).

TABLE 3.8. *Changes in borrowing from main banks*

	1970	1975	1980	1985	1987
Total borrowing (A) (billion yen)	13,180	35,598	43,687	52,628	54,296
Main bank borrowing (B) (billion yen)	1,804	4,813	5,133	6,432	6,446
(B) as % of (A)	13.7	13.5	11.7	12.2	11.9

Note: Coverage is of companies listed in sections 1 and 2 of the Tokyo Stock Exchange as having city banks as their main banks.
Source: Economic Research Association, 'Financial Institutions' Investment and Loans'.

as the main source of long-term primary capital meant they were or are an easy source. One now hugely successful entrepreneur said he had been refused by thirty-two banks before he found one to back him. As he pointed out ruefully, collateral is of great importance and significance to the banks when considering applications for loans (and it figured prominently in Ministry of Finance guidance). This has led to real problems for the banks in the 1990s when the value of property collapsed and local bankers, with no yardstick other than collateral, found it impossible to take decisions. The result was to push lending decisions upwards, which slowed them greatly.

The normal pattern is for companies to have a 'main' bank which will have the largest share of the company's business, although there are prudential limits imposed by the authorities on a bank's exposure to any individual company or group. The main bank will see itself as in a special relationship with particular obligations, notably to provide or co-ordinate support for the company in times of trouble. The value of this relationship to the bank is its profitability because of its hold on the customer for a wide range of its services. To the customer it is a convenience and an insurance policy, and he is often likely to pay a price for it, for instance, by depositing money with the bank at cheap rates. The 'insurance' aspect is crucial. One financial house said they would still not deal with a company which had no main bank. Another source said that some companies with big cash balances still maintained an overdraft with a lead bank to keep the relationship. All the evidence is that such a policy is justified. If a company has a main bank the umbrella stays up longer.

The obligations inherent in the customer/main bank relationship can bear heavily on the bank itself as is illustrated by the case of Ataka, a trading company which got into major difficulties in late 1975 at a time when, in the aftermath of the first oil crisis, the Japanese economy was under some strain. Because of the potential systemic implications of a failure by Ataka, the Bank of Japan became involved and a merger of Ataka with another trading company C. Itoh was arranged. As a condition for the merger, however, Sumitomo, Ataka's main bank, was obliged to take on liabilities not only of Ataka but also of related companies which amounted to several times its original exposure to the company itself. Ataka was saved from formal bankruptcy. Similar, though less far-reaching, cases of rescue operations to avert bankruptcy can be cited, for instance, Tateho Chemical Industries. Taiyo Kobe and six other creditor banks organized a restructuring of the company which lost $22 billion in Zaitech operations (actually government bond futures). The top management was replaced. A lead bank will try to rally support from any other banks or non-bank lenders, but it may have to take the lead by some sacrifice of its own rights, for example, by reducing its own rates of interest and charges to the customers. Such support operations are part of the system but even so may be difficult to set up and finalize. They may take a long time to bring to fruition: with banks themselves under increasing pressure the need to 'share the pain' may become more widespread.

The lead bank concept rests upon an important foundation—Japanese banks, whether long-term credit banks or city banks, view themselves as being in long-term relationships. To use the modern jargon, they are relationship not transaction oriented. Although some Japanese banks have the privileged position of borrowing and lending long-term money, other types of banks have found ways of moving into such operations even before the formal breakdown of the barriers now being organized by the authorities. The long-term business has some attractions, and although not by any means the only source provides a good flow of information. Some banks have extensive computer links between headquarters, local headquarters, functional departments, and branch managers, as a means of storing and making available the commercial intelligence they garner.

The long-term approach of Japanese banks affects staffing and training levels at the banks. As they expect to visit companies (nearly) daily, and aim to get to understand their business 'exactly well' as one banker said, and to know their people, the contact demands both time and knowledge; even so the switch away from collateral-based lending in the early 1990s is posing problems. Their basic concept, however, is to be able to provide some value added as well as funds: to assist in this, banks organize themselves to collect and dispense a flow of intelligence (gleaned from its client network) which its customers find invaluable about the economy in general but more especially about their own industry.

The role the banks play in corporate governance depends very much on the strength of a particular customer. In the case of an established and prosperous major company it will be minimal; the company does not need and would not brook interference. A company making its way will find itself in the warm embrace of its bank, with frequent visits from its officers. A company in trouble—of any size—may find itself losing its freedom of manœuvre and ultimately its top people if a bank decides to parachute in its rescue troops; in the very last resort it may face a total loss of identity as the bank negotiates a merger—which will at least save its staff's jobs. A typical case was Itoman (reported in the UK *Financial Times* (19/20 Sept. 1992)), an old-established business ruined by ill-judged property speculation beginning in 1988 which first came to notice in mid-1990. Its main bank, Sumitomo, arranged a merger with a steel trading subsidiary of Sumitomo Metal Industries.

It must not be supposed that banks are simply seeking opportunities to display their muscle; on the contrary, the escalation of interference is something they would much prefer to avoid. They will go to considerable lengths not to let a firm fail if it affects their reputation as lead bank. But the banks' safety net does not catch everyone. In 1991/2, there were 11,557 corporate failures (up 61 per cent on the previous year). A sectoral breakdown (of the year before) is illuminating (Table 3.9).

TABLE 3.9. *Corporate bankruptcies by sector* (Jan. 1990–May 1991; liabilities in 100 million yen)

	TOTAL		Construction		Manufacturing		Wholesale & retail trade		Transport & communication		Services	
	Cases	Liabilities	Cases	Liabilities	Cases	Liabilities	Cases	Liabilities	Cases	Liabilities	Cases	Liabilities
Jan. 1990	456	582	90	89	63	54	218	257	13	18	44	50
Feb. 1990	447	760	79	70	80	167	210	280	10	80	44	97
Mar. 1990	503	732	123	108	74	233	226	258	9	4	40	34
Apr. 1990	525	2,112	119	240	73	176	243	1,435	12	8	49	182
May 1990	502	1,862	109	160	78	93	226	356	9	31	50	983
June 1990	515	882	119	194	68	80	225	375	16	13	51	56
July 1990	493	867	108	150	59	126	232	300	9	9	45	77
Aug. 1990	513	1,253	107	135	84	341	236	407	14	19	38	54
Sept. 1990	532	892	111	160	68	75	242	363	13	12	60	82
Oct. 1990	645	1,479	144	207	94	191	297	877	15	13	59	68
Nov. 1990	634	3,153	132	2,029	105	149	287	366	5	5	57	119
Dec. 1990	713	4,870	144	225	86	169	292	1,886	22	35	90	164
Jan. 1991	646	6,423	119	210	86	642	292	610	18	63	73	141
Feb. 1991	676	3,292	125	278	100	404	302	580	9	3	55	136
Mar. 1991	773	7,913	133	299	103	162	354	1,608	18	25	72	206
Apr. 1991	835	8,551	179	377	112	777	362	1,496	21	7	85	2,878
May 1991	892	4,426	192	520	97	795	382	930	24	57	101	942

Source: MoF Statistics Bureau.

Summing up the banks' role as *lenders* it appears that they are *not* an easy touch; place much weight on collateral (this may be changing); take a long-term view; do not, judging by the number of bankruptcies, bail all companies out. They do, however, intervene actively where they think they should, generally when they are the recognized lead bank. And, at times of trouble, they may assume great responsibility for a company and its employees. The extent of their commitment will depend on many factors, not least that their relationship with a company may have been buttressed by reciprocal shareholdings.

In former days, when banks were prosperous, they could afford to act the patient nursemaid more often. Now pressure on their resources has made them more discriminating and they have tended, consciously, to sort out their customers into four categories:

those whose relationship they want to enhance;
those whose relationship they wish to maintain;
those to whom they want a reduced commitment;
those they wish to leave altogether.

The Banks as Shareholders

As we saw, German banks are substantial shareholders in industry, but most of their holdings were acquired *faute de mieux*, because a company was so distressed that its debt was turned into equity as a last resort. It was not an act of deliberate policy to take stakes in industry. In Japan it has been. Japanese banks took such stakes to cement their relationship with customers (especially when they were disintermediating). It was also useful to strengthen their position if the company encountered difficulties and they had to exercise influence. Nowadays they are limited to 5 per cent of the stock of any one company, but this does not preclude affiliates having holdings too.

In his paper on corporate governance, Yamamoto of Nomura (1992), put a different slant on the banks' purchase of equities:

To meet BIS requirements, many Japanese commercial banks issued equities very actively. However, banking stocks have been very illiquid on the markets. Thus, in order to issue new equities, commercial banks had to invest more in shares of business companies who bought new equities of the banks. Thus, the last column on the right in table [Table 3.10], A over B being more than 1, indicates that banks buy more equities than they sell their own equities. The cross-shareholding, with banks playing the core role, has been kept even during the active equity financing.

Companies for their part bought bank shares reciprocally from the proceeds of new issues at vertiginous PEs, thus acquiring them cheaply.

TABLE 3.10. *Equity financing and investment by major commercial banks*

	Net increase in amount of stock (billion yen) (A)	Equity finance (billion yen) (B)	(A) as % of (B)
IBJ	810	497	1.63
LTCB	505	186	2.73
Mitsubishi T/B	279	275	1.02
Sumitomo T/B	293	224	1.46
Mitsui T/B	323	107	2.73
DKB	933	390	2.39
Mitsubishi	729	359	2.03
Fuji	1,004	369	2.72
Sumitomo	747	290	2.58

Note: period is from March 1985 to March 1989.

The importance of the banks as holders of equity is shown in Table 3.10. Japanese banks are far and away the biggest shareholders among all countries studied (see Table 3.11).

Reciprocal holdings between banks and industrial companies can come under pressure if either party badly needs liquidity, but the general practice is not to reduce or dispose of holdings without prior consultation, so as to make sure the other party knows the score. The bank may well be able to place the shares in other friendly hands. Sometimes when an industrial company moves first, the bank may follow suit, especially if it is concerned about the company anyway; sometimes the embarrassment may be temporary, and if so the company will be expected to show its sincerity by building up its holding again when it has the resources to do so.

The power and influence of the banks is sometimes resented by industrial companies, and a few cash rich ones have shaken themselves quite free by discharging their main banks; things are, however, not always what they seem, and a relationship may nevertheless be maintained against a rainy day. In general, though, it is true that the banks must increasingly rely on influence, since their power has diminished as companies' indebtedness has declined and their access to improving capital markets has been facilitated. 1992 began to see a reversal of this trend because the surge in equity financing included a large slice of warrant bonds which mature between that year and 1996 (see Fig. 3.3). In the current state of the markets the warrants cannot be converted into equity, and must be financed by straight

TABLE 3.11. *Ownership of common stock* (as % of total outstanding common shares)

	USA (1990)	UK (1989)	France (1989)	Germany (1988)	Japan (1990)
Banks and other financial institutions	0.5	—	3.5	8.1	25.2
Life insurance companies	2.9	⎫	⎫	⎫	13.2
Other insurance companies	2.6	⎬ 20.0	⎬ 2.6	⎬ 2.7	4.1
Pension funds	26.5	32.0 ⎭	⎭	— ⎭	0.9
Mutual funds	6.6	8.0	2.5	3.4	3.6
Households	54.4	20.0	23.9	19.4	23.1
Non-financial business	n.a.	8.0	50.5	39.3	25.2
Government	—	3.0	4.3	7.1	0.6
Foreign	6.4	9.0	12.8	20.0	4.2
TOTAL	100.0	100.0	100.0	100.0	100.0

Note: The definition of common stock for each country is as follows:
  USA and UK: total market values of the securities quoted on the Stock Exchange.
  Germany: total par values of the securities of listed and unlisted companies.
  France: total market values of the securities of listed and unlisted companies.
  Japan: total par values of the securities quoted on the Stock Exchange.

  The following factors influence the allocation to categories of shareholder:
  USA: shares held in non-financial business are not counted here.
       shares held in mutual savings banks and by brokers and dealers are counted as Banks and other
         financial institutions.
       shares held in private pension funds and State and local government retirement funds are counted as
         Pension funds.
  UK: shares held in banks, by bankers and dealers and other insurance companies are counted as Non-
       financial business.
  France: shares held in CDC and other banks are counted as Banks and other financial institutions.

Source:
  USA: Federal Reserve Board (Flow of Funds Accounts 1990).
  UK: Confederation of British Industry estimates.
  France: Banque de France (*Bulletin trimestriel* 1990).
  Germany: Deutsche Bank (Monthly Report 1989).
  Japan: All stock exchanges.

bonds, borrowing, and asset sales (which would further add to the pressure on cross-holdings).

The final, but not least important of banks' relationships with companies is the outposting of bank staff—Amakudari of a different sort, and more widespread. Banks often arrange for a senior man to have a second career in an industrial company. When he goes there he becomes the company's man, not the bank's spy, but even so his previous connection can serve both parties well. Often he will get a directorship, but sometimes he may be difficult to accommodate and may find himself shunted around until a suitable niche is found. Even staff of the Bank of Japan move to industry on

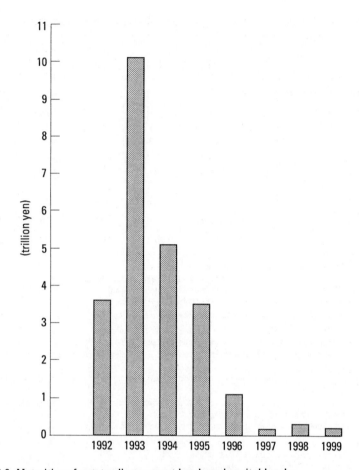

FIG. 3.3 Maturities of outstanding warrant bonds and capital bonds

occasion. There is reason to believe that they and other able bankers make a good contribution, and the moves of course strengthen the networking within Japanese commercial life.

Shareholders

As we know from the UK and USA, the stability of a holding does not automatically follow from its belonging to a particular class such as individuals, pension funds, or mutual funds. In the Japanese case, however, commentators feel that it is possible to make such a judgement, hence the bar charts produced by the Commercial Law Centre (reproduced in Fig. 3.3 above).

What these bar charts indicate is that a large proportion of the shares on the market are untraded, and that, correspondingly, few are available. This is often given as one of the reasons for prices being bid up so high. It means also that long-term shareholders have a real proprietorial interest in the businesses in which they hold investments. If they happen to be bankers too, they are in the fortunate position of being well informed and can thus exert timely influence if they need to. So can companies in Keiretsu. So apparently can other stable shareholders. How this influence is exercised is generally hidden from view, in accordance with the Japanese concern for relationships, though those who know the signals can doubtless read them.

We should not, I think, draw from this the conclusion that there exists in Japan endless and furious activity in which shareholders plot and plan how to interfere with management. This is the last thing they would wish to do. If, however, there is clear evidence of a problem which management appears unable or unwilling to address, the 'stable' shareholders may be so positioned as to play their part in remedial action.

Hideo Ishihara, then deputy president of the Industrial Bank of Japan, put it as follows in an address on 4 November 1991, at Duke University:

Shareholders, for their part, seldom make adverse comment on management and even less often do they make confrontational moves in shareholder meetings. With share holding in almost all cases mutual, corporations bask in an atmosphere of 'you scratch my bank, I'll scratch yours'. They are generally quiet and lenient shareholders unless management commits extreme blunders, negligence or excesses.

It is apparent that the existence of these stable corporate shareholders, who will not demand high dividend payout or sell their stake without prior consultation and who are prepared to judge management performance on a long-term basis, is a major factor enabling management to commit the company to large-scale projects which bring fruits only several years later. Nippon Steel's Kimitsu works, Honda's American plant in Ohio, NEC's semi-conductor plant in California and Komatsu's total quality control project are all examples of daring, long-range projects which would not have been possible unless the management was assured of the blessing or at least acquiescence of the shareholders.

Taking together the roles of the chairman and of advisers and the interests of the stable shareholders, one may conclude that Japanese management does operate within a framework of accountability, however quietly and tardily it may operate; add this to peer pressures and there is a coherent system (which is weakened where a company decides to do without a chairman). The Japanese themselves consider that the system is at its most vulnerable when dealing with a tough charismatic character who scorns peer pressure such as it is, and who has decided to dig in. He may be moved but it takes an enormous effort to do it.

The system works—but tardily. Japanese shareholders have traditionally been far more interested in capital appreciation than income, mainly on tax grounds: a whole generation has grown up since the mid-1960s to experience steady capital appreciation. If the 1990s show a different pattern, the level of dividend payments will assume greater importance. The life insurance companies in particular have to meet a minimum target investment yield of 5.5 per cent on their policy reserves; pressures on them have mounted since deregulation sharpened competition, especially in some companies, and there is even talk of their threatening to sell the shares of companies with a mean distribution policy, as an inducement to become more generous. In general shareholders do get occasional bonus issues or rights issues on favourable terms, but even so, yields are very low by UK/ USA standards. What all this means is that generally Japanese shareholders have not hitherto been spurred into concern, let alone action, by dividends or even profits—unless it is clear from a cut in the dividend that the company is in poor shape, which would indeed raise questions about the management. So Japanese management has not had to worry about increases in dividend, and even if the chairman had a moment of angst at taking an AGM when profits had fallen, he could generally depend on his shareholders not to intervene prematurely. He can even now depend absolutely on the absence of hostile bids, but not on continued acquiescence in a policy of distributional parsimony.

The Market

We have already considered how equity finance grew in the 1980s as a proportion of companies' external financing, and that a very high proportion of outstanding shares are in stable hands. 'Stable' means an unwillingness to trade in the market even if a bid is made for the company. Many mergers occur between willing managements and some shotgun marriages are arranged for failing companies, but no one, Japanese or foreign, has launched a successful take-over bid over the heads of incumbent management. It is entirely contrary to the whole ethos of Japanese commercial life, and the idea of 'buying and selling people' (as one interlocutor put it) is regarded as most unattractive. The unions would certainly be antipathetic to any 'hostile' bid, especially one from abroad, which they felt carried a threat of redundancies. If a Japanese company did want to launch a bid, it would need a great deal of Nemawashi with all the parties, including shareholders and unions.

The Japanese stockmarket, though very active, is therefore a market for shares but not companies; bid premiums do not exist. Company management pays no heed to any threat of take-over, and to that extent it is wholly entrenched, though while competition remains intense it is not lethargic. The absence of fear means that it can effectively disregard the effect on profitability of heavy investment. The system of asset allocation which a totally free stockmarket produces simply does not function—which has up till now given Japan a competitive advantage against countries where it does. Yamamoto (1992) is one of many commentators who note that Japanese management puts employees and customers miles before share-holders. As the shareholders have handcuffed themselves, this seems quite logical; as noted above, the shareholders have to be very roughly treated before they assert themselves.

The Unions

It is no disrespect to Japanese unions to have left them till last. They are not trade-based but enterprise-based. The great spring offensive for the annual pay claim is nearly genuine, but all companies have the same settlement date, which gives the government and employers a chance to conduct a *tutti* on the prevailing economic facts. The result is to establish clearly in people's minds where the band of expectation lies within which settlement is likely.

This short account of union activities is not intended to belittle their contribution. Although there were some fierce struggles immediately after the War, the unions became much more responsible from the mid-1950s onwards. There are occasional instances of confrontation, for instance at Nissan and Fujitsu—which certainly damaged Nissan for some time. Gener-ally speaking, the relationship between union and management is not bedevilled by folk memories of bitter battles and a long history of sour antagonism. Instances of confrontation are now rare. Commentators ascribe the reasons for the improvement to the better education and training the work-force receives which make the relations with management easier to handle, and to a more accommodating attitude on both sides. Management has made increasing efforts to make sure that the work-force understands its policies. The unions have reciprocated by trying to understand the companies' needs. There is as a result greater unity of purpose than there was; leaders of unions sometimes find themselves appointed to the board on retirement (quite common in the banking industry). In general it seems that although unions of course push their members' claims, they are *au fond* concerned with the company's prosperity and, given that dividends are meagre, there is less room for argument about how the cake should be cut. Indeed, there have been examples when the union has played a leading part in causing a president to stand down, notably in the case of Yamaha.

Litigation

Of all the countries studied, recourse to law figures least in Japan. Legal action is counted a failure in human relationships and is very rare—except in regard to foreign firms. The big firms nowadays tend to train employees so as to be able to do routine legal work in-house. Law firms therefore occupy a quite different place in regard to industry from their counterparts elsewhere. Directors and managers do not feel it necessary to conduct themselves on the basis that a writ may be served at the slightest provocation.

The Media

Surprisingly frank and apparently well-informed articles appear in Japanese newspapers, for Press coverage of companies is many times greater than in the UK, with special newspapers covering particular industries. Squads of journalists get to know how companies are organized, what their internal structure is, and what the personal profiles are. They seem to be uninhibited about defamation and write freely about what is going on and about the factions in the business. Even so they know more than they write and are thought to exercise restraint in the broader interest. The various Ministries and the Bank of Japan have their own press 'lobbies' made up of correspondents attached to each institution.

Summary

Now that we have examined the main components we can draw some conclusions about the corporate governance machine as a whole, bearing in mind the two principles set out at the very beginning.

Entrepreneurial Activity

If we look first at entrepreneurial activity, we can say with some certainty that it is not hampered by unnecessary impediments. There is no threat of legal action or take-over; as for government, Ministries work with industry and seem to help rather than hinder it. Within companies there are various structural features which may be positively helpful, of which three are worth a passing mention. First, that although our caricature of an inventor is a lonely man in an untidy room, genius may not always suffocate by existing in a more collegiate atmosphere; secondly, that it has long been thought (though it cannot be proved) that man's peak of inventiveness is reached young, and Japanese personnel practices seem to accept this and act on it; thirdly, that by using subsidiaries with a really separate existence and the opportunity of independent glory if they are good enough, the

Japanese may have found a better way of unlocking entrepreneurial skills in a big organization than by operating in divisions.

Accountability

The point about accountability—which will recur throughout this book—is not that it is desirable to have in place some pettifogging rules for detailed reporting or some cumbersome apparatus which kills entrepreneurial drive. It is to have a system in which there is proper control of the use of power, and that means above all maintaining the standard of competence and probity of those who exercise it. Whether this control is formal or informal or a mixture of both is of secondary importance to its consistent effectiveness. In Japan, as in most countries, the system has 'internal' components of control, that is to say, those within the company, as well as external elements.

Internal Influences

The internal system of accountability appears to work reasonably well, though the value of the collegiate and consensual approach can be argued either way. Its proponents commend its thoroughness and say that it is less likely to produce eccentric decisions; its critics dislike the diffusion of responsibility. These lines of argument apply at the highest level. Although the president himself is in a strong position, the normal Japanese practice of collective decision-making means that he is less likely to be personally exposed anyway—unless he gets his personal relationships wrong and fails to ensure harmony. But there are occasions when it becomes clear his leadership leaves something to be desired. Although he may be more dedicated to his company and less to himself than his Western counterpart (few hit the headlines; conspicuous consumption is for gangsters—he is less likely to go on an ego trip), he likes power as much as any CEO in the world. Even so, Japanese self-discipline has its limits. If he is the kind of man who is attuned to the views of colleagues he will sense from the tone and substance of questions at the top management committee that they are dissatisfied. And if it is clear that their dissatisfaction is deepening he may feel that he owes it to the company to stand down. Even if he does not, eventually he may find it hard to resist other influences that build up within the company, for example, from the chairman, or past chairmen and presidents, especially if they are still advisers, and especially if they have a proprietary interest. (There are tales of the founders of business still calling the shots in the 1980s and later, long after they had ceased to hold a formal position; generally, however, this is not so.)

   If, however, he does not want to listen, and has a dominant personality, the Japanese themselves seem to regard it as particularly difficult to get rid of him even though he has palpably gone off the boil and company results are deteriorating, until such time as trouble is well developed. The Itoman case is a classic example. The president, Kawamura, who was ultimately dismissed (itself unusual as we have seen), is alleged to have made most major decisions on his own. According to the London *Financial Times* (1 June 1992), this was the first formal sacking of the president of a listed Japanese company since 1982. In less dramatic circumstances, restraint and respect for authority make hinting embarrassing (to those who do not wish to listen), and more drastic action wholly unpalatable. It is in practice very difficult for a Japanese board to unship such a president unless they have external help. Occasionally it is the unions which act, as was noted earlier, and help bring the crisis to a head. There are several recent cases of their intervening effectively.

External Influences

The Japanese emphasis on enduring relationships means that all the parties have a much deeper interest in each other's continuing prosperity and generally a better base of knowledge on which to form judgements about whether it stands in danger of being impaired. Foremost among these parties are the banks, who do, as we have seen, foster close ties with industrial companies; some even have a desk of their own on the customer's premises. When times are good they have neither a basis nor a need to interfere; when they get bad they have both, for they stand to lose not only their money as lender and shareholder, but also a customer and reputation.

They are, then, in a strong position to influence management and they undoubtedly do, and continue to do so even when the company grows. Whilst the company continues to prosper advice will not constitute interference, but if trouble looms the borderline will be crossed. Pressure will be put on the company to make management changes; members of the bank's own staff may be parachuted in to help management or even run the company. Some banks have reservations about this, fearing that their staff are unqualified to run an industrial company, but even so there do seem to have been many occasions on which it has been done successfully. Finally, a bank may create the circumstances in which a company can put itself back on its feet, and it may even put in a whole management team to help it do so. If all else fails the bank will quietly negotiate a merger with another Japanese company, or very occasionally a foreign one. Meanwhile, and throughout this series of events, the main bank will have taken responsibility for co-ordinating action with other banks to keep the ship afloat.

Although it is the banks which so often instigate and orchestrate remedial action, troubled banks themselves may fall victim to the same process under pressure from their creditors or from the authorities. The chairman of the regional Hyogo bank, for example, has recently stepped down as part of a major restructuring, while a former official from the Bank of Japan has been appointed to the board, and a former Ministry of Finance official as an adviser.

It is difficult for an outsider to add up all the internal and external checks and balances and form any clear conclusion about their effectiveness. The Japanese I spoke to seemed to think they worked pretty well, if only because the process of selection was so thorough in the first place. Some interlocutors regretted the absence of outsiders at the top level of strategy determination and control, but my own observation is that this is connected with the ceremonial nature of the board's activities. If it has so little substantive business, what contribution could outsiders make? More broadly, experience suggests that any institution which retains its obligations but no longer carries out the function with which it is charged is a potential source of weakness. The networking arrangements involving elders, banks, and stable shareholders seem to function rather well, if slowly. But a determined tyrant clinging to power poses a real problem. Mr Nishikawa, a Sumitomo director, commented recently after the Itoman affair (*Financial Times* (1 June 1992)), 'When a person is at the top for a long time that is not an obstacle in itself. But when a person has a position of power for a long time, decay has a tendency to set in.'

Lord Acton's famous dictum applies in Japan as elsewhere, and so does its parody: 'All power is delightful and absolute power is absolutely delightful.' But the Japanese system seems for the most part adept at preventing the corruption of absolute power and limiting its delights.

iii. Trends and Issues

It is only too easy to confuse Japan's ability to react effectively and rapidly to world events (as, for instance, in the oil-price shocks) with the glacial rate of change or development in the fundamental structure of society. We should not assume that economic pressures—which are only too obvious in late 1992—will cause radical change, even though they may need to be accommodated, by various adjustments, which may in total be not inconsiderable.

Lifetime Employment

A good example of this is lifetime employment, a cornerstone of Japanese industrial practice in major companies. Already, by the end of 1992, firms were having to grapple with the fact that they had too many staff. I heard estimates that disguised unemployment which was running at a very high level, but the disguise itself makes precise figures unobtainable. As noted earlier, companies do have many options before having to declare redundancies. There was one, however, which could have knock-on effects, namely giving surplus staff jobs to other businesses and only charging enough for them to cover the cost or part of it with no profit element (thus undercutting the market). Even if trade deteriorates and companies have to take more drastic action, there is no reason to believe that the *principle* of lifetime employment will be abandoned, but it may be at risk. Overtime has in many cases been eliminated already; in others the core payment has been reduced. The room for manœuvre is shrinking.

Dividends

The lack of concern of Japanese shareholders, private and institutional, with dividends, and the soaring flight of the stock market in a gravity-defying orbit, irrespective of such mundane matters as the yield, have perhaps been more affected than currently appears. The role of the life insurance companies is critical here because their position in the market gets even stronger, but their financial position is not uniformly good; they need bigger dividends, and it will be interesting to see how hard they will push to get them. They have the satisfaction of knowing that government too supports bigger payments, for policy reasons of its own.

If the relationship between distribution and share price becomes less distant, it may have an effect in due course on decision-making within Japanese companies. The thought that *significant* shareholders could no longer be counted upon to be stable because they might sell their holdings may focus the companies' attention more closely on profits as a business objective alongside market share; indeed, there are already signs of a heightened consciousness of the importance of profits.

Cross-Holdings and Keiretsu Groups

Although subject to international pressures, there is little evidence so far of Keiretsu changing dramatically. There is an obvious tendency for cross-holdings outside Keiretsu groups to be reduced, not on grounds of principle but because companies, including banks, need to be more liquid and the cost of holding them may be felt excessive. If the underlying relationship is itself less stable, the reason for maintaining a holding weakens. But sometimes a holding is reduced temporarily for tactical reasons, for example, to boost profits before a year end. If so they may be repurchased later. This may only be a passing phase, but it could conceivably weaken some relationships at the margin. What it is unlikely to do is to leave such a high proportion of shares on the open market that contested take-over bids become possible.

Take-over bids

Merger activity is important and extensive; it will doubtless continue—and indeed, may increase. At the time of writing (1992), there were rumblings about mergers in the securities industry, where there was excess capacity. At the other end of the spectrum—automobiles—questions were being raised for the first time in many years, following Nissan's poor results, about over-capacity in that industry too. Even if some mergers do occur they will be 'friendly'. The ethos is still wholly antipathetic to 'hostile' bids.

Banking

The sub-section on banks in Section ii above has already indicated some of the pressures brought about by poor lending (overblown property values) and disintermediation by big companies. The banks will have to rethink their lending rules and training, paying more attention to such data as cash flows and the valuation of collateral. But they will remain the main source of cash advice and admonition for the very large part of industry that still cannot use the capital markets, and there is no reason to think their basic stance—'think long-term'—will change. It was said that the distinction between city banks and long-term credit banks has largely disappeared in this regard. How the banks themselves will withstand the stresses and strains of the downturn and what role the authorities will play is beyond the scope of this paper: it was observed that as risk appeared to increase the mood seemed to become more protective.

Whose Company is it?

Finally we ought to touch on the 'stakeholders' argument which is under discussion on both sides of the Atlantic and in Japan. Any company anywhere touches society at many points because it has customers, employees, suppliers, creditors, and shareholders, and it affects the environment in which it is located. They all have some interest in the company, though not to the same degree; they are—in the jargon—'stakeholders', though the importance of their stake varies both to them and to the company.

I have borrowed this paragraph heading from chapter 8 of one of the classic books on Japanese companies, *The Japanese Corporation* (Abegglen and Stalk 1985). The point is simply this. Shareholders everywhere own the company, but how important are they among the stakeholders? In whose interests is a company run?

In Western countries, as we shall see, for many years the Adam Smith observation about agency costs (no agent looks after your interests as if they were his own) was well borne out in circumstances where the Berle and Means analysis remained valid (that highly diversified ownership caused owners' power to atrophy). In other words, the managers of a business could run it in their interest, that is, the interest of the employees, and not in the owners' interests. The take-over boom of the 1970s and 1980s however, showed UK and US managers that they neglected owners' interests at their peril.

Japan is sometimes thought to be utterly different, but in this regard, as in many others, the difference is arguably one of degree not kind. There seems to be no doubt that Japanese companies put the 'family' first (or immediately after customers). They argue that an employee who devotes his life to a business has morally a bigger stake in it than a shareholder. Even so, they cannot totally neglect their owners. As we have seen ownership is concentrated, so the Berle and Means analysis does not hold.

What has made Japan different is not so much attitudes within the company—though these count—but the fact that outside the company the interested parties, banks and shareholders, share the company's view that the shareholders' interest does not have to be satisfied by a growing dividend stream. There is also a consensus that 'hostile' take-overs are impermissible on social grounds. The total absence of this threat means that management can pursue its objectives regardless of the shareholders—though not to the point where shareholders might be goaded into revolt (for example, by passing the already meagre dividend)—or of their own inability to tap the capital markets. Shareholders' interests, in other words, may be pushed to the back of the queue, but cannot be wholly neglected. Shareholders for their part have in the past been well served because the stock market took off regardless of companies' distribution policy (see Abegglen and Stalk, 1985: ch. 7). A Japanese shareholder may have had a poor income stream, but his capital profits more than made up for it (which suited him better because of the tax laws).

The Japanese feeling about the company as a family—in which shareholders are 'poor relations'—may in future be somewhat modified if shareholders assert themselves. And there are signs that some, particularly life insurance companies, are doing so. Since the Nikkei index suggests the stock market no longer seems wholly impervious to the laws of gravity, shareholders must be less satisfied. It would not be surprising to find some degree of convergence between the US and Japanese extremes about the place of shareholders at the table.

Government

As noted, Ministries' role has changed over the decade and will doubtless continue to do so. But there are no signs at all of any wish to do more than touch the tiller. The Japanese version of the market economy—and Japanese corporate governance is a critical part of it—will continue to reflect the general ethos: if there is a conflict between them, 'community logic' will continue to prevail over 'market logic' at its most important points. Where change—albeit at a glacial pace—may be on the cards is in the balance tilting a little towards 'market logic', simply because, in the end, it cannot be avoided. No one should imagine that drastic change is in the air, as the acid reception to the proposals of Akio Morita of Sony testifies. He suggested: fewer new models; more pay for workers; less overwhelming priority than in the past to 'victory in the market-place', but more responsible behaviour towards all the company's stakeholders (see the London *Financial Times* (26 June 1992)). But some of his points, like fewer new models, may well find general acceptance in the tougher economic climate.

The importance of the role of the Ministry of Finance should not be underestimated, as its actions in the second half of 1992 demonstrated. There was a support package in the financial system on 18 August, designed in part to stop the fall in share prices. The Nikkei index was 14309 by 18 August, but was back to 16216 by 21 August. One has the impression that the financial scene is carefully orchestrated. By December 1992 the Ministry of Finance felt comfortable enough to issue instructions to banks about further disclosure of non-performing loans, which had been announced at 12.3 trillion yen for the twenty-one major banks at the end of October. But unofficial estimates put the figure far higher, depending on definition. No Japanese I encountered was wildly enthusiastic about their political system and indeed seemed to regard it as of little practical significance to them compared with MoF and MITI, which were widely respected. No one indicated to me that they expected a rapid change.

Envoi

The euphoric conditions of the 1980s have gone and may not return for some time. The party is over and there is a price to be paid, in terms of adjusting to less buoyant conditions and financial excesses. Many commentators feel that most of the fundamentals are still sound, however, and there was nothing I could detect in my 1992 enquiries that would point to a conclusion that any major changes in the system of corporate governance were imminent. The joker in the pack is the degree to which a greater emphasis on profitability by banks and industrial companies will change the relationships and the assumptions that underlie them. Much will depend on the climate for economic growth, which is generally regarded as less favourable than it was in the 1980s.

4 FRANCE

i. Introduction

As elsewhere, corporate governance in France reflects the country's political, economic, and social history. It does, moreover, do so to a marked degree, not least because many people think deeply about the origins and development of their institutions in an analytical, political, and historical way. 'You must understand', one man said, 'that giving the président directeur-général [PDG] almost absolute power in a French company is in accordance with the French tradition of strong centralised leadership which goes back through de Gaulle and Napoleon to Louis XIV.'

We shall be considering the PDG's role later in this section. The point of including the quotation—whether or not my interlocutor was justified—is to illustrate the combination of the intellectual with the pragmatic, and also to show that the French sense of 'la politique' does not draw a clear boundary between government and industry. Absolute power as a concept is as applicable in the one as the other. It also illustrates the brooding presence of the idea of the State, 'la France', and this too has important practical consequences, as we shall see.

Because my interlocutors did have such a strong historical sense, and because they coupled the exercise of pure intellect with a pragmatic interest in the reality of power, discussions were of unusual depth. Their patience and frankness were likewise exceptional—the pure milk of Cartesian logic was well flavoured with anecdotes about individuals. No paper of this brevity could, however, possibly do justice to the intricacies of the power struggles within and between major French groups and the so powerful banks. Nor is it necessary, for this paper is about *principles*, and they are at work however gaudily they are overlaid by personalities. Indeed, it is not safe to draw general principles from particular cases, as so much depends on the personal attitudes of individuals, nor is it safe to make assumptions based on political party; a Socialist minister may well be less *dirigiste* than his predecessor.

The State

It is significant that in writing about corporate governance in France the logical point at which to start is with the national government, which 'is intimately involved in business organisation and governance. It participates significantly in economic endeavour ... and in *société d'économie mixte* ... (Bacon and Brown 1977).

The principle that power should be concentrated at the centre and that it should be strong seems to be pivotal in French assumptions about the organization of society and is reflected both in the constitution, in the authority of the President, and in corporate governance, in the authority of the PDG. Such a system is at the other end of the spectrum from a pluralist or collective approach or one based upon checks and balances. Americans sometimes say that their constitution was deliberately constructed to avoid what the founding fathers saw as George III's excessive authority. The French have had many constitutions since the time of Louis XIV, alternating sometimes between Bonapartism and weaker institutions; but the Gaullist constitution under which they now operate is definitely in the centralist tradition.

The strong central power is inclined to be *dirigiste*. When they wish, French governments seem good at getting things done quickly. The government's right to influence and where necessary intervene quietly and effectively behind the scenes is expected, respected, and it would seem admired; accountability is less of an issue. Like most governments it has many weapons at its disposal, including an armoury of regulations governing various aspects of industrial and commercial life. Additionally, however, there are less tangible sources of power and influence, particularly appointments: there are many anecdotes of how governmental influence is quite subtly brought to bear. 'Stay close to government' is advice that seems often given and generally heeded; for example, a leading stockbroker was careful, before it sold its private client business, to advise the Ministry of Finance. I asked one major conglomerate what connection there was between its very disparate parts. 'Virtually none', was the response. 'The only common thread is that every subsidiary has central or local government as its main customer.' While this report was being prepared the French government announced it was providing £590 million to Machines Bull and Thomson-CSF. The European Commission were required to rule whether this was an infusion of equity capital or a subsidy. The point is the investment, not its classification.

The French government has what I heard called 'la notion de place'—a concept which it is difficult to translate. It seems to amount to a conceptual approach to the establishment of a centre—in this case Paris—together with the provision by government of what are regarded as its essential institutions and services. The centrale des risques (see below), COFACE, and the Crédit nationale are all publicly funded bodies which form part of the apparatus of 'la place financière' in Paris which has been so regarded since 1945. Among the various services the French government supplies are:

(a) *Centrale des bilans.* The centrale des bilans, run by the Banque de France, is an information exchange. Twenty-eight thousand of France's bigger businesses (60 per cent of the manufacturing sector and 40 per cent each of the construction and retailing sectors) send in data voluntarily. In return they can buy reports about their own relative performance and balance-sheets. This is now supplemented with the more detailed AIDE analysis of a company's performance and financial health, which any company can request and which is available in a few hours at a cost of about FF10,000.

(b) *Centrale des risques.* This is an information exchange about companies' indebtedness. Banks which lend more than 30 million francs to a company report this to the Banque de France—and also all cases of repayment difficulties. Still regarded as useful, if less than formerly, as loans by foreign banks are not included.

(c) *Fichier bancaire des entreprises.* This provides ratings (*cotations*) on companies to banks. It is linked to the centrale des risques and normally only covers companies with an annual turnover of at least 5 million francs, but companies of all sizes with repayment difficulties are included if the banks have reported them.

Cotations are provided free; charges are made for supplementary data. Records of 750,000 SA/SARL companies are kept (that is, the approximate equivalent of PLCs and Limited companies in the UK) and 300,000 others. Information is also kept about 700,000 managers, to enable assessments of management quality to be made.

The Ministry of Economy and Finance and the Banque de France

The Trésor directorate of the Ministry of Finance or its equivalent is powerful in every country, by dint of holding the purse strings. Its degree of importance depends on its willingness to intervene and the influence it can exercise when it does. The impression I have is that the Trésor is very much at the interventionist end of the spectrum and its writ seems to run wider than, say, the Ministry of Finance in Japan (MITI is important there, as we have seen), but the important point about the Trésor is the remarkable concentration of power in its hands. In the financial sector it has driven Paris forward relentlessly, brushing aside solutions that it did not wish to air publicly (for example, the Bacot Report). Its control of the sector was so profound that it alone *could* be the engine of change. Its approach—in the financial sector— appears to be towards market solutions, but it is prepared to be *dirigiste* in organizing the framework in which the free market can best operate; a suspicion always lurks that dirigism is always just around the corner. Furthermore, the Trésor has performed over the years an important service for industry (in a similar way to the Banque de France's in respect of the banking sector): namely, it does its best to save companies in trouble. It operates by persuasion rather than legal powers, but has on occasions been able to hold creditors and banks at bay, and rally shareholders so that enough time could be bought for a viable company to be refinanced. The extent to which it becomes involved depends, of course, on how well industry is faring; in some parts of the economic cycle its activity will be much greater than in others.

The Ruling Class

The French revere intellect (and as a derivation, those whose brilliance is reflected by the examinations they pass). It is not surprising, therefore, that the single fact that was mentioned more often than any other as the key to the French system was education. It is not just that basic education is so uniform throughout the entire country, but that it creams off many of the ablest to the *grandes écoles*, particularly the Polytechnique, the École normale and the Écoles des mines and des ponts et chaussées (and, since the war, the École nationale d'administration—ENA). These *écoles* produce a cadre with a uniform set of values, dedicated to the nation, and with highly competitive instincts sharpened by a competitive educational system.

Their national attitude was that their role was to assist in the creation of a strong national economy, that quick money was immoral money, and that financial wizardry was less important than building up major industries. This thinking permeated the banking system too, as it was largely led by ex-inspecteurs des finances. But times are changing (see below).

I call them a 'class' rather than a 'group' because they now seem so clearly established as a permanent oligarchy, constantly refreshed it is true on merit, but by merit drawn from a relatively narrow stratum of French society, the upper middle class, much intermarried. It forms to this day a truly effective 'old boy network' which permeates French life, and its members move easily between public and private sectors (usually in that direction). This means that there is an empathy between government and industry and excellent lines of communication. Polytechniciens and Enarques move into politics and become Ministers; run the civil and diplomatic services; and now lead a sizeable part of French industry. There is even a word for the movement from the public to the private sector: 'Pantouflage'—that is, shuffling across in carpet slippers. Now it is not so much a shuffle as it used to be, more of a quick sprint, as people seem to move across younger. Some commentators ascribe this group's homogeneity to the enduring influence of the Crédit national, which used to make low-interest loans to industry, so that it was important for people to know each other, but most think it runs deeper than this.

It would be wrong to suggest that all French industry is run by members of this relatively small élite (fewer than 1,000). Many of the great French post-war companies, for example, Carrefour, Moulinex, Bouyges, have been built up by tough entrepreneurs with a quite different background. The French politico-industrialist system tends to be centralist, but there is still plenty of room in it for buccaneers and individualists. The 'University of Life' has its practitioners in France, but society's ideal for its captains of industry is to be highly educated and qualified.

ii. The Industrial Sector

Background

Throughout this section 'industry' should be construed broadly to include construction and services of all kinds: the picture is given at Appendix 4A. It is difficult to understand any society's view of itself. In France, if the layers of consciousness were stripped away perhaps the ideal would still be that of public service (whose status the École nationale d'administration has done so much to promote since 1945), or that of a predominantly agricultural society. Manufacturing industry is esteemed, in contrast to retailing which is not. To be a 'petit commerçant' is no passport to the Jockey Club. In terms of the comparative size of the French economy, French GDP (980 billion ecu) is bigger than the UK's (849.8), but smaller than Germany's.[1]

To give some indication of the relative importance of the stock market, it is interesting to compare London and Paris (see Table 4.1).

The Relative Size of French Companies

How French companies compare depends on how they are measured. In the *Financial Times* league table of 13 January 1992, based on market

[1] *European Economy* (Dec. 1990).

TABLE 4.1. *Comparison of domestic equity markets in London and Paris*

(*a*) *Relative importance of stock exchanges in 1991*

	London	Paris
Turnover (£ billion)	180	61
as % of GDP	31	9
Capitalization (£ billion)	543	181
as % of GNP	94	27
No. of listed companies	1,900	553 *

(*b*) *Comparison of trends in turnover* (£ billion)

	London (1)	Paris (2)	(2/1)%
1989	198	69	(35)
1990	157	65	(41)
1991	180	61	(34)

(*c*) *Comparison of trends in capitalization* (billion francs)

	London (1)	Paris (2)	(2/1)%
1982	1,394	203	(15)
1984	2,285	394	(17)
1986	3,011	990	(33)
1988	4,437	1,350	(30)
1989	4,796	1,952	(41)
1990	4,428	1,560	(34)
1991	5,407	1,850	(33)

* In Paris *and* provincial exchanges.

Sources: Bank of England Quarterly Bulletin (May 1991), LSE, FIBV, and COB.

capitalization of the top fifty European companies in the private sector, French companies stood thirteenth (Elf Aquitaine), twenty-third (Alcatel Alsthom), twenty-fifth (LMVH), fifty-first (Suez), forty-third (Générale dix Eaux), and fifty-second (UAP). Tables based on market capitalization tend to understate the importance of French firms in Europe because in the case of 'semi-nationalized' companies only the non-voting stock, in the form of certificates of investment, are listed and therefore counted. The State's voting shares are not.

The picture is clearer if turnover rather than market capitalization is taken as a measure and if nationalized companies are included. In *The Times* 1991/2 table of the top 1,000 European industrial companies, French companies come eleventh (Renault), fourteenth (Peugeot), sixteenth (Elf Aquitaine), seventeenth (Electricité de France), twenty-first (Alcatel-Alsthom), twenty-eighth (Total), thirty-first (Usinor Sacilor), thirty-seventh (Pechiney).

The Nationalized Industries

Many major firms have been through waves of nationalization and privatization (the last of each were respectively 1981–2 and 1986–8). Seven of the fifteen French companies in the European Top 100 were part of this privatization, though sometimes the government has retained control (e.g. with 54 per cent of Elf Aquitaine).

At the time the first draft of this book was prepared, much of French industry was still nationalized. The Mitterrand government, to bring stability after successive waves of nationalization and denationalization, had introduced what is known as a 'ni-ni' policy—neither more of the one nor of the other. What remains are two types of state-owned business. The first is the natural monopoly: electricity, gas, and railways, which are treated more like a branch of government service, controlled directly by the Minister, who has the power of appointment and dismissal of the PDG and board, which he might well exercise on political grounds. The second type consists of the industries which compete with other companies, domestic and foreign (e.g. Crédit Lyonnais; Thomson; CSF). These tend to have more autonomy, and seem less like a branch of the government service. The Trésor, for instance, is closely concerned in the minutiae of pay awards of some companies because of their repercussive effects, but does not interfere with them at Renault. The PDG of an 'independent' nationalized company like UAP will nevertheless consult his Minister about a major acquisition, but he would probably do this anyway even if the company were in the private sector. A proposal for a major investment or even a joint project may well be nodded through by the board. Many chairmen, for instance, have established a reputation of independence from government.

The government elected in 1993 soon announced an extensive programme of privatization including all those businesses mentioned above, which were on a list of 21 enterprises. Government ownership had not proved an unmixed blessing. The UAP, for instance, has been kept out of the USA because of it (as it is contrary to the US law). The extent of government influence on the nationalized industries is neither uniform nor clear: much depends on personalities. One ex-PDG contrasted his treatment at the hands of Balladur and Beregovoy—the latter seemingly being less authoritarian in practice. The government's powers are limited in practice as it does not relish having its permission sought too often: a refusal can be embarrassing. In loss-making industries it has leverage through its power to withhold funds, but even this is not absolute as some can and do, with the board's permission, borrow money direct from banks, or raise money in the markets. Even today the government may, however, feel that the national interest requires it to provide particular firms with subsidies, whatever international ire this may arouse. On the other hand, in a decree on 5 April 1991 the government somewhat relaxed the rule against private sector companies taking stakes in state-controlled businesses.[2] Finally, it was observed that the French nationalized industries would be better served if the PDG's appointment were longer than three years. It is true that many are re-appointed, but in principle the term is too short for the long-term nature of their industries. In one of the most venerable and respected of the French institutions, the important Caisse des dépots (see below) the Director is appointed for an indefinite period. Robert Lion caused a stir in 1992 by laying down office after a ten-year stint.

Private Sector Companies: The Structure of Shareholdings

In examining corporate governance in France I was advised 'to look at the shareholdings first'. Relatively few quoted companies have widely dispersed shareholdings as is the general rule in the UK and USA; it is so rare a phenomenon indeed that the names of leading companies of this kind, Air Liquide and Lafarge, recurred many times in conversation. All the others had major shareholders of one sort or another, either because they were floated subsidiaries (unto the third or fourth generation), or else because institutions or others had firm shareholdings (sometimes cross-share-holdings) and formed a 'noyau dur'—hard core (otherwise 'actionnaires de reference'). Indeed, Balladur's 1986 denationalization expressly provided for the creation of such holdings and insisted on five-year 'no-sell agreements'

---

[2] This permitted private sector companies, French or foreign, to hold up to 49.9% of many public sector companies, other than the utilities. These holdings will, however, have to conform to a certain commercial or industrial logic, of which the French authorities will be the arbiters. This modification is thought to be motivated less by principles of economic liberation than by a need to improve access to the capital markets.

(since cancelled). Sometimes, too, a company's original founders have hung on to sizeable holdings, as with Carrefour, whilst in other cases it is the State itself which has done so, as with Elf Aquitaine and UAP.

According to the Banque de France, the breakdown of shareholding was as follows at September 1991:

Institutional	17.4%	Individual	34.3%
Corporate	18.7%	Other	0.9%
Non-resident	28.7%		

'Individual' will include the shareholdings of proprietors and their families still running quoted companies.

French companies have typically been reluctant to tap the capital markets for all the familiar reasons, but have increasingly done so because debt-financing through the banking system left them exposed and they preferred to strengthen their equity base. Sometimes a founding family was forced into partial quotation by tax needs or by succession problems as well as by the thirst for capital; it is remarkable how many retain power even when their holdings have been whittled down to less than 5 per cent. The price for flotation of course includes a gradual dispersal of the shares and ultimately exposure to take-over (see below) if after a time the company graduates from a partial flotation on the second market to a quotation for more than half the shares on the Bourse. Floating subsidiaries is not just a gimmick: it enables them to use the capital markets separately. Share options are becoming more common among French management and this has increased interest in the Bourse and share prices. Individuals tend not to have personal portfolios or to hold shares in individual companies as investors (unless they are very rich). If they wish to participate in the equity market they generally do so through mutual funds.

The Spider's Webs

Apart from the cohesion of its élite ruling group, French industry and the financial sector are often linked by shareholdings. 'Les deux galaxies'—Suez and Paribas—stand at the centre of two networks. The biggest shareholders in the Paribas group, as shown in the 1991 report and accounts of the company, are listed in Table 4.2. The public held one-third of the shares, and its own subsidiaries had a smaller stake (in 1989 around 9 per cent). The list of Paribas's interests is given in Appendix 4B.

Looking back to September 1989 the Suez group held 18 per cent of Lyonnaise des Eaux, 4.7 per cent of St Gobain, 11.7 per cent of Bouygues, as well as stakes in Société Générale de Belgique and Groupe Victoire. UAP

TABLE 4.2. *Biggest shareholders in the Paribas Group*

	% shareholding	% of voting rights
Compagnie de Navigation Mixte	8.3	10.9
AGF	8.2	8.7
AXA	8.2	8.0
Parfinance-Frère & Power Groups	7.2	6.7
CIPAF	4.3	6.4
UAP	4.11	5.2

held a substantial stake in Suez. As an example of the way in which events occur there is the interesting case of St Gobain and Compagnie Générale des Eaux. A bruising take-over battle ended in failure ... but then the two companies took cross-shareholdings of 10–12 per cent.

Shearson Lehman Hutton Securities examined what they call 'The secret restructuring of European financial services'. They note that 'Certain groups, particularly those which incorporate Paribas and Suez/Confide/Mediobanca have become immensely powerful.' The first exhibit from their series of eight of the various networks follows as an illustration (Fig. 4.1): although quite recent this is now out of date, which shows that this situation is still fluid. The article is primarily relevant to the development of the international financial services industry in Europe—the motivations, natural characteristics, etc. It does not explore the wider effect on corporate governance generally.

There is another aspect to the increasing closeness of banks and insurance companies—'Bancassurance'—namely, the marketing of insurance products through bank branches and the provision of loans and guarantees by insurance companies. There used formerly to be a much clearer line of demarcation between the two industries than currently exists, a matter of considerable interest not only to the parties concerned but also to the French prudential authorities. French banks now take a third of life premiums; and some banks have bought insurance subsidiaries, for example, Suez buying Victoria.

iii. The Formal Structure of Corporate Governance

Introduction

French law provides for various kinds of company structure.

Sociétés anonymes (*SAs*). These are the French equivalent of the public

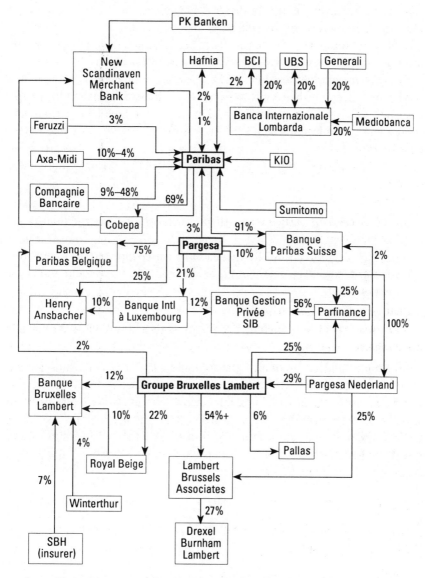

Source: Reprinted from a research article entitled 'The Secret Restructuring of European Financial Services' by Rodney Schwarz (1992), Copyright of Lehman Brothers.

FIG. 4.1 The secret restructuring of European financial services. The grouping shown is one of the most powerful and far reaching, and yet one of the best organized. This stems from the long-standing close personal and business relationships among the three core members: Paribas, Pargesa, and Groupe Bruxelles Lambert.

company, similar in concept to the AG company in Germany or the plc. in the UK. These alone are the subject of this paper. About 630 of them are quoted; any company with more than fifty shareholders, quoted or not, must be incorporated as an SA. It must have capital of at least FF 250,000.

Sociétés à responsibilité limitée (SARL). These are limited liability companies, similar in concept to the GmbH in Germany or the Ltd. company in the UK, and are, as elsewhere, numerous. They may not have more than fifty shareholders; minimum capital is FF 50,000. They are not obliged to have a board of directors.

EURL. Like a SARL, but with all the capital held by a single shareholder or entity.

Partnerships.

(a) SP: Société en participation (silent partnership). The traditional form of joint venture.

(b) Société en nom collectif. Rather like our partnerships, but still a company.

(c) Limited (société en commandite simple and société en commandite par action).

Civil company (société civile)

Succursale. This is a branch of a company with its head office abroad; it is not a separate legal entity.

Unusually—indeed uniquely—the formal structure of corporate govern-ance cannot be described briefly. Elsewhere there is one model for quoted companies, sometimes with particular provisions for those over a certain size (as in Germany). France is different. There is a choice of two quite distinct systems, one with a unitary board, the other with a supervisory board, for Sociétés anonymes. I have classified these as System I and System II and we will examine them in turn.

System I

This is the traditional French system for SAs and has two main components: the PDG and the board.

The PDG

In law the PDG is elected by the board which in turn is appointed by the shareholders. The reality may be the reverse of this: that is, the PDG picks the board (and the shareholders subsequently ratify its appointment) and selects his own successor—which choice the board formally approves.

In French law, executive authority vests in the PDG and he has the sole right to 'represent' the company, a power which only he can delegate. His authority is wider and greater than that of the CEO in the UK or USA. He may if he chooses create a management board as a type of executive committee, in which case it would typically contain his executive colleagues in charge of particular functions, product lines, or regions.

The board has the power to dismiss the PDG (though it very seldom exercises it). If it does he is not permitted to receive compensation—and the company cannot provide for it. He is not covered by the same arrangements as the other officers and staff, and is not protected by the social regulations: he is not even entitled to official holidays! (At the time of nationalization on 17 February 1982, thirty-one PDGs were summarily dismissed.) *En principe* he should retire at 65, but there are many exceptions where the board and the general meeting authorize an extension.

The way the system works depends mainly on the personality and disposition of the PDG. An able PDG tends to appoint able colleagues, but weak ones tend to appoint poor colleagues so as to be able to dominate them. PDGs vary in style. Some treat their boards with disdain, others keep them informed and consult them widely. A *Focus* article (7 Sept. 1992) says that Julien Charlier's board meetings, for instance, last several hours during which he discusses the group's progress and might consult them on the pros and cons of a new piece of machinery.

Some PDGs are professional managers who have come up through the business, but many are brought in from outside from the 'ruling class' and are selected for their general qualities rather than the managerial skills which derive from their background. Such people have great natural authority which lasts until they are proved to be inefficient. They are not chosen just for their coruscating brilliance. Some companies need their connections, particularly if they get business from government or need its support.

Another type of PDG is the 'founder chairman', many of whom have a controlling shareholding and some of whom do not have high academic qualifications. Their boards tend to be subordinates and play little part. Unless they are self-disciplined they may well stay on too long and damage the business they founded (as happened e.g. with Moulinex, resulting eventually in an employee-led buy-out); some are so powerful they can do wider damage (e.g. Dassault). There are often succession problems of the familiar sort—efficiency *v.* continuing the family line. Some companies have coped well with this problem (e.g. Carrefour).

The Conseil d'Administration (the Board)

Most boards meet about every two months, though many meet quarterly and a few monthly.

Except in the case of holding companies the board must have between three and twelve members and no more than a third can be executives (who must have had two years' service with the company). In other words at least two-thirds of the board must be non-executive. The size of boards of major companies seems to be generally between eleven and nineteen, with the twenty-eight of BSN rather exceptional. BNP, for instance, has nineteen; Pechiney eighteen, Suez seventeen; Schneider sixteen; Hachette thirteen; Peugeot and Paribas twelve; Matra and L'Air Liquide eleven.

The Conference Board reported in 1977 (Paper 728) that examination of sixty-eight major companies showed:

- The average age of board members was 58;
- The average formal term of office was five years, but re-election was generally automatic;
- 7 per cent of the board directors were former executives;
- In two-fifths of the companies the directors owned or represented 50 per cent or more of the stock.

The members of the board are proposed by the Conseil d'administration and are elected by the shareholders in the assemblé générale (the general meeting), but a strong PDG will have a considerable role in choosing them. How loud the shareholders' voice is depends on their relative strength. If they are powerful, their support will be essential so they will be consulted beforehand. As the board's role increases selection is becoming more important. Fewer PDGs now like to pack their boards with septuagenarian members of the French equivalent of the UK's 'Great and Good', taking their (substantial) fees but doing little else. Many deliberately choose people of substance from the commercial and industrial world whose counsel they would respect and whose influence they might harness. PDGs on the whole, it appears, like to have powerful bankers and shareholders aboard. The *Focus* article talks of a sort of 'nomenklatura'—a group of members of the establishment whose names tend to recur on many boards.

There is a French counterpart to Germany's Lex Abs: no one can sit on more than eight boards. Directors must hold at least the number of qualifying shares prescribed in the Articles ('actions de guarantie'). A body corporate may be a director and send a representative. The Moulinex report for 1991, for example, shows FINAP as a member of the board. FINAP was originally the personal investment company of the elderly owner of Moulinex, Jean Mantelet, which he used in the employee-led buy-out in 1989 as the buy-out and shareholding vehicle for the employers. In 1992, FINAP had 56 per cent of the voting rights.

The board's role is generally limited and it does not intervene in the day-to-day running of the business: indeed, its principal powers are:

- To hire and fire the PDG
- To authorize the raising of new capital. (It is natural for a PDG to try to evade this by seeking bank finance instead.)
- To authorize mergers or other links if either is significant.

If a business is running well the board tends to remain entirely passive and to defer to the PDG, even on major decisions. If, however, problems arise it will accept and exercise power even to the extent of dismissing the PDG—though it tends to do this late in the day. A recent article in *La Vie française* pointed out with approval how much slower the French are to fire PDGs than the US and UK are to get rid of CEOs. This thought was repeated in *Focus* (7 Sept. 1992), which contrasted the dismissal of Horton from BP in the UK with the survival, despite losses of 17 million francs in 1990/1, of Gilbert Trigano (PDG of the Club Mediterranée). As to the value of boards, the article went on to quote Antoine Veil, the old head of Wagon-Lits: 'Les conseils d'administration restent la façon la plus distinguée de perdre son temps.'

In recent times however, the board's role has increased, partly because its responsibilities in law have grown, which makes members more wary, and partly because of the fear of take-overs. No longer can it be said, as it was ten years ago, 'People all attended board meetings in rather the same way as they went to church.' This move towards greater activism by boards reflects the change in their composition that has gradually occurred since 1980. Since then institutions with significant shareholdings have begun to appoint nominees to boards. This in turn has led to greater consultation between the PDG and his major shareholders on the board—not without some disadvantage to the latter as it makes them insiders.

The change in practice is well illustrated in the *Focus* article: one PDG Bernard Tapie, who runs a finance holding company, telling his three biggest shareholders about a proposed bid; another (Pineau-Valencienne, ex-PDG of Rhone Poulenc and now PDG of Schneider) meeting regularly with the *noyau dur* shareholders and taking his relevant executives with him. And a headhunter (Beigbeder) has long wanted to create an association of professional directors. The tendency towards members of the board being able to speak for larger numbers of shares means that the board often controls enough shares to repel an unwanted approach. It is generally thought that their commitment implies an absolute refusal to consider a take-over offer, but this has yet to be tested. At the same time the board has the power to deal effectively with the PDG—not that it would do so lightly, as good PDGs are hard to find.

The legal imposition of an upper limit on board numbers has resulted in the appointment of 'Censors'—people who attend board meetings and can participate, but not vote. Some Censors are advisers who do not wish to join the board or whom the company does not wish to appoint. They may be paid for their services if the Articles permit. Ministerial representatives sometimes sit on the boards of nationalized industries as Censors and *their* role is to ensure that the correct procedures are followed in circumstances when formal authority is required for a decision.

System II

In 1966 the French government introduced legislation to provide companies with the option of an alternative structure, a supervisory system strongly reminiscent in some ways of the German Vorstand/Aufsichtsrat. Management is in the hands of a directorate (the directoire) which has two to five members appointed for a 2–6 year term by the supervisory board of three to twelve members (conseil de surveillance). Membership of the two bodies is separate. One of the directoire (any or all of whom may be executives of the company), is designated Président de directoire by his colleagues, but neither he nor they can be dismissed by the supervisory board. This can only be done (by a simple majority) by the shareholders in general meeting, so there is no particular problem for a purchaser of the company who has secured a majority of the votes. If they are dismissed without good cause however, they may be entitled to damages. The directoire is vested with full executive authority and is empowered to take decisions by majority; its members do not have to hold shares. One or more members of the directoire are appointed by the supervisory board to represent the company. Members of the supervisory board must hold qualifying shares and they too cannot sit on more than eight boards: they may sit as permanent representatives of a legal entity.

A smaller company (with capital of less than 1 million francs) may have a directeur général unique (DGU), that is, a one-person directorate.

In all cases the DGU or the directoire must submit a quarterly report to the supervisory board.

Unitary Board or Supervisory Committee: An Illuminating Comparison

The French themselves believe that the law which introduced the conseil de surveillance/directoire system is seriously flawed. Even so the reasons for a particular company making a particular choice are illuminating, especially as it is not irrevocable: it may change and change back as long as it observes the formalities, that is, an extraordinary general meeting with a two-thirds majority. Carrefour, for instance, has changed twice. LMVH has also changed.

Before the law was introduced in 1966 all French SAs had conseils d'administration, so for existing companies switching meant a positive change. Tradition and inertia being what they are, caution was evident until the new system proved its worth: by September 1990 only 7.6 per cent of French SAs[3] had chosen the new system. Use of the system has declined over the last decade, and in 1986 98.5 per cent of the SAs set up chose the old system. The new system has not generally caught on. Why is this so? Looking at this another way, what are the circumstances in which it does appeal?

The Advantages of System II

The circumstances in which most companies chose the conseil de surveillance/directoire system are related to personalities:

- At a turning-point in a company's life, e.g. after a merger in which it has absorbed another.
- To facilitate a transfer of management to a member of the family whilst retaining a supervisory control to ensure he is up to the mark.
- As a means of dividing power in 50:50 companies, i.e. where two families have equal shares.
- As a means of upgrading professional managers to a directorial level, i.e. on the directoire, whilst keeping a power of supervision among the shareholders (typically on a bank board or a family-controlled company like Peugeot or Calvet).
- To find directorships for a larger group of people after a merger, as members either of the directoire or the conseil de surveillance (17 seats in all).
- To limit the power of a PDG—or the reverse!
- To solve problems of personalities. Paribas is a recent example. It was felt that François-Poncet, the PDG, although valuable should relinquish his executive powers. So the structure was changed and he was made chairman of the conseil de surveillance, whilst a new chief executive was appointed to head up the directoire (Lévy-Lang).

[3] Much of this material is drawn from work produced by CREDA (the research centre of the Paris Chamber of Commerce and Industry).

- To cope with the transition from partnership to an SA. The partners are appointed to either the directoire or the conseil.
- To enable the executive directors to give themselves contracts of employment which ensure compensation on a take-over.
- To secure tax advantages for family businesses, since five directors can come under the tax system for employees whereas only three can with a conseil d'administration.

There are few reasons of general principle for preferring a conseil de surveillance or a directoire. It is immaterial, for instance, in the case of a controlled subsidiary: whichever the structure, power rests with the parent. Nor does it help establish collective responsibility among the executive. The Président de directoire or PDG seldom shares power with colleagues. It is doubtful whether the choice makes much difference to a nationalized industry, though there was a theory at one point that the new system would improve managerial autonomy. Some commentators believe the greater security of tenure enjoyed by members of the directoire to be an advantage (they can only be dismissed by a general meeting, whereas a PDG can be dismissed summarily and without compensation by a conseil d'administration). Others, however, see this as a disadvantage. Much depends anyway on how the shares are held: if the company is controlled by members of the conseil de surveillance there is not much security for the directors. An example of this was J. J. Servan Schreiber at L'Express. He introduced the system and gave power to a member of the staff. When he did not like the way it worked he simply changed the system again.

Members of the directoire need not be shareholders, but this does not confer much of a comparative advantage; members of a conseil d'administration may only have token holdings.

There are some advantages for small companies in that if their capital is less than 1 million francs they can have a sole general manager (DGU).

The system is nevertheless not wholly without its advantages. It is said to speed the process of decision-making because it is easier to get the directoire together than the conseil d'administration. In fact, it is said to enhance the power of the executives on the directoire because they meet jointly with the board from time to time.

German parent companies like to have the directoire two-tier system in their French subsidiaries because it reminds them of home and they are used to it. Foreign owners from other countries may also prefer the clarity of the line between management and supervisory board.

One area which may become more important is that of legal liability.

Members of the conseil d'administration have seldom been sued but are *en principe* liable if at fault: the members of a conseil de surveillance are not liable.

Summary

In terms of corporate governance the new system seems to offer little advantage over the old. Many small firms are pushed into it by legal advisers for tax and other reasons mentioned above, but these have nothing to do with dynamism and efficiency. The principal reasons for using it are to do with finessing problems of personalities often of a transient nature.

If the aim of System II was to ensure better accountability it has failed: it does not do so—though of course it may work if the PDG is complacent and the conseil de surveillance is powerful (particularly if it contains major shareholders). One critic said scathingly, 'The conseil de surveillance does not work. It is too static; too ill informed; and it never has a real grasp. As to the directoire, a dominant PDG may treat colleagues on it as mere cyphers and meet them perfunctorily four times a year to go through a charade of an agenda with no real consultations'.

And yet—— despite all its limitations the new system is used by some highly successful companies, such as Compagnie Bancaire and LMVH, though they use it in very different ways. It all depends . . .

Remuneration for Boards of Both Kinds

Members of both kinds of board receive attendance payments ('jetons de présence') fixed by the shareholders as a global amount which the board divides. The board may authorize extra payments for extra work. The board fixes the remuneration of the PDG.

French company law requires agreements between a company and its PDG or directors to be approved in advance by the board; and the statutory auditor must issue a special report to the shareholders' meeting for their approval.

As to the remuneration of board members, the *Focus* article presents some data (see Table 4.3), commenting that the examples given are particularly generous.

Credit Lyonnais, whose 17 board members share FF 111,390, is seen as a contrast, as indeed is BNP, whose board members apparently get no jetons de présence at all. The article seems to regard a normal sum for a big company as lying roughly in the range FF 30,000 to FF 50,000, i.e. (at end 1992 rates of exchange) about £5,000 or $8,000 ± 20 per cent.

TABLE 4.3. *Remuneration of board members*

	Sum shared among the administrators (million francs)	No. of administrators
L'Oreal	5.2	11
Bouygues	3.1	15
Hachelta	2.8	13
Lafarge Coppée	2.2	15
Société Générale	2.0	19

Source: Focus (7 Sept. 1992).

Subsidiary Companies

It was noted earlier that many quoted SAs have major shareholders with so large a stake as to make them actually or *de facto* subsidiaries. If quoted they must of course have a separate board in order to comply with the law. The board is in such cases largely ceremonial and its real business conducted between the PDG and the representatives of the parent company. The board of the parent company itself might well not have on it any of the PDGs of its subsidiaries.

The paradox is that the system of tiers of subsidiaries means that the shareholders have an active role—as many a French company has had cause to discover after a merger. The parent company sees its role as trying to get the best of both worlds for the subsidiaries—long-term thinking and efficiency.

Shares and Shareholders' Meetings

Share Structure

The minimum share capital for an SA is FF 250,000, and most companies have a single class of shares whose par value is set in the Articles. Some companies do have more than one class, for example, preferred or non-voting. Non-voting shares are entitled to priority dividends, may only be created if the SA has shown a profit for the two preceding years, may not represent more than a quarter of its capital, and cannot be held by the directors and officers.[4]

---

[4] 'Doing Business in France' (Price Waterhouse, 1989).

Shareholders' Meetings

In all SAs there must be an annual general meeting of shareholders to approve the financial statements within six months of the end of the financial year. There may be other meetings, ordinary and extraordinary. The business of ordinary general meetings would include management matters such as the election of directors or members of the supervisory board or the appointment of statutory auditors. Such meetings are quorate if a quarter of the capital is voted. If it is not, the meeting is reconvened a fortnight later and a quorum is not required; a simple majority of those voting will suffice.

Extraordinary meetings are required *inter alia* to amend the Articles or increase capital. For such important issues the quorum is half the capital, or if not available, at a meeting a fortnight later one-quarter of the capital (and a two-thirds majority of those voting).

Shareholders can attend in person or give proxies in one of three ways. They may authorize a spouse, or another shareholder, to attend for them; or give the chairman *carte blanche*; or tell the chairman to vote for the resolutions. (The third course is the one usually chosen.) In any given class there may be a limit of votes per shareholder; or there may be double votes for those who hold shares for more than two years. Under French law a vote to abstain counts against management's position. In Appendix 4C there is an example of a company's instructions to its shareholders about voting.

Even though some companies, L'Air Liquide for example, pay shareholders a token sum to attend, general meetings are sparsely attended and perfunctory, only coming to life if there is a change of ownership. Proxy fights are rare. It would be strange were it otherwise, as the boards so often have major shareholders on them, and as we see below, many private shareholders in practice do not have the foggiest notion when the meeting is or what the issues are.

The machinery for exercising voting rights may sound a boring and esoteric subject, but it may in fact be crucial. The influence, not to say power, of the German banks is much buttressed by it, as we saw in Chapter 2, because they so often in practice vote the shares deposited with them in the way they wish.

France has not gone as far as Germany. There used to be a clear distinction between bearer shares (keep under the bed; clip the dividend coupons; transfer secretly) and registered shares (company register; distribution of dividend according to the register, not dependent on coupons;

transfer documentation). Bearer shares had been more usual and were preferred by the public, more (allegedly) on privacy than tax grounds. Companies preferred registered shares, although more expensive to administer, as they could more easily discover who owned them.

The advent of 'dematerialization' in France has destroyed many of the differences between the two types of share. Paper certificates have gone and instead there is an entry in a central registry, SICOVAM,[5] which holds the records of ownership of securities. It operates a book-entry transfer system for the settlement of transactions, collects dividends and redemptions, and records securities lending.

Bearer Shares

A distinction does remain, however. Ninety-nine per cent of shares are held in bearer form. SICOVAM does not know who owns them, nor do the issuing companies, and neither has a right to this information. Only intermediaries authorized by the Trésor, such as custodian banks and brokers, hold this information. This means that French companies do not and indeed cannot routinely mail or contact their shareholders direct. Annual general meetings are advertised in the press and shareholders can write for a company report or notice of the meeting: the onus is on them. Most intermediaries do, however, offer such a service—at a price. In practice retail investors seldom vote. As intermediaries cannot do it for them, many general meetings are not quorate and the notices convening them include the subsequent date for reconvening them if this should prove necessary (see Appendix 4C for an example).

There are occasions when intermediaries must contact their clients who hold shares, for example, when a company needs to know whether shareholders want to receive a cash dividend or shares in lieu.

There are two processes for paying dividends. A company may choose to get SICOVAM to pay them in bulk to each intermediary, which will then divide or distribute them. This method is used by companies and intermediaries which think it preferable to earn a float on the payments. Alternatively, the company may ask SICOVAM to distribute dividends direct—a course that is often preferred as it is quicker.

---

[5] SICOVAM (Société interprofessionelle pour la compensation des valeurs mobilières) is owned by French financial institutions. It is a company whose articles and rules are subject to the approval of the Ministry of Finance.

Registered Shares

Owners of French registered shares cannot hide behind nominee names—in France; but this rule can be evaded by using an overseas agent as a 'front'. When registered shares are traded the intermediary bank or broker passes details to SICOVAM which forwards them to the company, on a daily basis. Companies routinely send reports and accounts to registered shareholders.

Identifiable Bearer Shares (TPI)

This interesting new hybrid was introduced in 1987 and stemmed from the government's concern that the beneficial owners of shares in particular industries about to be denationalized (e.g. TV, radio, etc.) should be identifiable. About 100 companies have followed suit (they have to amend the Articles at an EGM to do it). The details of individual holdings are still retained by intermediaries. The difference is that companies can ask SICOVAM to collect, collate, and reveal them. This is useful to monitor the early stages of stake building before an announceable threshold has been reached.

Foreign-Registered Shares

SICOVAM acts as a beneficial owner's proxy if the owner so instructs: instructions are centralized by the custodian banks. In such cases SICOVAM does, unusually, find itself receiving company reports and accounts.

Small Shareholders

The dominance of the big shareholders has created some concern among companies that small shareholders were being neglected and this has led to some improvements in the presentation of reports and accounts: in fact, as noted earlier, French shareholders usually prefer instruments of collective investment like unit trusts. As an article in Le Monde pointed out (4 Sept. 1990), some French companies now make strenuous efforts to contact shareholders to keep them up to date; L'Air Liquide, Essilor (optical instruments), and Minitel were quoted with approval, as were Suez and LMVH. The mode of communication seems to vary as it well might, given the company's ignorance about who owns its shares. The usual modes are by press announcements and by information being given to financial analysts. There may be direct mailings to registered or TPI shareholders. The cynical might feel that the urge to supply information is occasioned by the need to explain why the shares were performing badly; whatever the cause the practice is welcome.

The change in practice may owe something to pressure from the shareholder organizations which have emerged in recent years. Colette Neuville set up the Association pour la Defense des Actionaires Minoritaires (ADAM) in late 1991 to defend minority shareholders' interests in the take-over of Au Printemps. In 1992 she fought (and lost) against BSN's move to limit shareholders' voting rights to a set percentage however many shares they held. Her work has attracted support from foreign investors and much attention in the French press.

The Association national de actionnaires français represents small shareholders, and, despite its small membership, attends sharcholder meetings to voice concern on subjects such as pre-empting rights to dividends. Also worth monitoring are: the Fédération Nationale des Clubs d'Investissement—the first such group to be accredited by the government to represent shareholders in court proceedings against companies; Agir Ici, concerned with third world and social issues; and Association Éthique et Investissement, whose concern lies in companies' performance on social issues.

Despite the emergence of such groups, it seems that in general French shareholders have a conservative view of their expectations from dividends. They seem to feel that big payments are never justified. If a company is doing badly it cannot afford them; if it is doing well it should husband its resources. To raise a dividend so as to hike the share price (and deter a take-over) will be self-defeating as the market will mark down the shares after the payment. The model preferred is for steady unspectacular growth, which produces commensurate capital appreciation (more attractive for tax purposes).

From the company's point of view, there is naturally some anxiety about secretive stake building, though this is less than formerly now that purchasers have to disclose big holdings and state their intentions (see below). As we have seen, since the laws of 1981 and 1984, registered shares have to be held in accounts bearing the owner's name and must be held in that name. Companies can ask SICOVAM for this information. If the shares are in TPI form, SICOVAM must provide on request a list of the beneficial owners complete with name, address, number of shares, and voting rights. The fly in the ointment for the company is that SICOVAM cannot provide the information for foreign shareholders whose securities are held in the SICOVAM accounts of linked foreign national depositories.

Summary

Whether or not the SICOVAM system provides an economical and efficient way of transacting business in shares, what it certainly does not do is help most private shareholders play a part in corporate governance. They have either to pay the intermediaries to get reports and accounts and voting papers, or scan the press to know when to approach the company. The exceptions are the holders of registered or TPI shares, who are in very much the same position as their UK counterparts; but they are in a very small minority.

What seems to emerge is that the private shareholder in France plays little or no part in corporate governance, partly because there are relatively few of them (other than proprietors) and partly because the system strengthens the dominance of corporate or institutional shareholders since their resources ensure they get the necessary information. Revolts by private shareholders are so rare that no one mentioned them. Only in the case of contested take-overs do the private shareholders emerge from their burrows, because it is at this point that the system does ensure—at a cost—that they receive the material they need to make a decision.

The Role of the Unions and the Work-force

Two great changes have taken place in the last decade that have altered the atmosphere in which the unions operate. The first was the release of tension from 1981 after the return of the Socialists to power for the first time in thirty years. The second was the collapse of the politico-economic system in Eastern Europe with the public exposure of its inefficiency. No realistic person can offer a command economy as an alternative to the market, and the few diehards that do so are discredited. The unions, both internally and between themselves, have not wholly cleared their minds on which 'improvements' to the market system they would wish to see.

They feel that the State does have a natural and important role to ensure the market operates in the general interest. Only the State can set the rules or standards in such areas as competition, pollution, basic conditions of employment, and the constitution of enterprises. In many of these the State now has to operate in an international milieu—indeed, very many companies are now themselves multinational.

One fashionable line of approach is to see progress consisting of winning greater influence for the unions in three stages:

Information—Consultation—Participation

The prime vehicle is the comité d'enterprise which all companies over a certain size are obliged to have, and on which the work-force and unions are represented. But progress is not easy as there appear to be problems at all stages. There may be difficulties with information because of confidentiality: difficulties about the ambit of consultation; and the awkwardness of power-sharing which participation implies. The French temperament (and indeed the French unions) do not incline towards co-determination on the German model because they feel it leads to a confusion of roles. They tend to regard the German model as just the product of a particular phase of history, and to be comfortable to leave the power of decision with the PDG, maintaining at the same time collective bargaining. The boards of nationalized industries are an exception, as they have employee representatives on them; by some accounts their presence makes board meetings uncomfortable and difficult.

One or two members of the comité (six in a nationalized industry) attend board meetings, even though they have no voting rights. Their right to attend is significant because they know the business, but the PDG can sometimes get away with an inadequate presentation by transacting important business outside the board. In private sector companies many PDGs are so powerful that the comité representatives have a limited effect. The comité has a right to appoint its own financial adviser with powers to examine the accounts, which is valuable to it in collective bargaining. The employees want their share of the cake and management cannot easily deceive them (if it were so minded) about the company's profitability. Of course, this cuts both ways, when bad times come.

Despite all the drawbacks there seems to be a feeling by unions and managements that the arrangements do add value, because the formal framework is often supplemented by informal contacts just as they are in Germany. The area of consultation covers all fundamental changes, such as structure, closures, expansion, and diversification (out of fashion now in France).

Visions of 'L'Utopie' have faded and a more pragmatic and co-operative approach is in prospect but has yet to be fully developed. There are international developments too; *vide* COM(90)581—the EC Commission's proposal for a Council Directive which proposes the establishment of a European Works Council in community-scale undertakings for the purpose of informing and consulting employees: substantive negotiations seem certain to be protracted as attitudes vary so much across Europe.

The Banks and Savings Institutions

The main deposit-taking banks (banques des dépôts) historically did not take 'participations' in their industrial customers. Such shareholdings were avoided *en principe*, but occasionally resulted from a financial restructuring.

The banques d'affaires (merchant/investment banks) did take 'participations'.

In terms of structure, the number of French banks has been falling quite rapidly in recent years, mainly because of a restructuring of the caisses d'épargne which has reduced their number significantly. The number of bank branches, however, has stabilized rather than declined, and remains around 26,000. The concentration of French banking, which has long been a notable feature, remains as strong as ever. The largest five banks had at the end of 1991 a 58 per cent share of total deposits, and a combined 45 per cent share of total credit in the banking sector.

Two of the largest five—indeed two of the three 'vieilles dames', Crédit Lyonnais and BNP—remain state-owned. (The other 'vieille', Société Générale, was re-privatized in 1987 along with Paribas; the largest French bank of all by assets, and the world's largest non-Japanese bank, remains Crédit Agricole.) As well as these largest banks, the Caisse des Dépôts et Consignations is a state-owned institution with significant influence in the financial sector. It is France's largest institutional investor, managing retirement and health insurance funds for Social Security and escrow funds of the legal profession. It also has a life assurance subsidiary, the Caisse Nationale de Prévoyance, which uses the Post Office retail network, as well as the savings banks and Treasury networks. Its traditional retail role has been to transform tax-free savings collected by the savings banks and Post Office into long-term housing and local authority loans. Total banking assets under state control are now roughly 50 per cent of total assets, compared with approximately 90 per cent in the mid-1980s. At the end of 1991, the combined FF 3 trillion total assets of Crédit Lyonnais and BNP represented 21 per cent of total bank assets of FF 14.5 trillion.

In 1941 the Vichy government introduced legislation of such technical complexity that it survived the post-war bonfire of their measures: it virtually precluded the banques des dépots having shareholdings. In other words, it gave their normal business practice the force of law (which the banques d'affaires lobbied hard to maintain). For a fuller account of the history see a recent Bankers Almanac publication, reprinted in Appendix 4D.

Times have changed. The old distinctions had already been eroded by the time the Banking Act in 1984 (Clause 1) abolished them; all banks are now called 'établissements de crédit'. The paper 'Affaires' reported on 4 September 1990 that 'The FF 100 bn mark has now been passed.' The five big banks now hold between them FF 104 billion in industrial investments, excluding the insurance sector (Société Générale (18), Paribas (25), Suez (25), Crédit

Lyonnais (18), BNP (18)). Given the size of the stock market in France and the concentration of the holdings, this is a significant stake, which has been accumulated quite quickly. The figures are, however, suspect. The *Wall Street Journal* on 22 March 1991 reported that the Crédit Lyonnais portfolio was about FF 26 billion (including big stakes in Thomson, Rhône Poulenc, and Pechiney). They now regard themselves as a banque d'industrie.

It is not uncommon to find banques des dépôts taking part in take-over battles, for example, the Suez help for Société Générale de Belgique in defeating de Benedetti. And it can lead the banks into rivalry, for example, Crédit Lyonnais *v.* Paribas in the Navigation Mixte affair.

It is reported that most industrial companies like having banks as shareholders and often approach them to take an equity stake. The companies see it not so much as a source of cheaper capital, but more as an insurance policy for general support and for protection against take-over. The banks see it as a way of cementing a banking relationship rather than a source of short-term profit, though it is not without disadvantages because of potential losses, or alternatively, capital gains. It can create a conflict of interest for banks in their role as managers of mutual funds and as suppliers of credit. Some banks apparently intervene to stop their fund managers selling shares in a company which is one of the bank's prime customers.

The strategy behind accumulating industrial holdings was based on an evaluation of the comparative merits of the UK and German systems and a decided preference for the latter. Certainly it appears long term in its orientation and seems to envisage a multifaceted relationship which includes in some cases board membership. (In fact it is more deliberate than the German banks' strategy, since as we saw many of their shareholdings were acquired *faute de mieux* when their customers in the 1930s and 1940s had nothing else to offer.)

It remains to be seen if the French banks are as dedicated to the long term as their apparent policy implies; some people feel that if times get hard and they have to nurse companies through difficulties, with little immediate profit, their enthusiasm may wane. They point out moreover that the banks' shift in policy has taken place during the last decade, a period of unprecedented prosperity for French industry. There are those who are concerned about the effect of more adverse circumstances, fearing that even the banks may find it difficult to intervene early enough to prevent a collapse.

The involvement of Crédit Lyonnais and BNP in industry has not escaped comment because it smacks of covert state aid (e.g. Crédit Lyonnais's 10 per cent stake in steelmaker Usinor-Sacilor in July 1991; BNP's 9 per cent stake in Air France, cleared by the EC Commission in July 1992; Crédit Lyonnais's purchase in 1992 of 20 per cent of Aerospatiale). The deals sometimes have an interesting structure. A bank takes up a rights issue and the state gives it a tranche of its holding as well: so the company gets its money and the bank's capital base is boosted.

There is no equivalent in France to US or UK pension funds. The major French insurance companies led by UAP and Assurance Générale de France (AGF) are powerful, especially as they tend to concentrate their holdings. Eighty-five per cent of UAP's French equity investments are in twenty shares, and they hold between 3 per cent and 10 per cent of the capital in these companies. They have a nominee on the board of at least ten companies. Major shareholders in a company do concert action among themselves (but see below for a recent development). There is a tendency from time to time to place greater emphasis on bonds and less on equities. Relative yields and low inflation in 1992/3 may nudge the French insurance companies in this direction.

As has been mentioned earlier, such shareholders have a recognized status as core shareholders—the *noyau dur*—which may have some kind of informal agreement with a company.

The Caisse des Dépôts now manages a savings portfolio of nearly FF 1,700 billion. It has recently attracted criticism for being too entrepreneurial (e.g. cable TV), but it has 3–5 per cent of most French companies—holdings it is said to manage 'passively'. It keeps up with the trends. Stockholders generally have been looking for 'adossement', that is, a form of integration with banks, because of market developments. Caisse des Dépôts decided with UAP 'd'adosser' FMDA, one of France's largest stockbroking firms (Fauchier–Magnan–Durant des Aulnois).

The Stock Market

The French stock market ranks third in Europe but its market capitalization is small in proportion to the size of GDP: 24 per cent compared with 53 per cent in the US, 89 per cent in the UK, and 135 per cent in Japan. Of the forty-three member firms on the Bourse, nine are in foreign hands—that is, 21 per cent—compared with 38 per cent on the ISE, 19 per cent on the Tokyo Stock Exchange, and 9 per cent on the New York Stock Exchange. The domestic listed companies quoted on it are about one-third of the number of UK domestic companies listed in London, but even this may give a misleading picture since many companies have only floated 10 per cent or less of their shares and others are wholly controlled subsidiaries. In fact the market is not in any way as important as it is in the UK or USA. Family shareholdings control 60 per cent of the top 200 companies.[6] The government through the taking of strategic stakes holds between 15 and 20 per cent of total market capitalization 'in the national interest'. The Trésor has been instrumental in the operations of the Bourse, pushing it into modernization and sophisticated (if expensive) technology, but it is no easy task to deepen its roots.

Take-overs: The Role of the French Authorities

Theoretically the French have few formal barriers to take-overs (*offres publiques d'achat*: OPA) of their companies whether by foreign or French companies, though the formalities for non-EC purchasers are more stringent. The market has indeed been active. Taking mergers and take-overs together, there were 915 transactions in 1987 worth over $27 billion with 156 French acquisitions by foreign buyers and 196 foreign acquisitions by French buyers.

Ministry of Finance approval is required for non-EC acquisitions of more than 20 per cent of a company, and this has doubtless deterred many bidders because the Ministry has often tried to secure a matching French bid. It held up, for example, the International Paper Company's $300 million bid for Aussedat Rey to give time for a counter offer by Arjomari Prioux, and stopped 3M's bid for Spontex to give Suez a chance to arrange a management buy-out. These are not the only examples of the state's desire to find a French solution if possible, by whatever means are effective.

French commentators, however, do not see the government shield as all-effective. An analysis by Institut de l'enterprise in January 1991 investigates what they see as French firms' vulnerability. Some of the possible devices they consider have a familiar ring, for example:

- Loyalty premiums for long-term holders supported by tax concessions (especially on capital taxes);
- The formation of groups of stable shareholders big enough to form a blocking minority;
- Keeping shareholders better informed;
- Better representation of shareholders' views on the board;
- Greater power for custodian banks on the German model.

The Commission des operations au bourse (COB) (the French stock-market regulatory authority) clarified its requirements in April 1989 with changes to its code (which it drew up with the CBV, the Conseil des bourses de valeurs). The CBV is a self-regulating body mainly composed of members of

---

[6] *European Business Journal* (2 Apr. 1990).

the Bourse; its rules have to be approved by the COB, Banque de France, and Finance Ministry. Among the 1989 provisions are the following:

- A purchaser acting alone or in concert who holds more than 33 per cent of his shares must offer for all of them. If the purchaser stipulates an upper limit, those who tender shares will receive acceptances pro rata if an excess is offered. (The 'concert party' rule is having some curious consequences—see below.)
- Holdings must be publicly declared at various thresholds: 5, 10, 20 per cent; and the purchasers' intentions must be stated as soon as someone holds 20 per cent or more. If purchasers are acting in concert this, too, must be stated.
- If an offer is made it must stay open for at least twenty trading days: purchases on the market must take place at the offer price.

The French arrangements do not preclude litigation, but rulings are generally given within a week. So far lawsuits have been rare (generally concerned with the oppression of minority holders left out of a deal). It remains to be seen whether the new rules will produce more.

The Market

The French market appears more open than the German and Japanese, but much less than the US or UK. The main reason for this is the interlocking nature of shareholdings or the presence of major shareholders' representatives on the board, which separately or together make so many companies invulnerable.

It must also not be forgotten that the state sees itself as having a protective role, and its influence is by no means restricted to cases which do not 'endanger public order, health or national defence'. The French government may well use its influence discreetly to stop an agreed merger in favour of a 'French solution'; it is not just a case of keeping out a contested bid. But too much weight can be placed on the government as a factor, and the tendency has been for its intervention to lessen. Far more important is the 'network', which cannot be negotiated away by governments.

The Banque de France has special powers over the acquisition of French banks and it is not unknown for a conglomerate to buy a bank to get under the umbrella. This power resides formally in the Comité des établissements de crédit, chaired by the Governor of the Banque de France: its membership includes representatives of the government and the banks.

Mergers and Acquisitions

Table 4.4 gives some examples of how major French companies are using

TABLE 4.4. *Mergers and acquisitions by French companies*

Buyer	Target	Price ($ million)
Rhône-Poulenc	Rorer Group (USA)	3,298
BSN	5 units of RJR Nabisco (UK, France, Italy)	2,500
Alcatel	65% of Telettra (Italy)	2,200
Accor	Motel 6 (USA)	2,174
BSN & Ifil (Italy)	Galbani (Italy)	1,635
Pechiney	Triangle Industries (USA)	1,282
Elf Aquitaine	Pennwalt Corp (USA)	1,070
L'Air Liquide	Big Three Industries (USA)	1,054
Rhône-Poulenc	RTZ Chemicals (UK)	829
Hachette	Diamindis (USA)	712
Elf Aquitaine	Enterprise Oil	625
Hachette	Grolier (USA)	475

mergers and acquisitions as a way of securing sound strategic positions for the next century. This list is not exhaustive and most of the deals were not hostile or contested bids, but it provides a picture of French industrial strategy. The article in which it appeared (*M&A Europe* Jan.–Feb. 1991)) was making the point that profits had not yet grown commensurately, and it singled out Hachette and Rhône-Poulenc as cases in point. It noted that the latter is state-controlled—though the general public has a huge investment in it through non-voting preferred shares and other instruments such as 'perpetual subordinated capital notes'.

A similar point can be made in a different way. The French have acquired considerable interests in UK insurers and fund managers, thereby incidentally acquiring the voting rights in many UK industrial company shares (see Table 4.5).

The French lead Continental European countries in management buy-outs (MBOs). The *Investors Chronicle* (5 Apr. 1991), reporting a KPMG survey, put France a long way at the top of the list with fifty-two MBOs, value £3,470 million, between 1985 and 1990.

The tendency towards 'networking'—with banks and insurance companies taking bigger stakes in companies, and board representation with them—carries with it an increased risk, especially in hard times, of conflicts of interest. Does a banker for instance, as a board member of an industrial company, give preference to the interests of the company or his

TABLE 4.5. *French holdings in UK insurers and fund managers*

Year	Company	Foreign parent	% holding
1986	City & Westminster Assurance	AGF (France)	100
1986	Sentry (now City of Westminster) *	AGF (France)	100
1987	Equity & Law	Axa (France)	100
1989	Sun Life	UAP (France)	25
1989/90	General Portfolio Minister Insurance	} GAN (France)	100
1989	Touche Remnant	Société Générale (France)	100
1990	Gartmore	Banque Indosuez (France)	100
1990/1	Framlington	CCF (France)	51

* Sentry Insurance and its sister company City of Westminster Assurance were purchased from the Sentry Group of the USA, with the result that Sentry Insurance had to change its name.

bank—which may well not coincide? Potential conflicts of interest are the subject of some concern.

iv. Dynamism and Accountability: An Appreciation

Dynamism

Whether French companies adopt System I or System II, they pass the first test—that of unimpeded dynamism—with flying colours. There is no doubt that the executive, individually and collectively, has all the powers it needs. Formally power is heavily concentrated in the PDG, but as usual in any organization it may be distributed; anecdotal evidence suggests that the realities in any particular company may be quite difficult to fathom and have constantly to be checked when conducting business. The PDG in the old system (System I) combines the roles of chairman and chief executive. Even in the new system (System II) he remains the dominant figure, even though the conseil de surveillance has a separate chairman. The important point about the existence of two alternative systems is that in the end personalities matter more than structure, and that it is logical therefore to offer alternatives to fit people rather than force people to fit a single type of structure. That is clearly not how the choice was conceived, but that is how it has worked out, and there seems some advantage in having it.

In the nationalized industries the bureaucratic hand sits lightly on the PDG's shoulder—though there are exceptions which are most irritating to the PDGs concerned. On the whole, however, French governments seem to ride their nationalized industries with a loose rein.

The fear of take-over does not seem to affect PDGs because so few stand in danger of it—generally due to solid support from shareholders. The inference is that without such support they might—and this possibility restricts flotations.

As to fear of lawsuit, it will be recalled that the members of a conseil de surveillance cannot be sued. PDGs are seldom sued, and neither they nor members of the conseil d'administration seem much concerned about it. In February 1992, however, the Paris court of appeal condemned the members of the board of Nasa individually for their failure to supervise the management of the enterprise correctly.

Accountability

Until fairly recently boards of the old kind—the conseil d'administration— which are still used in over 90 per cent of French companies, did not really hold the PDG accountable in any consistent and timely way. They were often aged; they met seldom; were little consulted; and were quite content to cruise along passively unless and until the ship was nearly on the rocks. Even when it was clear they should throw the captain overboard, they did so with great reluctance, usually after the vessel was badly holed.

The same is true of the conseil de surveillance—indeed, they are probably more tardy because they meet less often; are more formal, more remote; and cannot enforce their will without shareholders' approval.

A considerable change has taken place over the last decade and is still developing. There were always many companies where the founding family held major holdings and were represented in the conseil (of either kind). The strength of such holdings means that the PDG has to consult the board— and does. For their part such boards tend to be knowledgeable, motivated, and prepared to act.

Nowadays it is not only family-controlled businesses that have important shareholders on the board. Many others have major shareholders represented on the board, typically banks, insurance companies, or other industrial companies. Sometimes such shareholders enter into a formal arrangement with the company, trading what is in effect a preferential position for an undertaking to support (which means not to buy or sell). By definition this does not infringe insider laws. But the change means that a PDG nowadays often finds himself with a cadre of well-informed and powerful shareholders in a fine position to exert influence if they choose.

The *noyau dur* shareholders pay a price for their position. They have to provide board members and concern themselves with their election. They are locked in, and lose flexibility as a result, producing a commitment which may not always suit them. For this they get—or can get—the information they need in order to ensure that the PDG is properly accountable. Does this arrangement work as planned? Will it result in the efficiency of French industry being maintained at a higher level? As far as it is possible to judge the verdict is open. As always, much depends on the personalities of the PDG and the key people on the board. On balance I felt that the French thought that the greater role of the board was a step in the right direction, but that accountability was still patchy and the boards' response to problems still tardy.

There is one interesting development which may not be precisely as intended. It will be recalled that the authorities have now introduced rules governing the accumulation of stakes in a company in preparation for a take-over bid, the idea being to ensure that shareholders are treated fairly. (Beyond a certain point a purchaser must make a comparable offer to all shareholders.) To stop conspiracies there is a rule against parties acting in concert to achieve a coup. It now appears that the rule may catch parties acting in concert even if they have no intention of bidding. So institutional shareholders who want to exert influence over a company's strategy (e.g. by stopping it making a bid) or who want to change the PDG are now concerned that if they act in concert with other shareholders they may be required to make a bid. This is odd to say the least, because there would be no price on the table, but it is apparently a factor of some concern.

The remaining checks and balances within the French system do not appear to be powerful, though there is some agreement that the involvement of employees has beneficial effects. The comité d'enterprise and the presence of employees at board meetings cannot stop a PDG but can give him pause—and the very existence of the formal structure opens useful informal channels of communication.

The role of shareholders without nominees on the board tends to be passive and minimal. General meetings are formal and perfunctory.

v. A Period of Transition

The study came at an awkward time (1991) in that the French are trying to steer a course between a command economy and a real market economy, and also between the corporate governance systems of Germany and the UK/USA. It was difficult at that point to see where their policies would take them. The change in political orientation in 1993 is leading to an extensive programme of privatization, including the major banks, Crédit Lyonnais and Banque

Nationale de Paris. Nevertheless, centuries of government stimulation of industry will not be washed away overnight; Colbert's ghost survives, and will not be easily exorcised. The background includes both change in the EC (bound to impact on French economic nationalism) and fierce competition in financial services. Views were mixed as to whether the end result would be a networked economy rather like Germany in which the banks, financial institutions, and industrial companies were closely interwoven: some thought this possible, others that it was unlikely given French philosophy and individuality.

Informed observers already saw signs that the ENA/Grandes écoles system might be losing its absolute domination, but the process would be extremely slow as no better alternative was in sight. It was generally remarked how far France had moved since 1983, and how much further it would move with the completion of the single market.

The attitude of the ruling class towards 'financial wizardry' is said to be changing, and interest in it is increasing. More of the best polytechniciens now go into the financial world. It used to be the case that most of the brightest from the Grandes écoles went into public administration; at a time when the banks were nationalized the government could post them there during the course of their career. Nowadays fewer such positions are available and the financial world must be entered by a more direct route.

More than any of the other nations studied, France seems genuinely uncertain about the direction in which it wishes its system to develop. It is less protective in many ways than Germany and Japan in regard to take-over bids, but more so than the USA and UK. Its banks and insurance companies seem to want to get closer to industry and create the kind of network that the Germans and Japanese have, yet this sits somewhat uncomfortably with French individualism and concentration of authority, and with the ever-present authority of the state and particularly the Trésor. What seems to me to be emerging is a temporary accommodation between the two systems which fits the French tradition and temperament and works well; the approach, for all the influence of Cartesian logic, is essentially pragmatic and most accommodative of personalities. It will always be on the verge of change, illustrating once again the validity of that old aphorism: 'Rien dure que la provisoire.'

Appendix 4A. *France: Structure of Output*

	Shares in GDP (%)			Annual change (%)			
	1970	1980	1989	1986	1987	1988	1989
Market GDP	84.0	84.0	84.4	2.7	2.3	4.3	4.0
Agriculture, etc.	5.4	4.2	4.2	1.1	1.2	−0.7	2.4
Industry	27.0	26.8	23.6	0.1	0.4	2.7	2.3
Foodstuffs	3.7	3.2	2.6	−0.2	−0.7	−3.1	−0.3
Energy	4.1	3.9	3.7	0.8	−0.4	−0.3	−2.4
Manufacturing	19.2	19.8	17.3	0.0	0.8	4.5	3.8
Intermediate goods	7.3	6.9	5.9	1.2	1.4	7.1	2.0
Current consumption	5.3	5.2	4.5	−1.4	0.1	2.2	3.6
Investment goods	4.4	5.4	5.0	−1.7	−1.0	3.4	5.7
Household equipment	0.2	0.3	0.4	6.1	5.1	2.7	8.6
Transportation equipment	2.0	1.9	1.6	5.0	5.4	5.1	3.7
Non industrial	48.6	48.4	51.4	3.9	2.9	4.8	4.4
Construction	8.7	6.9	5.9	3.0	1.2	6.6	1.2
Commerce	10.9	10.4	10.6	3.2	2.4	4.9	2.8
Transportation and telecommunication	4.7	5.8	7.2	3.7	5.5	9.8	7.1
Market services (non-financial)	18.2	20.4	23.4	4.8	3.4	5.0	6.1
Insurance and financial services	3.7	3.2	2.6	−0.2	−0.7	−3.1	−0.3

Note: value added in constant 1980 prices.

Source: INSEE, *Rapport sur les comptes de la nation.*

Appendix 4B. *Consolidated Companies of the Paribas Group*

Company	Country	Activity*	% Interest‡ 1991	% Effective ownership† 1991	1990	1989
FULLY CONSOLIDATED COMPANIES						
COMPAGNIE FINANCIÈRE DE PARIBAS	France	1	100.0	100.0	100.0	100.0
BANQUE PARIBAS GROUP						
Antin Contrepartie	France	1	100.0	96.9	95.5	94.7
Antrin Gérance	France	2	100.0	97.0		
Banque Continentale du Luxembourg	Luxembourg	1	50.0	34.6	33.4	
Banque de Bienne	Belgium	1	100.0	70.0	66.1	65.1
Banque Paribas Belgique SA	Belgium	1	79.4	71.5	67.7	67.2
Banque Paribas Canada	Canada	1	100.0	96.9	95.5	94.7
Banque Paribas Capital	West Germany					
Markets GmbH	Ivory Coast	1	100.0	96.9	95.5	94.7
Banque Paribas Cote d'Ivoire	West Germany	1	79.4	76.9	75.8	78.5
Banque Paribas Deutschland	Gabon					
OHG		1	100.0	96.9	95.5	94.7
Banque Paribas Gabon		1				34.8
Banque Paribas Luxembourg	Luxembourg	1	80.0	68.5	66.6	66.2
Banque Paribas Nederland NV	Netherlands	1	100.0	94.3	95.5	94.7
Banque Paribas Pacifique	Polynesia	1	85.0	64.0	68.2	67.7
Banque Paribas Polynesie	Polynesia	1	70.0	44.5	45.6	46.4
Banque Paribas Suisse	Switzerland	1	99.2	96.1	94.7	67.3
Banque Paribas	France	1	96.9	96.9	95.5	94.7
Banque Parisienne Internationale	France	1	60.7	59.6	49.1	67.0
Bureau d'Etudes & de Trans-actions Immobilières 'BETI'	France	2	100.0	96.9	95.5	94.7

Table cont.

Company	Country	Activity*	% Interest‡ 1991	% Effective ownership† 1991	1990	1989
Bureau Immobilier de Négociations Commerciales et Financières	France	2	100.0	96.9	95.5	94.7
Conseil Investissement	France	1	100.0	96.8	95.4	94.6
Courcoux—Bouvet SA	France	1	100.0	96.9	95.5	94.7
Cresscombe Realty Inc.	USA	1	100.0	96.9	76.4	75.8
Eural Spaarbank NV	Belgium	1				65.1
Euralunispar	Belgium	1	97.8	70.0	66.1	
Financière Gabonaise de Developpement Immobilier 'Figadim'	Gabon	1	64.9	44.9	44.3	43.9
Fipalux SA	Luxembourg	2	100.0	68.5		
Holnor	Netherlands	2	63.9	51.9	54.5	
Immo-Paribas	Belgium	2	100.0	71.5	67.7	67.2
Novolease NV	Belgium	1	100.0	71.5	67.7	67.2
Parbelux Finance	Belgium	2	100.0	71.5	67.7	67.2
Paribas Asia Ltd.	Hong-Kong	2	100.0	96.9	95.5	94.7
Paribas Asset Management Inc.	USA	1	100.0	96.9	95.5	94.7
Paribas Asset Management SA	France	2	100.0	96.8	95.5	94.7
Paribas Asset Management (Japan)	Japan	2	96.0	93.0		
Paribas Asset Management (Luxembourg)	Luxembourg	2	100.0	82.7		
Paribas Capital Investments Ltd	UK	1	100.0	96.9	95.5	94.7
Paribas Capital Markets Ltd.	Hong-Kong	1	65.0	63.0	62.1	61.6
Paribas Capital Markets Group Ltd.	UK	1	100.0	96.9		
Paribas Corporation	USA	1	100.0	96.9	95.5	94.7
Paribas Deelnemingen NV	Netherlands	2	100.0	91.3	79.0	
Paribas Deutschland BV	Netherlands	2	100.0	96.9	95.5	94.7
Paribas European Leveraged Investment	France	2	92.5	85.6	84.3	81.2
Paribas Finance Inc.	USA	1	100.0	96.9	95.5	94.7
Paribas Finance (Texas) Inc.	USA	1	100.0	96.9	95.5	94.7
Paribas Finanziaria	Italy	1	100.0	93.6	92.3	91.1
Paribas Futures Inc.	USA	1	100.0	96.7	95.4	90.2
Paribas Futures Ltd.	UK	1	100.0	96.7	95.3	87.8
Paribas Group (Australia) Pty. Ltd.	Australia	2	100.0	96.9	95.5	94.7

Table cont.

Company	Country	Activity*	% Interest‡ 1991	% Effective ownership†		
				1991	1990	1989
Paribas International	France	2	100.0	96.9	95.5	94.7
Paribas International Bond						
Management	USA	2	100.0	96.5	95.1	81.0
Paribas Investissement	France	2	84.9	83.2		
Paribas Investment Asia	Hong-Kong	2	100.0	96.9	95.5	94.7
Paribas Japan Ltd.	Japan	1	100.0	96.9		
Paribas Ltd.	UK	1	100.0	96.9	95.5	94.7
Paribas Management Services						
Ltd.	UK	1	100.0	96.9		
Paribas Net Ltd.	UK	1	100.0	96.9		
Paribas North America	USA	1	100.0	96.9	95.5	94.7
Paribas Participation BV	Netherlands	2	100.0	96.9	95.5	94.7
Paribas Privatbank AG	Switzerland	1	100.0	96.1	94.7	67.3
Paribas Properties Inc.	USA	1	90.0	87.1	85.9	82.5
Paribas South East Asia	Singapore	1	100.0	96.9	95.5	94.7
Paribas Technology Inc.	USA	1				94.7
Paribas Trust	Luxembourg	2	100.0	68.5	66.6	66.1
Paribas UK Holding Ltd.	UK	1	100.0	96.9	95.5	94.7
Paribus USA.	France	2	100.0	96.9	95.5	94.7
Paribas (Suisse) Bahamas Ltd.	Bahamas	1	100.0	96.1	94.7	67.3
Paribas (Suisse) Guernsey	Guernsey	1	100.0	96.1		
Parilease	France	2	100.0	96.8	95.5	94.7
Pasta Investment Ltd.	Hong-Kong	2	100.0	96.9	95.5	94.7
Polynésie Développement	France	2	71.0	63.3	64.0	65.7
Prominco Holding	Switzerland	2	100.0	96.1	94.7	67.3
Sireg	France	2	100.0	96.8		
Smurfit Paribas Bank Ltd.	Republic of Eire	1	50.0	48.4	47.7	
Société Anonyme de Gestion						
d'Investissements et de						
Participations	Belgium	2	100.0	96.7	95.3	94.7
Société Financière Paribas						
Suisse BV	Netherlands	2	100.0	96.9	95.5	47.4
Sociéte Gabonaise de						
Participations	Gabon	2	64.2	62.1	61.3	60.8
Société Néo-Calédonienne de						
Développement et de						
Participations	Polynesia	2	71.9	69.7	76.3	75.7
SNC Marché Saint-Honoré	France	2	99.9	96.8	95.4	94.6

Table cont.

Company	Country	Activity*	% Interest‡ 1991	% Effective ownership† 1991		
				1991	1990	1989
Wigmore Loan Finance Ltd.	UK	1	100.0	96.9		
COMPAGNIE BANCAIRE GROUP						
Arval	France	1	100.0	34.2	33.6	
Arval Belgium	Belgium	1	56.0	19.7		
Aurore Assurance	France	1	100.0	36.2	36.3	36.1
Banque Financière Cardif	France	1	100.0	29.3	29.5	30.3
Cardif Gestion (ex-Cartrois)	France	1	99.2	29.1	29.5	
Cardif SA	France	1	61.8	29.1	29.3	30.3
Carnegie & Cie	France	1	100.0	45.0	21.8	20.7
Cetebail	France	1	100.0	36.1	36.3	36.1
Credit d'Equipement des Ménages 'Cetelem'	France	1	75.6	36.2	36.4	36.1
Cetelem Expansion	France	1	100.0	36.9	36.3	36.1
Cetelem Nederland	Netherlands	1	100.0	36.2	36.3	
Clariance	France	1	100.0	36.1	36.3	36.1
Cofica	France	1	99.9	36.1	36.3	36.1
Cofiplus	France	1	100.0	36.1	36.3	36.1
Compagnie Bancaire	France	1	47.9	47.9	48.1	48.1
Compagnie Bancaire Pierre	France	1	99.0	46.9	47.1	46.6
Compagnie Bancaire Terme	France	1	100.0	41.6	41.8	41.8
Compagnie Bancaire UK (A)	UK	1	100.0	37.0	36.5	36.1
Compagnie Bancaire UK (B)	UK	1	100.0	46.4	29.6	28.9
Compagnie Bancaire US	USA	1	100.0	47.9	48.1	48.1
Compagnie de Placement & de Prévoyance	France	1	100.0	47.9		
Compagnie Financière Kleber	France	1	99.4	47.5	47.8	47.6
Compagnie Française Épargne & Crédit 'CFEC'	France	1	100.0	45.0	21.7	20.7
Cortal SA	France	1	99.4	47.3	47.5	47.1
Fimestic	Spain	1	100.0	37.9	38.0	38.0
Firem	France	1	100.0	30.2	30.4	31.3
Foncière de la Compagnie Bancaire	France	1	95.8	38.4	32.2	31.3
Gerfonds	France	1	99.4	46.9	47.0	46.2
Gestion Bail SARL	France	1	100.0	45.0	21.7	37.0
GAM—CB	France	1	88.6	33.9	48.1	27.4
GEP—CB	France	1	72.2	31.1	48.1	23.6

Table cont.

Company	Country	Activity*	% Interest‡ 1991	% Effective ownership†		
				1991	1990	1989
Klebail SA	France	1	100.0	38.4	32.5	31.7
Kleber Finance Conseil	France	1	100.0	47.2		
Kleber Portefeuille	France	1	100.0	47.9	48.0	47.6
Klecinq	France	1	100.0	47.8	48.0	47.6
Klepierre	France	1	42.7	20.3	21.2	18.3
Klerim & Cie	France	1	100.0	45.0	21.8	20.7
Kletrois	France	1	100.0	47.9	48.1	47.6
Loca SNC	France	1	100.0	34.3	33.6	33.2
Locabail UK	UK	1	100.0	34.3	33.6	33.2
Locabail Energie	France	1	100.0	34.2	33.6	33.2
Locabail International Finance	Bermuda	1	100.0	35.6	35.0	34.6
Logibail & Cie	France	1	90.7	38.3	31.5	29.3
Matradelme	France	1	99.6	34.1	33.4	33.2
Neuilly Contentieux	France	1	98.0	35.4	33.6	33.2
Neuilly Gestion	France	1	90.0	33.4	33.8	30.8
Savelme SNC	France	1	100.0	34.3	33.6	33.2
SC Centre Bourse	France	1	55.0	11.2	11.7	9.6
Secar	France	1				11.5
Secmarne	France	1	80.0	40.5	40.5	40.4
Segerim & Cie	France	1				27.9
Socappa	France	1	99.9	34.2	33.6	33.2
Solorec	France	1	43.6	8.9	9.3	7.7
Soservi	France	1	100.0	36.1	36.3	36.1
Société de Gestion	France	1	90.9	36.0	48.1	26.9
Systema Leasing	West Germany	1	100.0	36.9	36.5	36.1
Union Crédit pour le Batiment 'UCB'	France	1	94.1	45.0	21.8	20.7
UCB Bail	France	1	100.0	45.0	21.7	20.7
UCB Credicasa	Italy	1	100.0	46.4	21.6	21.2
UCB Group plc.	UK	1	100.0	46.4	29.7	28.9
UCB Locabail Immobilier	France	1	100.0	45.0	21.7	
UCB Pierre	France	1				23.6
UCB Socabail Immobiliare	Italy	1	100.0	46.4	23.5	21.6
UFB Assets Finance	UK	1	100.0	37.0	36.5	36.1
UFB España Grupo	Spain	1	100.0	37.0	36.5	
UFB Kredit Bank	West Germany	1	100.0	37.0	36.5	36.1
UFB Leasing Italia	Italy	1	70.0	25.9		
UFB Locaball	France	1	100.0	34.3	33.7	33.5

Table cont.

Company	Country	Activity*	% Interest‡ 1991	% Effective ownership†		
				1991	1990	1989
UFB Locabail Deutschland	West Germany	1	100.0	37.0	36.5	36.1
UFB-Group	UK	1	100.0	37.0	36.5	36.1
UFB-Humberclyde	UK	1	84.7	31.3	30.2	29.8
UCI	Spain	1	50.0	22.8	13.5	13.0
CREDIT DU NORD GROUP						
Banque Arnaud Gaidan	France	1	100.0	100.0	100.0	100.0
Banque Dupont	France	1	100.0	100.0		
Banque Kolb	France	1	51.0	50.9		
Banque Lenoir & Bernard	France	1	99.9	99.9	99.9	99.9
Banque Rhône Alpes	France	1	98.4	98.4	98.3	98.3
Banque Tarneaud	France	1	80.2	80.2	79.3	79.2
Banque Turgot	France	1	100.0	80.2	79.3	
Cageda	France	1	100.0	100.0	100.0	99.9
Crédinord Developpement	France	2	98.7	95.9	98.7	91.3
Crédinord Finance	UK	1	100.0	100.0	100.0	100.0
Crédit du Nord	France	1	100.0	100.0	100.0	100.0
Groupe Crédit du Nord	France	2	100.0	100.0	100.0	100.0
Norbail	France	1	69.7	68.6	65.7	65.3
Norbail Sicomi	France	1	100.0	99.4	99.4	
Norfinance	France	1	100.0	100.0	69.2	
Sedel	France	2	100.0	99.3	99.2	99.2
Société de Participations Tech- niques et Financières	France	2	100.0	95.9	98.7	91.3
Société Immobilière d'Invest- issement et de Coordination	France	2	90.4	90.4	99.9	99.9
Union Bancaire du Nord	France	1	64.4	63.7	60.5	61.3
COBEPA GROUP						
Agemar SAH	Luxembourg	2	100.0	32.0	31.7	29.2
Belgian Broadcasting Company	Belgium	2	100.0	64.0		
Cippar	Belgium	2	100.0	42.3	38.2	33.3
Cobepa Finance	Luxembourg	2	100.0	64.0	63.4	58.4
Citherm	Belgium	2	50.0	32.0	31.7	29.2
Compagnie Belge de Partici- pations Paribas 'COBEPA'	Belgium	2	66.8	64.0	63.4	58.4
Cocefin	Jersey	2	100.0	64.0	63.4	44.4
Compagnie de Développement International	Luxembourg	2	100.0	42.3	38.2	33.3

Table cont.

Company	Country	Activity*	% Interest‡ 1991	% Effective ownership†		
				1991	1990	1989
Compagnie de Participations Internationales BV	Netherlands	2	100.0	36.8	30.0	26.3
Compagnie de Participations Internationales NV	Netherlands Antilles	2	100.0	37.1	30.0	26.4
Compagnie de Participations Internationales SA	Belgium	2	64.8	37.1	30.0	26.6
Compagnie Financière & Mobilière 'COFIM'	Belgium	2	100.0	60.2	59.3	54.3
Compagnie Forestière 'COSYLVA'	Belgium	2	100.0	64.0	38.3	33.3
Compagnie Générale Mosane	Belgium	2	67.1	42.3	38.2	33.3
Coparin	Luxembourg	2	100.0	36.8		
Finagerbe	France	2	100.0	64.0	63.4	58.4
Financial Control International	Netherlands	2	100.0	36.8	30.0	26.3
Groupe Financier Liégeois	Luxembourg	2	100.0	42.2	38.2	33.3
Groupe TSA	Belgium	2	100.0	64.0		
Invest. Beleg. Maatschap. Lacourt 'IBEL'	Belgium	2	65.7	40.3	39.3	33.3
IIM	Netherlands	2	100.0	64.0	63.4	44.4
Leader-FM	Belgium	2	100.0	64.0	63.4	58.4
Libelux	Luxembourg	2	100.0	62.8	62.2	57.2
Libenel	Netherlands	2	100.0	64.0	63.4	58.4
Parfinasur	Belgium	2	65.3	41.8	44.4	38.0
Paribas Participation Limitée	Canada	2	100.0	57.0	43.1	39.1
Pollux	Belgium	2			62.2	
Regemea	Belgium	2	100.0	40.3	39.3	33.3
Regio Invest. Ontwik. Maats.	Belgium	2	100.0	40.3	39.3	33.3
Société de Développement & de Participations 'SODEPA'	Belgium	2				58.4
Société d'Investissements Internationaux (Nlle) 'SODINELE'	Belgium	2	100.0	64.0	63.4	58.4
Société Financière de Développement et de Participations 'FIDEPA'	Belgium	2	50.0	32.0	31.7	29.2
Société Financière de Réalisation 'SOFIREAL'	Belgium	2	100.0	64.0	63.4	58.4

Table cont.

Company	Country	Activity*	% Interest‡ 1991	% Effective ownership†		
				1991	1990	1989
Société Immobilière et Financière 'COFILM'	Belgium	2	58.2	24.6	21.9	16.9
Texaf	Belgium	2	82.1	52.5		
Vlaamse. Beleg. Maatschappij 'VIBEM'	Belgium	2				45.6
Vobis Finance	Belgium	2	50.0	32.0	31.7	29.2
POLIET GROUP						
Lambert Frères & Cie	France	3	99.2	79.3		
Poliet	France	3	80.3	79.9		
OTHER FULLY CONSOLIDATED COMPANIES						
Aubry-Gaspard	France	2	100.0	99.3	99.1	98.9
Avener Participations	France	2	30.0	34.8	34.8	34.8
Beltoren Holding BV	Netherlands	2	100.0	91.3	68.5	
Caisse Centrale de Réescompte	France	1	100.0	96.2		
Compagnie Auxiliaire d'Entreprises & de Chemin de Fer	France	2	100.0	99.4	99.1	98.9
Compagnie Centrale de Financement 'COCEFI'	France	1	100.0	100.0	100.0	100.0
Compagnie Foncière	France	2	60.8	57.5	56.9	56.4
Compagnie Franco Marocaine	France	2				41.6
CCR Participations	France	2	96.2	96.2		
Enelfi-Bretagne	France	2				43.3
Holding Franco-Britannique	France	2	100.0	100.0	100.0	100.0
Holpar Finance	Netherlands	1	100.0	100.0	100.0	
Nantes Navire Participations	France	2				42.9
Nouvelle Compagnie Financière pour l'Outre-Mer 'COFIMER'	France	2	100.0	100.0	100.0	100.0
Nouvelle Société Anonyme de Gestion Financière 'NEFICOM'	France	2			100.0	100.0
Opatra	France	2	100.0	100.0	100.0	100.0
Parfici	France	2	100.0	98.8	98.7	
Pargelux Holding SA	Luxembourg	2	100.0	100.0	100.0	100.0
Paribas Besse	France	2	100.0	100.0		
Paribas Domaines	France	2	85.5	85.3	82.0	73.2
Paribas Électronique	France	2	70.2	69.3	68.5	73.2

Table cont.

Company	Country	Activity*	% Interest‡ 1991	% Effective ownership†		
				1991	1990	1989
Paribas Électronique Développement	France	2	100.0	69.3	68.5	73.2
Paribas Environnement & Services	France	2	100.0	100.0		
Paribas Europe	France	2	100.0	100.0	100.0	100.0
Paribas Industries	France	2	100.0	100.0		
Paribas Participations	France	2	100.0	100.0	100.0	100.0
Paribas Santé	France	2	100.0	100.0	100.0	100.0
Paribas Santé International BV	Netherlands	2	100.0	100.0	100.0	
Poliet Group	France	3	80.3	79.9		
Société de Gestion & d'Inté-réts Petrolier 'SOGEDIP'	France	2	100.0	100.0	100.0	100.0
Société de Participations Bancaires & Financières Paribas	France	2			100.0	100.0
Société de Participations Financières Paribas 'ex-CSFL'	France	2	99.9	99.9	100.0	100.0
Société d'Études Immobilières & de Constructions	France	2	100.0	99.3	99.1	99.0
Société Européenne d'Études et de Gestion Industrielle et Financière 'SEDICECOM'	France	2	60.8	74.7	75.9	73.8
Société Financière de Gaz & Energie SA	Luxembourg	2	100.0	100.0	100.0	100.0
Société Financière de Saunes Châtillon	France	2	53.3	51.7	51.6	50.1
Société Financière d'Entre-prises d'Études & de Conseil	France	2			99.9	99.9
Société Foncière Mulhouse-Nord	France	2	100.0	57.5	74.2	73.8
Société Générale Commerciale & Financière 'SGCF'	France	2	100.0	100.0	100.0	100.0
Société Immobilière Victoire	France	2				100.0
Société Métallurgioue de Gorcy	France	2	93.3	93.3	93.3	93.3
Société Nouvelle de Banque Europe 'SNBE'	France	1				100.0
Sogimo	France	2	100.0	99.3	99.1	98.9

Table cont.

Company	Country	Activity*	% Interest‡ 1991	% Effective ownership†		
				1991	1990	1989
Union Financière & Bancaire 'UFIBA'	France	2	100.0	100.0	100.0	100.0
Valeurs et Rendements SA	Luxembourg	2	100.0	100.0	100.0	100.0

COMPANIES ACCOUNTED FOR BY THE EQUITY METHOD §

BANQUE PARIBAS GROUP

Company	Country	Activity*	% Interest‡ 1991	% Effective ownership†		
Banca International Lombarda	Italy	1	20.0	19.4	19.1	18.9
Banque Continentale du Luxembourg	Luxembourg	1				33.2
Banque Paribas Gabon	Gabon	1	43.5	35.6	35.1	
Ottoman Bank	Turkey	1	50.0	43.3	42.7	37.4
Smurfit Paribas Bank Ltd.	Republic of Eire	1				47.4

COMPANIE BANCAIRE GROUP

Company	Country	Activity*	% Interest‡ 1991	% Effective ownership†		
Capem	France	3	62.0	29.2	29.3	24.0
Cardif VIE	France	1	100.0	29.1	29.3	30.3
Cardim	France	1	99.0	28.7	29.3	
Cartrois	France	3				29.8
Cofidis	France	1	15.0	5.4	5.4	5.3
Covefi	France	1	15.0	5.4	5.4	3.7
Cybele RE	France	3	100.0	29.1	29.3	
Domi Equipement	France	1	35.0	12.2	11.8	11.5
Facet	France	1	38.5	13.9	13.9	13.5
Fedebail	France	1	33.0	11.3	11.1	10.6
Fimaser	Belgium	1	40.0	14.5	14.5	14.4
Finadis	Spain	1	15.0	5.7		
Finama	France	1	49.0	17.7	17.8	
Findomestic	Italy	1	35.0	13.2	13.3	13.0
Fipryca	Spain	1	34.0	12.9		
Fructivie	France	1	30.0	8.7	8.8	8.7
Helios	France	1	100.0	29.1	29.3	30.3
Helios RD (ex Cardif RD)	France	1	100.0	29.1	29.3	30.3
Lafayette Finance	France	1	49.0	17.7	17.8	17.3
Lecard BV	Netherlands	1	40.0	14.5	14.5	
Le Chene RD	France	1	40.0	11.6	11.7	12.0
Le Chene Vie	France	1	40.0	11.6	11.7	12.0
Marfina	Switzerland	1	35.0	13.2	13.3	13.0
Novecrédit	France	1	38.0	13.7	13.8	13.5

Table cont.

Company	Country	Activity*	% Interest‡ 1991	% Effective ownership† 1991	1990	1989
Orix Crédit Corp.	Japan	1	20.0	7.2	7.3	7.2
Pinnacle	UK	1	88.7	25.8		
Presbourg Étoile & Cie	France	1	95.9	38.8	30.4	
Sinvim SA	France	3	44.8	22.5	22.7	21.5
Sofrali SA	France	1	100.0	45.0	21.7	
Solveg	France	3	100.0	45.0	21.7	22.1
Soravie	France	1	10.0	2.9	2.9	2.9
Ste de Paiement Pass	France	1	40.0	14.5	14.5	14.4
SIS Croissance	France	3	48.0	23.0	23.2	39.4
Union Européenne d'Assurances	France	1	66.0	19.2	19.4	
Urba Gestion	France	3			48.1	33.2
UFB Leasindustria	France	1	30.0	10.3		
CREDIT DU NORD GROUP						
Banque des Marchés et d'Arbitrage	France	1	37.6	37.6	33.2	33.4
Banque Nuger	France	1	40.0	40.0	40.0	40.0
Banque Pouyanne	France	1	34.0	34.0	34.0	34.0
Société de Bourse Gilbert Dupont	France	1			34.0	34.0
COBEPA GROUP						
Assubel	Belgium	2	22.2	9.3		
Cable and Wire Assemblies 'CWA'	Belgium	3	20.0	8.1		
Calcitherm	Belgium	3	54.3	17.4		
Gerbe	France	3	99.9	64.0		
Gevaert SA (Group)	Belgium	2	35.4	17.6	16.9	15.1
Group Josi	Belgium	2	22.2	13.6		
La Floridienne	Belgium	3	25.4	10.7		
Sait Electronics	Belgium	3	70.1	42.6		
Sococlabecq	Belgium	3	30.0	9.6		
UCO	Belgium	3	48.3	27.7		
Vlaamse Uit Geversimj Maatschap 'VUM'	Belgium	3	25.2	10.2		
POLIET GROUP						
Bervialle SA (Group)	France	3	100.0	79.7	36.4	35.6

Table cont.

Company	Country	Activity*	% Interest‡ 1991	% Effective ownership† 1991	1990	1989
Ciments Française (Group)	France	3	86.2	68.8	10.5	9.9
Lambert Frères & Cie	France	3		27.7		
Menuiseries Lapeyre (Group)	France	3	100.0	79.9	36.6	35.7
Point P SA (Group)	France	3	100.0	79.8	34.8	35.7
Poliet	France	3		36.6	35.7	
SAMC (Group)	France	3			35.7	
Tuilerie Briqueterie Française (Group)	France	3	51.0	39.9	13.9	
Tuileries Briqueteries du Lauragais (Group)	France	3	100.0	79.1	27.5	
Tuiles Lambert (Group)	France	3	100.0	72.2	24.7	
Vachette	France	3	99.2	79.2	35.7	34.8
Weber & Broutin (Group)	France	3	100.0	79.7	36.5	35.6

OTHER COMPANIES ACCOUNTED FOR BY THE EQUITY METHOD

Company	Country	Activity*	% Interest‡ 1991	% Effective ownership† 1991	1990	1989
Axime (ex Segin)	France	3	34.5	31.8	45.0	58.6
Banque Franco-Yougoslave	France	1				24.9
Banque Petrofigaz	France	1	44.4	44.4	23.5	23.5
Caisse Centrale de Réescompte 'CCR'	France	1			60.0	32.5
Caisse Nationale a Portefeuille (Group)	Belgium	2	9.4	6.5	13.5	12.6
Cellulose du Rhône & d'Aquitaine (Group)	France	3				25.4
Compagnie de Fives-Lille (Group)	France	3	29.3	29.3	29.3	29.3
Compagnie de Navigation Mixte (Group)	France	2	29.4	29.2	29.8	
Compagnie Générale de Développement Immobilier Cogedim (Group)	France	3	55.6	48.9	49.0	50.0
Compagnie Luxembourgéoise de Télédiffusion SA CLT (Group)	Luxembourg	3	22.4	21.5		
Compagnie Metallurgique & Minière (Group)	France	3	39.0	39.0	38.7	41.5
Coparex (Group)	France	3	90.4	90.4	90.4	90.7
Erbe (Group)	Belgium	2	47.0	38.6	39.7	39.1
Euro Tungstene Poudre	France	3	28.2	28.2	28.1	31.8

Table cont.

Company	Country	Activity*	% Interest‡ 1991	% Effective ownership†		
				1991	1990	1989
Financière Fougerolle	France	2	48.5	47.9	46.5	
Finaxa (Group)	France	2	28.9	28.9	20.3	
Fougerolle (Group)	France	3	27.1	26.8	26.2	39.0
Guyomarch (Group)	France	3	96.8	93.3	97.0	
IHC Caland (Group)	Netherlands	3			28.4	29.0
La Rochette (Group)	France	3	28.0	27.8	28.1	
Maneurop	France	3				33.3
Matra-Communication (Group)	France	3	20.0	19.7	19.7	19.0
Mestrezat	France	3	80.9	69.0	64.0	64.1
Nord-Est (Group)	France	2	40.6	35.5	38.4	35.0
Pargesa Holding SA (Group)	Switzerland	2	17.8	7.9		
Régie Immobilière de la Ville de Paris 'RIVP'	France	3	32.1	32.1	32.2	32.2
SEMA Group	UK	3	35.9	32.8	33.1	32.4
SEPI	France	3	55.1	55.1	55.0	62.2
SCOA (Group)	France	3	50.0	49.4	29.4	27.3
Société Parisienne d'Entreprises et de Participations 'SPEP' (Group)	France	3	15.8	15.8	13.9	

* Activity: 1 = banks and financial companies; 2 = investment holding companies; 3 = industrial and commercial companies.

† % effective ownership: effective percentages held by Compagnie Financière de Paribas.

‡ % interest: sum of percentage held by majority-owned companies.

§ % equity method: percentage applied to determine the share in net equity or net income of companies accounted for by the equity method.

Appendix 4C. Shareholder's Proxy Form: An Example

MAIL BALLOT OR PROXY FORM

IMPORTANT : Before choosing between the three alternatives 1 2 3 please read the instructions on the other side.

AIR LIQUIDE

L'AIR LIQUIDE - Société Anonyme pour l'Étude et l'Exploitation des Procédés
Georges Claude au capital de 4 014 647 980 F
Siège social : 75, quai d'Orsay - 75007 PARIS
Code Postal : 75321 Paris CEDEX 07
RCS PARIS B 552 096 281

SPECIAL SHAREHOLDERS' MEETING on first call on Wednesday, May 5, 1993.
If that meeting fails for want of a quorum, it will be called anew for **Wednesday, May 19, 1993**, immediately after the **REGULAR ANNUAL SHAREHOLDERS' MEETING** called for the same date.

PLEASE DO NOT WRITE IN THIS SPACE

Identifier   Registered   VS

Number   Bearer   VD
of actions

Number of votes:

1   **I GIVE MY PROXY TO THE CHAIRMAN OF THE MEETING and authorize him to vote my shares.**

Date and sign below without filling in **2** or **3**

3   **APPOINTMENT OF A NAMED PROXY AGENT**

I give my proxy (see note 3 on the other side) to:

to represent me at the meetings on May 5 and 19, 1993

Stamp tax paid on statement

Authorization of March 29, 1993

Full Surname, Name, and Address (see note 1 on the other side).

Choose

1   or   2   or   3
To choose 2 or 3 you must choose the corresponding box

2   **VOTE BY MAIL**

I vote **IN FAVOR OF ALL** the resolutions recommended or approved by the board of directors EXCEPT those which I identify below by blackening like this ■ the corresponding box, which I vote AGAINST or on which I abstain, an abstention being tantamount to a vote AGAINST.
§ L. 161-1 (see note 2 on the other side).

REGULAR ANNUAL SHAREHOLDERS' MEETING

1	2	3	4	5
6	7	8	9	

SPECIAL SHAREHOLDERS' MEETING

1	2	3	4	5
6	7	8	9	10

If amendments or other resolutions are moved at the meetings:

- I authorize the chairman of the meeting to vote my shares.

- I abstain (tantamount to a vote against).

- I give _____ my proxy to vote my shares (see note 3 on the other side).

Date and signature

To be voted, this form must be received:

	on 1st call	on 2nd call
	special meeting	special meeting-annual meeting
- at the bank	by April 27, 1993	by May 13, 1993
- at the company	by May 3, 1993	by May 14, 1993

INSTRUCTIONS

IMPORTANT : If you cannot attend a meeting in person, you may vote by returning this form* specifying your choice of **one** of three alternatives:

1 authorizing the chairman of the meeting to vote your shares (date and sign on the other side without filling in 2 or 3)

2 voting by mail (check the box to the left of No. 2)

3 giving your proxy to a named proxy agent (check the box to the left of No. 3)

REGARDLESS OF YOUR CHOICE, YOU MUST SIGN THE FORM ON THE OTHER SIDE.

(1) The person signing the form is requested to write his last name (in block capitals), commonly used forename and address legibly in the space provided for that purpose; if that information already appears on the form, please check it and correct it if necessary. If the shareholder is a legal entity, write the last name, forename and title of the person signing the form. If the person signing the form is not a shareholder (for instance a receiver, life tenant, guardian, etc.), he must write his last name and forename, and specify the capacity in which he is signing the form. A form sent in for a given meeting is valid for the other successive meetings called on the same agenda (D 131-3-§3).

AUTHORIZATION OF THE CHAIRMAN OF THE MEETING 1
OR A NAMED PROXY AGENT 3
TO VOTE YOUR SHARES

(3) Trading Companies Act of July 24, 1966 (excerpt)
§ 161: "A shareholder may be represented by his spouse or another shareholder.
A shareholder may represent other shareholders at a shareholders' meeting as their proxy, without limitation other than those resulting from the legal or charter provisions specifying the maximum number of votes that anyone may cast in his own right or as proxy. Clauses contrary to the foregoing paragraphs are null and void.
If a shareholder sends a proxy without filling in a proxy agent's name, the chairman of the shareholders' meeting votes it in favor of the resolutions recommended or approved by the board of directors of the management board, as the case may be, and against all other resolutions. To vote otherwise, the shareholder must name a proxy who agrees to vote according to his principal's instructions."

N.B. If information contained on this form is used for a computerized name file, it is subject to the provisions of Act 78-17 of January 6, 1978 concerning the interested person's right of access and correction, and otherwise.

VOTING BY MAIL 2

(2) Trading Companies Act of July 24, 1966 (excerpt)
§ 161-1: "A shareholder may vote by mail, by means of a ballot, the wording of which is specified by decree. Contrary provisions of the certificate of incorporation are null and void. Only ballots received by the company before the meeting, by the deadline specified by decree, are counted for quorum purposes. Unmarked ballots or abstentions are counted as negative votes."

To vote by mail, you must check the box to the left of No. 2 on the other side. In such event, you are requested:
- in regard to the resolutions recommended or approved by the board of directors:
  • either to vote in favor of all of those resolutions by blackening none of the boxes,
  • or to vote against, or to abstain from voting on, some or all of those resolutions by blackening the boxes corresponding to those which you vote against or as to which you abstain (under the regulations, an abstention is counted as a vote against);
- in regard to the resolutions not approved by the board of directors, to vote resolution by resolution by blackening the box corresponding to your vote.

Furthermore, in the event that amendments of the resolutions or new resolutions should be moved for adoption at the meeting, we request you to choose between 3 alternatives (authorization of the chairman of the meeting to vote your shares, abstention, or appointment of a named proxy agent) by blackening the box corresponding to your choice.

* The resolutions and all other regulation documents (D 131.2 and D 133) appear in the enclosed notice of the meetings; do not use both 2 and 3 (§ D 1233-8).

Appendix 4D. *History of French Banking* [*]

Modern banking in France was born in the second half of the nineteenth century. Although the Bank of France was founded in 1800, legal paper currency was only introduced and established throughout French society after the revolution of 1884. This monetarization of the country, in which the banks played an important part, was a major factor in the realization of the Industrial revolution. From then until the present day, periods of growth in the economy and change in French society have been accompanied by a rapid expansion of banking activity.

Three distinct periods stand out in the development of the modern banking system. They are: 1850 to 1867—the beginnings of the modern bank, 1867 to 1941—the gradual specialization of banks, and 1941 to the present—the period of state intervention.

1850–67

In the seventeen years between 1850 and 1867 the lives of French people were transformed by the development of a national rail network which permitted the rapid growth of heavy industry and by the telegraph network linking Paris with every region and every departement. A national market had been created, but the existing banking system, was pitifully inadequate to service it. The role was filled by a completely new type of bank, the Banque de dépôts, created to cater for small savers, and intended to finance with their deposits the further industrialization of the country. In 1865 there were 1.2 million bond holders. There then followed the appearance of many of the institutions which still form the core of the French banking system—Crédit Foncier in 1852, Crédit Industriel et Commercial in 1859, Crédit Lyonnais in 1863, La Société des dépôts et comptes courants in 1863 and Société Générale in 1864. Banks covered a range of operations, short-term credit, discounts, advances on payments and goods, buying shares in industrial companies, all provided on an ad hoc basis with no financial safe-guards.

1867–1941

In 1867 Crédit Mobilier, which had been behind many of the new industrial companies, collapsed and shocked the banks into allocating their resources more carefully. Consequently the large banques de dépôts began to pull out of industrial

* This appendix is reproduced from the *Bankers' Almanac* (Dec. 1990), published by Reed Information Services Ltd.

operations, leaving these to newly created banques d'affaires such as la Banque de Paris et des Pays-Bas in 1872, la Banque de l'Indochine in 1875 and many more which appeared in the 1880s. In addition a new breed of cooperative banks sprang up to serve the needs of specific social groups—the etablissements mutualistes et cooperatifs which included le Crédit Populaire, created in Angers in 1878 to help small traders, le Crédit Mutuel established in Alsace-Lorraine, Brittany and Lyon and le Crédit Agricole intended to attract farmers suspicious of the big national banks. The Caisses d'Epargne, founded in 1818 to meet the needs of very small savers had acquired funds of FFr3 billion by 1888, compared with the banks' 1.5 billion, due to their very favourable conditions—a high interest rate and instant access which not only the modest savers had taken advantage of. In order to discourage wealthy depositors, the upper limit on deposits was lowered in 1895 and a period of stagnation followed for the Caisses d'Epargne until the deposit limit was lifted in 1913.

1941–1990

Following France's defeat against the Germans in 1940, the new government took charge of all aspects of the economy including the banking system. The laws of 13 and 14 June 1941 represent the first major state intervention in French banking. They created two supervisory bodies, (le Comité Permanent d'Organisation Profession-nelle and la Commission de Contrôle des Banques) and two professional organiza-tions which later became l'Association Française des Banques and l'Association Française des Sociétés Financières. After the war, the law of 2nd December 1945 transformed the Comité Permanent into the Conseil National du Crédit and formalized the specialization of banks which had been in practice since the 1880s by defining three categories: les banques de dépôts, les banques d'affaires and les banques de crédit à long et moyen terme. Most importantly the law nationalized the Bank of France, Crédit Lyonnais, Société Générale and the two banks which later became la Banque Nationale de Paris so fostering the close relationship between the government and the banks which still characterizes French banking. The banks became a vital part of the government bureaucracy, not only to implement monetary policy but to further social objectives such as supporting the agriculture industry or encouraging the residential home buyer. In the early 60s the government needed larger resources to meet the needs of the rapidly expanding economy and in particular to modernize the means of production. Although essential to this process, as they stood the banks were too restricted. The banking reforms of 1966 and 1967 therefore relaxed the division between the banques de dépôts and the banques d'affaires, allowed banks to open branches anywhere in the country and created the conditions conducive to bank refinancing. Following these reforms, many banques d'affaires disappeared because they lacked a branch network and were not equipped to accept demand deposits, while the banques de crédit à long et moyen terme flourished (8 in 1946, 60 in 1975), largely due to the growth of credit-bail (leasing). The overall result was the consolidation of the banking industry—by 1973 six main groups, including the three nationalized banks, accounted for 80 per cent of the banks' assets and 58 per cent of assets of the whole banking sector.

In 1979 the government of Raymond Barre commissioned an investigation into the banking sector. The findings of the resultant Mayoux report were that the structure of the French banking industry and the legislative framework within which it operated were inappropriate for the needs of modern banking. The banking sector was still impossibly fragmented with a whole network of different regulatory structures not designed to accommodate new financial methods such as leasing or factoring, or new hi-tech payment methods. In response to this the 1984 Banking Reform Act completely reorganized the banking system and brought all banking establishments, with a few exceptions, within the same regulatory framework. To a certain extent the financial system is still in a transitional stage embracing some specialized institutions and some establishments engaged in a wide variety of activities. None the less the general trend is now towards institutions that are market-orientated and less specialized.

The position of banks regarding public ownership changed dramatically in 1982 when President Mitterand nationalized two financial companies and all banks with deposits of more than a FFr 1bn, bringing to 39 the total of state-owned banking establishments. His move was countered by the Chirac government in 1986 when it introduced legislation providing for the privatization of more than 60 state-owned enterprises including the banks, industrial groups and financial holding companies. However, this privatization programme was prematurely arrested by the stock market crash of 1987 and Mitterand's return as president, followed by a Socialist victory in the 1988 legislative elections. Of the banks only Banque Paribas, Société Générale, Crédit Commercial de France and Banque Indosuez have returned to the private sector and President Mitterand has given an undertaking that there will be no further privatizations or nationalizations.

THE UNITED STATES OF AMERICA

i. Introduction

We have already seen in each country studied how corporate governance holds up a mirror to society in general. The USA is no exception. To understand the greatest of the democracies, therefore, we need to remind ourselves of what the relevant laws, assumptions, and attitudes are, so similar to those of others in many ways and yet so different. Societies in market economies have much in common, but who else would offer as two of their guiding principles 'Sunshine and due process'?

Federal and State Laws

Ever since Independence the States have fought to limit the role of the Federal government. Even today the basic laws governing company structure are State laws, with some significant differences between them. Wherever a company operates it may choose any State in which to incorporate, and the States compete for their business. The competition between these States is 'not one of diligence but of laxity' (Justice Brandeis 1933), or, in Professor W. L. Cary's words, a 'race for the bottom' (he had been chairman of the SEC) (Cary 1974: 663). If proof of this were needed, the example of New Jersey could be cited. In 1913 its legislature reintroduced a restrictive approach to corporations. The law lasted only four years because by that time most corporations had transferred to Delaware. Few returned.

Delaware, not an industrial centre by any means, is at the moment the clear winner, with half the top 500 companies registered there, partly because of its statutes, partly because the courts and lawyers there have long specialized in governance issues: the Delaware Chancery Court established in 1792 is undoubtedly pre-eminent. Delaware's statute is not substantially dissimilar from the Model Business Corporation Act (which was itself originally based on Illinois legislation) suggested by the American Bar Association and which a number of States use in whole or in part. (For the text see Soderquist and Sommer 1990.) That said, there is competition between States and this tends to favour management's interests, since it is management which decides where to incorporate and the States pander to them in order to attract them. State legislation is subject to some rather loose constitutional limitations, but the key point is a dislike of Federal intervention. Indeed, if a political head of steam builds up in Washington which might lead to Federal intervention a non-legislative solution is found wherever possible. An example of this was the incorporation in its listing requirements by the New York Stock Exchange of a rule that companies should have audit committees composed of outside directors. Deregulation is part of the same strand of thought, that is, rolling back the boundary of the central government's authority. There is a widespread feeling that those who govern least govern best. Of course, even this principle can be dented to protect vital interests, and there was a time before 1986 when there was pressure on the Congress to control or prohibit hostile take-overs. But this evaporated after the Supreme Court decision in *CTS* v. *Dynamics Corporation of America* restored States' rights in this area.

The SEC

The chief but not all-powerful machine for exerting Federal pressure is the Securities and Exchange Commission (SEC) which regulates many of the processes affecting companies, shareholders, and the market, and the traffic between them. Its staff are traditionally activist, and since its creation in 1934 it has been regarded as an 'élite' Federal agency. There are elaborate and important rules on what information must be provided, when and how it must be lodged, or whither sent and to whom. Although SEC regulation does go close to the heart of corporate governance because it largely controls information, substantive issues remain with the States and the Supreme Court has prevented the SEC encroaching. The SEC, for instance, rules on the disclosure of executive remuneration and States do not. While State laws govern what issues must be put to shareholders for approval, it is the SEC which requires companies to seek shareholder approval for employee stock option plans.

The Law

'Due process' has always been a crucial part of the US system, perhaps because it was a way of welding together people of many different races, traditions, and backgrounds. The legal system provided a common basis for them. Access to the system is facilitated by contingency fees (banned centuries ago in England as 'maintenance and champerty'), by class actions, and by derivative suits. The number of lawyers is high; recourse to the law is a normal part of life; and people do not move far without a lawyer at their elbow. This has a profound effect on corporate governance as it does on many aspects of US life. It is also expensive, and as all legal costs are borne somewhere in the price of goods and services, it makes them less competitive.

The King

The States have not of course had a king for 200 years, but the image of George III lives on in the tradition of distrust for a centralized governmental power and a desire for checks and balances; it has been reinforced by waves of immigrants with memories of truly despotic governments. For most of the last forty years the President's party has not controlled the Senate and House of Representatives—whether intended or not, a triumph for checks and balances over efficiency. The Constitution was concerned with public not private power, but a similar concern about concentrated power surfaces elsewhere from time to time, and has in the past led to legislation about monopolies, banks, banking, and insurance operations, and bank and insurance holdings in industrial companies. Whenever cabals threaten, hackles rise. These are the eyes through which some of corporate America views the potential power of institutional investors.

Size and Natural Wealth

Just as Japan's lack of usable land affects so many aspects of Japanese behaviour, the sheer spaciousness of America and the fact that it has so many industrial centres is reflected in US attitudes. To have such a rich and vast economic unity, with geographical diversity, encourages people to move. The attitudes of the old frontier have not yet gone. Those who move often must make friends quickly, and the basic assumptions are still of openness and hospitality. The possibility of renewal is always present. Failure is a setback but unshameful; Lincoln had failed in business twice, Truman once. It has been a world of vision of risk-taking, adventure. Perhaps, as the memory of the frontier dims, and the lawyers close in, the spirit of regeneration and adventure will falter. Americans fear both this and the decline of the entrepreneurial spirit and independent self-reliance. And the minerals are not inexhaustible.

Diversity

The plurality of US society is most striking in its ethnic mix. Unlike many other countries it cannot delve deep into its past to define the origins of its basic inhabitants. Those who originally lived there were largely dispossessed or annihilated, and the Europeans, who came from many countries, were *sub specie aeternatis*, a recent phenomenon. No one group could claim to be 'it', so all are equal (and the US constitution so decrees), though some, particularly the WASPS (White, Anglo-Saxon Protestants), are more equal than others. The Lowells may yet speak only to the Cabots, but neither would think of telling other immigrant groups to 'go back where you belong'—they belong there. Minority religious groups like Catholics and Jews did not take long to be emancipated, because they had never been as disadvantaged as they might have been elsewhere. The balance between the aristocracy of the blood and the plutocracy is different from countries in which there used to be or still survives a formal aristocratic structure, often linked to the land. The USA by and large has an aristocracy of wealth, to which all can aspire. Having said that, being a member of an 'old' family with 'old' money still counts for something and it also colours assumptions and thinking. The USA of course lacks an honours system which confers recognition without cash, and this has important consequences (as indeed does the retention of such a system in the UK).

The old order is changing in that the new waves of immigrants do not see the need to accept the British–US inheritance and its values, and some even balk at the language. Hispanic influences have grown at an amazing speed, and Spanish is the second language in very many places, the prime language for many, and the only language for some. The demographic centre of the USA has now for the first time shifted west of the Mississippi river.

It would not be surprising to find unevenness or some intolerance in such a heterogamous society and as a consequence to find pressures from groups who feel disadvantaged on account of race, colour, language, disablement, sexual proclivities, age, and sex—*inter alia*. This can give rise to egalitarian pressure for 'democracy' in many walks of life—at one end bilingualism in schools, and at the other representation on company boards. Today's motto is 'PC'—politically correct; curricula, for instance, in some universities are not allowed to concentrate on European cultural antecedents.

The UK Inheritance

The USA inherited, of course, the English language, the common law, a dislike of despotic systems of government, and, above all, a confrontational and individual approach—not a co-operative or collegiate one. What the USA did *not* inherit was UK envy. Perhaps this is because the country is so much richer that there is less cause for envy. Be that as it may, Americans do not resent success because they would rather use their energies trying to attain it. The unions want a bigger slice of a bigger cake and so can identify with the prosperity of the business. They have never seen themselves as the storm troops of socialism. But even though their industrial power is waning, they can and do exercise considerable political power.

The USA discarded monarchy and aristocracy and substituted a wealth-measured meritocracy. There are 'old boy' networks all over the place and the buddy system is considered by some to be the bane of boards. The Americans are so secure in their individuality that they can become great joiners without fear of impairing it. And boards are among the bodies they join, potential lawsuits notwithstanding.

The emphasis on individuality sits well with a pioneering entrepreneurial society, which needs heroes however tough, and powerful leadership whatever its darker aspects. The typical CEO is heavily personalized by the media (which in contrast to Japan, find it more profitable to make stories about personalities than products). The style at the top of USA companies to this day is more presidential/military than it is collegiate. We consider CEOs' pay below, but it is worth noting here that US heroes in any sphere tend to be exceptionally well rewarded.

The Political System

This is no place for a lengthy critique of the system as a whole and the salient features that affect corporate governance can be stated quite briefly:

- The division of power between States and Federal government noted above.
- The lesser importance of party and party programmes.
- The crucial importance of individuals' campaign funding, which often means their entering office burdened with obligations, and leaves them exposed to multivarious pressures.
- The major role of lobbyists. In recent years, divergent interests have mobilized support so effectively that in some areas an impasse has been reached, that is, 'lobbying gridlock'—for instance, on tort reform.

The sum of all this means that a subject like corporate governance normally excites little interest. Changes to the existing laws are bound to offend some interests and may produce no compensating political benefits. The Business Roundtable—which comprises CEOs of major companies—is one among many powerful lobbies. How powerful they are it is impossible to judge, but certainly sufficiently important and rich for politicians not to wish to antagonize them. The history of changes to company or banking law is of response to scandals or dramas when the political kudos for taking action was greater than the opprobrium for inaction would have been. There have been problems and scandals of late and there is a sense of unease at what now appears to be the excesses of the 1980s, but they have not produced pressures for root and branch reform, rather a general acceptance that current arrangements are worth reconsidering to see if improvements might be made. This is a far cry from saying that the reform of corporate governance would be a vote-catching programme. The solution was typified by the Sub-Council on Corporate Governance and the Markets—part of the Council on Competitiveness set up by President Bush in 1992. The subject was felt worthy of study and produced useful analyses, but its findings were not, to say the least, far reaching. I was its only European member.

US commentators have remarked that there is a lack of deference towards central government. Even if it is much less respected than elsewhere (and that is unproved), some opprobrium attaches to large corporations that disregard its laws. Helped by their control of the media, use of expensive lawyers, and funding of political campaigns, power in the USA now largely rests with these large corporations. But the entrepreneurial spirit has not been extinguished, so that if a big business in an industry is afflicted by bureaucratic sclerosis it will in time let in new thrusting companies who will take their share of power along with profit.

Openness

The 'sunshine' in the first paragraph of this section means openness. The Freedom of Information Acts in the USA give access to government papers that would be locked away elsewhere. The government in the Sunshine Act gives the public access to agency meetings. Openness pervades the atmosphere. The German and Japanese way of operating quietly and effectively behind the scenes to influence company management would strike Americans as underhand and wrong (and the lawsuits would start flying). American television programmes are amazingly frank and unrestrained by UK standards. Their laws of defamation do not seem inhibiting. The fear of adverse publicity in the media is a powerful prompter of self-restraint.

'Openness' affects behaviour but not human nature. The USA has its fair share of fraudsters, but they have to work on the assumption that discovery will be available. Warren Buffett, on taking the chair at Salomon, told the staff they should not do anything they would be unhappy to see on the front page of the *New York Times*. The fear of clandestine groupings, of conspiracy and cabals, is extreme and is strengthened by fear of ensuing lawsuits. The SEC rules permit up to ten shareholders to meet to discuss a company in which they have invested and about which they are concerned; they have seldom done so, however, for fear of the possibility that they may be sued for an alleged infringement of another SEC rule requiring disclosure by persons holding an aggregate of more than 5 per cent of the company's stock who agree to act together—even if the meeting decided in the event not to take common action. This particular situation was changed by the SEC in the second half of 1992 (see below). To take another example of openness, Schedules 14 D-1 (and 14 D-9) of the SEC regulations require both sets of advisers in a take-over to file details of the fees; if fees are to be fixed by a formula this must be stated.

Academia

The weight of literature coming from North American universities should not be underestimated. There are sophisticated articles and papers on many aspects of corporate governance. The measurable is measured, the rest described. The angle of approach varies—economic, legal, behavioural. Academia is more closely interwoven with the commercial world than in some other countries and is apparently influential, though advice tends to vary and some influences have not necessarily proved beneficial. Alongside the learned pieces (often complete with the mandatory algebra) are the popular books, apparently well researched, written like novels, but with better stories. *Barbarians at the Gate* (Burrough and Helyar 1990) and *The Predators' Ball* (Bruck 1988) are examples. Alongside these are serious and sometimes polemical works like *Power and Accountability* (Monks and Minnow 1991), *Bidders and Targets* (Herzel and Shepro 1990). It must never be forgotten that the lifeblood of academics is publication. In other words, the trees are numerous and the undergrowth tangled: to discern the wood, let alone describe it succinctly, is a far more difficult task than for other countries.

National Power

Commentators attempting a teleological assessment feel it would not be surprising if the twenty-second-century historian saw the twentieth century gradually witness the USA approach the zenith of its power and influence. It then became the undisputed military and economic world leader. It was the bulwark of free market democracy against centralist Communism and ended up the winner. But the victory had an economic and spiritual price.

The cost left the country heavily indebted at the same time as it became increasingly dependent on foreign oil. In 1980 the USA was the world's biggest creditor nation; by 1990 it was the largest debtor (Jacobs 1991). Others surpassed it technically in many industries and competition became ferocious. The Gulf victory of 1991 was no magic salve to heal the Vietnam wound. The massive self-confidence of the USA has dwindled, not as a result of foreign military might but by such mundane sights as foreign goods on the shelves and highly esteemed foreign vehicles in the streets. In the 1950s the foreign trade US companies did was a bonus and it accounted for a fraction of GNP; by the 1990s it was often significant to them and to the country. By the time of the Clinton presidency in 1993, the US was still the world's leading industrial power but isolation was not the option it once was. So there was a question in the minds of some whether under such stiff competition the USA can afford to maintain current practices.

David Halberstam in his book on the decline of the US motor industry (1986), identified three weaknesses: the public school system, the low level of industry, and excessive expectations. 'Few,' he concluded, 'were discussing how best to adjust the nation to an age of somewhat diminished expectations or how to marshall its abundant resources for survival in a harsh unforgiving new world or how to spread the inevitable sacrifices equitably.' This sense of relative decline has been felt much more widely in the five years since. It now colours the US approach to issues of corporate governance. There is much soul-searching about the effectiveness of the system. Americans ask themselves whether the Japanese and Germans are intrinsically cleverer, better motivated, harder working? Have they thrown up more geniuses? Surely not—in which case it can only mean that the USA is organizing itself badly. So what has gone wrong? Then they read *Bonfire of the Vanities* and *Barbarians at the Gate* (Burrough and Helyar 1990) and an old Puritan streak of conscience is aroused in them, if it has not already been by the ferocity of the take-over market, the junk bond débâcle, the appalling disaster of the Thrifts, and the unfolding problems of the commercial banks. At the same time, as the Council on Competitiveness has shown, the US share of high-tech industries has declined rapidly between 1980 and 1985: for example, in fibre optics from 73 to 42 per cent; in semiconductors from 60 to 36 per cent; and in supercomputers from 100 to 76 percent.

So it is that this paper is being written at a time (in 1992) when many of the issues are under the microscope and have been (or are being) considered by various arms of government, against an avalanche of articles from academe. Corporate governance has become a subject of wider interest, but there is no sign of any consensus on the need for reform or the direction it might take. Not much may be expected from a society which has not accepted the need for a systemic reform of anything in recent times—except the tax system in 1986—however badly it creaked. The recent débâcle over proposed bank reform is an obvious example of how difficult it is to carry reforms through Congress. From time to time, however, there are stirrings, and the *Wall Street Journal* reported on 10 January 1992 that Vice-President Quayle was working with Mr Breeden, Chairman of the SEC, 'to come up with ideas for greater corporate accountability'.

ii. The Machine at Work

As noted earlier there is no Federal Companies Act; companies incorporate under the laws of the state of their choice. The latest survey[1] by the Conference Board showed that 41 per cent of the respondents had chosen Delaware; New York was next with 7 per cent. The differences between States' laws have become more significant with their response to take-overs, as we shall see later. The main features are, however, common to all and familiar to the UK: namely, a board of directors elected by the shareholders and responsible to them for seeing that the company is properly run. Other common features include the directors' and officers' duties of loyalty and care to the corporation, and the right of any shareholder to sue on the corporation's behalf for breaches of duty.[2] The USA has many more unquoted than quoted companies, but this paper is confined to companies that are quoted on one of the US stock exchanges or on NASDAQ.

The Chief Executive Officer

When examining corporate governance in the USA, the place to start is not the board but the chief executive officer. To quote Herzel and Shepro (1990):

A reader unfamiliar with American company boards who walked into a board meeting [after reading our discussion of directors] might be surprised and disappointed. Under ordinary circumstances, what would be going on in the boardroom would correspond very little to the Delaware and other state law procedures. The CEO would probably be the chairman of the meeting and completely in charge. Generally, he controls both the agenda and the flow of information to the directors. He dominates the meeting and the board plays a quite secondary role.

---

[1] There are frequent references in this paper to the Conference Board (CB). The CB is a non-profit-making business information service, supported by an international research programme. More than 3,600 organizations participate as associates in its work. It is concerned with management practice, economics, and public policy.

[2] For a fuller exposition see Eisenberg 1989.

Shareholders and the market are far more interested in CEOs than directors. When we read about big businesses in the financial press, CEOs usually are the center of attention and directors are obscure. In fact, under normal circumstances very little attention is paid to directors by shareholders, the market or the press.

The CEO's Dominant Position

What the above quotation confirms is that US companies are run by their chief executives (whatever the formal title). The form of leadership is much more individual than collegiate. The balance of power between a CEO and his non-executive colleagues will naturally depend on the personalities. In most cases his position is far more exalted than theirs, in his own eyes, in theirs, and in the eyes of the world at large. The universal acceptance of his supremacy has a profound effect within his organization, not least in regard to his relationship with subordinates and their own aspirations. As noted earlier, he is frequently the outward and visible symbol of the business and treated as such by the media—a fact he usually enjoys and is sometimes seduced by. His pre-eminence is reflected in his pay. The figures (produced by the Conference Board) show that the second-highest-paid person gets substantially less than the CEO (see below).

The dominance of the CEO as a member of the board (which he always is) is virtually built into the general perception of the status of his position. When he assumes office he inherits a board, but gradually over the years his own power of patronage will affect its composition and this naturally tends to buttress his position. Even if he picks powerful independent CEOs like himself to serve as outside directors, he will know they will be inhibited because they owe their appointments to him and because of their fellow feeling for his position. These feelings permeate the board to the point where it is generally considered traitorous for the outside directors to caucus behind the CEO's back, and they seldom do it. *A fortiori* the members of the board— worthies all—who are less well equipped to understand the real significance of what is going on will tend to support him through thick and thin.

Viewed through a CEO's eyes such statements about their power might seem extreme. Their tenure of office is generally about six to eight years, and shorter therefore than that of many outside directors. Many are conscious of their vulnerability and do their best to make real colleagues of their board members. The reality seems to be, however, that it is generally accepted as the norm by all the parties concerned that on the spectrum which runs from individuality to collegiality, the place of the CEO is firmly at the end of individuality, and much of what follows for better or worse flows from this simple fact.

The chairman of the board is elected by his fellow directors. In more than three-quarters of companies he is also the CEO, and this is more prevalent in big companies. In manufacturing industry, for example, it was true of 92 per cent of companies with a turnover of $3 billion plus, but of only two-thirds of companies with a turnover under $100 million. This combination of posts—head of the company and head of the board—cements the CEO's power over the board—to whose structure and operations we turn below.

There is no US equivalent of the Confederation of British Industry (CBI), but many top CEOs belong to the Business Roundtable, which seems to be dedicated to defending and strengthening their position.

CEO's Compensation

There is a mass of data on what the British prefer to call remuneration, and the subject itself has become controversial, mainly because CEOs are well compensated through thick and thin and this does not seem just. Those interested in what they get and how it is organized are recommended to read the Conference Board's Report 1016, *Top Executive Compensation, 1992 Edition*. This shows that in addition to basic pay, CEOs and other executives get incentive compensation in one or more forms namely:

Annual bonus	Generally based on profits
Restricted stock	Shares awarded, but transfer restricted for n years: sometimes forfeit if executive goes
Long-term bonuses	Contingent grants payable on achievement performance plans of 3- or 5-year goals
Stock options	The right to purchase ordinary shares at a fixed price over a stated period of time

The figures for 1991 quoted below are the salary *paid* in 1991 plus the bonus *earned* for 1991, regardless of when paid. On this basis, the CEO's median current compensation in the survey was:

Manufacturing industry	$699,000
Commercial banking	$569,000
Energy and natural resources	$650,000
Diversified service	$582,000

Here are typical median figures from a range of industries to illustrate the relationship of the CEO's compensation to that of the next-highest-paid person:

	CEO	Next-highest pay
Industrial chemicals	$680,000	$400,000
Food etc.	$916,000	$625,000
Diversified service	$582,000	$409,000
Commercial banking	$569,000	$350,000

Given the CB evidence about quantum, it is not surprising that doubts have recently been expressed in many cases about the basis for remuneration, the level, and differentials.

Basically, the main grievance is that reward often fails to reflect results or personal performance. Jacobs (1991) quotes the specific case of General Motors and the general statistics in 1989 mentioned in *Business Week*, namely, that the average salary of the top 1,000 rose 7 per cent in a year when profits fell by 5 per cent and shareholders lost 11 per cent of the market value of their holdings. Boards have failed to implement reductions for poor performance.

There are some big figures about, Jacobs quoting Fireman (Reebok) and Siegel (Chris-Craft), both of whom drew over $10 million excluding stock-related gains (Steven J. Ross of Time Warner received a total of $151 million during the period 1973–90). And readers of *Barbarians at the Gate* will recall that Ross Johnson was somewhat above the breadline.

He is not alone. The top two executives in the 500 largest companies averaged more than $2 million a year in bonus and salary; the CEOs in the top 200 more than $3 million excluding perks.

On differentials Japanese Presidents earn 17 times the average base pay, British CEOs 35 times, and US CEOs 109 times (Graef S. Crystal, quoted by Jacobs 1991).

Given these facts it is understandable that shareholders should display dismay. Hitherto the SEC has prohibited their lodging shareholder resolutions on remuneration in company proxy statements. In 1992 it changed the rules on disclosure, broadening them substantially. (The changes are set out in the Federal Register, 21 October 1992; they are extensive and complex.) The general trend is to big picture disclosure:

- Disclosure would be consolidated into several tables, designed to be clear and easy to understand.
- A summary table would disclose all forms of compensation to the chief executive officer and the four other most highly paid executives for each of the past three years.
- The compensation committee (or the whole board) would issue a

report explaining the specific factors considered in determining the compensation for each of the executives named in the summary table.

- A performance graph would be required to compare the cumulative return to shareholders over the past five years to the return on a broad market index such as the Standard & Poor's 500 Stock Index and to the return on an index for a peer group of companies.
- Various forms of compensation will be broken down in the table.
- The table would distinguish between annual compensation and long-term compensation.
- Annual compensation would consist of salary, bonus (which can no longer be aggregated with salary), and other (such as perks, payments to cover taxes, deferred earnings on compensation, restricted stock, SAR, and stock option plans with above-market interest rates or preferential dividends, deferred earnings on long-term incentive plans, and preferential discounts on stock purchases).
- Long-term compensation would consist of awards of restricted stock, accrued dividends on restricted stock, pay-outs under long-term inventive plans, and stock options and stock appreciation rights (SARs).
- In addition to the summary table, there will be a table showing the potential values that can be realised by the named executive officers from the exercise of options and SARs, assuming various rates of appreciation of the price of the stock.

The most trenchant attack on CEOs' 'over-compensation' is contained in Graef S. Crystal's book, *In Search of Excess* (1991). No one is spared: CEOs, compensation consultants, and compensation committees. Anyone sanguine enough to put their faith in the present committees will be disillusioned; and the consultants do not escape the lash either. Crystal offers suggestions for the reform of compensation committees and their use of a consultant; and advises that the SEC regulations should be amended to reduce obfuscation. His main message is that too many CEOs get too much, absolutely and relatively, by any reasonable standard, through good times and bad. Harvard Economist Robert Reich asserts that there is no functioning labour market in CEOs, and Senator Levin proposed a Corporate Pay Responsibility Act to 'Reduce the Federal barriers to effective stockholder action on excessive executive pay'. This aroused strong opposition and the SEC was not prepared to support it. It is mentioned here only as an indication of the level of interest the subject currently commands.

Criticism tends to be shrill to command attention. It is not clear yet where the debate will end. There are pressures for *better* information and for better reflection of results in remuneration. Some critics would focus on the structure of remuneration packages rather than the actual sums. Others argue that top talent is rare and it matters greatly to a company to attract and retain it in a competitive market: the American CEO is not especially secure and his removal from office may in the end be abrupt, public, and wounding (so comparisons with regimes abroad where there is no mobility and great scarcity are unfair). The equilibrium which it is the function of the market to maintain depends upon information, and in the event this is often inappropriate or incomplete. The market for CEOs is in any case structurally imperfect and bound to be so. So almost everything depends upon judgements made inside and outside compensation committees. When all is said and done, however, there seems to be a widespread feeling that some judgements have failed to reflect the balance of interests which in the long run can only be disregarded at some risk to company and country.

The Business Roundtable acknowledges that 'there are problems in a few corporations', but generally considers that its 1990 dictum remains valid: 'Select, regularly evaluate, and, if necessary, replace the chief executive officer. Determine management compensation. Review succession planning.' This is supplemented by the following five principles:

(1) The committee of the board of directors designated to deal with executive compensation and share-ownership programmes, should be composed solely of non-management members of the board of directors.

(2) The overall structure of executive compensation and share-ownership programmes should directly link the interests of the executives, either individually or as a team, to the long-term interests of the shareholders.

(3) Executive compensation and share-ownership programmes should be designed to attract, motivate, reward, and retain the management talent required to achieve corporate objectives and increase shareholder value.

(4) Executive compensation and share-ownership programmes should be designed to create a commensurate level of opportunity and risk based on business and individual performance.

(5) Proxy statement reporting of annual cash compensation should be done in a standard format for all corporations in a manner that is easy for shareholders to comprehend. Share-ownership programmes should be separately reported in the proxy in a similarly understandable format.

The Business Roundtable's view is, broadly speaking, that shareholders already have all the powers they need including, as a last resort, replacing some or all of the board. It has also given advice on the format for reporting compensation in a way designed to be more helpful to shareholders.

Boards

The cornerstone of US corporate democracy is the shareholders' right to elect the board. In practice, this usually amounts to ratifying the board's nominations (which the CEO will have played an important part in formulating), but it can mean their proposing a slate of their own. This seldom occurs and even when it does, it usually fails. The boards to which directors are elected are single tier.

At one time boards were dominated by executives, but the tendency in recent years has been for 'outside' directors (the US term for 'non-executive' directors) to constitute a significant minority or, more usually, a majority. Indeed, it is not unusual to find that the CEO is the only executive on the board. The CEO may, however, have fellow executives on the board too, typically the president or chief operating officer (COO), financial officer, or a senior vice-president. The nomenclature for the top executives varies a great deal. Boards have shrunk in size since 1972, the median for big companies having reduced from fourteen to twelve and for smaller companies from twelve to nine.

Outside Directors

The movement towards a greater proportion of outside directors was given a great fillip in the late 1970s as a result of some cases of extensive misfeasance by executive directors. The response to this was that in 1978 the New York Stock Exchange made it a listing requirement that companies should have audit committees composed of outside directors. The American Stock Exchange has proposed a rule change requiring companies quoted on it to have audit committees with a majority of outside directors. NASDAQ/NMS require the same. The effect is that all quoted companies must have outside directors. In fact, the CB 1990 survey shows that they form a majority in 86 per cent of manufacturing industry boards and 91 per cent of the remainder.

Most outside directors have a background in manufacturing, services, or finance, but there is a good sprinkling of other backgrounds, including education (8–9 per cent). Forty-one per cent of companies have at least one woman on the board and 17 per cent have at least one foreigner. As PRO NED (Promotion of Non-Executive Directors; a UK body) has pointed out, outside directors are not necessarily 'independent'. In the USA the move towards their being so has been marked in recent years; all the outside directors can be so described on more than half the company boards. The biggest category of non-independent outside directors is lawyers.

US executives are paid as such whether or not they are members of the board. Fees are generally paid only to outside directors. These are covered in another Conference Board survey, *Corporate Directors' Compensation, 1993 Edition*. This shows that median total potential annual compensation for 1991–2 was as follows:

Manufacturing	$29,700
Financial	$24,000
Service	$24,500

Forty-five per cent of companies included stock in the compensation package: about a third had retirement benefit plans for their outside directors.

The outside directors' remuneration is founded on an annual retainer, which nearly all companies pay, plus a 'per meeting' fee, which well over 80 per cent pay. In companies that pay both, the 'per meeting' fee varies a great deal according to industry and size of company, but is likely to be somewhere around $1,000. Members of board committees generally receive 'per meeting' fees for them too, with the chairman getting more than the others. As in the case of CEOs' pay, board retainers and attendance fees are markedly higher in manufacturing industry than elsewhere.

It is said to be getting rather more difficult for companies, especially big ones, to recruit outside directors, partly because of exposure to liability, partly because of the time the office takes. The fear of lawsuits may be overstated, because the business judgement rule is in fact still highly protective, and because in June 1986 Delaware changed its corporation law to allow companies to eliminate or limit directors' liability for breaches of fiduciary duties—so long as they had acted in good faith and there was no breach of their duty of loyalty. In any event, many companies protect their boards with Directors and Officers (D&O) liability insurance. They also usually have provisions for reimbursing Directors and Officers for expenses incurred in defending litigation, amounts paid out in a settlement of an action, or—sometimes—because of a judgement.

The process of selection is changing too, with nominating committees beginning to play a bigger part both to reduce the CEO's influence and to make choice more methodical. Some companies invite nominations from shareholders, but the effective response has been insignificant—and that includes a response from institutions (see below). Despite the recruiting problem US companies have turned to professional help reluctantly and use it in less than a fifth of cases. All the rest of appointments come from recommendations made by members of the board, or the nominating committee, or professional advisers. And a very high proportion—around 90 per cent—are already known to the CEO even if he did not himself put the name forward.

Another recent change has been the trend away from one-year terms—only half as many as in 1972 (when it was 81 per cent). Three-year terms are now common (53 per cent), with staggered election. Cumulative voting has declined since 1972 from 32 per cent to 22 per cent (in this system shareholders get one vote per share per candidate and can give all their votes to a single candidate if they choose).

A myth persists that US boards are aged. The truth is that the median age is about 59–60, and this does not vary much with the size of the business except that they are two or three years younger in smaller companies (up to $200 million turnover). Two-thirds of companies have a mandatory retirement age of 70 or less.

Boards: Frequency of Meetings

There are two significant features of US boards that are so familiar to them that they seldom excite comment—geography and frequency of meetings. Compared with the USA, all the other countries studied, the UK, France, Germany, and Japan, have relatively concentrated industrial bases. Any major US company is likely to be widely dispersed at home, let alone overseas. With so many different industrial centres and so much dispersal, it is obviously sensible for US companies to seek their outside directors to match, and so they do. As a matter of mere logistics this would lead one to expect fewer meetings than elsewhere, and so it proves. In addition US companies are obliged to report quarterly, so the amount of public information directors have is greater than elsewhere. All these factors affect what boards do and how they do it.

In fact, most boards, smaller and younger and more independent than they were, meet about six or seven times a year. Data from the Conference Board Survey suggests that the boards of financial companies or very big companies of any type tend to meet more often—about nine times a year. Practice does vary greatly, some boards meeting only quarterly and some monthly. Meetings last about three hours—rather longer on average than they did, but neither this nor their frequency has changed much over the last decade. Most big companies have an all-day (or even two-day) board meeting once a year to review strategy and budgets. Korn Ferry, on the other hand, report that directors actually spend less time on board matters than they did—94 hours in 1990 against 125 hours in 1983.

Committees of the Board

Almost all US boards have at least one committee; about 85 per cent have two, and more than 50 per cent have three or four. In more detail, 98 per cent of companies have audit committees; more than 80 per cent have compensation committees, and about 50 per cent have nominating committees. In addition about 75 per cent have executive committees. The list of committees is quite long, including finance, public policy planning, human resources, etc. The main ones are sufficiently important to warrant further description.

Audit Committees

The New York Stock Exchange made audit committees a precondition of obtaining a quotation as far back as 1978, and companies met this requirement. In the early days there was much scepticism about their effectiveness: the imposition of a piece of machinery did not of itself ensure it was useful.

In a 1988 survey (Report 914), the Conference Board found that times had changed. Audit committees' responsibilities had generally been broadened. They were credited with having 'brought about improvements in . . . traditional core areas of their role—external audit, internal auditing, financial controls, and financial reporting. Many agreed that the committees' work has also improved both the full board's understanding of these matters and also its effectiveness.' In particular, audit committees were thought to have improved the procedures, practices and effectiveness of internal audit.

The terms of reference of audit committees vary between companies. The Conference Board Report 914 provides examples drawn from eleven different sectors. Common strands are:

- Recommending the auditors;
- Reviewing the scope of the external audit;
- Reviewing the results of the external audit with the auditors;
- Reviewing the results of the internal audit with the internal auditors;
- Reviewing the adequacy of the companies' accounting policies, practices, and systems of controls;
- Reviewing the scope and adequacy of the internal audit.

This list is by no means exhaustive. The terms of reference—generally provided in written form—may go into considerable detail and include various specific functions not mentioned above. Their essence is some reassurance about the effectiveness and integrity of the systems of financial control and information; a means of providing both internal and external auditors with a privileged and private forum in which to express doubts and concerns even (and perhaps especially) about top management; and a way of getting the outside directors closer to the business.

The Treadway Commission's 1987 Report did much to confirm the status and role of audit committees, though in fact its first recommendation was rejected (that the SEC should require all public companies to have audit committees composed solely of independent directors). Even so, there is no doubt which way the wind is blowing. The full recommendations are given in Appendix 5D.

Audit committees have tended to get larger (about four members now) and increasingly to be composed of wholly independent directors (about 90 per cent—the NYSE requires this). They still meet about three times a year on predetermined dates, but there are *ad hoc* meetings as well if necessary— and they commission enquiries if they feel it necessary. Nearly all meet the outside directors at least twice a year, usually in private session: it is understood that the outside auditors can request a private hearing with the committee when they want one.

In fact committee meetings are usually attended by key executives or other corporate employers, some as a matter of routine and some on a 'when invited' basis, but all may be excluded by the committee chairman for items it would be inappropriate for them to attend.

Audit committees do have in mind the danger of the outside auditors' independence being compromised by their consultancy work. Various procedures have been introduced to keep an eye on this, but the evidence seems to suggest that the effects of their surveillance have been limited. The committees are, however, much concerned in changes of outside auditors and these have crept up over the last decade from 5 to 8 per cent.

Compensation Committees

The use of compensation committees has risen sharply, and now nearly 90 per cent of companies have them. These committees tend to be a bit bigger than audit committees—about four to five people—and to meet about three or four times a year. Nearly all are composed wholly of outside directors, though the CEO is often invited to attend and may in practice do so for most meetings. About a quarter get help from outside consultants. The committee's remit covers only senior management and executive directors including the CEO, but its role is broad and covers the company's remuneration policy and guidelines—which takes it into questions of performance. Judging by the volume of criticism about many top executive 'compensation packages', the compensation committees concerned have failed in their prime task of reconciling the interests of management and shareholders by producing a 'fair' solution. Many reasons are suggested for their shortcomings, for instance, the indirect reciprocity between CEOs which tempers the severity of their judgement, and the desire of consultants not to lose business by producing unpalatable advice.

The 1992 SEC rules require a report from the compensation committee—or from the whole board if there is no committee—covering:

- A discussion of the compensation policies for the executive officers, including the extent to which it is performance-based;
- An explanation of the reasons for repricing the exercise price of options granted to named executive officers, if such options were repriced during the last year; and
- Disclosure of the identity of the members of the compensation committee, identifying any members that are employees or officers of the company or have certain other relationships with the company.

Nominating Committees

Many more companies—over half—have a nominating committee and it meets once or twice a year. Typically it might comprise one executive director and four outside directors. Again the CEO generally attends. Much of its work is concerned with screening the CEO's suggestions (or those others have put to him and he has endorsed), but it also increasingly puts forward its own ideas (some produced by consultants it has commissioned). Occasionally it may be asked to undertake a broader task such as conducting a review of the board itself or of the succession planning arrangements. There is still much disquiet about the CEO's dominating role in board appointments and a feeling that nominating committees have a larger part to play: indeed, their role has become a major focus of active attention for institutional shareholders.

A survey by Korn Ferry International, quoted by the United Shareholders Association in their September/October 1992 publication *Advocate*, shows that the recommendations of the chairman (who is usually CEO) is as ever the most important factor.

Executive Committees

Executive committees are found in rather more than two-thirds of companies. Their role varies and may include dealing with urgent issues arising between board meetings (remember there may be two or three months' interval between them). They can also be used as a sounding board on general management problems. Their nature means that executive directors play a large part on them and indeed have about a third of the seats.

The Board's Functions

Many bodies have pronounced on board functions. The Business Roundtable saw directors' duties as:

(1) Overseeing of management and board selection and succession.

(2) Reviewing the company's financial performance and allocating its funds.

(3) Overseeing corporate social responsibility.

(4) Ensuring compliance with the law.[3]

And the American Law Institute wrote in similar terms that their duties were to:

(1) Elect, evaluate and, where appropriate, dismiss the principal senior executives.

(2) Oversee the conduct of the corporation's business, with a view to evaluation on an ongoing basis, whether the corporation's resources are being managed in a manner consistent with enhancing shareholder gain, within the law, within ethical considerations, and while directing a reasonable amount of resources to public welfare and humanitarian purposes.

(3) Review and approve corporate plans and actions that the board and principal senior executives consider major and changes in accounting principles that the board or principal senior executives consider material.

(4) Perform such other functions as are prescribed by law, or assigned to the board under a standard of the corporation.

The Board at Work

Many brave words have been written about the accountability of the CEO (and the rest of management) to the board—not least by the Business Roundtable. Is this accountability real? Is the CEO an all-powerful boss and the board mere cyphers? Or is there a real balance? When Myles Mace wrote *Directors: Myth and Reality* in 1971, he had no doubt, describing them as merely 'Ornaments on a corporate Christmas tree'. There are undoubtedly boards today where this is largely true. But Jay W. Lorsch (Lorsch with McIver 1989) and others feel that the game has moved on in the last two decades, perhaps because of litigation, perhaps because of public comment and concern.

Directors who accept appointment to a board are not generally looking

[3] Business Roundtable, 'The Role and Composition of the Board of Directors of Large Publicly Held Corporations'.

for trouble. They are not, one gathers, doing it primarily for the money. They are more motivated by status and interest. Americans, in discussing the director's role, tend to turn to the old adage, 'If it ain't broke don't fix it.' The relationship between the CEO and the directors he has appointed, or who have appointed him, makes this a natural attitude. They trust him and like him and do not want prematurely to oppose him, much less eject him; they want him 'to provide strong leadership to pursue economic gains'. They realize his job in the market-place is tough enough anyway without the board holding him back. They are not unduly worried about this in normal times, will ask enough questions to satisfy their consciences, but accept the limitations imposed by their lack of information compared with the CEO. CEOs vary and the boards depend crucially on the role the CEO wants them to play. Some CEOs dominate and suppress; others encourage and create a collegiate style. It mainly depends on the personalities and their interplay: two similarly structured boards can behave in entirely different ways.

Directors will assert themselves more readily 'when push comes to shove'. In other words there may be a point beyond which even a complaisant board cannot be pushed. Readers of *Barbarians at the Gate* will remember this can be a long way down the track. We encounter in the USA the same phenomena described in other countries. First, that in times of trouble the tendency is to accord more, not less, power to the leader; secondly, that contrary to popular myth, there is no greater a tendency to fire the CEO prematurely in the USA than there is elsewhere. CEOs around the world tend to be given the benefit of the doubt for a long time, for reasons of inertia, cowardice, comradeship, and the sheer difficulty of organizing his removal and replacement. Many would go so far as to say (with the benefit of hindsight) that CEOs are often left in post too long.

So it is misleading to imply that US boards make little contribution. In many moments of crisis, including, for instance, the sudden death or resignation of a CEO, they may find themselves effectively in executive command for the interregnum. Their role is enhanced when take-overs threaten, not least because these have given rise to so much litigation. In the normal course of business, directors have little to fear from the courts because of the 'business judgement rule', that is, the courts are most reluctant to double-guess management decisions. In take-overs, however, the courts may well be heavily involved. As this is so, the directors are much more on the *qui vive*. Nowadays outside professional advice is invariably sought. The balance of power often shifts sharply and suddenly when a company is under attack. Even so, it is not necessarily always easy for

directors to reconcile their support for the CEO and the continued independence of the company with their overriding duty to the shareholders.

Those who serve on them assert that the USA has many excellent boards.
This is surely true, and reflects the will of those CEOs to make them work
properly. Even so, many Americans feel that there are few grounds for
complacency about the general effectiveness of their system and particularly
of the operation of the board. They know that they are faced with yet
another manifestation of the agency problem. As E. B. Rock put it, 'Because
directors do not generally have significant shareholdings and do not depend
on the shareholders, they lack any significant economic incentive to
discipline management. To the extent that they are economically or
psychologically dependent on management, they have significant incentives
not to act as the shareholders' champion . . .' (Rock 1991).

A quite different problem arises if the board as a whole does not work,
either because the directors cannot control the CEO when they should, or
because neither he nor they is up to the mark and the whole apparatus is
declining in a welter of reciprocal mediocrity. A poor CEO picks poor
directors and vice versa. In these circumstances, the old question arises, 'Quis
custodes ipsos custodiet?', and the answer is—the shareholders. We shall
examine their role a little later.

The Banks

As we have seen in the sections on corporate governance in Germany and
Japan, the role of the banks is central. The relationships between banks and
companies in both countries are subtle and complex; each reflects the
history of the development of the economy, as well as social and national
attitudes and behaviour. Naturally, the role the banks play conditions the
way they select, train, and deploy their staff.

There was a time when the USA might have developed on somewhat
similar lines (though early on it had more developed capital markets), but
the politico-social history of the USA worked out differently.

Rightly or wrongly, much of the blame for the intensity of the financial
crisis of the slump was attributed to financiers, and there was a reaction
against their abuse of power and influence. This led to legislative curbs on
banks in the 1930s. It is unnecessary to give a blow by blow account of
what occurred (Margaret Blair gives a short summary of the crucial elements
in the *Brookings Review*, Blair 1991). The Glass–Steagall Act of 1933
prohibited banks from underwriting stock or affiliating with investment
banks that do. The Bank Holding Company Act of 1956 restricts bank
holding companies from owning control blocks in companies not closely

relating to banking. Potential liability under trustee law encourages bank trust departments to fragment their holdings, and other rules make it difficult or impossible for the bank trust department to act in concert with other institutional stock holders.

Banks therefore do not come into the corporate governance picture except in so far as their trustee departments manage shares for clients. These are the record-holders of a significant portion of shares as custodian or fiduciary, in which case their preference is for their clients to vote their shares. Elaborate procedures have been introduced to facilitate this (under the 1986 SEC regulations pursuant to the Shareholder Communications Act).

Banks' own holdings are minimal because the law restricts them and they have few funds to spare; they neglect to use the influence they already have. The restrictions on their geographical spread cannot help them in serving major industrial customers. Furthermore, their biggest actual or potential clients are likely to have credit ratings as good or better than their own and are therefore able to get money on better terms and without their help (disintermediation). This has meant that the industrial and commercial companies which do still borrow are usually not the best risks. Banks have, however, been prominent in supplying some of the funds for LBOs or other take-overs (and costly this has proved when the overstretched borrower could not repay).

Some banks—the investment banks—have been key players, though not as shareholders. It is they who have acted as catalysts of change, not by assessing the quality of corporate governance, but by analysing companies to see if the market appeared to undervalue them. If so they hawked the company around (having produced a 'book' on it) among potential purchasers to whose greed and egos they might confidently turn. To the extent that the market's valuation did reflect the inadequacy of management, the investment bankers were assuming the shareholders' proper role, though the remedy they applied—a take-over—was often not as good for the parties as a straightforward change of management would have been. It suited the banks, of course, as take-overs and restructuring were infinitely more profitable to them than were changes of CEO or board. Investment bankers on the whole do not enthuse about really good boards or active shareholders—since both deprive them of an opportunity to make a killing by producing an inappropriate answer to a misguided question.

As if life were not already difficult enough for bankers, ingenious lawyers have exhumed the ancient Common Law concept of 'fraudulent conveyance' as a form of action against banks who loaned money to an LBO that failed.

(See the Revco case, 1990/1, *Wall Street Journal* (3 Jan. 1991).) But such claims are rare.

Despite all these problems, a bank may still form a close relationship with customers, and some still do. But 'relationship banking' depends on mutual trust and good information. It means a company being prepared to pay what is in effect an insurance premium for help in difficult times, and a bank giving its support if such times come. This goes against the grain when treasury departments are profit centres, straining to squeeze the last cent from every transaction. The trouble is that unless the board tells the treasury department to pay (within defined limits) the costs of relationship banking, it will not get it. Companies seldom think the price worth paying in good times and only regret the absence of an umbrella when the storm breaks. US banks, for their part, hemmed in by their law, seldom have the inclination, resources, and staff to try to sell the umbrellas—profitable though this might be. If a bank syndicates or securitizes debts, the tenuous connection between company and lender ceases to exist at all. In good times the company services its debt and repays when due. But if Humpty Dumpty falls off the wall there are likely to be so many pieces that even the marines cannot reassemble him. (See, e.g. the Federated Stores case in Lowenstein 1991: ch. 2.) It is not just the company that may get damaged—as the weight of non-performing loans on banks' books shows. An interesting account of Citibank's policy is given in *Institutional Investor* (Dec. 1991).

Shareholders

It is perhaps a sign of the times that one of the longest sections of this report is devoted to shareholders. For half a century commentators would have accepted the famous analysis by Berle and Means (1932) that the fragmentation of holdings had deprived shareholders of influence and power (in contrast to earlier days when proprietors retained enough stock to exercise both). The emergence of organizations which administer collective savings is gradually changing the picture, but there are many angles and complications, as we shall see. We take in order:

The form in which shares are held;
Annual meetings and the voting process;
Shareholders' duties;
Shareholders' diminishing rights;
Who owns what;

before turning to the role, if any, of shareholders in corporate governance.

It is widely appreciated that the USA has what Michael Jacobs dubbed a

'Board Centred' model (1991). Evidence suggests, however, that boards are not always self-correcting and self-renewing and that the take-over market is not always the right remedy for persisting deficiencies. Attention has therefore properly focused on shareholders in respect of the role they were originally designed to play—to ensure that the stewardship of their assets remained up to the mark, not by double-guessing management decisions, but by their interest in the composition of the board.

The Form in which Shares are Held

American shares are issued in registered form. Many are held by brokers in nominee names ('street names'). In fact, 70 per cent of all corporate stock was held in street name (by 1987), of which 30 per cent was held in broker name and 70 per cent in bank nominee name. The reasons for such arrangements vary from pure convenience to deliberate obfuscation. Arbs (Arbitrageurs) conceal; pension funds are held in trust. Whatever the cause the result is to complicate the process of voting proxies. There is no need in this paper to examine all its intricacies, but the curious sounding 'NOBO' rules may be cited as an example. These were introduced by the SEC in 1985, requiring brokers to tell issuers the names, addresses, and security position of shareholders who do not object (Non-Objecting Beneficial Owners). Some shares are held as ADRs (see Appendix 5G).

For many years the New York Stock Exchange refused to list common stock of companies which had unequal voting rights (the 'one share, one vote' rule). Some major companies have recently challenged this rule and the implied (or explicit) threat of their moving to another exchange has put the NYSE under severe pressure. The SEC sought to standardize the one share, one vote rule for all quoted companies by adopting Rule 19C-4 in 1985, but the Court of Appeals for the District of Columbia ruled that this was beyond the SEC's authority. The issue is still under consideration. US companies often have other kinds of share in issue and many debt instruments. This paper is concerned mainly with ordinary shares ('common stock'), because residual ownership attaches to them which provides their owners with potential influence on corporate governance. The issue of whether holders of senior securities should be enfranchised and if so to what extent lies outside its scope.

Annual Meetings and the Voting Process: Corporate Democracy in Action

As in most other countries the real business is not generally fought out at an AGM. J. K. Galbraith opined that 'The Annual Meeting of the large American corporation is perhaps our most elaborate exercise in popular illusion' (Galbraith 1967). But its very existence does produce certain consequences.

Companies must convene a shareholders' meeting annually. The NYSE expects companies to make certain that at least half of the outstanding shares are voted (to ensure a representative vote), and this has resulted in the appearance of proxy solicitors whose task *inter alia* is to help companies ensure that meetings are quorate and to afford shareholders a convenient method of voting. The SEC requires companies to send search cards to brokers twenty days before the record date so that brokers can tell them how many sets of proxy materials they will need for distribution together with the annual report, which has to be made public not more than three months after the end of the financial year.

The proxy voting system in the USA is a more important part of the governance process than in any of the other countries studied. In the UK, which is closest to the USA in style and approach, proxy contests rarely occur. As far back as 1934, the SEC was given powers to regulate proxies (the Securities Exchange Act), and its extensive rules cover both the process and content of proxy solicitations. Schedule 14B, for instance, lays down the information which must be given about candidates in a directors' contest. More importantly, the SEC was permitted to vet all proxy materials before they are mailed and insists on wide disclosure about those concerned, costs, and the issues. There is a good account of the whole subject, with cases, in a booklet by R. E. Shrager (1986), which noted: 'In any given fight, each side spends enormous amounts of time, effort and money, conveying its message to shareholders. . . . Both managements and dissidents retain a supporting cast of lawyers, investment bankers, and proxy solicitors . . . and often hire public relations specialists.'

Unless shareholders come under the ERISA legislation (which broadly speaking covers pension funds in the private sector), they do not have to vote. If they choose not to, management may vote the proxies provided that it has indicated how it intends to cast its votes and the shareholder has signed and returned the proxy and 'marked the boxes' in regard to specific items. If a properly signed proxy is returned without an indication of how to cast the vote, management can choose how to do so. Shareholders can use the proxy system negatively, that is, they can resist management's proposals. They can also launch competing proposals of their own—including candidates for the board. Indeed, this is a way of getting control of a company without a take-over bid. Some candidates put themselves forward on a platform of putting the company up for sale or liquidating it.

Shareholders' access to the proxy statement is limited via an SEC rule that confines shareholder proposals to matters that are not 'ordinary business'. Until recently it was impossible to raise the issue of excessive executive compensation, for instance (the SEC is in the process of changing this prohibition). Shareholder proposals are in any case generally 'precatory', that is, they do not bind management, though it does appear that management often heeds and acts on shareholder proposals that are passed, or might pass, even though there is no formal legal requirement for them to do so. Until recently proposals tended to be on politico/social issues like the environment and South Africa. There were twenty-one resolutions on Northern Ireland in 1990 (the New York Comptroller's Office was the most active in leading them). It must be irritating for the board to find general meetings raking over such issues, but they have the consolation of knowing they pre-empt the time and attention that might more fruitfully be spent on governance issues. These, however, seem to be more prominent than they were, and Appendix 5F shows, for example, how active the United Shareholders Association is in this area.

The 1980s saw proxy contests become more prominent (but not more numerous), and they were used from time to time as a cheap way of getting control of the board. The data on this type of proxy contest for the twenty years till 1977 show that about twenty-five contests occurred annually and that the dissidents were successful in getting full control in 15 per cent of cases or partial control in 32 per cent: about 20–5 contests per annum are thought to have occurred well into the 1980s. In 1983, for instance, there were twenty-five such contests, of which eleven were for full and four for partial control. Management won in 36 per cent of the cases and the dissidents in 40 per cent, an unusually high proportion. Proxy contests were also used in conjunction with a tender offer in an attempted take-over to put management on the defensive (e.g. AT&T/NCR), or were coupled with other take-over tactics—like 'Putting a company into play': that is, the dissidents' purpose was to force up the share price by attracting bids or restructuring.

Proxy contests also take place about other matters, for instance: contesting a proposal to increase Common Stock (Munsingwear, 1981); defeating a stock option plan (Aegis); defeating a proposed merger (Penn Central). Other typical subjects are proposals for restructuring and anti-take-over proposals of one kind or another.

Shareholders' Duties

In most countries shareholders have no duties once they have subscribed for their shares or bought them in the market. If they own the shares beneficially they may vote eccentrically or not at all. If they hold them as trustees they may still throw the papers away, and in the UK over 80 per cent of all holders routinely do so. In the USA the Labor Department requires the trustees of corporate pension plans which fall under the ERISA legislation (which covers most of them) to vote their shares or see that investment managers do so.[4] Trustees must monitor their managers to make sure they comply; unless the trustees specifically reserve the voting rights for themselves the managers must vote. What is more the votes must be cast in the interests of the beneficiaries.

Shareholders' Diminishing Rights

Shareholders' rights vary according to State statute, but usually include the right to elect directors as is general practice. The NYSE *Listed Company Manual* ensures a degree of uniformity and covers the frequency of reporting (§203). Most US public companies publish their results quarterly. They are not obliged to send copies to shareholders (except for the annual results), but usually do so.

Shareholders can bring a class action against the directors on behalf of all the shareholders (or those who bought or sold stock during a specified period). Alternatively they can bring a derivative suit—that is, they purport to sue on behalf of the company, which gets any ensuing benefits. Under Delaware law they generally need the board's consent to do this if it has a majority of disinterested directors—who can refuse if it is acting in accordance with the business judgement rule. If there is no such majority or if the action is not protected by the business judgement rule—for example, alleged waste of corporate assets—they do not need the board's permission to sue. If they win or settle the Court may require the company to reimburse their costs where the action conferred a 'specific and substantial benefit' upon the company; but they may well fail, because when they reach the substantive issues they may butt up against the business judgement rule which is designed to let directors run businesses without having to worry about shareholders with the benefit of hindsight suing them for mistakes.

The waves of take-overs during the last twenty years were only possible because control could so easily be acquired through open purchases in the stock market (without even having to offer to buy more than a bare majority of shares). There were no protective banks or interlocking shareholdings to stand in the way as there are in other countries; the NYSE had long insisted on 'one share, one vote'; finance became even easier to raise;

---

[4] For a full account see IRRC 1990.

and accounts (which had to be produced quarterly) lacked that enveloping opacity that shrouds companies' assets in some other regimes.

As this is so, incumbent management sought to protect its own position, partly from a genuine desire not to see its life work broken on the wheel of financial opportunism and a belief that they knew better than the shareholders how to protect their interests, partly from personal fear, greed, and love of power. To achieve their ends management was obliged to seek shareholders' permission to limit or reduce their power: and shareholders often gave it. The courts, however, generally permitted management to introduce poison pills without consulting their shareholders first (but we shall consider these later). Poison pills (see below) are a medicine with side-effects. To the extent they make purchasers pay a fair price they are beneficial; to the extent they entrench poor management they harm company and country alike. In recent years a significant number of shareholder resolutions have been aimed at clearing obstacles to tender offers by limiting or eliminating the effects of poison pills.

The SEC in its laudable aim to regulate the flow of information has in some cases made it far more difficult for the shareholders to monitor a company and take effective action to correct poor management. When it comes to proxy battles, management holds all the money and most of the cards, as Robert Monks's tilt at Sears showed. Amongst other devices it reduced the board and made access to shareholders' names and addresses difficult or hideously expensive.

In recent years, State legislatures have moved to protect their own, for example, Boeing by Washington; Norton by Massachusetts; and Armstrong World by Pennsylvania. We shall consider this further in the section on take-overs: the point here is that the protection of management led inexorably to a diminution of shareholder rights. And they may be further threatened by States introducing 'other constituency' provisions. These provisions have muddied the waters by permitting directors to consider the interests of other constituents than the shareholders—which can provide a convenient excuse for putting their own interests first. An incompetent management which does not wish to be dislodged can argue that it was resisting a bid which would have been to the shareholders' advantage on the grounds that other interests would not have benefited or had been harmed by it. In the long run shareholders can only prosper if all the other main interests—customers, employees, and creditors—have been satisfied first, but there is no excuse for neglecting the shareholders' interests and thus removing one of their effective means of redress.

Of course shareholders still retain their right to sell in the market, but if they see a board quite clearly under-performing or milking the company remorselessly, they cannot easily change its composition and they may not even get a chance to accept the offer if a bidder appears. The price of protecting good management from the depredations of the take-over artists has been to bring the mediocre within the corral and disarm the shareholders.

One kind of shareholder has been singled out by law for special attention—mutual funds. In the 1930s some began to act as monitoring intermediaries, but the 1936 Tax Act and the 1940 Investment Company Act forced them to stop. There were many contributing reasons but the main one was the general suspicion of the financial sector and the fear of its power over industry. American public opinion has always been mistrustful of accumulation of economic power and feels safer when it is fragmented. The regulations are detailed and need not be given here.

Shareholders: Who Owns What?

According to the New York Stock Exchange, 51.44 million individuals owned stock (including mutual fund shares) in 1990. Private shareholders hold 29 per cent of US equities in all—19 per cent in the hands of the general public and 10 per cent in the hands of owner founders. Many are totally passive; they are generally viewed as supportive of management, with good reason. They do not have to vote their proxies and management can usually do it for them. There are, however, organizations to 'brigade' private shareholders, of which the foremost is the United Shareholders Association (USA)* originally founded by T. Boone Pickens. Its objectives are given in Appendix 5E. This has 64,000 members who pay $50 a year to be able to enjoy the fruits of its research and campaigning: it rates 1,000 companies on their economic performance responsiveness to shareholders, and management remuneration. Each year it targets fifty of them in regard to some corporate governance issue. The 1991 list is given in Appendix 5F.

Institutional investors—mainly pension funds, mutual funds, insurance companies, etc.—have the lion's share of the rest, that is 53.3 per cent of the equity market in 1990. The latest data have been compiled by Dr Brancato as part of Columbia University's institutional investor project, and they relate to 31 December 1990 and give a reasonable but not totally complete picture.

- The institutions' share of the equity market has risen from 38 per cent in 1981 to 53.3 per cent in 1990. Pension funds held 28.2 per cent, mutual funds 7.2 per cent, insurance funds 6.9 per cent (much less

(* As this book went to press (November 1993) the USA announced it would disband, saying it had accomplished its objectives.)

than the UK), bank trusts 9.2 per cent. Appendix 5B shows fifteen top pension funds' equity holdings in 1988 and 1990. Appendix 5J lists the largest mutual fund managers—a group of growing importance.

- Major institutions hold 45.92 per cent of the stock of the top twenty-five companies (of which banks 17.10 per cent and investment advisers 16.54 per cent, public funds etc. 5.31 per cent, and insurance companies 2.32 per cent). The average number of institutions is 541. The largest concentration in the twenty-five is Eli Lilley & Co where institutions hold nearly 70 per cent; the lowest AT&T where they hold just about 22 per cent (this low figure is typical for utilities). Appendix 5A shows institutions' holdings by industry grouping, 1987–90.

- This increase reflects not only a growth in the total assets under the institutions' control but also a switch to equities from 32 per cent of their total financial assets in 1981 to 39 per cent in 1990; in 1950 the figure was 6 per cent!

The Columbia Study shows that the total assets of institutions at the end of 1990 were:

	$ billion	% in equities
Pension funds	2,491	38.6
Mutual funds	1,069	23.0
Life insurance	1,408	9.1

The major pension funds have substantial assets.

	$ billion	% in equities
TIAA-CREF	95	35.7
CalPERS	58	36.0
New York State LRS	45	47.0
AT&T	42	51.0
General Motors	41	43.8
General Electric	31	42.0

It should be noted, however that these are holdings in a very large market and that even TIAA-CREF only have 1.1 per cent of it.

Delving more deeply into ownership the Columbia study assembled data from the 13F forms which all investment managers and financiaries have to file with the SEC if they have investment discretion of more than $100 million. This showed that at 31 December 1990 those obliged to file held on average 45.9 per cent of outstanding stock in the top twenty-five corporations with—surprisingly—the banks holding the biggest block at 17.1 per cent. This shows the problem about gathering data—those obliged to file may have been given authority by pension funds. These figures, in other words, tell us about votes, not ownership, and therefore about control. On average banks keep sole voting authority over 70.8 per cent of the shares under their investment control. Appendix 5H sets out the details.

Interlocking corporate shareholdings are now conspicuously absent from the US corporate scene. It seems to be a case of all or nothing. Certainly the courts forcing du Pont to sell its 25 + per cent holding in General Motors was a discouragement to such a strategy, successful as it had been in that case. The nearest there is today is the Berkshire Hathaway Corporation, controlled by Warren Buffett, which has taken substantial stakes in a handful of US companies and is a long-term holder and active in its relationship with the businesses. To some extent some of the Management Buy-Out (MBO) funds perform the role of monitoring shareholders. There have recently been examples of funds being set up (like the LENS fund) with the avowed purpose of taking a large enough stake in underperforming businesses to influence management and secure improved performance.

The Role of Individual Shareholders

Except for the mega-rich or the proprietor who retains a substantial proportion of the stock, the situation is still as Berle and Means (1932) described it. Even if they had the knowledge and motivation (which would be rare), individual shareholders would be faced with the 'free rider' problem in relation to corporate performance issues. For them to be active would be costly, and they would be incurring a private cost for a public benefit. The only way they can act economically is by concerting with others. This is the basis on which the United Shareholders Association operates. Of course, individual shareholders can perfectly well support the initiatives of others and this means the institutions. It is to their position we now turn.

The Role of the Institutions

It is quite wrong to suppose that anyone concerned with institutional investment wakes up in the morning with corporate governance in his mind as the determining issue in choice of manager, portfolio strategy, or stocks. What they want of course is profitable investment, and the traditional way of achieving it is through straightforward market operations. If a stock disappoints one sells (EXIT). This is the so-called Wall Street Walk. The very idea that it is worthwhile contemplating governance issues is generally anathema, because

- it feels too costly;
- the free rider problem applies, as it does for individuals;
- one is not paid to do it or judged by having done it;
- there are concerns about the limits of legality.

In fact, such an analysis is seldom contemplated. Judging by what does not occur the subject is seldom addressed. Even where it is, the idea of using 'VOICE' (that is, attempting to influence a company rather than just selling its stock) is further inhibited by the size of the holding in a highly diversified portfolio. It would not so much be 'VOICE' as 'SQUEAK'.

The developments of recent years have, however, begun to cast doubts on whether such an attitude is justified. Perhaps the most significant of these is a question about the policy of diversification.

In principle institutional shareholders face the same basic choices as private ones, with one exception—their fiduciary duties prevent their taking certain kinds of risk. The US private shareholder may put all his money into a handful of local companies and stick to them through thick and thin. The institutional shareholder must to some extent spread risk (see Longstreth 1991). It is this—plus the never-ending pressure from brokers, analysts, and consultants—that has led to a somewhat indiscriminate acceptance of the principle of massive diversification, in which the golden rule seems to be 'Nothing succeeds like excess.'

Diversification to spread risk is therefore a well-established principle of prudent behaviour for owners and trustees (and their fund managers) alike. It might have been thought that diversification should at the very least be restricted by the capacity to understand what is being bought. In many cases this is clearly not so (one public pension fund has, for instance, 1,400 stocks and does more than 8,000 stock transactions a year). 'Since 1985 the use of stock index futures and other derivatives by pension managers has more than doubled. Corporate pension officers are the worst offenders. 34 per cent use futures of one kind or another, where the emphasis is not on companies but on market timing, switches in and out of different sectors . . . etc., etc. . . . with very little regard for the constituent companies' (Lowenstein 1991: 217).

There have been numerous studies which cast doubt on the benefits of trying to run a widely diversified portfolio by pro-actively managing it, for example:

- A US Department of Labor study of all 1,300 pension plans filed with them showed that between 1977 and 1983 they earned an average 75 BP less than unmanaged benchmarks.

- The 1988 Mercer Meidinger Hanson study of 137 major money managers found that on average investment managers underperformed major indices that year.
- A 1988 WM company survey of British pension funds found that on average the funds underperformed comparable indices over each of the previous years.
- The 1988 Forbes study showed that the busiest money managers returned 8.8 per cent, the most passive 11.3 per cent (taken from August 1989 newsletter of the Council of Institutional Investors).
- A study by William Mercer Asset Planning Inc. showed that in 1989 returns by 122 banks and insurance company investment managers were nearly 20 per cent below the S&P 500 index, making it seven consecutive years that they had underperformed the market average.

Annual turnover rates vary greatly. *Institutional Investor* reported in March 1991 that 26.3 per cent of funds had a turnover of 25 per cent or less; 41.6 per cent a turnover of 25–50 per cent; and 30 per cent a turnover of 51–100 per cent.

It seems gradually to be appreciated by owners or trustees that for fund managers (who are acting at one or two removes for beneficiaries) to over-diversify is neither helpful to the beneficiaries nor to the prospect of developing an interest in corporate governance. Coupled with heavy trading, it is costly and incompetent. The cost of trades shaves off the beneficiaries' capital; Lowenstein estimates that in 1987 $25 billion was spent in trading stocks, an amount equivalent to one-sixth of corporate profits and 40 per cent of all dividends paid out that year. What they trade is largely an unknown quantity, since they lack the resources to study the underlying companies in depth.

If funds continue to diversify, as they now do, beyond the range of both knowledge and resources, they are unlikely to have enough of either to play a part in corporate governance even if they wished to do so. In fact they are content not to bother as their eyes are firmly set on the criteria by which they are judged. They are not judged on their effectiveness in corporate governance matters—a different world from the league tables of performance which overhang them like the Sword of Damocles. No wonder so many funds simply replicate in their portfolios the firms that constitute a particular index, in the proportion in which the index is itself calculated: the managers do it in self-defence. They know that otherwise three-quarters of them will in any year underperform the index.

Indexation

Index funds started about twenty years ago and were the first investment product of the 'basket' variety. Many are based on the S&P 500—the 'plain vanilla' index (which comprises 400 industrials, forty utilities, twenty transportation companies, and forty financial institutions; 474 of the shares are listed in the NYSE). This index is capitalization weighted.

The growth of index funds is dramatic. The Columbia Project research shows that $342 billion of assets were so managed in May 1991 (up 25.8 per cent from December 1990) by the top fifty-three money managers: the top fifteen managers manage about $300 billion out of the total $342 billion, and nearly $100 billion was in the hands of the biggest, Wells Fargo Nikko Investment Advisers.

Concentration: 'Patience and Selectivity'

There is available to the institutional investor, within the law, a totally different strategy—concentration, that is, buying more of fewer stocks and holding them. The ultimate example of this kind of fund is Warren Buffett's Berkshire Hathaway Corporation. The principles behind it are, first, not to invest in a company until you thoroughly understand it—including its strategy; have a big enough holding for it to matter to you—and to them; maintain good contact with the company to ensure the board's stewardship is up to the mark—think long and trade little. The size of the holding must vary with the size of the company and the size of the fund, so the number of different shares in the portfolio will depend on both. Lowenstein (1991) calls concentration 'Patience and Selectivity'. Concentration incidentally does not mean putting all one's eggs in one basket. Twenty to forty stocks would be enough (in the views of some) for all but the biggest funds, where the resultant holding would constitute too large a chunk of the equity of all but the biggest companies.

Whether a heavily diversified portfolio is 'actively' managed or not is indeed relevant to costs and results, but not to the shareholder's power or interest in respect of any particular holding. Unless the fund is large he holds very little of each company. Besides, with so many holdings it costs too much to monitor all of them adequately. The manager of a heavily diversified portfolio, when it comes to corporate governance issues, is very much like a private shareholder, often ignorant, sometimes innocent, and generally helpless—unless he combines. The rationale behind the creation of the United Shareholders Association equally applies to him, indexed or not. Alone he squeaks; combined they may be heard.

As perceptions do change and the question of possible interest in corporate governance becomes more active, not unnaturally the legal dimension comes into view. This has been explored with great thoroughness by Professor Bernard Black of Columbia University, New York (1990, 1992, and forthcoming). Let Professor Black speak for himself (first from his 1990 paper):

Shareholder passivity is not inevitable even in large public companies. Instead, legal barriers, manager agenda control, and conflicts of interest may be important reasons why shareholders do as little as they do. Shareholders who would purchase large stakes, join forces with others to present voting proposals, or nominate and elect their own directors, face a comple web of legal barriers and risks. Many also face strong conflicts of interest, which are only weakly controlled by legal rules.

Collective action problems, while important, seem manageable for the large institutions who are today the dominant shareholders. Especially for issues with strong economies of scale, apathy may not be rational after all.

Shareholder monitoring *might* work, *might* become an important part of the larger web of legal and market constraints on corporate managers, *if* legal rules permit. Shareholders voice is an idea that hasn't been tried, not one that has failed. It deserves our renewed attention.

From Professor Black's 1992 paper I have selected the following:

Institutional voice is potentially valuable because of the need for *someone* to monitor corporate managers, with institutional shareholders as the only available candidates . . .

Corporate governance is, and will continue to be, imperfect. Shareholder voting is only part of the larger web of constraints on corporate managers, which includes the product capital labor, corporate control markets, incentive compensation, fiduciary duty, and cultural norms. But institutional voice rules can be a valuable strand in that web, and can serve as a partial alternative to relying on take-overs to discipline corporate managers. . . .

Institutional voice creates some risk that the institutions will abuse their power, but that risk is modest if particular institutions cannot control particular companies. If a half-dozen institutions exercise effective voice, the institutions can watch each other at the same time that they are watching corporate managers. . . .

The judgement here is that the upside from institutional voice is substantial and the downside limited. Perhaps institutional shareholders can become skilled monitors of corporate managers. And perhaps not. But the current system leaves much to be desired, and we will never know if there is a better system unless we try.

In one part of the legal jungle 1992 saw stirrings. The SEC has revised the proxy rules to make communication easier between shareholders who are not bent on acquiring control. However, there will still be managers or others suing shareholders who do decide to act jointly.

The modest changes were notable for the vigour with which the conflicting arguments were pressed. 'Leave us alone and keep off our backs,' said management, 'or you will inhibit our risk taking—and what do you know about our business anyway; you're just market gamblers.' 'We own you,' respond the shareholders, 'and as good Americans we believe in accountability. If you aren't accountable to us, where else is there? We don't want to run your business but we have a right to feel that the stewardship of our assets is in good hands.' This indeed is the crux of the US dilemma—a dislike of concentrations of power (in this case in the hands of the institutions), versus a respect for effective accountability. The conflict is nicely poised.

Which Shareholders are Active?

Action seems to rest on few shoulders—the prime moving force has been CalPERS (California state pension fund—with 950,000 participants). It has (1993) about $71 billion of assets with 80 per cent of US equities indexed, thus refuting the argument that indexation means the death of any interest in corporate governance. On the contrary, they feel it proves the old adage: 'If you can't sell, you must care.' CalPERS has not only prodded individual companies to some effect, but also initiated the movement to persuade the SEC to change some of its rules, in which it was able to muster some significant support. It remains to be seen whether or how much CalPERS' activism will be restrained by political influences.

Another public fund, CALSTRS, wrote to the SEC in the context of proxy reform in the following terms:

We wish to provide this presence (i.e. as real owners) because it is in the direct financial interest of our beneficiaries: our whole portfolio will do well only if the individual pieces in it do well. We have a legal obligation to try, since the obligation of fiduciaries to look after and maintain the assets in the trust is recognised both in statutory and common law. We are too large to escape by trying to buy and sell constantly to avoid poor (or simply under) performing companies. We have no interest in being confrontational, but we are afraid that the avoidance of confrontation is sometimes used as an excuse to avoid the legitimate activities that owners must undertake to protect and enhance their property.[5]

It is indeed the public pension funds which of all the US institutional groups have been the most pro-active—but not all of them. Some have no taste for it, others fear political interference, because the businesses they might wish to reproach may well have the ears of their political masters as contributors to campaign funds. 'Mr Governor, we have been generous contributors to

[5] Letter from J. D. Mosman to J. G. Katz, 15 July 1991.

your campaign funds—get your pension fund off my back.' In any case, the Columbia project research showed that in 1990 the public pension funds controlled only 8.3 per cent of equities. Most private pension funds—which have as we have seen a legal obligation to vote—have parallel fears, of upsetting suppliers or customers, or even simply because of an unspoken non-aggression pact, 'You don't vote against my company and I won't vote against yours.'

It is commonly argued that money managers are totally preoccupied with their place in the league tables, measuring their performance against that of competitors. This is true, but we should not draw the inference from it that dismissal waits round the corner. In 1989, thirty-two out of 427 were terminated with an average of 7.6 years service (cf. 1987, 8.7 years). The fact is that fund managers often build up good personal relationships with those who hire them, and will be given the benefit of the doubt for a long time ('he's going through a bad patch'). This is so although there is now a powerful new consultancy profession whose members help trustees pick fund managers—another manifestation of the pervasive tendency to diffuse responsibility in the face of possible litigation. In short, fund managers are not prevented by fear of dismissal from taking an interest in corporate governance. They simply do not feel they are paid to do it; are not measured by their success in it; and lack the skill and resources they would need to do it properly. Vote they must if they are managing funds covered by the ERISA legislation and the trustees order it, and they must follow whatever guidelines they are given. But that does not make them care. 'They vote woodenly,' as one commentator said of a big index fund manager.

What is more, when they are asked why they organize their funds the way they do—for instance, diversify or index as against concentration/patience—the response is seldom that the decision was reached after careful consideration of all the choices. Research tends to suggest that the reasons for present policy are lost in the mists of time and that it is pursued mainly by force of habit (see O'Barr and Conley 1992).

Money managers and even banks' trustee departments also come under pressure. They can find themselves with a conflict of interest. The Investor Responsibility Research Center knows how widely attempts at persuasion occur. The answer often suggested is for voting to be confidential, but this is widely opposed by some business groups precisely because it is likely to be effective. Proxy solicitors oppose it as it weakens their position; and there are certain technical problems.

Apart from the strenuous efforts of a handful of public sector pension funds and the work of some representative organizations, there are few signs of shareholder activism. On rare occasions a public-spirited private shareholder (with sufficient means) enters the lists. A notable example mentioned earlier is Robert Monks, who founded Institutional Shareholder Services in Washington DC after a successful career in industry and the Administration. Among his more spectacular forays (mentioned earlier) was a tilt at the board of Sears, a company whose results had been mediocre for some time. He failed to win a seat on the board, but his attempt hassled the company into defensive actions of a questionable nature and certainly drew the attention of the investing community to the alleged shortcomings of the board. It may have been pure coincidence, but the company made some radical structural changes not very long afterwards.

Among the representative organizations for individual shareholders, the United Shareholders Association (USA) is worth a further mention. USA targeted fifty companies for 1993 which will be subject to activism on a range of issues from USA members, including:

- adoption of confidential proxy voting;
- termination of poison pill devices;
- reform of executive compensation policies;
- delimitation of gold parachutes;
- ensuring the independence of board compensation and nominating committees.

USA claims record results for the 1992 proxy season with majority votes in favour of shareholder rights at Hartmax International Foods and Polaroid: 40 + per cent votes at twenty-four other companies; and agreement with fifteen other companies to update shareholder rights.

There seems little doubt that US management is angry at the hint of greater shareholder activism and perhaps a little frightened, judging by the vigour of its reaction. They may also be alarmed at the prospect of its becoming politicised. Sixty years ago they were emancipated by Federal legislation from domination by financiers, whose stakes in their businesses were severely limited if they were allowed at all. More recently, they have succeeded in getting many State legislatures to pass laws making take-overs more difficult—as if poison pills were not a sufficient delaying mechanism. This latest threat seems to them particularly dangerous because it is legitimate. If the owners of the business are not entitled to have their say about the stewardship of the board, who is?

They would argue that the temporary holders of share certificates bought as mere counters for trading purposes are not and cannot be true owners in any real sense of the word. But this argument would not apply to any shareholders or group of shareholders who deliberately set out to implement the alternative strategy—concentration rather than diversity—holding rather than selling—meaningful stakes rather than penny numbers—knowledge and loyalty rather than ignorance and unconcern. With such a policy which emphasizes VOICE as a useful alternative to EXIT goes a natural desire to reduce the legal constraints which now impede it, particularly as joint action by shareholders may on rare occasions be desirable. There are indeed already straws in the wind. Some big funds do intend to concentrate their portfolios. And 'concentrated' funds have been established as a vehicle for a number of investors (private or institutional) to get together so that the sums they put into any one company require attention and interest by all the parties.

The Stock Market

The US stock exchanges provide an important primary market for raising capital and are an essential piece of machinery for businesses over time to move smoothly away from family control. About $10 billion of equity was raised in 1970 and over $40 billion in 1988. A record $55 billion was raised in 1991 and $532 billion in debt instruments of one kind or another, including bonds and mortgage-backed securities. They and NASDAQ also provide the vital secondary markets in which securities are traded. At the end of 1990 there were 6,765 quoted companies in all (Congressional Research Service Report).

The development of businesses naturally leads to changes in their requirements for capital, so it is not surprising to see shares being repurchased or disappearing in a take-over. By the end of the 1980s, however, the retirement of equity from these causes greatly exceeded the raising of new capital. In 1988, $118 billion of equity was drained from the system (after $40 billion referred to in the last paragraph was taken into account (Lowenstein 1991a)).

This apotheosis of leveraging naturally led to interest costs absorbing more of corporate cash flows in 1989 than at any time since 1945: namely, over 25 per cent. In fact US industry finances itself mainly by retained earnings and debt; new issues of stock for cash only amount to about $25 billion per annum. Debt exploded in the 1980s—from 30.5 per cent (ratio of credit market debt to net worth at book value) to an all-time high of 56.2 per cent in 1990 (Blair 1991).

Trading on the NYSE was about three million shares per day in 1960; 14 per cent of the shares listed were traded during the year. By 1987 the total of transactions was 95 per cent (including those that took place away from the exchange). This was dwarfed by trading in the derivative instruments. Just one of these contracts, the S&P 500 stock index futures in Chicago, traded in March 1990 at an average weekly rate of $45 billion, twice the dollar volume of the NYSE.

As noted earlier, Lowenstein estimates that in 1987 the total cost of commissions and other trading expenses exceeded $25 billion—more than one-sixth of corporate earnings that year. Unfortunately high turn-over does not guarantee that liquidity will be maintained in times of finan-cial disruption. Less than 1 per cent of the total float was traded on Black Monday (19 Oct. 1987), that is, $21 billion, but the Dow fell over 500 points.

No analyst or stockbroker ever made a cent in the short term by advising clients to 'hold' even if that was the best advice (in the long term their honesty might well produce rewards). Action is the name of the game, with every morsel of information used to titillate clients' palates. The US trading machine is greased by soft dollars, that is, a rebate on commissions paid to a fund manager by the broker in the form of services of various kinds. The subject is shrouded in secrecy and the fund managers' employers often do not know, or shut their eyes; published guesses are that the soft dollar business is worth $1 billion per annum and involves a third of all institutional brokerage business. The practice encourages churning, but those who benefit of course defend it, and it is not illegal. The SEC published a release indicating permissible limits and investment managers who do it or intend to do it must make disclosure.

Take-overs

As we have seen, control of a US company can pass by replacing enough of the board through the proxy process, but the more usual route is by acquiring a majority of the votes through a tender offer.

Take-overs of all kinds rose from $12 billion in 1975 to $268 billion in 1988, the *annus mirabilis* for investment bankers. The figure has dropped sharply since; in 1991 it was less than $100 billion.

There is no equivalent to the UK's Takeover Panel to police the process, though the SEC imposes certain requirements and constraints; for example, the secret accumulation of stakes is regulated by Section 13(d)(1) of the Exchange Act, which requires beneficial owners to make a Schedule 13D filing with the SEC within ten days of crossing the 5 per cent threshold, and give full details of their identity and intentions. Changes of more than 1 per cent thereafter or of intentions must be promptly notified; but bigger stakes can legally be accumulated during the so-called '10-day window'. In the

Norlin case (1984), a 37 per cent stake had been accumulated before the notification date. Since then the introduction of poison pills has made it difficult to accumulate a large stake in the open market.

Contested bids, or as Americans call them, 'hostile takeovers', first became common in the 1960s.[6] They were, and are, an invitation to shareholders to accept an offer, whether or not the board recommended it. At first they were welcomed as an instrument for sharpening or replacing poor management, and their increasing numbers put corporate America on notice that management could not disregard shareholders' interests (for instance, by building up cash mountains whilst being mean with dividends). Naturally management did its best to persuade shareholders to refuse an offer, blandishing them with stock splits, raised dividends, and optimistic news. The tender offer was for control, not necessarily for total ownership. There used to be no US requirement that such an offer must extend to all the shareholders. Viewed in that light they were a step forward from proxy contests, which do not necessarily imply any shares changing hands.

Incidentally, unequal treatment for shareholders took various forms. It might mean paying a lower price to the minority shareholders after control had changed, or depressing the stock price by cutting the dividend or by other means. It could mean paying a premium to a predator for the stake he had accumulated (greenmail), or it could mean freezing the predator out by paying a premium for everyone else's shares (the Lollipop defence used in 1985 by UNOCAL against T. Boone Pickens). Fairness it appears is at a discount, but less than in those days. The SEC now requires an offer to be made to all shareholders, but not for all the shares.

The final step in the developing take-over saga came in the mid-1970s after Morgan Stanley decided to break with what had been accepted practice and act for a 'hostile' bidder. This marks an important turning-point. The focus was no longer a correction to a defective system of corporate governance—it was to do with empire-building: the skill of the management of the target company became an irrelevance (though it might affect the price). (A study by Herman and Lowenstein showed that there was a change about 1980. After then, broadly speaking—though there remain many exceptions—the target companies were as well managed (and sometimes better) than the bidders.) The dual nature of the market, which meant that there was generally a premium for control over the normal trading price, meant also that shareholders' attention was focused on the premium and scarcely on the quality of the management they were abandon-

---

[6] Much of this material is drawn from Lowenstein 1988.

ing by tendering their shares (or for that matter on the bidder's management).

Many professional fund managers thought the premium irresistible; indeed they felt legally obliged to accept a tender offer. It was as if a 'For sale' notice hung over most of corporate America.

With finance available mergers multiplied—from $12 billion in 1975 to $180 billion in 1985. The businesses sold that year were 10 per cent of the stocks listed on the New York Stock Exchange. But the effect of this activity—restructuring, other voluntary mergers, stock retirements, and so forth—were wider still.

Beleaguered corporate management cast around for ways of defending itself, and the ingenious legal profession produced some brilliant answers. In essence they were all based on a single principle. A company would set in place an arrangement which in normal times would lie dormant. Only a tender offer would activate it. Then, once the alarm bells rang, management could set the machinery in motion to change, grant extra shares, etc., etc., the result of which would be to make it virtually impossible for the bidder to succeed. These were the so-called 'poison pills'. An alternative strategy was 'Crown Jewels', that is, to give a third party an option to buy a prime asset to stop the bidder getting it. Yet another was a 'supermajority' provision, for example, a requirement that there be a 75 per cent majority to remove a board of directors. These devices were often challenged in the State courts (which might not necessarily produce consistent judgements), but generally they seem to have survived—at least in certain forms. And in most cases management introduced them without consulting the shareholders. 'Supermajority' provisions (which have in any case proved a less effective tactic) have to be approved by the shareholders.

Opinion is divided on whether the shareholders have benefited. Two things seem to be true—that entrenching management means that if there is a take-over bid the board can usually exact a bigger premium (from an opening price that would probably have been higher but for the protective mechanism). On the other hand, if no take-over bid is in the offing, shareholders fare worse if management is deeply entrenched. It must be remembered that two-tier offers were permitted and that any resultant non-accepting minority might be mercilessly squeezed at a later date: the principle of equal treatment for shareholders was and is notably absent. Poison pills have rarely if ever been swallowed—it is not their purpose, which is delay, but they have been effective in preventing hostile two-tier offers, which have all but disappeared. Companies with poison pills tend to fetch better prices than those without, because they strengthen management's bargaining position and bidders cannot go direct to shareholders over management's heads. On the other hand they may deter bidders from attacking a company where management is incompetent. They are based on the principle that it is right for management to nanny shareholders and understate the agency costs implicit in management's personal interests. To gain some idea of the nature of the fortifications that management can erect around their position please turn to Appendix 5C, where I have reproduced from Michael Jacobs' book (1991) the take-over defences actually implemented by Boise Cascade.

After poison pills has come legislation. There have been some recent instances of normally leaden-footed State legislatures galvanized into instant action to protect some beloved industrial enterprise at the behest of the unlikely combination of its management and its labour unions. (The protective legislation for Armstrong World Industries and Norton are cases in point.) Indeed, some State legislation has been so over-protective that many enterprises, in Pennsylvania for instance, exercised their right to opt out, perhaps through fear that it might affect their share price adversely.

The Pennsylvania Statute is one of the most extreme and enshrines in law an 'other constituencies' clause: that is, directors are empowered to take into account constituencies other than shareholders when they make decisions—especially relevant in a take-over bid. The directors are exempted from suit from *any* interested party. The Statute also contains a 'disgorging' provision which makes a failed bidder who sells his shares at a profit within eighteen months give it to the target company. Moreover, shareholders who acquire more than 20 per cent of the shares are disenfranchised unless 'disinterested' shareholders have first approved their purchase (of more than 20 per cent).

During the 1980s imaginative methods of financing take-over bids proliferated, of which the most prominent was the issuing of bonds graded as being below investment level (junk bonds). Very often these were used as part of the arrangements by which existing shareholders were replaced by management in some combination with those who financed them (management buy-outs/leveraged buy-outs). LBOs are not new in the USA and were known in the old days as 'bootstrapping'. What were new were their number, size, and sophistication.

The LBO movement started quite quietly and was conservatively managed. Kohlberg Kravis and Roberts (KKR) were one of the leading firms organizing them. The principles on which they operated were to avoid cyclical industries, ensure margins were adequate, and maintain careful supervision. From the point of view of corporate governance, the resulting structure could be compared either with a holding company or an active supervisory board whose meetings had substance. Operating management of the new entity (itself well motivated by its substantial equity stake) was generally given a free hand, but KKR (and other firms) stood in the background keeping a fatherly eye on the success of the new enterprise. Because of the conservatism of the original choice of targets many early LBOs were wildly successful. Companies which had been taken private were refloated a few years later at a vast profit.

One of the main points of divergence between the interests of shareholders and CEOs is the quality of growth. Shareholders want long-term increases in income and value and may be prepared to make short-term sacrifices to achieve it, provided it is soundly based. US shareholders are perhaps less patient than their German and Japanese counterparts in this respect, but they too have respect for increasing market share based on quality and design. That is, however, a slow grinding business, often beyond the span of office of a CEO. The temptation in the 1960s was to try to take the short cut—growth by diversification, aided by some accounting rules that often created an illusion of growth where little or none existed. With growth the CEO's status (and his rewards) could be enhanced rapidly; acquisition was quicker and easier than organic growth. However, the idea that management skills were always transferable across industries proved not to be true and led to the markets tending to price down conglomerates on the convoy principle—that is, a disparate group moves at the pace of the slowest main business in it. (Cf. the Japanese Keiretsu group, where the individual companies are sufficiently separate for this not to apply.)

By the 1980s, therefore, some of the unwieldy conglomerates assembled in the 1970s were looking vulnerable and duly became targets of 'bust up' LBOs (55 per cent of completed LBOs in 1988). Tears need not be shed; what investment banks had cobbled together in unholy conglomeration, LBOs might legitimately rend asunder. Some of the early break-up artists made fortunes.

All these well-publicized successes attracted more players into the game and competition became fiercer. Money was pumped in until at one time there was enough to buy 10 per cent of quoted companies. The prices rose to amazing levels, so the financial burdens on the new entities became heavier. Less attention was paid to the cyclical nature of business so that cash flows and profits could very easily become insufficient to service the debt. And supervision became laxer. The results of these excesses are well known and with us still—restructuring and bankruptcies for businesses, bad debts for bankers, junk bonds for investors living up to their name. Such movements come in waves. At the moment (1992) the tide is ebbing still because credit is short and memories of failure still vivid. Indeed, as I was correcting this draft the world-famous department store group Macy's sought the protection of Chapter 11 (the provision in the bankruptcy law which enables a company to seek protection from its creditors whilst the management formulates proposals for its future; some companies subsequently fail, but others 'come out of Chapter 11' and continue in business).

The effects are more widespread than first appears and are not confined to companies for which bids were actually made. Many others sought to render themselves unattractive by 'restructuring' and were aided and abetted in this by investment bankers. One said in my hearing at a public seminar in 1986, 'Restructure or our 26-year-olds will get you.' Restructuring or recapitalization meant borrowing vast sums (which were paid to share-holders), often at the same time retiring equity. The present shareholders had a windfall, but the company was often so weakened that it could not sustain a downturn in business. Academics who had preached the virtues of leveraging as a new faith, found gearing a dangerous god. Sad to say, the effects of the last decade have not yet worked themselves out.

This book is about corporate governance and it is unnecessary to explore the financial excesses of the 1980s in detail, fascinating though they are. Lowenstein, writing in 1988, was among the commentators who felt that whatever virtue there may have been at one time in using the market to secure management changes had long since been outweighed by the cost and damage inflicted on US industry by those who exploited apparent imperfections in the market to make massive short-term gains. Displacing poor management is one thing; replacing good management at great cost with a group that is no better, in a structure which has less industrial logic, is quite another.

iii. Commentary

It would not be fair to attribute the relative success or failure of US industry wholly to its system of corporate governance, any more than it would in other countries: it may not even be a main cause. There is simply no certain way of knowing. As elsewhere commentators have identified many other contributing factors such as the deficiencies of the educational system, the insidious corruption of the political system, and the excessive use and cost of the legal system, and even medical costs. A further cause may be the cost of capital, which is high compared with some leading competitors (Jacobs

1991): this in itself may lead to shorter investment horizons. And yet, with all these alleged handicaps, the USA still has some of the finest companies and best technology in the world, able to hold their own in a fiercely competitive industrial environment. As this is so it is difficult to argue that externalities are the prime cause of relative US industrial decline. We must look inside companies themselves for at least some of the causes. One possibility, which lies outside the scope of this paper, is that US companies are not making as good a use of people as they might; Japanese success (since they have virtually no natural resources) must owe much to this skill. People are their only resource. Technical skills are a subset of this, but much depends on how people are trained, led, and motivated. When all is said and done, however, many commentators have reached the conclusion that it is not sufficient to blame or give credit to the leadership of particular US companies. There is a question mark over the *system* of corporate governance—under which companies are managed and controlled.

When times are good and industry is flourishing, no one takes an interest in corporate governance in general or in particular boards—however ominous the signs or flawed the hero in charge. As Margaret Blair puts it, 'In good times, with markets growing, capital cheap, and competition limited, almost any governance system can seem to work well. The test comes when markets are flat or shrinking, capital costs are high, and competition is tough' (Blair 1991: 13). This test is here now. That is why there is so much interest in the subject.

Having said that there is no system of corporate governance in the world that is perfect. Companies like people are born, grow, and die. In the economic sphere what needs to be emphasized is the capacity for renewal and the avoidance of waste, in an ever more competitive environment. It would be facile to suggest copying our successful competitors' systems, since these are part of their heritage and are themselves imperfect, and sometimes more fragile than contemporary success would lead us to suppose. Instead we need to look at each and every system, including that of the USA, in the light of the two universal criteria, which, as we have seen, are surprisingly straightforward: dynamism and accountability.

Dynamism

We have already noted—but it is convenient to restate it—that management, however individual or collective, must be able to drive the business forward without undue bureaucratic interference, or fear of litigation, or fear of displacement. This is the first and crucial principle for an entrepreneurial free-market economy in a competitive world. This is or should be the management's right and its charter. One can only have sympathy when it is infringed.

The first potential source of infringement of this Charter is government. No one doubts, however, that it is the government's task (whether at Federal or State level) to hold the balance between the competing interests in the economy—producers and consumers; employers and employees; providers and users of capital. I encountered very few complaints from the CEOs' side that government or State law as manifested by bureaucratic interference was considered an undue or unfair handicap, even though many governmental requirements impose costs (c.g. in respect of the environment). I did find and have quoted severe doubts about the boundary between State and Federal law. 'The race to the bottom' is not universally admired.

The ground is less certain in regard to litigation. The contrast between the USA and Japan could not be greater. In the USA the law is seen as a unifying force, a way of ensuring equality for all the heterogeneous elements in society. In Japan with its homogenous society to go to law is regarded as a shameful failure of relationships. Lawyers play little part in company affairs—except perhaps in their relationships with foreigners. I noted earlier the cost of lawyers in the USA, but have seen no evidence of their value or the effect on behaviour of the fear of litigation. At one time the business judgement rule provided directors with a nearly impregnable defence against lawsuits alleging they had made a poor decision. In the case of *Smith* v. *Van Gorkom* a considerable dent was made because the Court ruled that the process by which the decision had been reached was inadequate. Over the last few years cases have moved further down this track—only for judges to retreat of late. The rule still lives, dented it is true. Perhaps the feeling that litigation lurks in the wings is pervasive; it might be worth a behavioural study. The Delaware amendment in 1986, noted above, also put into corporations' hands a powerful weapon to protect its directors from lawsuits. And if it can be obtained in the market there is always directors' and officers' insurance, expensive as it is.

There was much talk about outside directors being inhibited from accepting office because the threat of litigation outweighed any potential reward, though it was impossible to measure the effects. My own judgement is that it is an element to be considered, but not yet a matter for deep concern. If it became really difficult to find good candidates it would be truly serious because sound boards are the keystone of the structure.

As regards displacement, US CEOs do not in general look more vulnerable than their counterparts elsewhere—except in a take-over. There is a great deal of discussion on the effects of the fear of take-over, and it is difficult to determine to what degree it exists, and what its effects are. To those who deny the existence of what they cannot measure, it is insignificant. From many conversations I have had, this conclusion would be mistaken, though how much fear of take-over matters depends on many variables, such as the vulnerability of the company, the personality of the CEO and his age, the stockholding position. Certainly Americans' traditional robustness about picking themselves up and starting again would suggest that fear of displacement would not generally loom large—were it not for the vigour of their defence against bids, often far in excess of what might profit their shareholders, not just in the short or medium term but on any reasonable timescale.

There is an interesting analysis of this issue in Porter 1992. Porter links the capital allocative function of the market with the investment decision process in a company. To my mind the main issue is one of time-scale. It is the speed with which the market wants returns (or at least a company's perception of the speed) that exerts pressure, under fear ultimately of displacement. The evidence I have for such an assertion is thin enough and rests on the many statements made to me about the relative strength of such pressures when a company can be bought in the market, and when it cannot (by people who have experienced the transition). We are dealing here with a psychological issue, in which the subjects may not themselves realize how deeply their thinking has been affected. A robust CEO who prides himself on his macho view of life may assert vehemently that market pressures mean nothing to him; he invests what he and his board feel essential for the long-term well-being of the company. And he may be wrong simply because subconsciously he has set his sights too low, in unknowing recognition of what his instinct tells him the market will stand. The important point to make is that the market, which in some ways acts as a spur, in others acts as a shackle, because of the complexity of managerial motivations.

Business may be an economic activity, but man is not just an economic animal. He looks to his job for other satisfactions—the pride of construction, the warmth of camaraderie, and the excitement of mental stimulation. It is a source of power and influence and a means of recognition. These multiple satisfactions account for people working long hours after they have accumulated more riches than they could spend in a dozen extravagant lifetimes. They are the cause of CEOs defending their territory and achievements so fiercely, often in the face of economic logic. These are the reasons why the fear of take-over is so damaging—it absorbs the nervous energy that would otherwise go into the proper task of driving the business forward. My own view is that on balance the excessive fear of take-overs has been damaging, though many a fiercely combative CEO will assert that he has never been deflected an inch from his chosen course as a result of it. What we do know is that the Japanese and Germans do quite well without it.

Be that as it may, what are we to make of the economic consequences of take-overs? It is easy to accumulate a mass of literature on US take-overs and take-over defences and funding, some set out as blueprints, others as factual accounts, and others as drama like Bruck's 'The Predators' Ball'. The language is colourful: 'Poison pills', 'Junk bonds', 'White Knights', and 'Black Knights'; and many of the principal players larger than life, dealing in billions. Some are disgraced; many bask in luxury. Is the US the richer? The creation of real wealth can only come from investment and production, but the transfer of wealth is justified if in fact a better use of resources ensues. Hard evidence on whether $2 + 2$ sum out to 10, 5, 4, 3, or less, is hard to come by. But there is no doubt that in the opinion of many US commentators (Eisenberg 1989 is one example of many), a large number of good businesses have been destroyed and many others emasculated

It is part of the function of the market in the USA to re-allocate resources to those who will make best use of them—over a reasonable time-scale. The time-scales of decision between investor and industry are totally different. An investor may decide to switch from a chemical company into textiles and achieve the change in a single telephone call. Company management, hemmed in by its present plant, people, and commitments, may take a decade to change direction radically. A system which places so much emphasis on shareholders' *immediate* values may be at a competitive disadvantage with others which take a longer-term view. The impression with which I am left about US corporate governance is that the entrepreneurial spirit is free but not quite as free as it thinks it is; and the proof of that can be seen on American streets and in American shops any day of the week.

Accountability

The greater executives' freedom of action, the greater the need for account-ability. The two go hand in hand. The concept of accountability in this context derives to some extent from its counterpart in the political sphere, where it is the main prophylactic against tyranny. A strong board and vigilant shareholders may be crucial in stopping a dynamic and powerful CEO from running amok. In business, accountability is essential as a means of maintaining standards of competence. The way in which it is exercised is of secondary importance: it may be quite informal and private as in Germany or Japan (though their styles and arrangements would not suit the USA or UK).

The general feeling in the USA among thoughtful commentators is that US management is often not accountable enough. The board does not often work properly, and shareholders seldom work at all: management may fear the market but its tendency will be to entrench itself in the ways described earlier and reward itself well enough to reduce the financial consequences of displacement. I have chosen one of the many quotations on the subject selected by Professor Lowenstein (1988):

Directors have some information but not enough. Besides, most of them have other things on their minds. Inside directors work full-time for particular parts of the company, and the great majority of outside directors have other jobs. The outside director has many reasons—practical, philosophical, emotional—for playing a more passive role than the one we espouse. It is easier to be a permissive parent than a disciplined one. And in their permissive and passive stance, most boards . . . have a tendency (1) not to appraise the performance of CEOs critically enough; (2) to overestimate the ability of managers to manage different kinds of businesses well; (3) to allow managers to build enterprises that may be too large and diversified for anyone to manage well; and (4) to wait too long to respond to ongoing political, social, and economic change. (Quoted from W. Knowlton and I. M. Millstein, 'Can the Board of Directors Help the American Corporation Earn the Immortality it Holds so Dear?' (Apr. 1987).)

We can appreciate the gloomy summary at the beginning of Jacob 1991:

Lack of communication prevents investors from understanding management's long-term goals and objectives. Shareholders trade stocks so often and hold such broadly diversified portfolios that they cannot possibly keep up with the business activities of the companies they own. Because most US investors are detached from the businesses they fund, they rely on outward manifestations of what is really going on within the company; namely, quarterly earnings and other accounting measures of performance. These numbers only measure the past; they do not explain the future. When they are dissatisfied with corporate performance shareholders sell stock, rather than trying to discern the causes of poor performance and using their collective voice to communicate their concerns to management.

Companies exacerbate the problem by stacking their boards with directors handpicked by top management and insulating themselves from the oversight traditionally provided by shareholders and lenders. In recent years companies have consistently disenfranchised their owners; they want access to capital with no strings attached. But a lack of trust makes investors hesitant to fund projects with no visible results for extended periods of time.

The problem breaks down into two parts, the first and more important of which is the quality of US boards, *as an entity*. There is always a danger of making the mistake that because the quality of the people individually is high, the quality of the board *as an entity* necessarily follows suit. It does not. Many a company has foundered despite having good talent aboard. The dynamics of the board are largely in the hands of the CEO, who can make or mar it. In my conversations with many able ones I was struck by the way they seem to fall into two camps: those who were very powerful and admitted it, and those who were very powerful and did not—though I cannot say with certainty which group used its board better! If some boards work better than others it is because the CEO wills it.

All the devices of recent years, like audit, compensation, and nomination committees, have as an unspoken objective the task of improving the board's dynamics, of giving the outside directors a real role, of spreading the flow of information. The potential importance of the nomination committee is sometimes underestimated by those who do not understand the far-reaching consequences of the CEO's grip of patronage. The acid test of the balance of any board is its capacity to stand up to the CEO when really necessary. Of how many US boards is this actually true today? This capacity does not imply constant friction but the degree of reciprocal respect between CEO and director necessary for real accountability.

The second part of the problem concerns the accountability of the board to shareholders. In the USA, as elsewhere, weak CEOs and weak boards allow companies to drift and decline in a welter of reciprocal mediocrity. In cases where shareholdings are widely dispersed the Berle and Means' analysis (1932) is still valid—no one has the interest and few the knowledge to intervene. Now when shareholdings are becoming more concentrated the analysis no longer holds—there are many signs of action. In looking at the vast panorama of US companies and the regiments of institutional shareholders, it is clear that at the moment action is confined to few of the latter in relation to relatively few of the former. But the situation is changing and to that we now turn.

iv. Developments

More Effective Boards?

Given that Americans see their system as being one of 'Board-centred accountability', the first question for them is how to make boards work better, given that the concept of a supervisory board has been little discussed. This largely turns on the role of the outside directors.

The problems they feel need to be faced are, first, how to ensure the directors are truly independent without destroying the cohesion of the board. This has implications for selection and patronage to shift the focus of directors' loyalty from the CEO to the company. Of course, this strikes directly at the CEO's power base. Even so, if the issue is not faced, it is safe to predict that all other changes will prove disappointing, since the vital balance between CEO and board is bound to be wrong.

Secondly, there is the clutch of issues concerned with the board's dynamics. Should the CEO cease to be chairman? If he does continue to fill both roles, should the independent directors have a leader of their own who can call them together for a separate meeting when needs be? A CEO may find himself by accident or design behind an invisible moat created by his power and patronage, which bad news cannot easily cross. Such insulation is potentially dangerous, and if it is coupled with a lack of integrity may be most damaging to the company. The plain fact is that if the CEO does not run his board with integrity the directors stand little chance. What integrity means is proper selection of the board, proper presentation of the important issues supported by the necessary background information, proper conduct of meetings, and proper levels of remuneration. Many commentators believe that this can be better achieved if the chairman's role is separated from that of the CEO. But the acid test is the capacity of the board to stand up to the CEO not routinely but when it should.

The Competitiveness Sub-Council Report charts a particular path:

(a) Boards should insure they have processes in place which enable them to function independently in their task of monitoring and evaluating corporate performance. Key aspects of this independence include:

(i) establishing an appropriate structure for the operation of the board including the number of directors to serve and their qualifications, the selection and accountabilities of committees and their chairs, a process for selecting, where appropriate and necessary, a director(s) with special responsibilities, and the establishment of special requirements such as age or term limits for directors;

(ii) establishing appropriate procedures at the full board level to oversee the formulation and realization of the long-term strategic, financial, and organizational goals of the corporation;

(iii) establishing appropriate committees comprised solely of independent directors to oversee the auditing, compensation and nominating responsibilities of the board; and

(iv) establishing appropriate procedures to insure the board receives appropriate information from managers upon which to base decisions, devotes sufficient time to the review and discussion of such information, and is able to independently evaluate such information.

(b) Boards should establish criteria and procedures for evaluating their own processes and performance, as well as that of the CEO. These criteria should be based on a clear understanding of the board's accountability to shareholders and, as appropriate, to various other constituents of the corporation.

(c) Boards should be informed of and approve management practices to impart information to shareholders while insuring against insider training abuses. Where appropriate and, considering the resources involved, designees of the company should hold periodic meetings with shareholders.

Heavy emphasis is being placed on the directors' monitoring role. The distinguished head of the Court of Chancery of Delaware, William T. Allen, the Chancellor, put the point thus (1992):

Conventional wisdom says that boards should select senior management, create incentive compensation schemes and then step back and watch the organisation prosper. In addition, board members should be available to act as advisers to the CEO when called upon and they should be prepared to act during a crisis: an emergency succession problem, threatened insolvency or a management buyout proposal, for example.

This view is, in my opinion, badly deficient. It ignores a most basic responsibility: the duty to monitor the performance of senior management in an informed way. Outside directors should function as active monitors of corporate management, not just in crisis, but continually; they should have an active role in the formulation of the long-term strategic, financial and organisation goals of the corporation and should approve plans to achieve those goals; they should as well engage in the periodic review of short- and long-term performance according to plan and be prepared to press for correction when in their judgment there is need.

For outside directors to assume a more active role in corporate monitoring may require implementing changes of many kinds, but most basically of all it requires that outside directors understand that their duty requires more of them than simply acting as advisers and requires more than acting once a crisis has arisen. It requires that directors understand and assume the burden of active long-term monitoring.

Effective long-term monitoring also requires a sympathetic and productive relationship between the outside board members and the CEO, and the acknowledgement by the CEO of the legitimacy of the monitoring role and its requisites. More than this, effective sympathetic monitoring requires a commitment of time and resources especially information, and sometimes independent advice. A few hours a quarter may satisfy the role of passive adviser in good times; it is never sufficient to meet the obligation to act as a monitor. Furthermore, in my opinion, the demands of the director position, if properly understood, are inconsistent with service on an impressively long list of boards.

The focus of attention on the way US boards work will not go away, though as the economy picks up it will inevitably become less sharp. In times of prosperity anything goes; it takes adversity to highlight weaknesses. My view of the developments is that nothing really radical—like a two-tier system—is on the agenda. What is likely is a heightened awareness of the importance of the sound structure and good dynamics.

Another Take-over Boom?

It is impossible not to sympathize with CEOs who see a lifetime's work threatened for little sound economic cause, except perhaps a sacrifice on the altar of 'shareholders' immediate values'. The concentration on the short term, which provides an opportunity for the take-over artist to exploit any passing market imperfection, is surely not to the country's long-term benefit. CEOs have defended themselves in the ways indicated earlier, but that is not necessarily the right long-term response. Some CEOs do rip off their corporations. Some management ought to be replaced, and take-overs ought to be available as the instrument of last resort. Take-overs were excessively easy and the response has been to make them excessively difficult. Is it beyond the wit of man to devise a better regulated system which produces a better balance?

Using take-overs to replace managers is an unnecessarily expensive and illogical solution anyway, but essential if neither boards nor shareholders have played their parts adequately, and the company is decaying.

The takeover boom of the 1980s did as we have seen produce its own reaction—in the wake of poison pills and State legislation. This in turn has produced a counter-reaction exemplified by the programme of the United Shareholders Association designed to protect and enhance shareholder rights. A whole series of judgements in the courts has swung this way and that. At the moment (1992/3) the economic and financial circumstances are not propitious for another take-over boom anyway—too many people are licking their wounds from the last one. So the groundswell of feeling that was all for putting a little grit in the gearbox has abated. Many commentators seem to think that any further tampering with the take-over mechanism would be worse than the disease and would introduce an element of rigidity more injurious to the economy than the exuberance of hyperactivity. But it is as well to remember who makes a living from restructurings: Wall Street is the abattoir of industry and butchers, generally speaking, are carnivores.

More Active Shareholders?

Until recently the very idea of shareholders being able to monitor companies effectively was considered impractical; the ghosts of Berle and Means still haunted the debate. But the concentration of holdings in the hands of the institutions has gradually changed that perception. And the nearer the possibility of real accountability has become, the more the unaccountable have resented it. Whether a more active role is practical and whether it would actually lead to improved corporate performance are subjects that are widely discussed, but so far there is more heat than light. Many commentators believe that actions taken to enhance management account-ability to directors or shareholders increase shareholder value. But these are early days and we cannot yet see the subject in proper perspective.

Having said that, there is a wealth of evidence about US disquiet over shareholders' unwillingness or inability to ensure that accountability to them is meaningful. Martin Lipton, the prominent lawyer who invented poison pills, produced a quinquennial scheme to improve accountability: the Honorable Edward V. Regan, Comptroller of New York State, lodged a proposal with the SEC that shareholders should be able to have a statement included in a company's proxy material criticizing management (after prior discussion: management would have a right of reply). Robert Monks, the former architect of ERISA and long-time critic of non-performing manage-ment, has been deeply concerned about the shareholders' role. At the end of the day, however, few really advocate legislation except on minor matters.

The disquiet is far from universal. One CEO told me there was nothing wrong with the system: 'There are recourse options which are very effective when they are used.' Neither he nor most others want to banish take-overs, and as we saw earlier the combination of State legislation and poison pills has made hostile bids more difficult to mount. To the extent that that is so, the need both for better boards and some element of active shareholder monitoring becomes greater. The Competitiveness Sub-Council Report recognized the point, recommending:

(a) That institutional investors seek to influence the management of corporations and make corporations accountable for poor performance through their boards of directors by using the processes discussed in this paper, but not by attempts to 'manage' the companies.
(b) That measures be adopted to open up the process to improve communication among shareholders and between shareholders and corporations. In this context the proposed SEC rules facilitating such communication were discussed though not critiqued. Subsequently, the Sub-Council members indicated their approval of these rules except for a few members who voiced their disagreement.
(c) That companies and shareholders recognize the potential for improved, constructive shareholder monitoring as employees acquire and hold increased amounts of stock of the firms in which they work. In the 1000 companies where employees have significant holdings, these employees now own an average of 12 per cent of stock—with stakes in Proctor and Gamble, Chevron, and many other corporations even higher. Employees will soon own an average of 15 per cent of the stock in these corporations as savings and share ownership plans expand. Participation on the plant floor could turn to participa-tion in the boardroom as a critical mass of employee ownership approaches.

Employee/shareholders are one of the new shareholder groups most likely to play an increased and potentially positive role in corporate governance.

(d) That no change be made in the current restrictions on the corporate holdings of common stock by various types of institutional investors. Under these restrictions defined benefit plans covered by the Employee Retirement Income Security Act (ERISA), mutual funds, and bank collective investment funds are prohibited from investing more than a limited amount of their assets in one company. ERISA also requires that plan assets be diversified; many plans, however, own stock in more companies than are needed for optimal diversification, and others are taking the ultimate diversification step of replicating indexes such as the S&P 500.

The Sub-Council recognized that action was growing, but not extensively:

Shareholder Monitoring in the Corporate Governance Process

Shareholder resolutions involving corporate governance procedures are now amassing an increasingly sizable percentage—frequently in excess of 30 per cent—of the vote at annual meetings. Thus, shareholder activism as to voting procedures and board organisation is now an established fact. What is more important, however, is monitoring the performance of corporations, not just by boards of directors, but also by informed and effective shareholders.

An evolving system of institutional oversight clearly appears to be working. Some public pension funds and shareholder organisations have begun to focus their attention on specific company financial performance. These groups have increased their participation in shareholder meetings, in drafting statements, but mainly through increasingly successful use of the proxy voting system. A new institutional investor model—which has been referred to as 'political'—embodies an approach in which active investors seek to change corporate policy by amassing voting support from dispersed shareholders. While still only marginally focused on performance, it is gaining support among corporations, boards of directors and institutional asset managers. Through a well defined public process, 'insurgents' seek to educate shareholder voters and propose alternatives to the policies of 'incumbents'. The process is still largely unorganised and episodic. But the ensuing debate, when focused on issues relating to performance, promotes an informed, participatory and substantive approach to institutional investor oversight of management, without pursuing the more acrimonious destructive transactions-based market for corporate control of the 1980s.

Informal oversight tactics available to shareholders are remarkably varied. There are numerous examples that have led to changes in corporate governance, while the more important ones have led to changes in management and performance. For example: active private and public institutional shareholders have solicited votes for a proposal urging a company to engage in a spin off; articulated an alternative business plan and showed that the company can do better by sticking to its core business; and supported independent director nominees. . . .

Shareholder oversight is being conducted by just a few organisations. Some question whether institutional investors have the expertise or the will to provide an optimal level of corporate performance oversight. The Sub-Council takes note of this. It believes that optimal oversight requires heightened responsibility from all parties in the corporate governance process. The quality of the leadership and expertise of institutional investors is as important as the quality of management and expertise of the corporations whose securities they own. As the focus shifts to the performance of the corporations, the spotlight must also be directed on the management of the activist institutions.

Certain public and private funds and other asset managers already actively monitor their investments and do not hesitate to express their views on company plans and performance. There are signs that others are adding analytical and communications capabilities, which is a welcome development. On the other hand, most do not generally make use of the communications and monitoring opportunities already available. They have not yet developed the staff or consultants necessary to monitor actively, nor are they expected to.

All this is interesting, but there is room for doubt about its real significance. We already know, for instance, that those who are required by the ERISA rules to vote, do so; but the rules cannot make them care. We know that many institutions' holdings, whether in index funds or not, are so fragmented that to all intents and purposes the Berle and Means analysis is still valid for them. We observe that private sector pension funds seldom play an active part, presumably on the 'Dog does not eat dog' principle. We can see no evidence of institutions wanting to get together (though as the SEC rules on this have only just been relaxed it is perhaps early to judge).

The institutions may think again about their portfolio strategy. It really is odd that so many trustees put up with 'active' managers who do not understand what they buy, who trade excessively, and who under-perform the index. 'Active' management should surely move steadily towards concentration—larger parcels of fewer stocks, traded less. The shift cannot take place overnight because it means adding to the skills of short-term market trading a better understanding of fundamental values and the quality of management. Communication between company and investor should improve as it would matter more to both, and the economies realized by less trading should release resources for it.

The alternative strategy—passive—means indexation, which is cheap but 'safer'. It is followed because managers know that three-quarters of active portfolio investors in any year do worse. But indexed fund-holders are long-term share owners, so they too have the platform on which to build an interest in corporate governance as CalPERS does. Small funds can only act effectively if they too get together. For institutions, therefore, the commentators' message boils down to this, 'Get big or get together.'

The fourth and final range of issues concerns standards of behaviour but these generally emerge in commentaries as a sort of moral body dressed up in lawyers' or economists' clothing. The issue of integrity is a prime example. Clearly boards cannot work properly without it; nor can other parts of the system. Extraneous pressures on managers of funds, for example, both in the private and public sector to vote their stock in a certain way can present them with difficult conflicts of interest and strain their duty to the beneficiaries. There again, to talk of integrity in the fetid atmosphere of a contested take-over bid would be to excite contemptuous ribaldry. It is not for foreigners to judge, but US commentators often seem concerned not just about the effectiveness of parts and processes of the system, but about their rightness. It makes one wonder if there may be one of those sharp reactions which periodically convulse American society. One example of an argument with such moral overtones concerns confidential voting. Without it shareholders can always be subject to pressure—sometimes extreme—political or commercial, which is covert and as such un-American. In US society as in many others it is common to cut every issue up into little parcels neatly labelled: economic—political—legal—moral. But life is not like that, and corporate governance which means much to many is in its effect a large piece of life. Citizens can no more ignore issues of integrity than the accuracy of costings. What thoughtful US commentators seem to suggest is that the long-term prosperity of industry requires at its heart a system of corporate governance which produces a reasonable balance between the often conflicting interests of the parties, and that one of the ingredients which makes it possible to strike and maintain that balance is integrity.

The Clinton Administration

This chapter was written during the last quarter of President Bush's administration, when it was too early to gauge which way his successor would want to go were there to be a change of administration. The immediate Bush legacy in corporate governance was a change to SEC rules which facilitated shareholder activism in a modest way. There were relatively few clues about changes in policy. The United Shareholders Association reported (Sept./Oct. 1992) Clinton's concern about CEO pay and the accountability of management to shareholders, but there was no whiff in the air of fundamental reform. It was common gossip during the campaign that some of corporate America had supported his candidacy. He will have many other more pressing issues to face and may not be in any hurry to antagonize American businessmen on one like corporate governance which does not carry wide popular support. There is a feeling that US industry is leaner and fitter than it was and that Japan and Germany have troubles of their own; even so, the concern about imperfections in the US system will not be easily dispelled. It is therefore possible that what may emerge in the next four years is a slow measured series of changes along the lines indicated in the previous paragraphs. It will be Webbs' 'Inevitability of Gradualness' in a new setting.

Appendix 5A. *Institutional Investor Holdings in US Corporations: Average % Holdings by Industry Grouping, 1987–1990*

Industry Group	Average institutional holdings as % outstanding stock				% change 1987–90
	1987	1988	1989	1990	
Aerospace	54.6	58.0	55.5	55.6	1.0
Automotive	53.8	52.1	52.3	52.2	− 1.7
Banks	39.6	41.5	44.4	43.6	4.0
Chemicals	55.7	55.2	54.6	54.7	− 1.0
Conglomerate	42.6	50.3	48.6	53.5	10.9
Consumer	48.8	49.0	47.6	51.1	2.3
Container	46.1	41.0	39.3	40.6	− 5.5
Electrical	58.6	59.0	58.9	58.8	0.2
Food	43.8	42.0	43.3	41.5	− 2.3
Fuel	46.5	47.0	46.6	51.6	5.1
Health Care	50.0	52.0	53.2	54.5	4.5
Housing	41.4	36.0	44.9	45.9	4.5
Leisure	43.4	44.0	44.6	52.0	8.6
Manufacturing	53.2	53.0	56.1	57.7	4.5
Metals	46.5	43.0	46.6	50.1	3.6
Non-bank Finance	50.9	54.0	58.2	54.2	3.3
Office Equipment	53.0	54.0	53.2	55.3	2.3
Paper	55.7	58.0	59.2	62.2	6.5
Publishing/TV	44.5	39.0	42.4	40.2	− 4.3
Retailing	45.1	43.0	48.6	53.5	8.4
Services	45.0	48.0	49.1	47.1	2.1
Telecommunications	36.6	35.0	39.8	37.5	0.9
Transportation	54.9	58.0	53.1	61.1	6.2
Utilities	34.5	35.0	36.3	39.2	4.7
Average: All corporations in Top 1,000 Group	46.6	46.8	48.1	50.6	2.9

Source: C. K. Brancato, *Institutional Investors in Capital Markets: 1991 update* (Columbia, Sept. 1991), based on *Business Week*'s Database on Top 1,000 Corporations ranked by stock market value.

Appendix 5B. *Top Fifteen Pension Funds with Investments in Equities*

Fund	Indexed equities	Total equities ($ million)*	Total assets ($ million)	Indexed equities (as % of total equities)	Indexed equities (as % of total assets)
At 30 September 1990					
New York State	13,914	18,938	43,737	73.5	31.8
California Employees	13,800	21,508	54,000	64.1	25.6
New State Teachers	13,019	14,145	26,689	92.0	48.8
California State Teachers	9,175	11,122	30,140	82.5	30.4
AT&T	7,639	16,312	38,876	46.8	19.6
Florida State Board	5,868	8,863	19,268	66.2	30.5
General Electric	3,641	9,386	27,108	38.8	13.4
NYNEX	3,372	6,300	14,383	53.5	23.4
Du Pont	3,246	6,182	17,728	52.5	18.3
Ford Motor	3,000	9,295	20,800	32.3	14.4
Virginia Retirement	2,869	5,434	10,687	52.8	26.8
Maryland State	2,485	3,067	10,761	81.0	23.1
Washington State Board	2,439	3,800	12,839	64.2	19.0
Southwestern Bell	2,382	4,249	8,303	56.1	28.7
Minnesota State Board	2,188	5,010	12,098	43.7	18.1
Average				60.0	24.8
Total	89.037	143.611	347,417		
% of $ total				62.0	25.6

Fund	Indexed equities	Total equities ($ million)*	Total assets ($ million)	Indexed equities (as % of total equities)	Indexed equities (as % of total assets)
At 30 September 1988					
New York State	12,600	17,550	37,920	71.8	33.2
New York State Teachers	9,520	9,800	22,780	97.1	41.8
California State Teachers	9,290	11,590	24,720	80.2	37.6
AT&T	8,770	15,780	28,690	55.6	30.6
New York City	7,650	12,790	35,540	59.8	21.5
NYNEX	4,110	6,530	11,260	62.9	36.5
California Public Employees	4,110	20,170	45,940	20.4	90.0
General Electric	3,700	9,700	21,100	38.1	17.5
Florida State Board	3,320	6,020	14,410	55.2	23.0
Teamsters, Central	2,670	3,630	8,470	73.6	31.5
Ford Motor	2,500	8,600	15,100	29.1	16.6
Minnesota State Board	2,390	3,490	9,660	68.5	24.7
Maryland State	1,810	2,780	8,710	65.1	20.8
Virginia Supplemental	1,740	4,260	8,040	40.9	21.6
Exxon	1,720	2,140	350	80.4	49.1
Average				59.9	33.1
Total	75.900	134.830	292,690		
% of $ total				56.3	25.9

* Total equities are total defined benefit plan equities.

Source: Brancato and Columbia Institutional Investor Project. Based on data from *Pensions and Investments*.

Appendix 5C. *Take-over Defences: An Example (from Jacobs 1991)*

Exhibit 3.1

Boise Cascade Takeover Defenses

Charter Provisions

Classified board	Directors divided into three classes with overlapping three-year terms. Thus, it would take two years to win control, even if someone owned a majority of the shares.
Fair price provision	Requires a bidder to pay all shareholders a 'fair price' (the highest price it paid for any shares acquired during a certain period before it commenced its offer) unless the offer is approved by a majority of the board not affiliated with the acquirer or of the disinterested outstanding shares. A vote of 80 percent of the outstanding shares is required to amend or repeal this provision.
No shareholder action by written consent	Prevents shareholders from taking action without a meeting, and only the board may call a meeting (see Bylaw Provisions below).
Eliminated cumulative voting in 1984	Cumulative voting enables minority shareholders to win token board representation by cumulating their votes for one or two candidates rather than spreading votes across the entire slate.
Blank check preferred stock	Preferred stock for which the board has broad authority to set voting, dividend, conversion and other rights. May be used for ordinary business purposes such as acquisitions, but may be used in connection with a shareholder rights plan (poison pill) or issued to a friendly party to block a takeover.

Bylaw Provisions

Shareholders prohibited from calling a meeting	Guarantees that only the board can call a meeting of the shareholders, even if a majority of the shares seek a meeting to oust the board, consider an offer or for any other reason.

Board-Adopted Protections

'Shareholder rights plan' (poison pill)	If triggered by the board during a hostile bid, allows shareholders (except for the bidder) to double their holdings at a bargain rate, causing such dilution of the bidder's equity and voting power that to continue with the takeover would be economically unviable.

Other Corporate Governance Features

Golden parachutes	Twenty-six executives have severance agreements contingent on a change in control, as of the 1990 annual meeting. The value of the top five was $10 million, if they were fired, demoted or resigned within a certain period after the change in control. While cushioning executives against job loss, parachutes also make a takeover more expensive.
Pension parachute	Provides that surplus pension assets be distributed to employees and retirees if an attempt is made to terminate or merge the pension plan or transfer its assets within a specified period after a change in control. This prevents an acquirer from using the money to help finance the acquisition even though *excess* assets legally belong to the company.
Limited director liability	Charter amendment eliminates personal financial liability of directors for breaches of the fiduciary duty of care.
Director indemnification	Charter amendment indemnifies officers and directors against legal expenses and/or judgments incurred as a result of actual or threatened lawsuits relating to their conduct. In addition, the company has indemnification contracts with certain officers and directors.
Employee stock ownership plan	The company's ESOP holds 15 percent of the voting power, sufficient to block a takeover under Delaware's anti-takeover law.

State Anti-takeover Law

Delaware three-year business combination (freeze out)	Bars a business combination with a shareholder owning more than 15 percent of the company for three years after the 15-percent acquisition unless the acquirer had board approval, acquires at least 85 percent of the shares or the combination is approved by the board and two-thirds of the outstanding disinterested shares at a special meeting (which cannot be called by the shareholders). This prevents someone from being able to finance a transaction, because lenders will not fund a buyout in which the bidder cannot secure title to the company's assets.

Source: Investor Responsibility Research Center.

Appendix 5D. *Recommendations of Treadway Commission on Audit Committees (1987)*

1. The board of directors of all public companies should be required by SEC rule to establish audit committees composed solely of independent directors.
2. Audit committees should be informed, vigilant, and effective overseers of the financial reporting process and the company's internal controls.
3. All public companies should develop a written charter setting forth the duties and responsibilities of the audit committee. The board of directors should approve the charter, review it periodically, and modify it as necessary.
4. Audit committees should have adequate resources and authority to discharge their responsibilities.
5. The audit committee should review management's evaluation of factors related to the independence of the company's public accountant. Both the audit committee and management should assist the public accountant in preserving his independence.
6. Before the beginning of each year, the audit committee should review management's plans for engaging the company's independent public accountant to perform management advisory services during the coming year, considering both types of services that may be rendered and the projected fees.
7. All public companies should be required by SEC rule to include in their annual reports to stockholders a letter signed by the chairman of the audit committee describing the committee's responsibilities and activities during the year.
8. Management should advise the audit committee when it seeks a second opinion on a significant accounting issue.
9. Audit committees should oversee the quarterly reporting process.

Appendix 5E. *Objectives of the United Shareholders Association*

What is USA?

- USA was founded in August 1986 to serve as a grassroots advocacy organization for shareholder rights and to promote corporate competitiveness through a return to the basic principles of American capitalism.
- Today, USA has more than 64,000 members in all 50 states.
- Local USA chapters in 39 major metropolitan areas form a nationwide network of shareholder rights activists.
- USA headquarters and staff are based in Washington, D.C.

What are USA's Goals?

A more vibrant American economy, based on free market capitalism, is USA's major objective. USA works to achieve this objective by advocating public and corporate policy focusing on management accountability to shareholders. Specific goals are:

- Guarantee a universal one share, one vote standard for public corporations.
- Reform the proxy voting system to require a confidential vote in corporate elections, independent tabulation of voting results and equal shareholder access to the proxy statement.
- Eliminate abusive management tactics such as greenmail, poison pills and golden parachutes.
- Create federal minimum standards for state tender offer regulation to replace the jurisdictional maze imposed by more than 30 inconsistent state statutes.
- Stop wasteful corporate investments and ill-conceived diversifications by returning more corporate profits directly to shareholders.
- Encourage new equity investment by providing favourable tax treatment for dividend payments and capital gains.

Appendix 5F. *1991 Target 50 Results (United Shareholders' Association Survey)*

Company	Sponsor	Proposal	Support (%)
Allied Signal	Charles Morse	Confidential Vote	34
	Gregory Jones	Opt-Out	21
Amax	Bill Steiner	Poison Pill	53
Am. Ship Bldg.	NYCERS	Confidential Vote	(No meeting yet)
Armco	CalSTRS	Poison Pill	59
Bethlehem Steel	Alfred Haindl	Opt-Out	26
Caterpillar	NYCERS	Confidential Vote	30
	CREF	Share Placement	30
Champion Intl.	CREF	Confidential Vote	38
	Frank Boushee	Golden Parachute	23
Control Data	Edwin Season	Poison Pill	43
Crane	John Duncan	Poison Pill	44
EG&G	Leighton Laughlin	Confidential Vote	35
	Jennifer Cherniss	Poison Pill	32
Eastman Kodak	James Sefried	Golden Parachute	34
Great Western	Robert Einkauf	Confidential Vote	48
Greyhound Dial	Robert Barbieri	Golden Parachute	34
	Frank Martin	Poison Pill	40
Grumman	Henry Jasen	Poison Pill	37
Hercules	CalPERS	Confidential Vote	50
	Bill Steiner	Poison Pill	57
Intl. Paper	Aaron Martin	Poison Pill	40
	Howard Thompson	Golden Parachute	30
K mart	SWIB	Poison Pill	95
Lubrizol	NYCERS	Confidential Vote	31
Nalco Chemical	Preston Haglin	Poison Pill	29
Natl. Education	Yana Bridle	Poison Pill	43
Navistar Intl.	Edwin Hogan	Confidential Vote	49
	Norman Lien	Golden Parachute	45

Company	Sponsor	Proposal	Support (%)
Ogden	Bill Steiner	Golden Parachute	30
Pfizer	Kelvin Pierce	Confidential Vote	42
	SWIB	Poison Pill	45
	CREF	Share Placement	40
	Marvin Beyer	Golden Parachute	32
PHH	George Duncan	Poison Pill	(No meeting yet)
Pittston	Bill Steiner	Golden Parachute	25
Polaroid	Vincent Theisen	Poison Pill	40
Raytheon	Evelyn Gillin	Poison Pill	45
	NYCERS	Confidential Vote	45
Ryder Systems	Roger McNeill	Poison Pill	59
Santa Fe Pacific	Richard Foley	Confidential Vote	21

Appendix 5G. *American Depositary Receipts (ADRs)*

ADRs were invented in 1927 by the forerunner of the Morgan Guaranty Trust Company to facilitate trading in the USA of foreign securities, usually ordinary shares but sometimes debt instruments. The concept is simple. An American depositary holds the stock and issues ADRs for a specified quantity. The depositary notes changes of beneficial ownership but these changes do not have to be registered with the issuer. Holders have full shareholder rights yet do not have to face problems of currency conversion or settlement delays. Leading depositaries include the Bank of New York, Citibank, and the Morgan Bank.

There are two types of ADR, 'Sponsored' (where the scheme is set up by the issuer) and 'Unsponsored' (when it is organized by the depositary). There are procedural differences in setting up these schemes but the total effect is broadly the same, save that as there is no formal agreement between issuer and depositary in an unsponsored scheme, the depositary is not required to distribute shareholder communciations to ADR holders.

ADRs may be traded on a US Stock Exchange quoted on NASDAQ or traded over the computer. For a full description of ADRs see Meyer, Brown and Platt 1991.

Appendix 5H. Percentage Holdings by Type of Institutional Investor in Largest Twenty-five US Corporations (31 December 1990)

Rank	Company	Total institutional holdings	Banks	Insurance companies	Investment companies	Investment advisors	Corporate	Public academic & foundation	Other
1	Exxon	35.81	18.62	1.52	0.56	9.36	0.58	4.01	1.16
2	International Business Machines	48.55	17.27	2.63	3.05	18.09	1.02	5.74	0.75
3	General Electric Co.	47.39	20.01	2.10	1.69	16.17	0.91	5.45	1.07
4	Philip Morris Cos. Inc.	59.07	16.76	2.28	3.76	29.26	1.11	4.27	1.63
5	Bristol Meyers Squibb Co.	56.69	19.46	2.86	3.58	25.11	1.07	3.46	1.14
6	Merck & Co. Inc.	52.99	21.02	2.80	2.86	20.19	1.08	4.53	0.50
7	Wal Mart Stores Inc.	28.86	8.12	1.07	1.33	13.62	0.75	2.89	1.07
8	American Tel. & Teleg. Co.	21.98	8.19	1.17	0.84	6.60	0.56	3.54	1.08
9	Coca Cola Co.	52.12	22.04	1.28	0.96	14.87	8.01	4.36	0.59
10	Proctor & Gamble Co.	43.35	18.85	1.71	1.38	14.88	0.72	5.17	0.65
11	Amoco Corp.	47.80	24.36	2.07	1.59	13.60	0.86	4.72	0.60
12	Bellsouth Corp.	24.76	11.25	1.17	1.17	5.62	0.49	3.97	1.08
13	Chevron Corporation	40.28	11.36	2.48	1.34	11.27	9.89	3.00	0.94
14	Du Pont E.I. De Nemours & Co.	37.75	17.37	1.52	1.62	13.20	0.76	2.69	0.59
15	Johnson & Johnson	55.73	17.10	4.67	2.18	19.58	1.20	9.98	1.02
16	Mobil Corp.	48.79	16.97	2.07	2.73	19.38	0.97	5.82	0.87

Table cont.

Rank	Company	Total institutional holdings	Banks	Insurance companies	Investment companies	Investment advisors	Corporate	Public academic & foundation	Other
17	Bell Atlantic Corp.	29.06	12.12	1.37	1.15	8.14	0.80	4.38	1.10
18	General Motors Corp.	38.09	11.31	1.10	1.82	16.99	0.64	5.25	0.98
19	Pepsico Inc.	57.82	17.86	2.75	2.96	27.24	1.31	4.36	1.35
20	Atlantic Richfield Co.	51.28	19.64	4.01	1.91	17.85	1.44	5.92	0.52
21	GTE Corp.	53.09	24.02	1.94	2.42	16.36	0.94	6.29	1.12
22	Eli Lilly & Co.	68.96	17.89	3.45	2.88	21.59	1.65	20.34	1.16
23	Abbot Labs.	50.29	18.79	2.93	2.16	20.61	1.12	3.50	1.18
24	Minnesota Mng. & Mfg. Co.	62.27	26.46	4.87	2.51	21.75	1.11	4.40	1.17
25	Pacific Telesis Group	35.13	10.66	2.09	3.65	12.21	0.62	4.77	1.14
	Average	45.92	17.10	2.32	2.08	16.54	1.58	5.31	0.10

Note: Holdings are those of delegated 13F filing institution and do not necessarily represent ultimate owner or fiduciary.

Source: C. K. Brancato, 'Institutional Investors: A Widely Diverse Presence in Corporate Governance' (paper for Columbia Institutional Investor Project; 25 Feb. 1993). Table 4; based on CDA Spectrum Data Base of 13F filings.

Appendix 5J. *The Largest Mutual Fund Managers (September 1992)*

Management company	Assets* ($ billion)	Market share* (%)
Fidelity	164.3	10.2
Merrill Lynch	107.6	6.7
Vanguard	92.6	5.8
Dreyfus	75.8	4.7
Franklin†	64.6	4.0
Capital Research	62.1	3.9
Dean Witter	52.9	3.3
Kemper	45.4	2.8
Federated	45.2	2.8
Shearson	45.1	2.8
Putnam	41.4	2.6
Prudential	34.2	2.1
IDS	27.9	1.7
Scudder	26.2	1.6
Nuveen	25.8	1.6
T. Rowe Price	25.3	1.6
Provident Institutional	24.3	1.5
MFS	23.2	1.5
Goldman, Sachs	23.0	1.4
Alliance Capital	20.9	1.3
Painewebber	20.5	1.3
Oppenheimer	19.8	1.2
AIM	18.7	1.2
20th Century	17.3	1.1
American Capital	13.8	0.9

* Includes mutual funds and closed-end funds as of Sept. 1992.

† Has since acquired Templeton funds, which would bring Franklin's total to $76.9 billion, with a 4.8% share of the market.

Source: C. K. Brancato, 'Institutional Investors: A Widely Diverse Preserve in Corporate Governance' (paper for Columbia Institutional Investor Project; 25 Feb. 1993), Table 5; based on Strategic Insight as reported in *Business Week* (18 Jan. 1993), 64.

6 THE UNITED KINGDOM

i. The Background

> O wad some power the giftie gie us
> to see oursels as ithers see us.
>
> (Robert Burns)

It may seem perverse to cover the United Kingdom last of the five studies, when historically it was the first country in which industrialization on a massive scale made corporate governance important. The reason for doing so is that my years in industry—and much later in PRO NED (Promotion of Non-Executive Directors)—which together afforded opportunities of seeing corporate governance in action (or inaction!), and of interviewing literally hundreds of leading industrialists, brought home to me how difficult it was to be objective about the familiar. The decline of great firms and whole industries made me wish to analyse corporate governance systems abroad so as to shed some light on the UK's strengths and weaknesses.

A few years ago the subject of corporate governance was little discussed, certainly not under that name. The word 'governance' itself was revived by Harold Wilson in the title of his book *The Governance of Britain* (1977): it was not in popular usage before then. There is to this day some doubt about what 'corporate governance' means. R. I. Tricker defines it as 'the processes by which companies are run'. The Committee on the Financial Aspects of Corporate Governance (Cadbury) said 'corporate governance is the system by which companies are directed and controlled' (2. 5). This book has concentrated on the system in each country.

It is the belief—or concern—that the system may be inadequate that has sparked such interest on both sides of the Atlantic. The main spur has been and still is lack of competitiveness, but there are other causes such as a doubt about the huge wave of take-overs and management buy-outs in the 1980s which superficially, at any rate, seem to have done so much damage and so little good. The doubt may be misplaced, but it extends beyond the immediate economic effects to the social consequences. If others can prosper without such 'excesses', have their systems something to teach us? We are probably too close to events to form a sound judgement on any of these issues, but concern about them is surely not misplaced, nor is the desire to understand better what a country's system of corporate governance is, and what its strengths and weaknesses are. Emphasis has been heightened in the UK by a series of corporate failures where the weakness of corporate governance was clearly a contributory factor (Polly Peck; Maxwell; Coloroll; etc.).

The Cadbury Committee addressed some of the issues, but as its terms of reference suggest, not by any means all of them. Cadbury however was set up (May 1991) because its sponsors (the Financial Reporting Council, the London Stock Exchange, and the accountancy profession) 'were concerned at the perceived low level of confidence both in financial reporting and in the ability of auditors to provide the safeguards which the users of company reports sought and expected' (para. 2.1). In fact the committee (of which the author was a member) found that its work inevitably took it deep into many aspects of the UK system of corporate governance. This chapter contains many references to its findings but extends beyond them; the Cadbury Code itself, together with Appendix 4 on audit committees, is included as Appendix 7A.

In the UK as elsewhere, corporate governance is set in the framework of its political and social history and attitudes. It very soon appears that the differences between the UK's version of the market economy and corporate governance owe less to the calm intellectual choices made by legislators and businessmen than to attitudes and prejudices cherished and nurtured across centuries. We cannot hope to interpret the British system without taking some of these into account. I have tried to condense the most relevant into a few paragraphs. To attempt to trace every influence would take volumes. Among the works which helpfully shed further light on industrial development over the last 140 years are those by Wiener (1981) and Barnett (1986).

The consequences of being an island are so well understood as to be worth only a passing reference for the sake of completeness. 'Fog in the Channel: Continent cut off' is the newsboy's proper appreciation of where the centre of the universe is (borne out by the Greenwich meridian). Psychologically the sense of 'going abroad'—because Britons have to cross water to do it—is different from crossing what is palpably an artificial check at a Continental border post. The UK sense of its own insularity is markedly different from the French view of 'La France'.

Land-locked powers with ill-defined and often disputed borders which presented no physical obstacles to marauders lacked this sense of definition and security. Britain needed a navy but not a standing army to serve its ends. Insularity has bequeathed the UK a sense of welcome separateness which no amount of foreign entanglement can destroy; some of the distrust of the Channel tunnel stems more from a fear that this separateness has been compromised than from more rational causes. More seriously, it impedes commitment to the EC and its institutions, as the Maastricht debate shows. The UK's geography has provided military security and the land has been free from invasion for nearly a millennium, despite many threats. There have been internal power struggles certainly, some bloody, but few cruel. Taking a long view, there has been a gradual and continuous development of most of the main institutions, which has imparted a high degree of confidence in them and makes the UK suspicious of violent innovations, especially if introduced by those whose history is more chequered. The UK prefers gradual evolution to rapid change—let alone revolution, and this applies as much to its corporate governance arrangements as anything else.

Confidence in its institutions has its flip side in an affection for obsolescent forms and an acceptance of outmoded attitudes. One of the most striking features of the UK is that the aristocratic settlement, which goes back to William I, still persists. Its consequences are not simply that the UK still has a monarchy, peerage, and honours system, important though all of these are. It is that it fundamentally affects the value system. Ownership of land conferred status as well as wealth, though Adam Smith noted that successful businessmen in fact managed the land better than many of those who inherited it. Trade, and later manufacturing, were always seen as inferior occupations, though there was a short period after the beginning of the Industrial Revolution when so much wealth was produced that the country's pride as well as its pocket was affected. But this attitude, which found its greatest expression in the Great Exhibition of 1851, soon weakened under various pressures, secular and ecclesiastical.

The consequences of these attitudes are still manifest in the relative esteem in which manufacturing industry is held, which in turn affects the attitudes of many educationalists (and education itself), and so, perhaps, helps to predetermine the choice of career of so many of the ablest youngsters. These attitudes are pervasive and account, for instance, for the paucity of industrialists' names in works of reference (such as *Who's Who*); they pass away unsung, as the obituaries in *The Times* show. Much of the recent outcry about industrialists' 'excessive' remuneration is due to this discrimination. Fewer attacks are made on professional salaries, yet the top partners in solicitors and accountants' firms (and in some City houses) earn sums which would make most industrialists (from whose companies they derive their living) green with envy.

There have been many recent pronouncements on the anti-industrial culture. Here is how the House of Lords' Select Committee on Science and Technology summed up the problem:

Improving the status of manufacturing

Success in manufacturing industries is essential in a very competitive international world if we are to maintain a rising standard of living and quality of life. But how widely is this recognised?

The most urgent need is for a change in our culture. Unless we revise radically some of the attitudes which permeate our society, the factors which help to make industry competitive—of which innovation is a most important one—will continue to be neglected. Antipathy to manufacturing industry runs deep in our society. Industry is held in low esteem and so attracts too little of the country's talent and other resources. The conditioning which leads to a belief that making things is a second-class occupation does us all a disservice. Our competitors in Germany, Japan, and elsewhere rightly regard manufacturing as a prestigious and worthwhile occupation. They have pride in their industrial achievements. Once and for all we must shed the national attitudes which deter us from a vigorous pursuit of economic growth and progress through increased sales of competitive manufactured goods.

There are those who would argue that status is less important than reward: that is, if industry paid better, the quality of its recruits would improve. Although there is obviously some connection between choice of career and expected rewards, perceived risk, status, and expected job satisfaction also come into the equation.

The Anglican church now appears to disown anti-industrial attitudes. The Bishop of Oxford in his 1992 Stockton Lecture said:

... as you know the Church has been severely criticised in recent years for its alleged failure to support the mechanisms of wealth creation. In fact, a negative attitude to business has been one aspect of our culture for a long time. In Trollope's novel Dr Thorne, the author writes: 'Merchants as such are not the first men among us: though it perhaps be open, barely open, to a merchant to become one of them. Buying and selling is good and necessary; it is very necessary, and may, possibly, be very good; but it cannot be the noblest work of man; and let us hope that it may not in our time be esteemed the noblest work of an Englishman.'

This passage, written in 1858, reflects the importance of trading in a trading nation but its aspiration, the noblest work referred to, is still directed towards the great landed estates of the countryside. It is an attitude that owes much more to the Romantic Movement of the early 19th Century with its idealisation of nature and plain old-fashioned snobbery than it does to Christianity.

From a Christian point of view the values inherent in a market economy: the stress on consumer choice, the inevitability of risk-taking, the attempt to meet stated wants, are congruous with our understanding of what it is to be a human being in society, made in the image of God.

Providing the mechanisms for gathering savings for investment and providing the goods and services society needs both render a valuable service to society. In the UK, however, it has long been more acceptable socially to make money rather than things. Being 'something in the City', or in a profession, or the public service, would pass muster, so that is what the younger sons of the nobility (kept off the land by the rules of primogeniture) and the aspiring middle class generally did if they were going to enter commercial life. Their natural habitat was the partners' desk, the bank, or the stockbroker's office, rather than the management mess or boardroom of manfacturing companies. On the other hand British society has always been and still is pragmatic. If people did choose industry and made an overwhelming success of it, most doors would open to them. Hugely successful retailers earn and get respect and honour to go with their riches, but 'petit commerçants' are not to be found in *Who's Who* any more than they are likely to become members of the Jockey Club in Newmarket or Paris.

To be fair, some realized the importance of trade and industry as far back as the mid-eighteenth century. The 'Plan' for what is now the RSA in 1755 had the following preamble:

Whereas the Riches, Honour, Strength, and Prosperity of a Nation depend in a great Measure on the Knowledge and Improvement of useful Arts, Manufactures, Etc, several of the Nobility and Gentry of this Kingdom, being fully sensible that due Encouragements and Rewards are greatly conducive to excite a Spirit of Emulation and Industry, have resolved to form themselves into a Society, by the Name of *The Society for the Encouragement of the Arts, Manufactures, and Commerce*, by bestowing Premiums for such Productions, Inventions, or Improvements, as shall tend to the employing of the Poor, and the Increase of Trade.

The limitations of the domestic economy pushed Britain into overseas trade from earliest times, and the development of a merchant marine (with a navy to protect it, from Henry VIII's time onwards) meant that traders' horizons were broad; the world was their oyster. Many who lacked land at home ventured abroad in search of fortune if not fame, and this was socially acceptable too—indeed, admired, especially as the empire slowly and absent-mindedly developed so that the traders could confer on people who in their opinion needed both, the joys of Anglicanism and honest administration. Despite all the faults, the benefits conferred were far from negligible. The breadth of perspective of the old Empire lives on in 'British' companies today. The successors of those who ran the East India Company, planted rubber in Malaysia, built railways in the Argentine, constructed Sydney Harbour bridge, are the new and committed in great multinational companies. Britain has for centuries looked outwards across the world and does so still. Two of the world's great companies, Shell and Unilever, are bi-national (UK and the Netherlands, as it happens). Very many 'British' companies now do more business abroad than at home. Britons do not yet suffer from strangulated mobility; they mix well in any cultures which will tolerate foreigners and take them to their bosom. UK companies generally have a promotion policy that depends mostly on merit and little on national-ity. Foreign companies which operate from the UK are welcome, and if they deserve admiration receive it.

This brings us to the variety of nationalities within the British Isles. There is a difference between being British (a broad concept) and the narrow concept of being English, Scottish, Welsh, or Irish, as everyone knows, and the UK's sports arrangements demonstrate. The crucial point is that the two concepts co-exist. The unseen benefit of this duality has been a residual tolerance and open-mindedness, especially since the seventeenth century, towards the different nationalities within the UK and towards immigrants from other countries' cultures, which has shown itself in an ability to accept and assimilate minorities as part of Britain which in their turn have added much to the country's cultural and commercial life. Huguenots, Jews, Muslims, West Indians, Indians, and others, have successively arrived and joined in. They have been able to preserve a certain sense of separateness whilst feeling themselves British. From such people (uninhibited by the more enervating influences of the British aristocratic value system) have often come ideas and energy, thrust and entrepreneurial desire. The com-mercial strength of the UK has drawn advantage from the willingness of both majority and minority alike to accept this duality.

Commentators tend to concentrate on natural mineral resources, of which the UK has a fair share. Minerals, fertile land, and a teeming sea are valuable, but not if in the long run they distract a country from the use of its main resource—its people: nothing else is remotely important compared with that, as Japan, Singapore, and Hong Kong demonstrate.

The anti-industrial bias of the ruling class/aristocracy was mirrored for many years by the Luddite or Communist attitude of trade unionists, many of whom were at best indifferent to the success of the enterprise which employed them. They felt alienated from it, not at all surprising given the past attitudes of so many owners and managers, and the fact that they did not greatly participate in its prosperity. This hostility or indifference sprang from the concentration of most nineteenth-century owners and managers on technology and production and their neglect of people. The UK has changed radically since 1979, to be sure: management has improved and so have attitudes generally. The unions have changed constructively both in approach and structure. The practices in the best UK plants now demonstrate that the indigenous work-force is second to none if well led, trained, and motivated. Japanese companies operating in the UK often find that the plants they run are as efficient as those at home or even better. Even so, concern for people is not ubiquitous. They are dealt with like chattels in take-overs, regarded as 'structural imperfections' in some of the effects of macro-economic policy, and sometimes called 'liveware' in the computer world. Their right to be informed—even about matters which affect their vital interests—is not enshrined in law as it is in Germany.

The stability of UK institutions was, and indeed is, a tremendous benefit but can induce complacency—which the miners have not been forgiven for disturbing in 1972. One area in which governments of both parties have consistently failed industry is in not providing reasonably stable macro-economic conditions with minimal inflation. These are things which only governments can do, and they cannot do it all; the UK could never be immune to a world slump whatever its own government did. But the toleration of stop–go policies for short-term electoral reasons is a betrayal of trust. UK companies have been forced to operate against a backcloth of macro-economic inconsistency for most of the period since the War. And draconian monetarist policies have latterly been implemented in a way which was bound to savage industry, although their objective—to eliminate inflation—was thoroughly laudable. Looking back, however, it is evident that the blame cannot be heaped too high on inconsistent policies. UK industry was declining in relative terms in the decades before 1914 when no such accusation could be made of government.

It used to be popular to talk about 'class'. In this respect the terminology now owes more to Madison Avenue than Karl Marx, since modern classifications are marketing-based 'A/B', 'C1', 'C2' and so forth. Equally negative in many ways is the division between sectors: Academe—Finance—Industry—Professions—Public Service (in alphabetical order!). The UK lacks the mobility of the Americans and the French: there is some movement at the margins, but not much. Consequently each sector seems to resent at least some of the others and finds it hard to view life through their eyes. It is true that the more any particular calling requires professionalism, the less time there is to move to another: it would never be desirable or practical to have wholesale migrations. It is much more a question of the readiness to move, the preparedness to receive a move willingly, and the willingness to regard others not as adversaries but as members of the same team. Were the UK better at this it would find it easier to see general problems in the round and not as the exclusive preserve of a particular faction or sector. Jealousies and rivalries between sectors often inhibit people from making common cause; envy and suspicion between those from different sectors almost always prove negative and damaging. The way, for instance, in which most industrialists think about those who might contribute to their boards precludes proper consideration of academics and public servants *as a class and irrespective of ability*; and I cannot count the number of industrialists who have complained bitterly to me that government, industry, and finance still have not found a way of playing together as if they were in the same team.

The movement upwards and downwards through the social scale has up to a point always been relatively common and easy: but the classification of class by accent (which the BBC has done well to reduce) and by other signs, perpetuated by a double-decker schooling system, lingers on. Humble origins are still played upon by the media far more than they would be elsewhere. One cannot blame the industrial revolution for this—it existed before it and seems destined to survive vestigially for ever. As far as industry and commerce are concerned it matters less than it did, and in most firms not at all. It is now one of the weaker undercurrents, but we catch a glimpse of an odd eddy here and there.

One division merits particular attention: the City and industry. Many City figures—mainly merchant-bankers like Lord Keith—have performed with distinction as company chairmen. Even so, historically the reciprocal perception has been to see each other as a world apart, even though industry used the City's services and the City made a good living from it. Many industrialists were (and some still are) deeply suspicious of the City. They felt the City was at best indifferent towards them. For an interesting historical account see Kynaston 1990. Kynaston believes that there are four historical characteristics which have contributed to industrialists' negative attitudes (which he illustrates), namely, the City's

- traditional indifference toward industry, shading at times into repugnance;
- conservatism;
- periodic exploitation of industry;
- short-termism.

And he concludes by quoting Lord Kearton (former chairman of Courtaulds):

This [i.e. the Japanese] system which involves a degree of day-to-day meshing of industry, banking and government, would I think be complete anathema to the City here, certainly to the Conservative party and certainly to a great many people in business.

The divide existed because on balance the parties preferred it. Judging by the efforts to bridge it today, however, the preference is neither as strong nor as usual as it was.

All societies have to decide the extent to which individual freedom must be curtailed in the general interest. The fundamental British attitude is that freedom is the natural state which should be staunchly guarded against proposed derogations by governments or others—even in hours of the nation's mortal peril. The burden of proof lies on those who would propose restrictions—like abolishing or limiting the right to silence in a criminal trial. Lawyers may not be popular (see below), but the Rule of Law is so familiar a part of the national landscape that few espy it, and this applies although the British Isles are the home of two quite different legal systems. The English (for in this one must exclude the Scots) feel a great sense of pride in the Common Law. Its gradual and pragmatic 'discovery' by the judiciary is in direct contrast to the systems based on codes like Roman, Dutch, or French law. The same contrast can be observed in regard to the constitution. The encroachment of statute law on both has narrowed the gap, but even so there is a distinct preference for organic development rather than tidy revelation which to this day affects the UK approach. The law once enacted generally commands respect: the UK may not always welcome EC legislation as effusively as its partners and may argue both the merits and details more thoroughly, but when it does accept it, it implements properly what it enacts. Confidence in the legal system has never, however, been matched by affection for lawyers. From Shakespeare's 'The first thing we'll do, let's kill all the lawyers', to Dickens's 'Jarndyce and Jarndyce', there runs a theme that wherever possible one should keep out of court. The laws of maintenance and champerty (which stop contingency fees) were designed to restrain the legal profession from inciting the litigious poor; whilst the expense deterred the litigious middle class. Again, the development of the modern corporation and the involvement of the insurance industry have changed the picture—not, some would say, wholly for the better. We shall encounter the debate about the role of the law at various points, for instance, in considering the Take-over Panel.

The working of many UK institutions reflects a preference for the adversarial approach. We see this pattern in Parliament, industry, the law, sport. The UK distrusts committees, co-operation, combinations, and cartels, because it fears they will act primarily to their own advantage. Charles II's coterie of advisers—Clifford, Arlington, Buckingham, Ashley, Lauderdale—caused a word to be added to the language, and it was a word of opprobrium: cabal. The rituals of destructive collective bargaining are matched by the adversarial nature of the customer/supplier relationship. It is a great relief for the UK that some of the worst excesses of both are diminishing.

Behind the adversarial style lies a principle in the constitution for which one monarch was humbled by his barons and, four centuries later, another was executed and a third deposed. The principle was accountability, at least to the extent that the standards of the age suggested. It is not perfect even today, given the control by the executive of the House of Commons, but it is palpable and Ministers ignore it at their peril. It is one of the more curious features of the UK's arrangements that accountability, which has been so great a consideration in the political sphere, counts for so little in the economic. This is a subject worthy of deep study, for it may be to blame for many of the UK's problems.

Accountability should not be confused with publicity. The media understandably have a preference for a good story built around individual people. Tales about personalities sell more papers than paragraphs about products. They find their subjects generally willing, not to say eager, to co-operate. A few shrinking violets apart, the UK may be divided into two groups: those who enjoy publicity and admit it and those who enjoy it and pretend otherwise. The emphasis on individual responsibility which such publicity implies might be admirable were accountability real. As, generally speaking, it is not, the mixture of power and publicity often observably leads to problems. The media can exploit the fall of their heroes as effectively as they facilitated their rise.

The steady development of crafts from earliest times through the Middle Ages left its mark on the UK mode of thought in one important way. Craftsmen tended to group together, and in London and elsewhere their associations became formalized, often as Livery Companies whose function it was to supervise and set standards for training, pay, quality, and often—price. There was a concept of the 'fair' price (not just the price the market would bear), and this fits with the general concept of 'fairness' which is deeply embedded in the British psyche. 'Fair play', 'Felt fair pay' are familiar phrases. Dickens, in his brilliant but unsparing attacks on the excesses of the industrial revolution and the harshness of aspects of Victorian society, did not hanker after a new scheme of things but a less unfair and more caring society. The concept lives on, in the (now fading) idea of the minimum wage, the sanctity of the National Health Service, and in all kinds of welfare for the disadvantaged. In an undoctrinaire and practical way it is the British response to the consequences of the full rigours of the market and competition. It can be a real force.

Gambling seems to enjoy rather a special place in the UK. Merit is on the whole rather suspect because meritocracies are for the meritorious and most people are neither able nor energetic enough to qualify. Luck on the other hand is impartial, in that all can aspire to the fortune it bestows, whatever one's capacity or station. Fewer envious eyes are cast on the pools winners than the keepers of 24-hours-a-day convenience stores who accumulate wealth by toil and application. Gambling, whether on the races or the tables or in stocks, has always therefore been acceptable. Indeed, gamblers in shares are said to be positively virtuous by adding liquidity to the market: how much liquidity is optimal and how gamblers help in a crisis has never quite been explained. Even the terminology is confusing: many a bookmaker calls bets 'investment'. Many of the derivative instruments have their origin in risk management and are generally used for this purpose, but the risk they are hedging may itself be of the nature of either an investment (or trade) or a gamble. The borderline can be blurred. Many fund managers treat their investments as bets: they do not take much of an interest in corporate governance. A 'punter's' view of a horse is vastly different from that of a bloodstock agency: it is no coincidence that people are often said to 'take a punt' in shares. Perhaps it is the same the world over. In the UK it is as well to remember what an honoured place gambling has amongst its activities: 'If you do not speculate you cannot accumulate' is an old adage. All enterprise is a risk; a gamble. As an element it is vital—and often fun; as a way of life, it is short term and negative. Getty when asked whether he gambled replied, 'In business I take risks, having measured them; in your sense, if I wanted to gamble I'd buy a casino.' As a typical example of the UK's attitude we need look no further than the section on take-overs. The UK's system is so constructed as to ensure that any bid made without the target board's agreement is bound to lack crucial information—it is, in other words, a gamble.

The picture is now becoming clearer. The primacy of the importance of land, plus primogeniture, was 'long-termism' *in excelsis*, though the system was prevented from becoming scelerotic by the 'rule against perpetuities' quite early on. Those who did not inherit land wanted to make their fortunes as quickly as possible—the shorter-term the better. Some industries, notably brewing and milling, which were closely associated with the land and its produce, lent themselves to a long-term perspective, and many of their proprietors were eventually ennobled (the so-called 'beerage'). Some industrialists coming from a totally different background also wanted to build up businesses for their children to run. Alas, industry is more demanding, and 'clogs to clogs in three generations' was only too often true, perhaps because the education system provided such a poor background to commercial life. But others had no desire to found industrial dynasties and aimed to use their industrial wealth as a means to landed respectability.

Industry does after all, and always did, require technical proficiency to compete. In the early days of the industrial revolution the UK produced a stream of geniuses whose ideas and inventions gave the country a generation or two's start. These were the practical men, with little formal training for the most part, but masters of their craft with great imaginations. Their successors were not short-term in just wanting to make money as fast as possible to buy land and status; they were short-sighted, which is quite a different matter. Their distrust of first-rate formal qualifications and modern scientific training went hand in hand with a dislike of any overt display of intellect. The practical men were no match for overseas competitors who were better trained in ever more complex technologies.

The lack of foresight of British Industry and Government alike during the last century is only now beginning to be understood.

The truth is that the British establishment's whole approach to the question of industrial strategy was rooted in a Victorian mercantile conception of a myriad firms competing in a market place—industry was still often referred to as 'trade': 'the coal trade; the steel trade. The establishment—politicians, civil servants, hired economists—had not yet grasped the twentieth century concept, pioneered by the great American and German corporations, of the massive technology-led operation that conquers its own market almost on the analogy of a great military offensive. (Barnett 1986: 275.)

There was a time when some UK manfacturers took pride in getting production from old machines because it showed how sensible their original investment had been even when better ones were available. Does such an attitude still prevail in regard to the UK's corporate governance system, which is a more important part of industrial machinery than any item of capital equipment ever was? As we now turn to consider how the system works and then evaluate it, it is as well to remember how deeply set in its ways it is possible for the UK to become. At the point when pragmatic conservatism becomes an article of faith, distasteful evidence may be set aside as heresy. There is nothing sacred about the Companies Act. The Joint Stock company is a creature of Parliament not the Book of Genesis. The pragmatic questions for the UK are whether the system works as well as others, and whether it works as well as it might, and they need to be faced with an open mind.

ii. The Machine at Work

The Legal Framework

Small companies are the most numerous in the United Kingdom as elsewhere. Although the principles of good corporate governance apply to the corner shop as well as to ICI, the way in which a company will give effect to them will differ according to its size and complexity and whether its shares are privately held or quoted on the Stock Exchange. This chapter, like the others, deals primarily with quoted companies.

Apart from a relatively small number of big enterprises incorporated under Charter or Act of Parliament, businesses in Britain up to the middle of the nineteenth century were run by sole traders or partnerships (often a family); their common characteristic was unlimited liability, which although not an absolute bar, was a considerable disincentive to expansion. The Acts of 1855 and 1862 enabled companies to incorporate and introduce the principle of limited liability. The directors were usually managers and owners as well; the 'board', if it met at all, was a perfunctory and formal affair—and it stayed that way even when in the effluxion of time some of the shares found their way into other hands. Only at a later stage, when the business grew, did formality creep in, and the concept of a board became a reality.

Such businesses often stayed private for a long while, and either died or were absorbed. Of the successful a relative few were floated later; even so, they retained most of the characteristics of the family business with few if any outsiders on the board. Many of them, if truth be told, made the transition without changing habits, in the mistaken belief that it was they, the proprietors, who were conferring a favour on those who subscribed for some shares in their business, an error which occasionally persists.

There was another type of enterprise from early times: the joint stock company where ownership and management were separate from the start. The Muscovy Company founded in the sixteenth century is one of the first examples. Some businesses were incorporated under Statute or Royal Charter. In the nineteenth century, major enterprises like the railway companies needed to attract capital from a wide range of subscribers, and were financed by public subscription from the beginning. They had formal boards of directors composed mainly of the 'Great and Good', which were quite separate from management. The directors of such enterprises may have held some shares but were not the sole or even controlling proprietors; and most of them had no management function.

The way in which people think about companies in the UK reflects this double ancestry and accounts for the continuing debate about boards and the role of directors. There is a world of difference between a committee of owner-managers in a private company and a board of a great public company on which no one owns more than a few shares. The UK uses the same laws for both. A company can organize the kind of board it believes it needs if it needs one at all; its shareholders can dissent if they wish.

The present UK law is contained in the latest of a series of Companies Acts, which seek to balance the interests of those concerned, for instance would-be subscribers, shareholders, and creditors. The 1948 Act was regarded at the time as a milestone: the 1985 Act is the latest version, which must be read with the Statutory Instruments which supplement it, including Table A. It provides for various kinds of company including companies limited by guarantee and unlimited companies. These are not significant in the economy and are outside the scope of this book. All the rest are joint stock companies as defined in Section 683, with limited liability. Such companies are divided into two types, 'Limited' and 'Public Limited', and the Act provides that their names shall end with Ltd. or PLC respectively. Contrary to what is sometimes believed, being a PLC does not mean that the company's shares are publicly quoted on a stock exchange. It does mean that the company has capital above a certain size (£50,000 (sect. 118)), and that it may, if it acts in accordance with the law, issue shares to the public, a thing which a Ltd. company is expressly forbidden to do. There is, however, no restriction on the size of a Ltd. company. Some Ltd. companies and some unquoted PLCs are big: we shall examine some issues that arise from this later.

It is, however, quoted PLCs that are the subject of this paper, and there were roughly 2,000 of them at the end of 1991. They must conform to a single set of rules; there is no choice of structure as in France. Many other Acts bear on the way companies are run, for instance the Insolvency Act 1986 which, *inter alia*, defines the point at which it is unlawful for a director to continue trading. (And in effect removes from someone who does so the protection of limited liability, as well as imposing other penalties.) Certain other aspects of the conduct of a company's affairs are controlled by rules and regulations (e.g. the Stock Exchange's rules entitled 'Admission of Securities to Listing', known as the Yellow Book; the Take-over Panel's code; the accountancy profession's rules and conventions). Codes of best practice proliferate. We shall encounter the Institutional Shareholders' Committee's pronouncement on the role of shareholders. The code proposed by the Cadbury Committee is a recent and significant addition (see Appendix 6A). Codes illustrate the point made in the introduction about the UK's preference for gradualness, and the dislike of legislation. Unfortunately codes usually affect least those who need them most: the good follow them, the bad avert their gaze. Excessive legislation may be counter-productive, but voluntarism has its limitations.

The legal structure rests on very simple principles. The owners (shareholders) appoint agents (directors) to run the business, and the directors report annually on their stewardship. The directors can delegate their powers but cannot abandon them. In practice in PLCs there is therefore a two-link chain of accountability, management to directors, and directors to shareholders.

Directors and Boards

Introduction

The Company Act 1985 (sect. 282) requires all companies registered after 1 November 1929 to have at least two directors. There is no distinction between classes of directors, for instance, between 'executive' and 'non-executive', only obscure references to a chairman[1] and little mention of a 'board'.[2] Any duties laid on directors, for instance, to prepare annual accounts (sect. 227) and laying and delivering annual accounts (sect. 241), are laid on them all, and they are *all* guilty of an offence (sect. 243) if sect. 241 is not complied with. On this extremely narrow legal base, which Table A does little to widen, is the whole edifice of UK corporate governance constructed. The superstructure as we know it: boards, board committees, chairmen, non-executive directors—are pragmatic adaptations. In law none is essential; to this day ICI could legally be run by two directors, like the Consulate of the Roman Republic.

Language often contains important clues about attitudes and sometimes about misconceptions. The popular term for an 'outside' director in the UK is a 'non-executive director'. The use of the negative implies that *not* having executive powers is special. In law the reverse is true. The Companies Acts do not require directors to be managers; they require directors to see that

---

[1] A chairman is referred to in sched. 6, para. 3 (amended 1989) as a person elected by the company's directors to chair their meetings.

[2] Boards are not mentioned where they might be expected but in odd places like sched. 6, para. 17 as amended (re whether a connected exposure is sufficiently material to be reportable).

the business is properly managed, which is quite a different matter. There is indeed only one class of director and all are equal in the eyes of the law—or, at least, nearly equal. Any qualifying adjective is descriptive but not in law definitional. A 'finance director' or 'marketing director' is simply a director who has executive responsibility for specific executive functions. Strict logic would render the term 'non-executive director' superfluous. *In law* it is the norm. This may sound like an exercise in semantics, but it conveys an important reality—that being a director imposes a quite different set of responsibilities from those which attend any specific executive function, a fact which is not always appreciated by directors who are also executive 'barons' with responsibility for sections of an enterprise.

Although the Companies Act and other legislation lay specific duties on directors—as do other regulatory bodies like the Stock Exchange and Take-over Panel—they say nothing about what directors should do in respect of the running of the business. There is an enormous range of literature on every conceivable aspect of management, and extensive training is available around the world in business schools and other institutions of learning. There is little specifically addressed to directors. Few companies give any training in direction to those they promote to the board; it is assumed that a director's skills are a natural development of those of a manager. This is not necessarily true, and many a good manager has failed to shine on the board. At the time of writing (1992), new courses are being developed to supplement those already available. There is a growing number of useful documents for directors to consider, among which are:

- *The Role & Duties of Directors: a Statement of Best Practice* (Institutional Shareholders' Committee, 1991).
- *A Practical Guide for Non-Executive Directors* (PRO NED, 1987).
- *Guidelines for Directors* (Institute of Directors, 1990).

Some of the data in the following paragraphs comes from a survey conducted in 1992 on behalf of 3i, to which 215 companies responded (the 3i Survey).

The UK, unlike Germany, never developed a formal two-board system. There was a separation of function of a sort on the boards (or courts) of Chartered companies and many of the early Joint Stock companies, as few if any of the board had executive functions (and the same was true until quite recently of some of our joint stock banks), so it acted in effect as a supervisory board. The chief general manager (whatever his title) gathered round himself the group that managed the business. This informal kind of two-tier system persists within the UK to this day in many companies, but few have wanted to formalize it. The idea became anathema because it became complicated by concepts of employee representation (e.g. in the Bullock Report 1975). We shall return to this issue later. With the UK system in its present form there is always a danger of the management board (if one exists) seeing itself as a mechanism *mainly* to caucus before board meetings, which makes it more difficult for executives on the board to do other than toe the party line, and more difficult for the non-executives to get at the heart of the matter since so much of the real discussion will have been pre-empted.

The Size of the Board

Anyone who is used to committee work knows that the bigger the committee the more difficult it becomes for each person to contribute. Size is inhibiting and time runs short. A cynic might suspect that this realization has inspired company chairmen to over-populate their board rooms. Significantly Japanese boards are huge (often over 60 strong), but their functions are, by common consent, mainly 'ceremonial' (see Chapter 3).

Of course, chairmen have to ensure balance and the range of experience they need for the board's deliberations, but they will know that after a certain point the dynamics deteriorate. Views vary about the optimum or maximum sizes. At the time of writing, ICI had sixteen directors, British Telecom fifteen, Grand Met. eight, Sainsbury twenty-two, BP sixteen. The average for the top ten companies was sixteen. Smaller companies sensibly tend to have smaller boards: the Bank of England *Quarterly Bulletin* in May 1988 showed that of 549 companies in *The Times* 1,000, 39 per cent had between six and eight and 29 per cent between nine and eleven. The 3i Survey shows that 172 of the 215 companies in it had boards of six or fewer, and that this was typical of companies with a turnover of less than £100 million.

Frequency of Board Meetings

Two-thirds of UK boards meet monthly or ten times a year (3i Survey). There are many variations, including two-day strategy meetings in some comfortable retreat; and peregrinations to less comfortable seats of distant operations. 14.4 per cent of company boards meet quarterly, but it is surprising to find among them that the boards of some quite substantial businesses meet quarterly or less often. Meetings of the board committees tend to cluster round main board meetings for convenience.

The Chief Executive Officer (CEO)

We shall use the title CEO for the person with the top executive authority, though his title varies and he may be called the 'chief executive', the 'managing director', or the 'chief operating officer'. In fact, 'CEO' is an importation from America and has presidential overtones: 'managing director' used to be the common term in the UK, and is in some ways a better designation. The trouble with the 'CEO' title is that it implies the summit of power and almost by definition makes the chairman's role 'non-executive'. This, however, is a contradiction in terms. A chairman always has some executive powers, certainly in relation to the board and usually others too. The titles of 'chairman' and 'managing director' convey more felicitously the division of duties at the top of the business. Be that as it may, the title 'chief executive' or 'chief executive officer' is now too embedded to be dislodged, and the top executive will be titled 'CEO' for the rest of this section. In fact, the roles are often combined and one meets the titles 'executive chairman' or 'chairman and chief executive officer' quite frequently—far too often for many who believe the roles should be split (a point considered below). All UK companies do have a top executive, whatever his title. The PRO NED 1990 survey revealed that 26 per cent of the top 100 companies in *The Times* 1,000 combined the chairman/CEO roles.

As noted earlier we are used to thinking in terms of individual accountability and for directors to have among them a dominant individual, clearly identifiable as the leader—and not just a *primus inter pares*. The UK prefers individual leadership, with personal responsibility, risks, and rewards. Annual reports often look like a CEO's scrap-book; I counted thirteen photographs of the CEO in one! The media thrive on this cult of the individual on which they can build drama and romance; CEOs enjoy the limelight and are sometimes corrupted by it, gradually getting to believe the hyperbole of their public relations department. The over-dramatization of their rise and fall seems to represent the industrial interpretation of 'A crowded hour of glorious life is worth an age without a name.' But it does not seem in the long run to benefit the business, whatever excitement it may temporarily produce. Some companies, like the Royal Dutch/Shell Group, are exceptions to the general rule, have no CEO, and draw strength from avoiding the personality cult.

As to CEOs' rewards, here are some figures taken from a recent survey (PE International, Summer 1991). The average basic salary of CEOs in UK companies with a turnover of more than £500 million was £140,000 plus a bonus. The median bonus was 8.3 per cent of salary. A Korn Ferry survey shows that 81 per cent of the 196 companies in their sample (from *The Times* 1,000) gave their CEOs cash-related bonuses. The Office of Manpower Economies shows that in large firms the CEOs' salary and bonuses had risen from £110,000 in 1981 to £329,000 in 1989 (large meant minimum turnover of £1.1 billion in 1981 and £2 billion in 1989).

A rather different picture emerges from a study carried out by B. G. M. Main and J. Johnston (University of Edinburgh: updated April 1992). In the year 1990, in companies with sales of more than £1.5 billion, the highest paid director received a salary of £387,904. He also had share options which were calculated at £1,251,845 (the number of options times the share price at 31 December 1990), and held shares worth £5,851,972. For the highest paid director in a company with sales of less than £500 million the corresponding figures were £154,732 salary, £311,130 options, and £1,973,532 shareholding. The sample which was used was drawn from companies in the top 500 which were listed on the London Stock Exchange. Allowing for incomplete data, foreign ownership, etc., the size of the sample was about 220 companies (these are listed in the survey and include most large, publicly held UK firms).

The Chairman

The chairman's position is indeed a strange one. In law there is no such post as chairman of the company. There is no requirement in law to have a board, so it follows there can be no requirement to have a chairman of the board, let alone a chairman of the company. In practice, of course, directors tend to meet in committee—that is, the board—and they choose someone to chair it. From this has sprung the notion that the chairman of the board is something more. We find that almost every company report contains a chairman's statement, sometimes as if he or she personally had something to say that was in some way different and separate. Shareholders welcome a succinct report on policy, progress, and prospects, and it does not matter who puts a name to it—as long as it is clear they are writing on behalf of their co-directors who ought at least to have a chance to clear it. It may hurt their vanity to say so, but chairmen have no authority in law save what they derive from the support of their colleagues.

The role of the chairman varies greatly, depending on the size, complexity, and nature of the business, the division of duties with the CEO, and the amount of time devoted to the job. There is no set pattern in the UK. Most chairmen are part-time, giving perhaps a day a week to the company or even less: others are full-time, or nearly so. Circumstances alter cases: if there is a crisis, like a take-over bid, even a part-time chairman will find himself in over-time.

The division of duties with the CEO will reflect their respective capacities and inclinations. A chairman will often handle some or most external relations and be so to speak the public face of the company. But this is not clear-cut, and the cake is observably cut in various ways. So much depends on personalities. Even when a powerful CEO is the person most in demand the chairman may find himself with a substantial ambassadorial role. The chairman may have a crucial contribution to make in setting the tone for the business externally and internally; his example is of the greatest importance. There is one responsibility every chairman has and it is of vital importance—the running of the board.

It is impossible to over-emphasize the chairman's role in regard to the board (whether or not he is CEO). It is his task to get the size, balance, and composition of the board right (with his board colleagues' help, of course). He is responsible for the agenda—nothing important missed, nothing trivial included. He must insist on appropriate and timely information (which emphatically does *not* mean swamping directors with wheelbarrows of computer printouts of peripheral value). And he must conduct the meeting in such a way as to ensure he gets the best from those present. In many of these things he will be working closely with the CEO, but one thing is absolutely personal, he must display at all points the utmost integrity. Any chairman can 'fix' the composition of the board or the agenda or the information or the meeting. It is no wonder that two boards with identical structures may be quite different in their effectiveness. It is the possibility of such extreme variation that underlines the importance of the role of the non-executive directors—and as we shall see later, requires the active vigilance of the shareholders.

With such a range of responsibilities the chairman has considerable power. There is a growing feeling that the duty of running the board well is too onerous to combine with the even greater burden that a CEO has to bear, quite apart from the excessive concentration of power that results. Here is a quotation from a paper by the Institutional Shareholders Committee on their responsibilities:

Institutional investors should take a positive interest in the composition of boards of directors with particular reference to:
  (i) Concentrations of decision making power not formally constrained by checks and balances appropriate to the particular company;
  (ii) The appointment of a core of non-executives of appropriate calibre, experience and independence.

The Cadbury Committee felt strongly that a separation of powers was desirable in principle (para 4.9 of the Report), but stopped short of making a firm recommendation because it felt that it would be excessively prescriptive to rule out having a concentration of power under any circumstances. Even so, it had severe reservations about it, as the Code makes clear (para. 1.2):

There should be a clearly accepted division of responsibilities at the head of a company, which will ensure a balance of power and authority, such that no one individual has unfettered powers of decision. Where the chairman is also the chief executive it is essential that there should be a strong independent element on the board, with a recognised senior member.

Another reason that some people are not prepared to be absolutely categorical about dividing the roles is that many companies are excellently run, at least in the short term, with roles combined—generally because they have good strong boards as well, fully capable of keeping the top man in check. If the concentration of power exists without such checks it is only too easy for the unscrupulous to be corrupted by it. An analysis of many recent cases of company collapse shows that the two roles were combined and the boards tended to be weak. It was often the case that the principal character was also charismatic, and generally at one time or other, a darling of the media. The first intimation of corporate mortality may indeed be a public award, such as 'Entrepreneur of the Year', to a company's leader.[3]

Board Structure: The Importance of Non-Executive Directors

It is observable that a board's dynamics are as important as its structure. Structure is the handmaiden of dynamics, not vice versa. What matters is that the board should operate effectively as an entity. This is difficult even for its members to ascertain, let alone outsiders: three people who have attended the same meeting often have a totally different perception of how effective its process was. Some chairmen who regard themselves as models of unassuming collegiality are regarded by colleagues as unreconstructed autocrats. What matters is that the board should consider and take decisions in an informed way on what counts; that the executive should be competent enough to drive the business forward, and that the board should be strong enough to say 'No' when it feels it must. Because dynamics are so difficult to judge, we do have to fall back on structure to give us some guide about whether they are likely to be satisfactory—but it is only a guide. Boards of all shapes, composition, and size have been known to work—or not. But if they fail the acid test—the saying 'No' test—they are not really boards at all but advisory committees. The acid test sounds negative but it is based on an important principle—that of reciprocal respect. If a CEO and the board do not respect each other the system will not work as it should. The only people in a position to judge whether the board passes the acid test or not are its members. We shall consider later the difficult dilemma board members

---

[3] For a fuller discussion of the role of the chairman see Cadbury 1990 (not to be confused with the committee report named after him).

often face in the UK's system when they have concluded that it functions poorly.

As far back as 1973, the Watkinson report for the CBI commended the use of non-executive directors. (The US term 'outside' directors is in some ways preferable because it sounds less negative. Best of all is 'independent', but it is not accepted because some 'non-executive' directors are deemed valuable to companies even though they are not wholly independent in view of their past or present connections with the company.) In 1980, City institutions led by the Bank of England, together with the banks, the Stock Exchange, the Confederation of British Industries, and the British Institute of Management, set up PRO NED to promote the wider use of non-executive directors.

The effect of the Cadbury Code is to make non-executive directors mandatory in quoted companies (unless good cause is shown), since they must have audit committees (para. 4.3) with at least three non-executive directors. This reinforces the requirement (para. 1.3) for a board to have non-executive directors 'of significant calibre and number for their views to carry significant weight in the board's decisions'. All this supports the line taken by the Institutional Shareholders' Committee in December 1991 in *The Responsibilities of Institutional Shareholders in the UK*, which states:

(e) ii. . . . Institutional investors should take a positive interest in the composition of boards of directors with particular reference to . . . the appointment of a core of non-executives of appropriate calibre, experience, and independence.

(f) Institutional investors support the appointment of compensation and audit committees.

In the twelve years since 1980 there has been evidence of an improvement in quality. According to the Centre for Business Strategy analysis, of seventy-four of the first 100 companies in *The Times* 1,000, 62 per cent of non-executive directors are executive directors of other companies, and 12 per cent are professionals or from the financial sector. The fictional Duke of Plaza Toro who used to 'sit by selection upon the direction of several companies' bubble' would get fewer offers than he did. Quantity has improved too. According to PRO NED's 1990 survey of this top 100 UK companies, 96 per cent had two or more non-executive directors and 82 per cent three or more. Broadly speaking the larger the company, the higher the proportion of NEDs. The picture has changed much in the last decade. The 3i Survey showed that two-thirds of the respondents boards had three to six non-executive directors.

Even so, some companies still have none, and many have supple reeds who bend to the wind. Some chairmen feel that their boards are so clever and operate in such a collegiate style that the wisdom of the rest of the world is superfluous, and no other checks are necessary. Others feel that a committee of one is best and treat their colleagues as cyphers—the so-called mushroom boards, with directors kept in the dark and nourished with a little fertilizer occasionally: the last thing such chairmen want is a penetrating questioner.

As we have seen, the law permits total flexibility and chairmen make the most of it, each according to his character. The UK has what are probably some of the best boards in the world, with able executives and non-executives chosen on merits and not plucked from the nineteenth hole; well-constructed agendas supported by adequate and timely information; a style of conduct of business which encourages all to have their say; and a decision-making process which is clear, brave, and robust. At the other end of the spectrum are companies which are run like private fiefdoms (even though public money has been subscribed), where the boards are weak and ill informed; where the decision-making process is obscure; and where either venality is concealed or the board is seduced by participating in the goodies.

The UK system imposes severe strains on all participants, but particularly the non-executive directors. They share in full the responsibilities of their executive colleagues, yet their knowledge of the business is bound to be far less. They must contribute positively to discussions. They must share in the directors' general function of supervising the running of the business—in the knowledge that although their duties are nominally the same, the executive directors cannot easily supervise themselves. Of course there is a trade-off between knowledge and objectivity, but there are crucial times when a person's intense commitment to a project fatally warps judgement. A non-executive director will often feel alone, fearful of raising what seems an obvious point or checking a basic assumption which everyone else treats like the laws of the Medes and Persians. It is not a job for the bashful or timid and requires courage; and yet he or she is part of a team so that firmness must never degenerate into abrasiveness. Non-executive directors must position themselves correctly knowing which issues to consider and which to ignore; not for them the crystalline delineation of authority that goes with the formal powers of a supervisory board. I wrote this passage not to add to the many manuals for non-executive directors but to illustrate what a difficult role the system gives them to play. I hear many people say nowadays that the role is always difficult and sometimes impossible, because the co-operative and supervisory modes are simply not consistent. The idea of the member of the team who has a referee's whistle in his pocket to blow when necessary is a picturesque sporting metaphor but an awkward concept to practise effectively.

Their value to the board lies in part in considering difficult issues with sympathetic objectivity, seeing them in the broad context of the company as a whole, and questioning the critical assumptions on which proposals are based. If they become unnerved they may find their critical faculty dulled. Theirs is not a negative function, for they must contribute positively to discussions, but it requires skill, tact, and courage which over-familiarity and personal friendship must not weaken.

At least NEDs are a little better paid than they were. A P-E international survey (Summer 1991) found that the average remuneration of a NED was £12,400 for about 12–15 days' work in a year. PRO NED say that currently (Spring 1992) companies that brief them generally envisage remuneration of £12,000 to £15,000 per annum.

Ever since the Bullock Report of 1975 the issue of employee representation on boards has been dead; neither employees nor unions wanted it then and few would advocate it today, although the Fifth Directive which would make it mandatory still hovers in the wings. Employee representation probably works better in practice associated with a supervisory tier, which the UK does not have or seem to want, than it would in a unitary board. This was certainly the view in Germany.

A Corporate Governance Report

Even before the Cadbury Report, some of the better-governed UK companies had begun to include statements on their governance arrangements. In Appendix 6A is the passage in ICI's 1991 report and a statement from that of the National Westminster Bank. The Cadbury Report recommends that listed companies in respect of accounting years ending after 30 June 1993 should state in the report and accounts whether they comply with the Code and identify and give reasons for any areas of non-compliance. The London Stock Exchange intends to require such a statement as one of its continuing listing obligations, but it will be up to shareholders to take up with a company any points of non-compliance that concern them.

The Appointment and Dismissal of Directors

In practice all directors are appointed by the board and elected by the shareholders. Shareholder nominations are rare for quoted companies (except perhaps when companies are in deep trouble), though quite common for small companies where a supplier of venture capital may wish to nominate a director or two.

In the case of executives appointed as directors the dominant voice is that of the CEO, whose subordinates by definition the others are. By the same token it is he who will in practice have the prime responsibility for removing them if they prove unsatisfactory and sometimes, power being what it is, if they are exceptionally good and a threat to him. The CEO himself can be removed by the board; strangely enough this happens more often when the board is dominated by executives than when it is dominated by non-executive directors. There have been occasions where the shareholders have intervened directly to unseat a CEO and change a board by exerting pressure (with the stated or implied threat of a vote), but this is rare; there are on the other hand many examples of board *coups*. It is the UK style for these things to be managed rather noisily; not for the UK the quiet tap on the shoulder and the discreet shunt sideways that typifies the Japanese system. One of the consequences is a considerable reluctance to do the deed, since it may affect publicly an old colleague and friend whose past service has been good enough to make a public *congé* seem harsh.

Non-executive directors are a different matter. The old way of identifying them (which still persists) was for the CEO to consider successively people known to him personally; to his colleagues; and to his advisers and friends. If all else failed he might seek professional help. The search tended to put status and compatibility before relevance and acuity; the candidates often preceded the specification; like the Queen in Alice in Wonderland, the verdict preceded the evidence. All that is gradually changing and the appointment of nominating committees is starting to have an effect. The use of professional help from PRO NED and from headhunting firms is increasing. As to formal election, in practice the board appoints and the shareholders ratify—a perfectly sensible arrangement, though it is a pity the shareholders are not always given, and do not seem to demand, better information when a name is proposed for the first time.

The dismissal of non-executive directors is an important and neglected subject. In law directors can only be dismissed by the shareholders. On this crucial fact rests the shareholders' main power and directors' independence. Unless the articles so permit a board cannot dismiss a director (though it can strip him of executive powers if he has any), though I notice an increasing tendency to introduce such a provision. Of course, if they wish him to resign they can make his life uncomfortable, but they have no right to force him out—not even after a take-over. In practice the unwanted generally go, often with a *douceur*. And sometimes the shareholders' interests are badly served by their leaving. The chairman is chosen by his fellow directors and they can equally cause him to stand down; but in practice cases are rare of a chairman being removed against his will and yet remaining as director.

Where some members of the board—or an individual—is or are actually or effectively the controlling shareholder, no other director has any security of tenure; all are there at the will of the shareholders. This was true of Robert Maxwell's directors on MCC and Mirror Newspapers, and remains true of many a smaller PLC where the family retain control. What this boils down to is that in such companies, rather as in private companies, the board is basically an advisory committee to those who exercise power. This may be extremely useful to the company and is to be welcomed; many a company of this sort will acknowledge the debt it owes to directors whose experience and wisdom have proved invaluable. They can only act as monitors to the extent that those with power permit it. They themselves may have influence, but they have no power. Those who control the business are in effect accountable to no one but themselves. The presence of outside directors should mislead no one that they have power.

Resignation on grounds of fundamental disagreement is a non-executive director's ultimate weapon and it appears to be most useful as a deterrent or if it is feared it may make a big bang. A quiet retreat 'to concentrate on other interests' has generally not helped to protect shareholders' interests: arguably it would have served the company better had the resigner stayed on, however uncomfortable, to continue the struggle. Few directors have resigned noisily, partly because of potential damage to the company, which is the last thing they want, partly because of an understandable lack of relish for a fight. Few resignations signify. If there is only one director, no one notices. If there are more than one, and one resigns, it seldom makes a stir. Resignation is a weapon of dubious value; any virtue it may have is associated with publicity and, if there are several directors, with joint action. Cadbury proposes that the non-executives should have 'a recognized senior member' to whom the non-executives can turn if the chairman is also the CEO. This should help to make non-executives more effective in action—and action is undoubtedly better than resignation.

I have known cases where a sole non-executive director has felt his position to be untenable, disliking the board's actions but without support or even an avenue of communication. Resignation seemed the only course. At least in respect of quoted companies there should be no companies with only a single NED after the Cadbury Code comes into effect.

Committees of the Board

All committees of the board serve two purposes, not just the obvious one of facilitating the dispatch of business; the other is to involve the non-executive directors by familiarizing them in detail with some important aspect of the governance of the company. Membership of a remuneration committee, for instance, may well mean considering both performance and succession. Greater involvement is important. It gives the non-executives a chance to work together and to caucus alone if they feel they must, and it gives them the confidence to intervene when they should and the knowledge when not to. Let us look at the most important committees.

(1) *Audit committees.* Audit committees first came to prominence in the USA in the late 1970s as a riposte to some cases of financial abuse. The New York Stock Exchange made them a listing condition in 1978 and stipulated that they should be composed of outside directors (thereby changing the shape of American boards—at least for the minority of companies that did not already have outside directors). Their formal functions, which are the same as in the UK, are to do with the scope of the external audit, the appointment of external auditors, the internal audit system, and liaison with the internal auditors, examination of the financial statements, and discussions on them with the external auditors. And—if necessary—investigations including the problem of the dishonest CEO. If dishonesty occurs at lower levels, it is relatively easy for the CEO to deal with it. But what do the auditors, internal or external, do about a CEO they suspect? Fraud, by its very nature, is often carefully concealed, so they lack proof. The audit committee's power to require an investigation eases the problem: it should rarely be needed, but it is nevertheless useful. Of course most CEOs, being honest, have nothing to fear.

In the USA the financial director usually attends the audit committee, but formally this is by invitation not as of right. And others, including the CEO, may be invited too. When the Americans began, there was much scepticism, but a decade later surveys there showed that this had faded. They are felt useful. Audit committees are at the heart of the Cadbury report, and paragraph 4.3 of the Code says:

The board should establish an audit committee of at least three non-executive directors within terms of reference which deal clearly with its authority and duties.

Note 11 to the Code sets out the recommendations more fully, namely:

(a) They should be formally constituted as sub-committees of the main board to whom they are answerable and to whom they should report regularly; they should be given written terms of reference which deal adequately with their membership, authority and duties; and they should normally meet at least twice a year.

(b) There should be a minimum of three members. Membership should be confined to the non-executive directors of the company and a majority of the non-executives serving on the committee should be independent of the company, as defined in paragraph 2.2 of the Code.

(c) The external auditor and, where an internal audit function exists, the head of internal audit should normally attend committee meetings, as should the finance director. Other board members should also have the right to attend.

(d) The audit committee should have a discussion with the auditors at least once a year, without executive board members present, to ensure that there are no unresolved issues of concern.

(e) The audit committee should have explicit authority to investigate any matters within its terms of reference, the resources which it needs to do so, and full access to information. The committee should be able to obtain outside professional advice and if necessary to invite outsiders with relevant experience to attend meetings.

(f) Membership of the committee should be disclosed in the annual report and the chairman of the committee should be available to answer questions about its work at the annual general meeting.

Appendix 4 to the Cadbury Report covers the ground in much more detail: I have included it at the end of Appendix 7A.

The University of Exeter recently carried out some research into audit committees in financial institutions and discovered that of the forty-four who responded (out of fifty):

80 per cent had audit committees;
The norm was three to four members;
Two-thirds were composed wholly of NEDs;
They met three to four times a year;
Meetings lasted about 2 hours;
Functions were broadly as stated above.

The details are given in Appendix 6B.

Korn Ferry, looking at a different sample, found that the proportion of UK companies with an audit committee had risen from 13 per cent in 1980 to 45 per cent in 1990.

(2) *Remuneration committees.* In recent years the pay of top executives has excited public interest in the UK as it has in the USA, particularly when increases were not matched by increases in profits. (For instance, Robert Evans of British Gas had an increase of 18 per cent to £435,000 in 1991 when profits fell 5 per cent; there were queries from shareholders at the AGM. Questions were also raised at the AGM of the Prudential, whose chairman, M. Newmarch, received a 43 per cent increase in 1991 against a fall in profits of 37 per cent.) Sometimes, however, the comment was about

quantum even when a company had been hugely successful. (Sir Ian MacLaurin had the highest percentage increase in 1991—330 per cent—which took him to £1.48 million.) Press attention has also focused on other big salaries, such as Lord Hanson (Hanson PLC, 1991 salary £1.4 million); Tiny Rowland (Lonrho PLC, 1991 salary £1.6 million); Ian Vallance (British Telecom bonus in 1991, £225,000, out of a package of £675,000). The average chairman of a company in the FTSE 100 now gets about £400,000, and the range as of December 1992 was from £148,000 to £6.2 million. Since 1980 pay for male manual workers has risen 239 per cent: pay for chief executives has risen 324 per cent.

Against this background there has been increasing pressure to find a more objective way of determining the emoluments of executive directors, recognizing that their personal interests are not necessarily the same as those of the shareholders and that the board must reconcile the two. The solution is increasingly seen to lie in the operation of a remuneration committee—what the Americans call a compensation committee—manned by the non-executive directors, who may be trusted to take an objective view of the competing interests. This is what Cadbury recommended (para. 4.42), and PRO NED recently produced a booklet on their role. This may be a step forward, but it must be admitted that the committee has a difficult task. The forces of upward pressure are for the most part more vigorous than those for containment: consultants are not loved if they recommend parsimony; there is an inbuilt ratcheting effect because review dates vary; and maintaining both internal and external relativities is never easy and usually results in the choice of the more favourable indicator. Meanwhile, there is external pressure to relate remuneration to performance—and that is not easy either. There is no such thing as a 'right' level of remuneration; judgements may be 'informed' but they are nevertheless judgements, and they are unlikely to please everyone—especially in hard times. There is scepticism about the effectiveness of remuneration committees and shareholders seem increasingly to realize the need for vigilance not out of distrust but because this is technically a difficult area in which the answers inevitably depend on somewhat subjective judgements. Shareholders seem to be more prepared to let a company know if they are dissatisfied—not necessarily by a public démarche.

The Korn Ferry Survey (1990) shows that 62 per cent of their sample of listed companies had remuneration committees, compared with 26 per cent in 1980. The Main/Johnston study showed that far from curbing remuneration, companies with remuneration committees paid more than those without—about 14–18 per cent! So as a way of keeping remuneration down they are not the answer (if that is in itself a desirable objective). Their study concludes that much depends on the quantity and quality of non-executive directors on the board from whom the remuneration committee is drawn. 'Simply grafting on an additional board sub-committee will of itself do little either for the disciplines of top executive pay or for corporate governance in general.'

(3) *Nominating committees.* Patronage is such an enjoyable and satisfying pastime that one cannot expect anyone who has the chance to exercise it to deny themselves that pleasure. Besides, the chairman (or CEO) would be less than human if he did not prefer to be surrounded by like-minded and congenial spirits, rather than by those of an angular personality, however clever. The chairman/CEO inevitably has great influence on the choice of colleagues and this can result in the appointment of sycophants or buddies: my impression is that as the spotlight on non-executive directors has brightened, the selection process has improved. Now that companies have to describe their background in the annual report the world can at least share the chairman's wisdom in his exercise of patronage. A nominating committee is really designed to do three things: give the chairman a conscience when he picks buddies; offer alternatives; improve the selection process. In the best-run companies specification precedes search and choice; in many the reverse often happens. At the very least a nominating committee brings an element of discipline into the process. Smaller companies may hesitate to have one because of the work load, but PRO NED and other agencies can fill the gap at modest cost. The service they can render makes the exercise of patronage not only respectable but also effective—in the sense that candidates have to evince other qualities besides ingratiating themselves with the chairman.

The Boards of Private Companies

To some extent different principles apply to unquoted companies. Although the obligations to the shareholders remain, there are by definition no 'public' shareholders to be affected, and private ones may be assumed not to need the same degree of protection. Some private companies do have outside directors mainly to broaden the range of experience available to management and the board. My impression is that in this role they are extremely valuable and that more companies might with advantage appoint them. Their monitoring role in practice is no more or less than those who control the company desire.

Dynasties

Many private companies have remained not only in family control but also under family direction for two or three generations. It would be interesting to have some hard facts on this, but the general impression is that the old saying 'Clogs to clogs in three generations', mentioned in Section i above, is still not far wide of the mark. The most promising members of the family often want other careers; or the line does not produce the requisite talent. Being succeeded by one's offspring gratifies an understandable human desire to defy mortality, but appears only too often to hasten the mortality of the business.

Some families succeed in maintaining their central role long after the company has floated and their shareholdings have dwindled or been diluted; it is surprising to learn that they sometimes hold less than 5 per cent. It seems to be more widely recognized than it was that succession should be governed more by competence than by heredity. My impression is that boards are increasingly reluctant to allow CEOs/chairmen to hand over the reins to an offspring or relation unless he or she is really qualified for the post. Some of course are, and when this is so, turn out to be among the very best because of their exceptional dedication to the enterprise.

Even so, Sir Lewis Robertson (1993), doctor to many ailing companies, warned his audience to beware:

Management imbalance comes in many forms. One of these is the area of family and family deference; a true entrepreneur can build up a remarkable business, to the advantage of investors' staff and customers, but it can be disastrous if his (or his family's) influence continues too long. On more than one occasion I have seen a very good company brought close to disaster by this . . . Beware of families; press for the professionalization of family businesses, be they smaller or large.

The European Dimension

In Chapter 2 there is a description of German arrangements which combine two quite separate principles.

(1) That it is better to separate the functions of management and supervision.

(2) That the employees are entitled to play a part in the governance of the company.

Because the Germans have combined these two principles, it has become fashionable for others to follow down the same track, but this is not necessary. We saw from Chapter 4 that French law provides for a two-tier system without adding employee representation to it. The Dutch, in a different way, have a two-tier system; in their case the direct involvement of employees is limited to having a role in the selection process. Unfortunately the report of the Bullock committee in 1975 was so universally opposed that dispassionate discussion has been difficult ever since in the UK.

The success of German industry and Germany's important role in the Economic Community even before the UK joined meant that German influence with the Commission was considerable. The early drafts of the Fifth Directive owed much to the work of Germans on the Commission's staff. Later drafts give companies a choice between a single and dual tier structure. Even so, the unitary board option currently envisaged requires a majority of non-executive directors (art. 21A), and that at least a third of the board shall be appointed by the employees or their representative. The UK predilection for fudge has caused it to take the view that the *de jure* creation of two classes of directors is unacceptable even though its *de facto* existence is not only tolerable but positively to be recommended. Other aspects of the draft Fifth Directive have excited UK opposition, such as prescription about arrangements involving employee participation and involvement. It lauds best practice among its companies, but feels they should be free to do what they wish (even if it is the worst). The UK position appears to reflect the attitude mentioned earlier of a hatred of excessive prescription and over-definnition, besides a deep-seated mistrust of formalized employee involvement. It does not see any overriding need for European uniformity: if the Americans can have variety between States in the same country, why should not EC countries with their vastly differing histories and traditions have variety too? It offends the UK sense of the practical. There is no point in going through the motions. Let there be flexibility; let the parties work it out for themselves. If minimum standards are set too high, companies could be priced out of the market. Quite apart from these general points there are some specific problems, such as the effect of Article 33, which would as drafted have an adverse effect on some UK companies because of their present structure (this is the article which proposes equal voting rights).

As mentioned earlier, the European Company Statute (ECS) provides an *additional* option for companies in the Community. This differs from the Fifth Directive in that its use is conceived as being voluntary. Even so, it has aroused opposition on the 'Thin edge of the wedge' argument. If the UK were to accept the features in the draft ECS which it dislikes, such as co-determination, it would weaken its argument against similar provisions in the Fifth Directive. And there is always a fear that once the ECS is in place, its use could be encouraged by favourable tax treatment.

Shareholders

Shareholders' Rights

One of the advantages of a joint stock company and the concept of limited liability is that a person may venture his savings in an enterprise without putting at risk a penny more than he has staked, and without either a duty or a right to manage the enterprise. The bundle of rights with which the shareholder is left include a share of money distributed by way of dividend; a share of any surplus if the enterprise is wound up; a vote in the election of those to whom its stewardship is entrusted—the directors; a supply of information as laid down by the Companies Act and supplemented by the Stock Exchange's rules; the right to subscribe when new capital is sought. A shareholder's main right is, of course, to dispose freely of stock at the best price. Most rights are proportionate to the capital owned—a vote per share, not a vote per shareholder. This proportionality leads to a differentiation between shareholders which is based on the reality of power, not on status. A shareholder with ten votes is entitled to the same status as one with a million; but a platoon was never equal to a regiment, except in fairy stories. In Orwellian language, all shareholders are equal but some are more equal than others.

Individual Shareholders

Individual shareholders are numerous—about 9.26 million according to PRO SHARE. Of all UK shareholders 62 per cent own shares in privatized issues only; 7 per cent own only the free shares they were given with the Abbey National flotation; and 10 per cent own shares solely through employee schemes. PRO SHARE estimate there are only 1.6 million shareholders with a portfolio of shares. Limited though their relative power may be, it is not negligible. They have as much right at an annual general meeting to hold the floor as the representative of Omnium Gatherum Insurance plc, and if they have the wit to ask the right questions with the media present, may cause quite a stir (though the media only cover an AGM as a rule if they expect a story). That private shareholders seldom speak reflects their feeling of overwhelming odds, timidity, and ignorance. They have the Report and Accounts and newspaper comments; they may have their broker's advice. Unlike professionals they lack the power or knowledge to delve into the figures or peer behind the mask. Their only sight of company management is at the AGM itself—and this would often tell them quite a lot were they to take the trouble to attend—but few do. If the company is big, rich, and forward-looking, it may make a presentation in different localities, but this is rare.

These obstacles are on the whole treated by private shareholders as insuperable. If they lose confidence in the company they either sell or hold on and wait for better days. There is nowhere for them to turn for help if they feel that what is wrong is the board; they can vote against the directors of course, but feel as they do as if they were shaking a pepper-pot' on to desert sand. Who notices? Who cares? All this was seen and analysed 60 years ago by the American professors Berle and Means, who understood the implications of shareholdings being dispersed and fragmented. It meant accountability by the board to the shareholders was effectively dead.

Today we find individual shareholders beginning to resent the power of the institutions; they ought in fact be grateful for it, for it is the institutions who have begun to invalidate the Berle and Means analysis, as we have seen in the USA (Chapter 5). It is absurd to pretend that the small shareholder has the knowledge or clout of a major institution, or that the market treats such shareholders 'fairly'. It costs them more to trade *pro rata* because of dis-economies of scale. They cannot know as much. They cannot expect a company to care as much about a handful of votes as it does about a million. They should hope that the institutions do have sensible and close relations with companies which will keep an eye on them for everyone's good; and they should trust the insider trading laws to trap those who abuse their position.

The private shareholders could write in to the company more often; few companies ignore sensible enquiries, which may produce an effect. They could but seldom do ask penetrating questions at AGMs; if they speak it is often on extraneous matters like the environment or (in the old days) South Africa, not about the way the company is run. They have to face the 'free rider' problem, that is, that individually they would have to bear all the costs of actions whose benefits mainly accrued to others. The logical answer is for them to get together with other private shareholders and make common cause. Britain lacks a means of bringing this about. People are encouraged to own shares but not to combine to protect their interest; they could do it if they had a mind to (see Chapter 5 for the United Shareholder Association of the USA by way of comparison). A body which represented individual shareholders and held their proxies would find itself with similar access to company management as the institutions—to which we now turn.

Institutional Shareholders

Partly because the UK's tax arrangements favour collective savings—particularly pension funds—the proportion of equity shares in the hands of those who administer them now predominates. When inflation was non-existent or low, funds could largely meet their obligations by investing in fixed interest securities; inflationary pressures made fund managers seek better, if riskier, returns. With the exception of a short period in the Great Depression equities have been a better investment. By 1989, 18.4 per cent of UK equities were held by insurance companies, 30.4 per cent by pension funds, 5.9 per cent by unit trusts, and 3.2 per cent by other financial companies (source CSO 1989 share register survey). In 1991, life insurance companies held 42 per cent of their assets in UK equities and 9 per cent in other equities (source CSO). The pattern, in other words, is like that of the USA, only more developed in favour of the institutions.

Institutional investors are no more homogeneous as a class than individuals. They vary greatly in size. A pension fund may be a million pounds. A big insurance company may manage forty billions. They vary in purpose—pension funds, insurance companies, unit and investment trust managers serve differing purposes, have different obligations, and are under different pressures. They can discharge their obligations in various ways, choosing to manage funds in house, or employing external managers. The one thing they all have in common is that the managers are investing someone else's money, which imposes on them and those who employ them standards a private individual can choose to ignore if he is acting for himself. Not all their funds go into the UK equity market by any means. The proportion allocated to it flows from strategic decisions about the proportion that should go into property, or bonds, or into other equity markets. With capital flows now unrestricted the world is their oyster, though of course they need to be able to match their obligations in the currency in which they have to be paid.

Portfolio Management and Corporate Governance

An examination of portfolio management would seem at first sight to be an odd digression in a book on corporate governance, but it is not. The capacity and willingness of investors to take an interest in the subject depends greatly on what portfolios they have, how they manage them, and what their perceptions are of their tasks. So we must at least glance at the different main approaches, realizing as we do so that the text simplifies for the sake of brevity an immensely complicated and sophisticated subject.

Fund managers cannot put all their eggs in one basket and must diversify to spread risk. There is, however, no magic formula for deciding how much to diversify or what basic policy to adopt. There seem to be two main choices.

(1) *Active investing*. This covers a range of policies from highly diversified to concentrated portfolios; and from 'keep and hold' to 'active trading'.

(2) *Passive investing*. This means 'buying the index', that is, the investor buys all the shares in a given index, e.g. the FTSE (or segment of an index). The funds will be weighted identically to the index itself. It is difficult to get precise figures, but it is estimated that about 8 per cent of UK equities are now in indexed funds.

As noted above, active investors can approach their task in a wide variety of ways: here are two examples from opposite ends of the spectrum. The first is M&G's published policy statement.

[A] M&G's investment philosophy is to concentrate on long term value with an emphasis on income and recovery, and a general reluctance to invest in highly rated fashionable stocks. M&G funds have holdings of 5 percent or more in the equity capital of about 220 companies. We believe that as substantial investors we should have a firm and lasting relationship with the managements of companies in which we have a large interest, and we make a point of getting to know the people who run those companies. We do not presume to tell the management how to run their business but, if a company's actions are likely to jeopardise the interests of shareholders, we find that constructive intervention can often be preferable to disposing of a holding. This means that we take a long term view of performance and try not to be deflected by short term considerations. This seems to us to be in the best interests of both industry and our own investors. M&G is independent of any organization which could influence our policy-making or day-to-day decisions. As a further safeguard, the equity proportion of our Group reserves is always invested in M&G unit trusts rather than individual shareholdings. When we deal in the stock market we do so as agents for our various funds and clients, not as principals for our own benefit.

Here is a contrasting view from a top fund manager

[B] I do not believe that it is sensible to expect shareholders to step in and sort out management problems, except as the very last resort. We do not have the resources nor are our clients likely to be willing to pay for them. More important though, our overriding responsibility is to our clients, who judge us on the investment results achieved each year. Unless that objective is changed, then we are bound to prefer selling shares in problem companies to the costly and very lengthy business of organising management change ourselves.

Neither envisages interfering with everyday management decisions. In Example A the role of the shareholder is to be informed sufficiently to exert influence in the rare cases where an obvious lapse of general standards makes this essential in the interests of all the stakeholders, including the shareholders. There is no implication that the board is neglecting its duties: it may be doing its best, but not be good enough.

Type A's characteristics are:

- Concentration of the portfolio on fewer stocks;
- Large stakes in individual companies;
- Close (and often direct) communication with companies in which such investments are held; and the exercise of influence where appropriate;
- High loyalty factor to the companies;
- Few dealings in those shares and less freedom to deal with whole stakes because of the effect on the market;
- General interest in corporate governance matters.

Type B is the opposite in almost every way:

- Wide diversification—many different shares;
- Small stakes in each;
- Communication, if any, with companies mainly about matters which will have a short-term effect on the price;
- Low loyalty factor;
- Frequent dealing;
- Interest in corporate governance virtually non-existent.

The most celebrated exponent of Type A is Warren Buffett with his Berkshire Hathaway Corporation (see Chapter 5). Many of the UK's major insurance companies see themselves as far closer to Type A than Type B, and so do some of the major pension funds that are managed in house. My impression is that most UK fund managers who pursue an 'active' policy are closer to Type B than to Type A.

If we take pension funds as fairly typical of institutional investors (and they involve external fund managers, including life insurance companies), we can get some useful indication of activity from the *WM Annual Review* for 1991, which analyses 1,424 funds comprising over 2,000 portfolios with a market value of £241 billion at the end of the year—about three-quarters of UK pension funds. Of this money 56 per cent was invested in UK equities, whose value rose in the year by 20 per cent—0.7 per cent below the FTA–All Share Index. Over the last ten years the funds in the WM sample have returned an increase of 19.1 per cent compared with the FTA–All Share Index 19.7 per cent. WM said that '[This] largely reflects the costs of trading and investing new money'. This small difference means £144.6 million (i.e. 0.6 per cent of £241 billion).

As to who actually manages pension funds, the 1991 *WM Review* shows that 30 per cent are managed internally and 32 per cent part internal, part external—and these groups alone show above average returns over five years (10.1 and 10.0 respectively). External managers who managed the rest had returns varying from 9.3 per cent (life company segregated funds) to 9.9 per cent (life company managed), with others between these last two figures. Activity levels have tended to grow, but internally managed funds at 29 per cent are far lower than for all the rest—the highest being life company segregation funds at 123 per cent, followed by life company managed, 112 per cent, and two or more external fund managers, 101 per cent.

What all this tends to show is that there is no correlation between high activity and success, nor indeed between 'active' management and success. In an average year active managers run very hard to keep up with the index and few of them manage to do so—rewarding for intermediaries but not for beneficiaries!

As noted above, one of the characteristics of 'active' fund management is a widely diversified portfolio. Of course risk must be spread—but how far? Active traders want to be able to sell without moving the market against themselves; the size of the total portfolio and the market capitalization of the companies in which they invest are obviously relevant considerations. One is still left wondering why they diversify as much as they do. Richard Brealey and Stewart Myers (1991: 137) write:

Even a little diversification can provide a substantial reduction in variability. Suppose you calculate and compare the standard deviations of randomly chosen one-stock portfolios, two-stock portfolios, five-stock portfolios, etc. Diversification can cut the variability of returns about in half. But you can get most of this benefit with relatively few stocks: the improvement is slight when the number of securities is increased beyond, say, twenty or thirty.

Wagner and Lau (1971) suggested that most of the benefits of diversification could be achieved with between 10 and 15 stocks.

Graham and Dodd (1934) reached a similar destination by a different route, that of 'value investing' based on a patient, disciplined approach to the selection of stocks. Lowenstein (1988: 32–5) gives a summary of the main thrust of their argument.

It would be interesting to establish why particular institutions diversify to the extent they do. Have they calculated what the optimum would be for them? One is left with the feeling, which the data in the last paragraph supports, that in most cases they would be better off to go for index

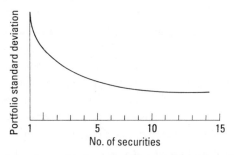

Fɪɢ. 6.1 Diversification reduces risk (standard deviation) rapidly at first, then more slowly

matching. It would be less costly to administer and produce a better result in most years.

One possible explanation has been put forward by US commentators. They point out that many fund managers are part of a group of which a merchant bank is the parent company. It could cause acute embarrassment to the merchant bank were its investment arm to become active as share-holders in a way which upset the management of one of the bank's clients, as could very easily happen. There ought, it is true, to be a Chinese wall between the merchant bank and its investment arm, but in real life a client company would not regard this is a satisfactory excuse. So it is easier, as a matter of practice if not of policy, for the fund managers in such groups to ignore corporate governance issues altogether.

One of the effects of present practices for the Type B operation is to put an impenetrable wall between the fund managers and issues of corporate governance. They routinely buy shares in companies they do not properly understand. What concerns them is not a company's fundamentals, which take time to explore and particular skills to understand, but market timing. Most shares fluctuate markedly in any year, so investment in them means for many fund managers focusing mainly on trading signals. What matters is timing, which attracts great interest (see e.g. the article in *Investors Chronicle* (19 June 1992) called 'Secrets of Investment Timing', which deals with seasonal influences). The UK has an efficient stock market, so fund managers can, they believe, trade out of their mistakes. With such an approach there can be no interest in corporate governance: all shares are *in principle* held for the short term (even if in the event some part of some holdings remains in the portfolio for years). The skills of such fund managers may be great as traders, and they could no doubt switch them to any other commodity from cocoa to pork bellies: they are right to be modest about their capacity to act as if they were real owners. That is not how they consider themselves and they are not equipped for it.

Perhaps the surprising part of all this is its obvious costliness and inefficiency. As more than two-thirds of UK equities are in the hands of institutions, the counter-party is usually another institution. Every transaction is at the cost of someone's beneficiaries. Viewed in aggregate, this is not a zero sum game for beneficiaries, but a minus sum game. It is interesting to consider—and we shall return to the point—why trustees do not consider carefully the related issues of diversification and turnover. They should. A restriction on the percentage of a portfolio that could be traded in any one year would in principle have a beneficial effect on performance, since it would reduce costs and focus fund managers' attention more sharply on selection.

The Institutional Shareholders' Committee gives a steer in the right direction, indicating perhaps that the tide is turning. It says, in a recent policy document,

It is considered important that institutional shareholders support boards by a positive use of their voting rights unless they have good reasons for doing otherwise. Such shareholders should register their votes wherever possible on a regular basis. Where a board has received steady support over a period of time, it should become a matter of concern to the board if that support is not forthcoming on a particular matter.

The document suggests that:

(a) Institutional investors should encourage regular, systematic contact at senior executive level to exchange views and information on strategy, performance, board membership and quality of management. . . .
(e) Institutional investors should take a positive interest in the composition of boards of directors, with particular reference to:
   (i) Concentrations of decision-making power not formally constrained by checks and balances appropriate to the particular company.
   (ii) The appointment of a core of non-executives of appropriate calibre, experience and independence.
(f) Institutional investors support the appointment of compensation and audit committees.
(g) Institutional investors encourage disclosure of the principles upon which directors' emoluments are determined.

How practical is such a policy? It is already followed to some extent by many of the biggest houses, but not by all. Some believe their staff lack the necessary skills: that they are good at trading and expert at numbers; that they understand charts and market timing in a highly sophisticated way; but that they are not trained to consider issues of corporate governance. In a bull market such fund managers may be happy to shut their eyes to obviously flawed corporate governance and even on occasion to dubious behaviour. Even if a house wished its fund managers to shift from a Type B to a Type A policy it would need to ensure that they had the appropriate skills—not a daunting or expensive prospect, and easily soluble given determination.

Having said that, we must not lose sight of how many institutions there are, how small some are, and how little power, by themselves, all but the biggest have. It takes a lot of time and effort to reach the degree of confidence in one's judgement at which action would appear to be justified: it takes more time—and expense—to take action. Standing alone only the biggest institutions will be heeded when they speak, and sometimes not even they.

Even when, unlike small private shareholders, large institutions have the information to support some form of approach or action, they, like them, still have to consider the free-rider problem. Even if they hold 2 per cent of the equity, why should they accept the burden to benefit the other 98 per cent as well? Their solution, too, is joint action to share costs and gain 'muscle'. So far this has appeared unattractive to the institutions, probably because of rivalry between them. There were attempts to set up machinery in the 1970s and 1980s, but they fizzled out.

To understand why fund managers behave this way we must consider the influences upon them. They are judged by relative performances (the league tables), so they are motivated both by fear and hope. If they perform consistently badly they will be dropped; if they do exceptionally well they will attract much new business as well as keeping what they have. 'Active' investing is therefore a gamble for them, and if it fails it may cost the fund manager his client but not as quickly as might be supposed, especially if he has established a good rapport. Changes are themselves likely to be expensive, and there is no guarantee that a successor will perform better, but even so the pressures are intense.

One distinguished fund manager approaching retirement recently voiced his concern about the amount of value added compared to the level of activity. In his view fund managers, particularly younger ones, were under great pressure to perform and to justify their existence. Brokers applied strong psychological pressures on them to do business, carefully building up personal relations and offering 'freebies'. Consultants tended to advise trustees to change fund managers—which then often meant turning over the whole portfolio: his own institution's US portfolio had had six different managers since the early 1980s. It would have done better had it been index matched.

Given these pressures it is not surprising that index-matched funds have grown more popular. A fund manager who turns to them may not yet be high enough in the league tables to attract much new business, but he will be sufficiently high to avoid dismissal. It is a safety first policy and can be regarded as diversification *in excelsis*: a fund manager realizes that if he can only know less about more and more, he might as well accept that he knows nothing about everything, trust that market theory is right (as the market reflects all available knowledge), and join it rather than try to beat it. This then is the fund manager's choice (if he has decided not to be a 'value investor').

It might have been thought that passive investing meant passivity in relation to corporate governance; after all, one is locked into whatever index has been chosen. In fact, it is possible to argue—as some big US funds do—that indexation and being locked in means logically that one *should* take a proprietorial interest as a means, ultimately, of improving company performance and hence the index as a whole. The administrative savings realized by indexing can be partially redeployed to this end. This argument appeals much less to small funds. They too are dogged by the free-rider problem mentioned above. The answer must be for them too to make common cause with others similarly placed so as to share costs.

The Role of Trustees

There are those who believe (and not just in the aftermath of the Maxwell collapse) that too little attention has been paid to the role of trustees, which is or should be significant in pension funds and in other forms of collective savings. It is not just that the trustees should obviously assure themselves of the safety of the funds, but that they have a responsibility for managing them prudently, either themselves, or more usually through professional managers. Even if they delegate, they remain responsible for the terms on which the delegation is made. This is not easy to do in an informed and knowledgeable way. How many trustees feel themselves competent to instruct their fund managers on the appropriate degree of diversification and the maximum proportion of turnover? Do they really appreciate what excessive trading costs the beneficiaries? Do they understand the cost of splitting a portfolio between too many managers? It has been estimated, for instance, that the cost of managing a fund of £100 million with four managers rather than one might typically rise from £195,000 to £320,000, excluding extra consultancy and custodial fees.

Indeed, to do the trustees' job effectively requires considerable knowledge, skill, and judgement. They should know how to use consultants and what terms of reference to give them. They should decide what their fund's strategy ought to be; how many managers they will need to execute it; whether the fund managers should have particular skills in specialized sectors or countries; whether they should be Type A or Type B operators; and what proportion of the fund should be entrusted to each. In reality trustees of big funds (over £0.5 billion) tend to employ more than three managers; smaller funds (average £115 million) tend to use only one. Some now consider that the role of the trustee is now so complex that it requires training (as the lay magistracy now does) and that the government should consider as a matter or urgency how this would best be organized.

In a celebrated judgement in April 1984, Megarry J. told the National Union of Mineworkers that its trustees must put the interests of the pension fund's beneficiaries before union policy. It was not for them to make 'moral gestures'; they had a duty to obtain expert advice and to act on it prudently. Mere prudence is not enough.

The paradox is whether this singleness of purpose in favour of the beneficiaries extends to the company itself. The trustees of a company pension fund must ensure that it can meet its obligations when they fall due (for which they will receive actuarial advice). If, however, a manager of the company is, as so often, a trustee of its pension fund, he has another aim. He wishes to maximize the value of the pension fund so as to minimize the firm's contribution ('pension holidays'), and to minimize its obligation to put in more money if the fund needs topping up. If the fund is in surplus he would like to take this back into the company to swell its profits.

This duality of objective has important consequences for corporate governance. The pressures a trustee and company director exerts on his fund managers are related far less to the pension fund's beneficiaries than to the pension fund as a 'profit centre'. All directors want their own shareholders to belong to the Type A school and exhibit loyalty based on long-term perspectives. To the extent that they put pressure on their own pension fund managers for short-term results they stand in danger of pushing them towards Type B behaviour. There is in fact an unresolved question about who 'owns' a pension fund—and until this is settled the trustee/company director is bound to have a difficult role. Some critics believe that all trustees should be 'independent' of the company—or at least, a majority should.

It is often claimed that one of the factors that drives fund managers into Type B behaviour is performance measurement. Consultants have an important part to play, for it is they who often guide trustees into their choice of managers, and they do so largely on the basis of limited product differentiation that the league tables quantify. American research, however, suggests that once a manager is appointed—and provided he sticks to whatever strategy he has 'sold'—he is unlikely to be quickly displaced if he takes trouble to court the trustees and establish a strong relationship with them. Of course, if he performs disastrously for long enough he will be sacked, but a good salesman who sticks to his guns will often find trustees making excuses to continue backing him. Besides, knowledgeable trustees realize there is often 'performance drag'—new managers tend initially to under-perform.

Performance measurers are increasingly influential, often attending reviews between trustees and investment managers and counselling trustees on selection—that is, both sacking and replacement. Some commentators consider the measurers' influence has been on balance malign, a criticism which measurers have been anxious to refute, by advocating *inter alia* longer-term contracts for managers.

Performance measurement has been blamed for 'short-termism' in that it drives fund managers into frenetic action which in turn destroys any possibility of Type A behaviour. It makes them look on their shares as gaming chips, not part-ownership of real companies performing a useful service. This is an exaggeration. Most intelligent trustees tend to want to think in terms of a cycle despite the difficulty of deciding when a cycle starts and ends, and they want to give managers a fair chance. Measurement is inevitable. It may be abused or used foolishly; or as an excuse for consultants to earn themselves a fee. But gunning for performance measurement is aiming at the wrong target. The right inference is once again the skill, knowledge, and training of trustees. This is a book that has scarcely been opened; it should be.

Companies and Shareholders: Communications

As noted above, the main opportunity for shareholders of all kinds to communicate with the directors is at the annual general meeting, though there is no obligation on all the board to attend or on the chairman of the meeting to answer questions. Shareholders can write to the company at any time. Individual shareholders cannot expect the directors to agree to meet them separately. Institutions vary in the audience they can command, broadly in proportion to their potential power (through their shareholdings) in relation to the relative size of the particular company. In practice smaller companies find themselves addressing relatively junior members of an institutions' staff; and smaller institutions cannot expect to command the presence of the chairman of a major PLC unless their shareholding warrants it. Neither companies nor institutions have unlimited resources.

There is widespread agreement that it serves the interest of both shareholders and company for there to be regular communication between them; numerous bodies have warmly commended it (including, for instance, the CBI's City Industry Task Force). It is realized that this leaves the non-communicators (particularly the small shareholders) at a relative disadvantage, but it is argued that this is less important than the absolute advantage which good communication brings both to the market and to the company by making them better informed.

The conventional UK position is that investor relations' activities are useful for company, market, and investors and should be encouraged, and that problems about price-sensitive information are containable.

There is now some information on what actually occurs. C. Marston's study (1993) for the Newcastle and Glasgow Business Schools produced responses from 337 companies among the top 550. These showed that a very high proportion of CEOs attend company meetings with analysts and fund managers (83.83 per cent), and finance directors are almost always present (95.81 per cent). Other senior members of a company also attend meetings, including chairmen and managing directors and marketing directors (where companies have a separate person in these positions). In other words, companies attach much importance to the meetings. The mean numbers of sell-side analysts and buy-side analysts/fund managers on companies' circulation lists were twenty-six and fifty-three respectively.

The sell-side analysts' reports usually contain profits forecasts. Companies always face a dilemma if these are grossly inaccurate. Should they remain silent and let the particular analyst look foolish when the figures appear? (Meanwhile, those who put faith in his judgement will have been misled.) Or should they in one way or another tip him off (and in doing so inevitably give him by inference price-sensitive information)? The Marston Survey shows that the companies were evenly divided: 49.11 per cent did offer comments on the accuracy of analysts' predictions; 53.43 per cent gave some guidance regarding the size and direction of the error in the forecast (Marston 1993: tables 6. 6 and 6. 12).

More broadly the survey shows that companies attached great importance to investor relations and thought that generally analysts' work was acceptable or good (sect. ix), even though there were many reservations about the pressure the sell-side analysts exerted (para. 9. 9), and a feeling that they were too concerned with short-term profit opportunities (para. 9. 10).

It is impossible anyway to set a dividing line between all information that is price sensitive and all that is not. There is nothing illegal in having price-sensitive information as long as one does not trade on it until it is generally available; an investor may always consent to become an 'insider'; that is, to accept information on the understanding he or she will not trade.

In countries where there are no insider trading laws (or they are weakly applied), none of these problems obtrude, so bankers and shareholders can get to know (and may feel they cannot do their job properly unless they do know), and yet feel no inhibition about trading, though doubtless many, particularly bankers, do not do so any more than they would in the UK.

The pragmatic solution in the UK is set out in the pamphlet published by the Institutional Shareholders Committee in the following terms. Those who criticize it as a fudge should be required to produce a formula that confers greater advantage on all the parties:

Institutional shareholders have a responsibility actively to encourage contact with companies which will include contact at senior executive level on both sides. Such dialogue will enable shareholders to gain a better appreciation of the management's objectives, the problems confronting it and the quality of those involved, while also focusing the attention of management more sharply on the expectations and requirements of shareholders. Institutions do not wish to be made insiders, and such contacts should not include the transmission of price-sensitive information. Where, exceptionally, there are compelling reasons for a board to consult institutional shareholders on issues which are price-sensitive, those shareholders may have to accept that such consultation would involve the receipt of confidences which will require that they suspend their ability to deal in the company's shares. It is important that such confidences are not disclosed to investors by companies or their advisers inadvertently or without the investors' prior consent.

The situation does, however, remain unsatisfactory in certain respects. In the first place some shareholders quite properly refuse to receive information that might inhibit them from trading because they would be insiders. This, incidentally, is a further argument in favour of Type A behaviour, because such institutions are much less concerned to trade and may be more content to accept the inhibitions which go with the receipt of price-sensitive information. As an extension of this, an institution or group of institutions which had decided to exert influence on a company might also feel themselves under an interdict until they had completed their action and its consequences were in the market.

The degree of delicacy various parties feel about giving, receiving, and using price-sensitive information varies greatly even today. As we saw from the Marston study, many companies routinely help analysts with their profit forecasts: there has to be a question mark about the propriety of this practice.

Annual General Meetings

UK companies are run by an elected oligarchy, that is, the board; an Athenian type of democracy would be totally impracticable. 'Democracy' is limited to the prescribed rights of the electorate (i.e. the shareholders) to choose or dismiss the oligarchs. Additionally, the directors may convene general meetings which all shareholders may attend: if a tenth of the shareholders require it in due form, the directors must convene such a meeting (Companies Act 1985, sects. 368 ff.). And a company must call an annual general meeting (AGM) (sect. 366) on pain of fines; if it does not the court may call one.

Having thus assured shareholders of a day's democracy, the Companies Act gives it substance by requiring the directors to lay the accounts before the AGM with the auditors' report (sect. 241). The shareholder does not have to attend in person but is entitled to appoint someone else as proxy or lodge a proxy vote (sect. 372).

To the general observer, the AGM is on the surface a non-event. In normal circumstances they are poorly attended. Penetrating questions are seldom put. Institutional shareholders prefer to ask quietly on another occasion rather than give an appearance of public confrontation: besides, if they have fastened on to an interesting point they may not wish to reveal it to their 'competitors'. Private shareholders are more likely to be concerned with peripheral social issues or with their own experience as customers. Few shareholders bother to complete their proxy cards; figures of 11–13 per cent are typical. *The Economist* (7 Sept.1991) suggested that apathy is diminishing and cited Flemings, Philips and Drew, and M&G among the fund management firms which intended to use their votes more regularly; the article also pointed out that the insurance companies claim to have a good voting record. Votes at EGMs tend to be higher—in the range 30–50 per cent—but even at these levels apathy is manifest.

There is no required quorum at an AGM, so no profession of proxy solicitor has emerged. Even when a contentious issue arises and both parties are trying feverishly to marshal support, it is rare for half the shares to be voted.

Shareholders rarely exercise their right to make the company circulate a resolution and accompanying statement of up to 1,000 words, even though it only needs 5 per cent of the vote or a hundred members with £100 each of paid-up capital to do it (sect. 376).

At first blush AGMs appear a total waste of time. Few attend them. The proportion of votes cast is pathetic (usually less than 15 per cent). Even when a company's management has not covered itself with glory a public *démarche* is rare (but may be effective if carefully mounted). Companies do not on the whole seek to evade responsibility by arranging the AGM for an awkward time on an inconvenient date in an inaccessible place: some go to the opposite extreme and offer refreshments to restore the weary. It seems that institutional shareholders generally prefer the privacy and discretion of private contact rather than public questions or declarations, while private shareholders tend to miss the point or cut little ice. Despite all this, many chairmen I have questioned are far more sensitive to the potential problems of an AGM than their shareholders might imagine; it concentrates their minds far more than might possibly be supposed.

It is the privilege of the UK's kind of democracy for voters to abstain, however much doing so weakens the system. As we saw in Chapter 5, US law now requires the trustees of private pension funds to see their shares are voted. Both the USA and France have rules about AGMs needing a quorum. Is there anything that could be done in the UK to breathe life into AGMs or are they doomed to remain statuesque tableaux until, once in a blue moon, something occurs which galvanizes one of them into life? It is not as if all UK companies perform so well there is nothing to answer for; nor is it the case that messages delivered in private even by major institutions always produce results. Some well-directed judicious questions, adequately reported in the press, could well have a salutary effect. Even if chairmen do not fear losing control of an AGM, they respect penetrating and apposite questions and views.

There are various slightly curious aspects of the conduct of AGMs. The auditors, who are appointed by the shareholders and who report to them, are present, but they have no right to speak unless the chairman invites them to do so, even though a shareholder may direct a question to them. Chairmen would defend their position on grounds of retaining control of the meeting: is this stand justified? Chairmen indeed can make a mockery of the whole proceedings by declining to answer questions or let anyone else answer them. Perhaps the time is right to reconsider the form of the AGM to make it a more significant occasion and to improve the accountability of the firm's executive management. More fundamentally, perhaps it is time to face the reality that for many small shareholders it would simply be uneconomical to inform themselves on how to vote; perhaps there might be a way of providing them with a service, through an intermediary. The banks do this routinely in Germany, as we have seen. Could not the arrangements in the UK be improved?

Corporate Governance and the Suppliers of Capital

Governments use part of the proceeds of taxation for capital projects—in effect pre-empting private saving and investment. Apart from this it would be fair to say that no job exists anywhere except as the result of a conscious decision by someone to save. In the UK private savings were from early times marshalled in two distinct ways. For much of the population the principal mechanism was through deposits with the huge number of small banks: visitors to the headquarters of the National Westminster at Lothbury still see in the hall a tree which indicates how many banks it has absorbed over the centuries, and much the same is true of Barclays and the other major banks.

At the same time there was a parallel process well described in outline in the *History of the London Stock Exchange* (ISE 1992). It notes that the first joint stock company where the public subscribed to ownership in equal shares was founded in London in 1553. This was a trading venture which in due course became the Muscovy Company. The Bank of England was established in 1694 and funded by public subscription, and the South Seas Company followed in 1711. The development of the secondary market in stocks followed hard on the raising of capital through the market. Stocks could be easily traded, so one's investment could be efficiently realized. Investment and speculation were bedfellows from the outset and led to wild excesses. The bursting of the South Seas bubble set back the joint stock company for a hundred years.

The industrial revolution hastened developments. Even for smaller enterprises the limitations of partnerships were exposed. Secondly, the bigger ones, like railways, needed to cast the net for capital more widely. In due course there were new Acts of Parliament governing joint stock companies. The stock market grew in size and importance both in its primary function (of raising capital) and its secondary role, of trading shares already issued.

The two sources of capital complemented each other. Local banks tended to support local business on a long-term basis. For medium and large enterprises, the stock market came to be seen as the primary source of longer-term capital; for such companies the banks saw themselves and were increasingly seen as suppliers of funds for shorter-term purposes, such as financing seasonal stocks—in much the same way as they had financed harvests. In all cases retained earnings were probably the most important source of capital, as they are to this day.

TABLE 6.1. *Sources of finance for UK industrial commercial companies*

Year	Total (£ billion)	Internal sources (%)	External sources (%)			
			Bank borrowing	Ordinary shares	Other capital issues	Other sources*
1979	33.4	76	12	3	—	10
1980	29.0	66	22	3	3	6
1981	33.2	64	17	5	4	10
1982	29.4	62	23	4	1	11
1983	33.7	76	5	6	3	10
1984	34.8	80	20	3	3	− 6
1985	44.3	68	17	8	6	1
1986	47.9	57	19	11	7	5
1987	70.7	49	17	19	8	6
1988	86.2	41	36	5	7	11
1989	89.8	31	37	2	15	15
1990	66.7	37	28	4	14	17

* Other loans and mortgages, other overseas investment, capital transfers, and import and other credit sources.

Note: In 1991 £1.6 billion of stock was newly raised by UK companies, plus £10 billion by way of rights issues.

The Banks

As we have seen, mainly for historical reasons the banks play virtually no part in corporate governance in the USA; have a significant role in France in some cases; and a key role in Germany and Japan. Although we classify our system like that of the USA as 'market based' in contrast to the 'bank based' systems of Germany and France, the true facts about the sources of industry's finance are more complex. Table 6.1 is based on a table produced by the Bank of England's Economics Division, and gives sources of finance for industrial and commercial companies.

The table shows that the banks play a larger part, and the market a smaller part, than popular belief would lead us to suppose. In theory the markets provided long-term capital; companies came to the banks for short-term trading resources. The main instrument was the overdraft, which was extremely flexible and which had to be repaid on demand. It was generally, but not always, secured, usually by a floating charge over the company's assets—again a flexible instrument. To this day, this kind of finance is the one most used by small and medium businesses. Their preference for it rests n its simplicity and flexibility, and the fact that they do not have to surrender any equity. From the banks' point of view it simplifies lending decisions and is a perfect instrument in a 'stand off'. As the main question is ability to repay, what matters is the quality of the collateral and the character of the borrower.

In reality short-term loans were rolled over so long that they effectively became medium- and long-term hard core capital. This did not matter to either party until things went wrong. If they did, the injudiciousness of funding long-term investment with short-term money was harshly exposed. Many of the complaints against the banks in the 1989–93 recession related, at bottom, to this basic fact. The instrument which borrowers and lenders were both happy to use was unsuitable for the purpose.

If a loan is *ab initio* going to be medium- or long-term, different considerations apply from lending short-term. The medium/long-term lender needs to explore in much greater depth the market in which the borrower is operating and the borrower's place and aspirations in it. The lender, as for all lending, must be able to satisfy himself about the competence and integrity of the borrower. But if the lender knows from the outset that if the borrower is successful (and why lend if one thinks he will fail?), he will be called on for more funds, until such time as the borrower no longer needs the intermediation of the banks to raise capital—then the degree of care he must exercise and knowledge he will require will be correspondingly greater.

In recent years UK banks have developed different types of funding— including medium- and longer-term loans—and they haven made organizational changes to look towards industry more constructively. Even so the attitudes and behaviour of some bank officials and some companies still reflect the old divide, that is, short- rather than long-term; arms' length rather than co-operative; secretive rather than open. And severe competition between banks has arguably impeded change, because pressure on costs and profits inhibits them from providing the resources necessary to sustain better relationships—and to give enough of their staff the deeper training and wider experience that more complex relationships demand. They are not unique, for instance, in finding that their previous dependence on collateral is inadequate when the value of collateral, particularly property, is uncertain. The collapse in realty values in Japan, the USA, and the UK caught bankers on the hop in all these countries as their provisions against bad debts so amply demonstrate.

In the UK there is no comprehensive system for collecting data about a borrower's total indebtedness, or a central bureau such as Centrale des Risques to which a lender can refer. It is evident from many cases where a company has collapsed that most of the lenders did not possess the full facts—severe competition had doubtless impelled them to lend without asking the right questions, however injudicious this may with hindsight now appear. With banks lining up to lend, companies could refuse to borrow from the inquisitive, but that is no excuse.

Just as competitive pressures made banks lower their guard, so they forced companies to hit them as hard as possible by squeezing the last ounce from every transaction. Treasury departments were turned into profit centres; relationships became secondary to securing the keenest terms. Syndicated loans became common, and in them relationships disappeared altogether except perhaps with the leading bank, whose responsibilities were minimal and who might, indeed, retain virtually none of the debt on its own book. Companies did not seem to accept that banks had to make profits too, overlooking the fact that forcing a marginal existence upon them was not costless. Complaints about a lack of loyalty when a bank financed a bidder (and some did) seem singularly ill placed from those who gave neither loyalty or headroom. If the value set upon a relationship is low, one cannot expect too much from it in an hour of need. Loyalty had not been earned and the companies got the relationship they deserved. Other companies which had told their finance directors to maintain the key relationship even at a price have observably found they had bought a bargain. Companies in trouble have often found it very difficult to deal with syndicated loans where many of the banks were quite unknown to them and difficult to hold in line whilst problems were being settled or variations agreed in the terms of the loan agreement.

One of the consequences of the present 'stand off' between UK banks and companies is that when the going gets rough the banks can find themselves in the awkward position of being the arbiters of a company's survival. At the moment a lack of information and reciprocal confidence often means that the crisis is sharp and sudden. As the relationship has been tenuous and information poor, the bank has had no inkling of the oncoming storm or opportunity to nudge the company into timely action (admittedly not an easy thing to do if the real trouble is a wilful but erratic CEO).

It follows from the nature of companies and banks' views of one another that UK banks do not take equity stakes to cement the relationship with a customer or to secure influence. Historically the acquisition of such stakes has often been accidental; that is, they have been taken in lieu of debt as part of a restructuring. Many UK banks have found themselves doing just this recently. The general UK stance is that such interdependence is potentially dangerous. The banks consider equity stakes a poor use of funds and unnecessary for a relationship with clients: besides, there could be a conflict of interest between their role as lender and their role as shareholder. Moreover, if a bank has too much of its balance-sheet in company shares it may be vulnerable if their value declines.

There are no doubt varying views within the UK banking system about the role of the main banks. At a debate on 27 March 1992, Wyatt of the Midland Bank spoke in the following terms:

Short-term unplanned liquidity requirements and working capital are clearly where we should be offering services. We should not be used for long-term lending, while being happy that refinancing for long-term lending requirements in the market place can be carried out by treasurers of corporates who can borrow as cheap or more cheaply than a bank. However, relationship bankers should be given a more than equal chance at capital markets business. If banks are in a long-term enduring relationship of mutual trust then capital markets business is an area in which most relationship banks will want to be active.

What of the corporate governance of the banks themselves? Their own performance has not always sparkled, which suggests that they share the frailties of other businesses. The governance of some insurance companies has also let them down, even whilst their own investment managers were quite properly concerned with it in the companies whose shares they held. Both banks and insurance companies have supervisors whose task is to guard against systemic risk and to protect the depositors or policy-holders against failure. They do this by monitoring prudential or liquidity ratios and other data. In so doing they protect, to a limited extent, shareholders' interests too, but only as a by-product. It is up to a bank's shareholders, as in the case of any other company, to assert themselves if the board's performance requires it.

In the case of banks the supervisors ensure that the members of the board are 'fit and proper' within the meaning of the Banking Acts, but this does not imply that the board as a whole is either competent or effective. It is up to the chairman to attend to this and up to him and the non-executive directors to ensure executive management is up to the mark. If it looks as if this task is not being adequately performed, it is the shareholders' right (and it would be very much in their interests) for them to monitor the banks and insurance companies in which they were invested and do whatever was necessary. The idea that the shareholders should leave it to the supervisors is ill founded. The market for corporate control may be inhibited because a few particular institutions give the impression of being partly or entirely protected from 'hostile' bids: but recent events show that this protection, if it exists at all, is at best partial. The shareholders still have a real role to play.

Table 6.2. *Market capitalization of quoted companies*

	Domestic equity market capitalization (£ billion) *	GDP (£ billion)	Market capitalization as % of GDP
London	602.1	684.0	88
Federation of German Exchanges	217.9	1,154.2	19
Paris	216.9	880.0	25
Swiss Exchanges	129.2	159.8	81
Amsterdam	113.1	211.3	54
Milan	76.2	810.5	9
Belgium	42.4	142.3	30
Luxembourg	7.9	6.9	114

* Market capitalization figures include investment trusts, listed unit trusts, and UCITS.
Note: £/$ exchange rate: 1991 = 1.77, 1992 = 1.53; £/ECU exchange rate: 1991 = 0.7161, 1992 = 0.7982.
Source: European Stock Exchange Statistics, Annual Report 1992; OECD Main Economic Indicators, May 1993.

The Stock Market

The London Stock Market has been active since the sixteenth century—albeit in the early days on a limited number of stocks. By 1697 the authorities found it active enough to want to regulate it 'to restrain the number of ill practices of brokers and stock jobbers'. From those days to the present, with various vicissitudes, the market has continued to flourish.

Although we noted above that the stock market provides a small proportion of industry's funds, Table 6.2 shows how much more important it is in the UK than in most other European countries

Market capitalization of quoted companies as a percentage of GDP, in 1987, was as follows:

United Kingdom	86.3
Netherlands	43.7
Belgium	37.3
Spain	27.1
Denmark	16.6
West Germany	16.0
France	12.8

The turnover of domestic and foreign equities on the London Stock Exchange in 1992 was £381.7 billion (of which £164.7 billion was in foreign equities). The comparable total figures for other centres, expressed in pounds, single counted, were:

Federation of German Exchanges	£249.7 billion
Paris	£72.2 ,,
Tokyo	£269.9 ,,
USA (NYSE)	£1033.4 ,,
USA (NASDAQ)	£513.6 ,,

Thus the function of intermediating between savers and industry is shared by banks (and similar institutions) and the stock market in the UK as elsewhere; broadly speaking, the bigger companies get the more likely it is that they will want and be able to tap the capital markets direct and also to see their shares quoted.

Although the UK has a relatively large number of quoted companies (2,006 in 1991, as noted earlier), many of them are quite small and in any case they only constitute a fraction of the total number of companies trading (most of which are private and unquoted). As in other countries the choice of when to take a company public rests with its shareholders, some of whom are likely to be directors with significant holdings. They contemplate flotation as a means of:

(a) Improving the capital structure (by replacing debt by equity or by improving the debt–equity ratio).

(b) Realizing part of their investment so as not to have too much of their wealth in one company.

(c) Dealing with succession problems.

(d) Dealing with taxation problems.

(e) Enhancing their status.

(f) Making take-over bids more easy.

For many years those who sought flotation had little to concern them except the costs of the transaction. They had to conform with the regulations of whatever stock exchange(s) they chose and to the Companies Act, but they did not have to worry about officious non-executive directors (since there was no pressure to appoint them, and if any were chosen they were likely to be old friends or great names or both). The attitude of many proprietors was that the public were exceedingly fortunate to be able to participate and they themselves fully intended to carry on as before. The public were free to buy their shares or not; if they purchased they must be deemed to accept the package as it was, because of and not despite the company's leadership.[4] Many directors have told me over the years that

---

[4] Much the same argument is used to defend the issue of non-voting shares; namely, purchasers should understand what they are getting and not complain that it should be something else.

times have not much changed in that respect. One thing however that did not worry the old guard was the possibility of a take-over—even if they were minority holders after the flotation.

It is not axiomatic that the price of shares in the secondary market should have any direct effect on corporate governance, since movements may be due to extraneous influences. A consistently poor performance will obviously affect the share price and the cost of new capital (and the readiness of shareholders to subscribe). Shareholders have tended to react to bad news by selling out to those presumably of a more optimistic disposition or by holding on and like Mr Micawber waiting for something to turn up. Direct intervention was rare, and until comparatively recently 'take-overs' were most unusual, as they are to this day in Germany and Japan. It is a consideration of this subject that takes us into one of the most troubling and disputed areas of the UK corporate governance system.

Mergers and Take-overs

As in all other countries mergers have been frequent in the UK. The term 'take-over' tends to be used in regard to a specific form of merger, namely one in which a company seeks to acquire another against the will of its board. Some would-be 'friendly' mergers turn into take-overs because the 'target' company's board does not wish to proceed: some 'hostile' bids end in negotiated terms, so the distinctions are not necessarily clear-cut.

'Take-overs' began in the 1950s and gathered pace in the 1960s. They really took off in the 1980s (see Table 6.3). According to *Acquisition Monthly*, UK bids completed in 1990 summed to £12 billion in 1990 and £10 billion in 1991.

In the twenty-year period 1969–88 take-overs accounted on average for 1.6 per cent of the replacement cost and 2 per cent of the market value of the UK capital stock per annum. The peak years were 1972 and 1988, at around 4 per cent of the market value of the capital stock.

The reasons for the growth of merger activity are many and various. Companies aspire to growth and there are only two basic ways of achieving it—organic development or merger/acquisition. Some like Marks & Spencer PLC have chosen the former; others like Hanson PLC or BTR mainly the latter. Some, including those two, have tended to diversify across a wide range or industries; others like Morgan Crucible PLC have tended to have a narrower range. Growth has both offensive and defensive advantages. Many a CEO has ridden down the acquisition trail to give himself and his group the protection of size; whatever the theory about take-overs being a remedy for inefficient management, the market actually works mainly one way—

TABLE 6.3. *Mergers and take-overs of UK companies, 1969–1988*

Year	No. of all completed mergers and acquisitions	Total value of bids (£ billion)	Value as a proportion of market capitalization of securities %
1970	614	1.00	2.3
1975	200	0.22	0.6
1980	368	1.26	1.7
1985	340	6.30	2.8
1986	537	12.13	4.0
1987	905	11.28	2.7
1988	937	16.87	4.2
1991 †	512	10.2	
1992 † (1st quarter)	124	2.2	

† Based on Bank of England estimates.

Source: Department of Trade & Industry Business Monitor MQ7, 1989.

big companies buy smaller ones, not vice versa, so the big one faces a much shorter list of probable predators. Or as Dr Ajit Singh puts it, 'In the market for corporate control a large unprofitable company has a much higher chance of survival than a small relatively much more profitable company' (Singh 1992).

Acquisitions, moreover, serve various other purposes. For those in mature industries, like BAT in tobacco, they may lead to diversification. For those with aspirations to improve their share of the world-wide market like Forte, they may lead to judicious purchases at home and abroad in one's basic trade. For those who feel their home market is too small a base, since they already have a substantial market share, like Tate & Lyle or Nestlé, it may lead to major acquisitions abroad. Some companies like BTR relish the challenge of squeezing more profit from businesses, even those already competently managed; others like Hanson seem to be expert at spotting undervalued companies and either managing them better or reselling them or both. In none of these cases can acquisitions be said to be undesirable in principle, though some worked better than others, and there remains the stubborn question whether companies with cash to spare should give the shareholders a chance to reinvest it rather than doing it for them.

We must not overlook the CEO's personal motivation. Size carries status, and eventually perhaps Honours. Their time in office may be short so they may be in a hurry. They found (especially in the 1980s) an atmosphere conducive to their operations, with deregulation in the air and funds readily available. The accounting conventions in the UK did not, to say the least, hinder them, so that acquisition (where goodwill and provisions could be manipulated) looked more attractive than organic growth, where the early stages of development of a product or market could eat into the profit and loss account. But the stage had been set rather earlier by a simple perception about the stock market.

In the 1960s it became generally recognized that the stock market was in effect a market for companies as well. There were at that time no rules about concert parties or secret stake-building, and a patient purchaser could secretly build up a commanding position. Once a purchaser had pounced and assumed control he was under no obligation to bid for the rump of the shares or to offer as much for them as he paid for those he had already bought. Some purchasers bought companies to break them up to realize an immediate gain made possible by some perhaps temporary market imperfection, with scant regard for any other consideration or the longer term (the 'asset strippers').

The Process of Take-overs: A Digression

The pioneering buccaneers of the 1950s and early 1960s caused a reaction which led in 1967 to an announcement by the Bank of England of the establishment of the Take-over Panel (TOP), which came into being the following year when the Code had been drawn up. In its first twelve months to March 1969 it handled 575 cases. The Panel is a non-statutory body which commands the support both of industry and the financial world. It is managed by a director (seconded for a limited period from one of the financial houses), who is supported by a small professional staff (one of whom is usually seconded from the Bank of England). The Panel itself is drawn from leading members of the financial, professional, and industrial worlds. The chairman is usually a prominent lawyer. (There is an excellent account of the Panel and Code in Johnston 1980.)

The TOP is both legislator and court. It makes the rules which are promulgated as a code. Being non-statutory it can change them rapidly if needs be. It hears cases and makes decisions. The courts have been reluctant to interfere with the substance of the TOP's decision, so appeals to them are rare (though of course there is always judicial review). The TOP has its own appeal procedure. Cases are heard by three members of the Panel who did not hear it at first instance; they are chaired by a prominent lawyer. It is a matter for conjecture whether the TOP will be able to continue on its present basis if the EC's Take-over Directive ever becomes law: the idea that such an important body can work effectively (as it clearly does) without a formal statutory framework is odd to non-British eyes—especially as it has no formal powers to enforce its rulings. Its rulings are, however, almost always observed, because the power of those who support the Panel cannot be ignored: the Stock Exchange might, for instance, suspend the listing of a company which flouted the Panel. One or two securities firms in the 1980s became so full of themselves that they felt they could treat the TOP with scant respect—for instance, by exploiting what they saw as gaps in the rules—but their reputation was, to say the least, not enhanced as a consequence.

The TOP Code has had an important effect on the process of take-overs. It has now become a substantial document of seventeen sections, thirty-eight rules, plus appendices. The General Principles, however, are quite short and are stated here for convenience (edition of 25 October 1990):

1. All shareholders of the same class of an offeree company must be treated similarly by an offeror.

2. During the course of an offer, or when an offer is in contemplation, neither an offeror, nor the offeree company, nor any of their respective advisers may furnish information to some shareholders which is not made available to all shareholders. This principle does not apply to the furnishing of information in confidence by the offeree company to a bona fide potential offeror or vice versa.

3. An offeror should only announce an offer after the most careful and responsible consideration. Such an announcement should be made only when the offeror has every reason to believe that it can and will continue to be able to implement the offer: responsibility in this connection also rests on the financial adviser to the offeror.

4. Shareholders must be given sufficient information and advice to enable them to reach a properly informed decision and must have sufficient time to do so. No relevant information should be withheld from them.

5. Any document or advertisement addressed to shareholders containing information or advice from an offeror or the board of the offeree company or their respective advisers must, as is the case with a prospectus, be prepared with the highest standards of care and accuracy.

6. All parties to an offer must use every endeavour to prevent the creation of a false market in the securities of an offeror or the offeree company. Parties involved in offers must take care that statements are not made which may mislead shareholders or the market.

7. At no time after a bona fide offer has been communicated to the board of the offeree company, or after the board of the offeree company has reason to believe that a bona fide offer might be imminent, may any action be taken by the board of the offeree company in relation to the affairs of the company, without the approval of the shareholders in general meeting, which could effectively result in any bona fide offer being frustrated or in the shareholders being denied an opportunity to decide on its merits.

8. Rights of control must be exercised in good faith and the oppression of a minority is wholly unacceptable.

9. Directors of an offeror and the offeree company must always, in advising their shareholders, act only in their capacity as directors and not have regard to their personal or family shareholdings or to their personal relationships with the companies. It is the shareholders' interests taken as a whole, together with those of employees and creditors, which should be considered when the directors are giving advice to shareholders. Directors of the offeree company should give careful considera-tion before they enter into any commitment with an offeror (or anyone else) which would restrict their freedom to advise their shareholders in the future. Such commit-ments may give rise to conflicts of interest or result in a breach of the directors' fiduciary duties.

10. Where control of a company is acquired by a person, or persons acting in concert, a general offer to all other shareholders is normally required; a similar obligation may arise if control is consolidated. Where an acquisition is contemplated as a result of which a person may incur such an obligation, he must, before making the acquisition, ensure that he can and will continue to be able to implement such an offer.

It will be seen that the underlying themes are those of openness, timeliness, and even-handedness.

Openness means revealing the accumulation of stakes (in accordance with the Substantial Acquisition Rules), plus the rules about 'concert parties' (i.e. where various parties act together in secret concert). In less picturesque language its rules promote openness and limit conspiracies. As a more general point, it is interesting to note how standards have changed. The Companies Act 1948 contained no provisions about disclosing interests in shares. The 1985 Act devotes the whole of Part VI to the subject, sections 198–220. The obligation to disclose ownership has become more stringent. At the time of the 1985 Act a 'notifiable percentage' was 5 per cent. This has been reduced to 3 per cent.

Timeliness means conducting the bid according to a timetable, thus saving the bidders the cost of keeping finance in place indefinitely, and the target company the uncertainty of an extended battle. Anyone who has received an unwanted bid will attest to the amount of management time and nervous energy it pre-empts. On the other hand, there are those who feel it wrong that businesses which it has taken generations to build should be dispatched with indecent haste. If a bid fails, however, the bidder may not normally bid again for a year.

Even-handedness means, first, that it is the shareholders not management who decide the outcome of the bid: management may not put a wall around them to stop a purchaser (e.g. by using poison pills), or frustrate the bid in other ways (e.g. by a Crown Jewels defence[5]). Second, it means fairness

---

[5] A Crown Jewels defence is an arrangement where a company arranges to sell one or more

among shareholders. Offers must be made for *all* the shares on equal terms and the price must not be lower than the bidder has paid before or after he made the bid. Furthermore, if someone acquires more than 29.9 per cent of the shares, control is deemed to pass and he must bid, in cash, for the rest. If, however, the purchaser is foreign it may get away with unequal treatment. (Bosch bought the Worcester Group for £71.8 million, but gave management shareholders—38.4 per cent—different terms from the others.)

Although the Code is now detailed the Introduction to the General Principles makes it clear that what is intended is not a legalistic search for loopholes but an approach which is consonant with the Code's general spirit. 'It is impracticable to devise rules in sufficient detail to cover all circumstances which can arise in offers. Accordingly, persons engaged in offers should be aware that the spirit as well as the precise wording of the General Principles and the ensuing Rules must be observed.'

In fact, clever merchant banks have often searched for cracks in the brickwork into which to insert a knife—a legalistic approach not in keeping with the spirit of a system that does its best *not* to be legalistic. Big money is at stake—enough to dull the sensibilities of the unscrupulous. Not everyone likes the system: some British companies do not like the TOP's ability to change its own rules and would prefer a statutory system, despite the risk of court battles to accompany it. No one has taken a vote on this, but I suggest this view is not widely held.

Take-overs and Corporate Governance

The theory behind the relationship of take-overs to corporate governance is quite straightforward. If a company is thought to be badly run over time, its share price declines and provides an opportunity for a purchaser to acquire it and make better use of the assets. There have been take-overs which fall into this category, the purchase of Distillers for instance. The inducement to the existing shareholders to sell to a purchaser is the latter's readiness to offer a price above that ruling in the market at the time of the bid— 'the bid premium'. *Acquisitions Monthly* in February 1990 showed the average premiums as a percentage of the share price a month before the bid as follows: 1987—37 per cent; 1988—37 per cent; 1989—38 per cent.

It is, however, now apparent that the existence of a bid premium does not

---

of its prime assets to a third party (the 'Crown Jewels'), on the basis that the deal will only be completed if an unwanted bidder tries to take the company over.

depend on the target company being badly managed. There are always two pricing systems at work on a stock exchange, one for parcels of shares, one for control, and control always carries a premium. (For fuller discussion of this, see Charkham 1989.) However good a management may be, a bidder prepared to offer a premium is bound to have some appeal to shareholders—how much depends on the size of the premium divided by the sense of loyalty shareholders feel less their fears about the market. The case of the DRG group is informative. A special vehicle was used for the bid, organized in such a way as to take the fullest advantage of the tax laws. Shareholders were more or less evenly divided about accepting the bid, which offered a premium over the previous market price. At the last moment, just before the closing date of the offer, the whole stock market fell for some general reasons and DRG shares fell in sympathy. A small number of wavering shareholders thereupon accepted the offer, thus sealing the company's fate.

Superficially it appears as if take-overs are a game which everyone wins: the target company's shareholders collect their premium, the bidding company collects an asset of which it can (in principle—or why bid?) make better use. A more careful look reveals the losers. A. Shleifer and L. H. Summers (1988: 33 ff.) draw attention to the losers in a chapter entitled 'Breach of Trust in Hostile Takeovers'. They argue that a corporation is a nexus of long-term contracts between shareholders and stakeholders' customers and suppliers, many of which are implicit, and that these contracts are generally of value to the parties. Sometimes, however, shareholders stand to benefit if a contract is broken, and this in effect is payment in advance for the benefits the bidder hopes to get by repudiating a whole series of implied contracts. Many of the contracts could equally well be breached by new internal management (imposing greater efficiency). The reason why this does not happen is that shareholders find it easier to sell to a bidder than organize a change of management. I argue that this is currently true, but that shareholders have the remedy in their own hands, that is, to combine effectively.

One of the interesting features of the UK scene is how many contested take-overs actually fail even though the defenders have no poison pills. Paper 11 for the Peacock Committee, by E. V. and A. D. Morgan, records the interesting results of a survey they concluded among fund managers. Respondents were asked to indicate on a scale of 'very', 'moderate', 'little', or 'none' 'the importance of various factors that might influence them to accept or reject a bid': 69 per cent of respondents rated the long-term prospects of the bidder as very important; 87 per cent rated the long-term prospects of the target likewise; and 67 per cent rated the immediate value of the bid in the same way. To my way of thinking this means that fund managers do weigh the factors, but in the end everything has a price—which is what one would expect. The price is often not high enough to stop the target's management being given the benefit of the doubt.

One can understand private shareholders refusing an offer on non-economic grounds—sentiment, loyalty, dislike of the bidders, and so forth. But the institutional manager cannot properly allow himself such latitude. He must decide on economic grounds what is in the best interests of his beneficiaries, whatever view he takes of the parties. Quite probably he will already hold the purchaser's shares as well. In strict logic he ought to hold on if a bid contains a premium which looks as if it will evaporate, only if he cannot do better by investing the proceeds elsewhere (or perhaps by buying back in if the bid fails and the price drops); and in many cases he would do well to sell the shares of both bidder and target, especially if the price is full.

The figures do not provide proof absolute but seem to show that sentiment and loyalty do influence the course of events. Shareholders do not, it appears, readily abandon a management that has kept them informed and whom they trust; they will often be given the benefit of the doubt (e.g. in BTR's bid for Pilkington). Sometimes they live to rue their refusal; sometimes they benefit from their loyalty. There is nothing cut and dried or mechanistic about bids except, to repeat, that every company has its price. Sometimes, as the Lex column of the *Financial Times* put it on 11 June 1990, bids are better lost from the bidder's point of view, if not the country's; they quoted as examples Blacks' Leisure bid for Goldbergs, Williams Holdings' bid for Norcros, and Mountleigh's bid for Storehouse. In all these cases, and others, the market value of the target had dropped dramatically (in Goldberg's case to zero) in the months after the bid failed; and now Mountleigh itself has failed. Pronouncing on mergers that did, or did not, occur, however, is making a judgement on half the evidence, since no one can say what would have happened had merged companies remained separate or unmerged companies come together. In general, however, we can say for sure that differences in company culture, let alone problems of personality, are likely to make mergers difficult, and a change of leadership—though this too can have dramatic effects—is probably a much more effective and less costly solution to problems of corporate governance than a change of owner-ship.

It is not the purpose of this paper to try to evaluate take-overs. There have been many attempts at this, not least in the aftermath of the Nestlé purchase of Rowntree. A committee under Professor Sir Alan Peacock (on which I sat) steered some helpful research for the David Hume Institute's Inquiry into Corporate Take-overs in the United Kingdom, and many of its papers are well worth reading.

In the tenth paper for that inquiry, E. V. and A. D. Morgan touched on the question of costs. Take-overs do not come cheap. *Acquisitions Monthly* gives an estimate for 1989 of £800 million *for financial advisers alone*. The abortive Elders IXL bid for Allied Lyons in 1986 cost the bidder £30 million and the target £14 million. When examining and comparing the UK corporate governance system with others, we should take into the reckoning the total costs of the friction that the take-over process generates in the UK, and not just the costs of the duel but also the price for the people it affects. In the last few years some ill-considered acquisitions have had disastrous consequences: for example, the Ferranti purchase of ISC; the British and Commonwealth purchase of Atlantic Computers; many of Maxwell's purchases; and some of Polly Peck's. The list is too long for comfort. Even so, that is not the real point, which is: what is or should be the role of the take-over, if any, in corporate governance?

As we have seen there are many reasons for 'legitimate' take-overs which have little to do with rectifying poor corporate governance. Nestlé bought Rowntree because its management had been good, not bad, and had created an enterprise and brand names worth having. Deutschebank gave the head of Morgan Grenfell a major role and a seat on the Vorstand in recognition of competence.

In theory, management should never be allowed to under-perform for long. The board ought to see to that; and if it fails to do so the shareholders should address the problem. The role of the market only becomes possible for this kind of take-over because both board and shareholders have failed. The market does have this role as a sort of long-stop, although it only provides a fraction of the funds companies employ (see Table 6.1). It does not play it in Germany and Japan because, as we have seen, others, notably the banks, do, but even the banks are fallible.

The picture in the UK is not very rosy since neither boards nor shareholders play their parts properly and many take-overs have not been industrially motivated. A CEO receiving an unwanted approach is naturally concerned about its motivation for various reasons, including the extent to which it may affect his personal future. Even so, few I have met complain. They say that they buy companies themselves and are content to live with the risk of being forcibly acquired. These are brave sentiments, but there is room for doubt about whether they tell the whole story.

As noted earlier (and in the US section), it is impossible to measure the effects of the prospect of being taken over. In one respect it will usually provide a benefit—economy. Head offices in the UK are noticeably less opulent than they were: they now tend to be small and sparsely manned. What about investment? Most CEOs will assert that their investment programmes are unaffected by fear of take-over. And yet no CEO ignores his share price. Are these points compatible? My doubts are reinforced by the apparently greater robustness of attitudes in private companies which do not have to worry about a public share price: directors who have 'gone private' tell me of their relief at being able to concentrate on the longer term without fear of a hostile bid. Much can be done by directors making sure their shareholders understand the company, but even so they are nervous about their share price. It is difficult to escape the conclusion that the emphasis the market naturally places on 'shareholders' immediate values' is likely to lead to management opting for shorter-term payback wherever possible.

If the world all worked to the same rules this would not matter, but as we have seen, it does not. In some respects UK industry is at a continuing competitive disadvantage against countries in which market pressures are not so severe. Much of this is a paraphrase of the US situation, but just as much a matter of concern to the one country as the other. The UK is vulnerable against those who play with different rules, in that their networked systems of accountability work effectively without managements having to live in fear of the market: these tend to have more latitude for investments which take longer to pay off.

If this thesis is correct it is predictable that the UK will progressively be forced out of businesses which have longer-term horizons (unless, as in oil, it has built up a strong position over nearly a century). It will tend to gravitate to areas in which short-term gains can be secured by efficiency or where the figures can be massaged (legally) to cast them in the most favourable light. Efficiency is always to be welcomed, and the financial massage parlour is already under the spotlight. A cursory glance at the industrial scene suggests that it is indeed the case that the UK's relative strength in long-term business has been declining, with one or two honourable exceptions.

The TOP rules help the process of take-overs but do not bear on the above arguments. It only took Hanson PLC to acquire $2\frac{1}{2}$ per cent of ICI's shares to set all the alarm bells ringing. Salutary? In some eyes possibly. But such a threat is not calculated to make companies think longterm. Franks and Mayer (1990) set contested take-overs (which apply only to PLCs) in context for the year 1986, showing that by value they accounted for 19 per cent of all take-over activity (only 4 per cent by numbers). In that year, 180 PLCs were taken over—10 per cent after a contested bid; furthermore, thirty-one contested bids were launched but were not completed. Franks and Mayer also showed that more than half the directors in target companies resigned after acquisition. In the case of executive directors 64 per cent resigned after a contested bid, against 24 per cent in the case of an uncontested bid.

Such figures are only to be expected—contested bids are often acrimonious. What they indicate is a solid basis of concern about being bid for. It is not surprising that bids are feared and fought. It is not just a matter of money or compensation. Society wants its enterprises to be run by people who are motivated and dedicated, not just economic machines that suck what they can from an enterprise and leave it happily for a golden hello. Strong motivation is consistent with a fear of being displaced, of having to abandon the spiritual investment of many years, not because of one of the normal calamities to which business may be prey, but for a convulsive response of the stock market to a rich raider.

Because it is so important it is worth repeating that it is impossible to measure the effect of fear on the individual members of company boards, for this would take us into deep psychological waters. As noted above, CEOs often assert vigorously that they carry on regardless, doing what is best for the company, ignoring the share market. And yet ... may it just be that they are now so conditioned by its continuing pressures that they factor them into their subconscious without even knowing it? May the standards they set themselves be lower than they would otherwise be? Is not fear a poor motivator, distracting and destructive? The physical systems of mankind equip us to respond to danger in one of two ways: to stand and fight or run like hell—not, however civilized we may think ourselves, to ignore the threat and get on with planning for our children's futures.

There is another consequence of the threat of take-over which has been particularly evident in recent times and the subject of much comment; for instance, the article by Will Hutton (1990). He noted that the Bank of England had reported that by the fourth quarter of 1989 the dividend pay-out ratio had reached an unprecedented 62 per cent. The Bank wrote 'there is quite substantial empirical evidence that the growth in dividend payments has been strongly associated with the boom in hostile bids.' This distribution took place in a year when the corporate sector's financial deficit was £24 billion and indebtedness to banks rose by £33 billion. Hutton wrote, 'The monetary squeeze has been tighter for longer as companies have borrowed to pay dividends: and when the recession comes it will be amplified by higher than needed cuts in investment and workforces so that dividends, having reached ever higher levels do not suffer.' In fact, and some would say belatedly, we have now (Spring 1992) seen many companies cut dividends. In Japan and Germany shareholders receive relatively small dividends, though in the former this was compensated for some years by share prices being raised to unsustainable levels by incomprehensible levitation; in the UK, by contrast, shareholders riding on the back of the fear of take-over have often probably been paid more than is strictly good for the medium- and longer-term health of the business. The *Financial Times* leader of 4–5 January 1992 made a similar point in different language: 'The result is that dividends enjoy priority in a recession over capital investment, pay and jobs. German corporations by contrast operate on the reverse set of priorities with dividends coming bottom.'

It may be argued that in the UK system dividends have an important signalling function; that is, they convey to the investing world how management views prospects as well as performance. If, as in other systems, the shares are closely held or controlled, the signalling function is less important. Critics assert that UK industry pays a high price for its signalling mechanism—that is, a weakening of the company beyond what a prudent management would consider ideal were the function unnecessary.

Adam Smith still casts a long shadow. In the final chapter of book 1 of the *Wealth of Nations* he wrote, 'On the contrary it [the rate of profit] is naturally low in rich and high in poor countries, and it is always highest in the countries which are going fastest to ruin.'

Leveraged Buy-outs, Management Buy-outs and Buy-ins

No mention of take-overs would be complete without reference to LBOs, MBOs, and MBIs, which have become so important in recent years. As recently as 1979 there were only nineteen, with a total value of £14 million. A decade later when they were at their peak there were 522 with a value of £7,502 million. By 1991 this had declined to 595 with a value of £2,809 million. Although the number was still rising, the average value had fallen from £14.4 million to £5 million.

Like many good ideas, LBOs, MBOs, and MBIs were so swamped by fashion that caution and prudence were lost. In the four years to 1984 gearing was 1 : 3 (i.e. debt + mezzanine : equity). By the second half of 1989 it was 5 : 9. Then sense prevailed; the ratio for the second half of 1991 was 1 : 8. Sense came at a price. Of the 1989 transactions 8.8 per cent of MBOs and 21.0 per cent of MBIs have already ended in receivership (*Investors Chronicle* survey, Apr. 1992).

What the failure of so many MBOs and MBIs tells us about corporate governance is that some risks are excessive and that motivation is not enough by itself. MBOs and MBIs are based on the principle that if management owns a big enough stake the agency costs (in economists' parlance) are reduced; performance will improve with motivation. It ought to have been clear that motivation needs to be accompanied by competence: if that were not so, no family business would ever fail as long as the directors remained fully motivated—but as we all know, many do collapse. So the general principles of good corporate governance apply as much to MBOs and MBIs as in other companies, and investors ignore this factor at their peril. This is all the more important because there are so many cases of successful MBOs and MBIs scurrying back to the market and getting a new quotation, thereby presumably to some extent re-opening the issue of agency costs.

Litigation

Although we share with the USA systems based on the common law, we do not have derivative suits, class actions, and contingency litigation (see Ch. 5), so the opportunity for suits is much less and they are quite rare. I never knew a director contemplating appointment in normal circumstances who was concerned about it.

There have, however, been enough awkward cases in recent years (e.g. Guinness) to cause directors to realize that there could be abnormal circumstances when they might need legal or other professional advice; this is a subject PRO NED has covered in a leaflet, and which the Cadbury Report has addressed (para. 4.18). Both favour procedures which give directors a right to get the independent professional advice they need at the company's expense as long as it is in furtherance of their duties. Cadbury advocates there being in place an agreed procedure laid down formally: for example, in a Board Resolution, in the Articles, or in the Letter of Appointment. In fact, all directors probably have a Common Law right to get the professional advice they need at the company's expense. The point of having an agreed procedure is to make sure that they can exercise this right without recourse to the courts.

The Insolvency Act 1986 has made directors more wary of their role in troubled companies lest they trade wrongfully and so open themselves both to a suit for damages and the prospect of disqualification.

There has been an increasing tendency to sue auditors, especially after a company has failed unexpectedly shortly after its accounts have been passed, though the well-known judgement by the House of Lords in the Caparo case restricted the right of suit by defining narrowly the persons to whom auditors owed a duty of care. This again is a subject which the Cadbury Committee addressed (appendix 6 to the Report).

In short, litigation does not play an important part in corporate governance in the UK—even in or after take-overs.

Reporting to the Shareholders

The information which the directors are obliged to provide under the Companies Act, though not negligible, falls short of providing a complete picture of their stewardship. To do this would mean their furnishing shareholders with a coherent account of how their company had performed in the last accounting period, what its position was, and what its prospects were. Figures would not be enough, for they are at best a snapshot, an approximation of past facts. The often-held view that numerical data enshrine the truth and words are equivocal is the reverse of reality. Many numbers have perforce to be based on subjective judgements: for instance, provisions for bad debts, incomplete contracts, and the value of stock and real estate. Furthermore, all the numbers, even if accurate, do not necessarily add up to the whole story.

The numbers themselves have to be calculated in accordance with the conventions the accounting profession has adopted. The Financial Reporting Council and Accounting Standards Board are revising reporting standards, and the Financial Reporting Review Panel now monitors companies whose accounts fall below accepted reporting standards. At the end of the day, whatever standards are adopted, it will be the primary responsibility of directors to see they are followed. The auditor's role is secondary, despite the propensity to sue them on the 'long pocket' principle when something goes wrong.

The Cadbury Report covers financial reports in paragraphs 4.47 ff. recommending in para. 4.50 'that boards should pay particular attention to their duty to present a balanced and understandable assessment of their company's position. Balance requires that setbacks should be dealt with as well as successes, while the need for the report to be readily understood emphasises that words are as important as figures.'

The kind of issue that troubled the Cadbury Committee was the concept of 'going concern'. Odd as it may be, directors are not obliged under the Companies Act to check whether the company is a going concern when they sign off the accounts. They are entitled to assume it. Cadbury in paragraphs 5.18 ff. seeks to change the present rule and recommends in paragraph 5.22 that directors should state 'that the business is a going concern with supporting assumptions or qualification as necessary'.

The pressures on company boards to provide ever more numerical data spring from the natural desire of investors and analysts to produce what can easily be compared. Charts and league tables can be constructed from numbers (however suspect) more easily than words (however reliable). The plain fact is that qualitative data requires judgement and that judgement requires both skill and experience—hence the urge to provide data which reduces the importance of both. Interestingly exactly the same problem surfaced in the USA as a search for series of data which would cover the aspects of the accounts now omitted (e.g. quality and market share). The problem will not go away. A company's report and accounts cannot be rendered automatically interpretable without judgement. Judgement can be assisted—at least for those prepared to exercise it—by a coherent narrative about past, present, and future. In regard to the last this means describing what the company is doing by way of personnel policies to provide for it, such as recruitment and training, together with sketching its investment and development plans in as much detail as commercial confidentiality will allow.

The Institutional Shareholders Committee (ISC) (which represents pension funds, insurance companies, unit and investment trusts, and some fund managers) have made a particular point about the disclosure of research and development costs in the belief that this gives a good indication of the depth of commitment. Their April 1992 recommendation is worth reproducing in full:

Why Disclosure of R&D Costs would be Helpful

A company's commitment to R&D is an important indication of its future prospects and investors are keen to learn as much as they can about this topic, including the record in recent years, since any information on successful innovation in the past is indicative of the likely success of current and future expenditure.

Investors would particularly like to know, of course, about future plans, and here they come up against a company's understandable need to keep secrets from competitors. Often, however, secrecy is maintained as a matter of routine, without regard to its necessity. Where details cannot be disclosed without giving away too much to competitors, a lot can be done to strengthen the confidence of investors by speaking in general terms of major projected launches. *The rule should be to be positive and to reveal as much about research and innovation as is consistent with competitive prudence.*

Institutions are interested in how much is spent on R&D by any one company in comparison with its competitors in the same sector.

Our recommendation is that within any one sector, the definition of R&D used should be spelt out in detail, in a way that is relevant to patterns of research and development in that sector. *All companies within each sector should be encouraged to use the same industry-specific definition.* If this could be achieved, comparisons within each industry could legitimately be made, as could analyses of year on year changes. Comparisons between industries could still be difficult, but the ISC recognises that appropriate levels of R&D investment vary greatly from one industry to another, and consequently considers that comparisons within an industry are more meaningful.

To achieve the above recommendation, a high level of cooperation within each industry would be required, firstly to establish a standard industry-specific definition of R&D and secondly, to secure a sufficiently wide commitment to using that definition when disclosing the level of R&D. Here the Trade Associations of each industry would have a key role to play.

It will be seen from the above that the precise definition of R&D used in any one sector is of less importance than that all companies in that sector should use the same one. The ISC will not, therefore, attempt to suggest its own definition, on top of those already put forward by others. However, with regard to the three categories of R&D identified in SSAP 13 (pure research, applied research and *development*) the ISC suggests that figures for all three should be given, but that the third category should be interpreted in its broadest sense. *All costs relating to the development and improvement of existing products and processes should be included as well as all costs relating to new products and processes.*

Of course R&D and people are only two aspects of the future, albeit of critical importance. The picture would be incomplete without an account of investment of other kinds—plant, machinery, marketing. What will matter most will vary from industry to industry. This reinforces the point about the supreme importance of the narrative. What shareholders need to know is what really matters.

The old tale of the new finance director voicing an opinion at his first board meeting and being put down: 'Shut up lad, thou are nowt but scorer', has long been unfunny. The accounts and accounting conventions bear directly on directors' and managers' actions (e.g. in regard to an acquisitions policy). The accounting profession is working hard to resolve some of the more intractable problems about the treatment of financial data in a wide range of cases ('true and fair': 'going concern'; acquisition/merger accounting; off balance-sheet transactions; and so forth).

It is unnecessary in a book on corporate governance to examine the auditing function in detail, although it is part of the process by which accountability is maintained. It goes without saying that the users of reports and accounts need to be able to rely on them; the recent tendency to sue auditors when such reliance has proved to be misplaced does, perhaps, require a reminder that the prime responsibility for accuracy rests with the directors. The Auditing Practices Board, whose aim is to ensure public confidence in the auditing process, published a paper in November 1992 on the *Future Development of Auditing* which addresses *inter alia* the questions of:

Independence of auditors from pressures;
The scope of the audit;
The contents of the audit report;
Competition, cost, and quality;
Litigation and its effects;

Progress will benefit individual companies, the profession, and the market.

iii. An Evaluation

Introduction

It does not seem that history has disadvantaged the UK. On the contrary, it has enjoyed priceless benefits in many respects—defined boundaries, effective government, the rule of law (without having a surfeit of lawyers), great tolerance, liberal attitudes towards trade. So why has its performance been relatively poor for so long? There are some who would argue that it is actually doing rather well and that it does not matter if others are doing better. Such a position is optimistic, not to say unsustainable. The constant grind of international competition poses a threat of the UK being marginalized industry by industry. Commentators with liberal views about the internationalization of industry would not like *all* the major companies operating in any country to be controlled from abroad, because of the head office effect (so much of the most interesting work takes place in the home country), the home front principle (when times are hard, look after the home front first, not least because of the political consequences of doing otherwise), and the implications for careers (practice is improving but not yet good enough: far too few companies operate a genuine international meritocracy all the way to the top).

Many of the great multinationals with manufacturing or distributional companies in many countries have arranged for their shares to be quoted on several stock exchanges and are accustomed to a significant proportion of their shares being held abroad; and indeed welcome the fact. A wide distribution of ownership, as long as control remains unaffected, presents no issue of principle. Control, however, is another matter. No one can put an exact measure on how much of a country's industry should be controlled from abroad in this ever more international world. The proportion is probably rising sharply. Even so there does still seem to be a point at which countries feel uncomfortable: this is certainly true of France, judging by the search for 'French solutions' to restructuring problems, and to some degree it is true of the UK too.

The analysis begins with two propositions—first, that the UK is not content to see its commercial and industrial companies slowly sink into insignificance (and this applies as much to insurance as it does to cars); and, second, that it cannot attribute their relative decline overwhelmingly to external factors. The remedy in other words is in its own hands. What are its elements? In my view there is no magic bullet, no simple answer. The solution does depend partly on matters that lie outside corporate governance, like the educational system and macro-economic conditions including, for instance, the cost of money. A paper produced for the National Economic Development Office in 1990 (CF(90)3) stated: 'A comparison of real bank borrowing costs in the UK and Germany revealed little difference for the period 1979–87; however the nominal cost of debt (which has direct implications for companies' cash flows) shows UK industry to have been at a considerable disadvantage relative to its competitors in the 1970s; nominal borrowing rates have been both high and more volatile in this period.' Of all the external elements which serve industry ill, perhaps the most pervasive and intractable is the one that is the most difficult to pin down—esteem.

Esteem

What we can discern from all the other societies examined is that commerce and industry have an honoured place in them. That is not to assert that materialism is or should be all conquering or that money is or should be the only target in life and measurement of value. It is simply that everyone enjoys the products and services that industry and commerce provide, and that it is hypocritical to pretend that supplying them is inestimable: it is fair to scorn what is useless or superfluous, but absurd to extend this to what one uses and enjoys. And it betrays the mentality of a bygone age to pretend that somehow these things can be produced by Untermenschen, whose lives and contributions can be regarded by any element in society, whatever their self-esteem, with disdain. The surplus wealth their efforts provide fund all the laudable objectives the high principled (correctly) wish to pursue, from care for the aged to support for struggling artists. This wealth can only be won by being successful against international competition. Those who compete are like the country's champions of old, worthy of esteem and support. In time every society will get, more or less, the commerce and industry it deserves. All starts with esteem, for without it nothing else will be made available. Nor must esteem be reserved wholly for success, for if it is, faliure even with herioc efforts will earn neglect and opprobrium. The industrialists' apparent disdain of educationalists ('ivory tower ... those who can do, those who can't teach'), is matched by reciprocal feelings: 'You have the intelligence to seek a career in the civil service or professions; you do not have to go into industry.' If these trite caricatures did not have so much truth in them they would be pitiable.

Many people in the UK know this—the Royal Society of Arts' 'Industry Matters' campaign is evidence. Many industrialists are respected, some honoured. And yet ... there is still among many an echo of that Treasury official who years ago said to me, 'Why must we always be making things?' A basic change is needed, and perhaps it can only be attained by a sustained and sincere lead from the very top. For some time the cares—and the illusions—of empire (not to say the investments) sheltered the UK from having to face economic reality, but no one can argue convincingly that the even looser ties of the Commonwealth (important though they are) merit more attention than the cause of trade and industry. It is not just a question of more Queen's Awards—valuable though these are—but leading a widespread and sincere change to the value system, to elevate commerce and industry and all those who are employed in them. Their place in the public esteem in France, Germany, and the US is far higher than it is in the UK, yet there is no evidence that they are any abler or more expert.

The UK has long valued the gallant—and properly so. Members of the Armed Forces command great respect. Nowadays, they, like almost everyone else, can only be as effective in action as their technological support permits. That is what makes engineers so important in function today as in their historic contribution to the UK's industrial past; that is why their position in society is symptomatic. The UK is approaching the twenty-first century without a serious international contender among the major players in the electronics and computer industries; and even in its traditional industries it is surpassed. Any tour of UK factories reveals that most of the sophisticated capital equipment in most industries is made abroad. This is the end of a long road which started when influential sections of society began to feel that many of the malaises of their day could be attributed to industry, so those who dirtied their hands with production had somehow slipped socially. The Classics formed the spine of education; lines like Horace's 'Beatus ille qui procul negotiis'[6] both reflected and inspired the anti-industrial culture. All is not lost if these basic attitudes linger still, but unless they are relegated to the sidelines of history the UK cannot expect to be among the world's economic leaders in the twenty-first century. The UK loves sporting metaphors: it cannot expect to win a game it only plays half-heartedly or like an amateur among the professionals. Much helpful and constructive work is going on at the level of individual schools to link them to firms and restore the image of industry. Such a 'bottom upward' approach is valuable, but society needs a 'top down' effort from its leadership if the malaise of a hundred years is to be remedied.

The Purpose of Business: In Search of Consensus

In the early part of this chapter I commented on the divisions in Britain between commerce and industry on the one hand, and academe on the other, and quoted Kynaston and others on the great division between commerce and industry, and the financial world. This has more immediate consequences, for it starts with a different perception of the very purpose of commerce and industry.

The basic question which divides UK society is 'What are companies for?' The financial world sees them as a source of profits, almost irrespective of function. Academia (economists in particular) sees them as users of resources subject to the competing claims of other potential users in a constantly optimizing model: assets ought to be used by those who can make the best returns. This is the objective of enterprise and the yardstick of success; as to time-scale, the answer is 'The quicker the better.'

To a businessman the purpose of an enterprise is to produce the goods and services people need or can be induced to want. Profit is crucial for survival and continued employment, growth (and promotion), and invest-ment, and in order to be able to satisfy lenders about their capacity to repay and investors that they are a worthy choice among competing opportunities.

The difference in the end is not great. The businessmen in choosing between available investment opportunities must take their relative profit-ability into account in absolute and time terms, remembering always that time increases risk. They know too that short term is better but that in a particular industry it may be long term or not at all. It depends what time-scale competitors are using. But managers do not want to lose their jobs by being taken over if the competition forces them to be long term and this

---

[6] 'Blessed is he, who a long way from business . . .'

affects profits. (The UK industries that succeed in long-term sectors—oil and pharmaceuticals—have built up commanding positions from which they cannot easily be dislodged. Even so, a determined onslaught on the pharmaceutical industry would create pressures.)

As a result of the power of the 'financial' view of the purposes of a business, many managers have become adept at manipulating and massaging balance-sheets. Their MBAs have made them feel they can run anything; the slow slog and the patient development of a business career whilst they become infused with a company's culture is not for them. Change for them is cerebral not visceral, yet all effective change must be both. They are the choppers, cutters, and squeezers, but not often the patient builders, the incremental developers. The boards of the companies in which they work will run the subsidiaries and divisions under strictly financial controls and care little about what is done as long as the bottom line is right. They do not visit group factories for fear their judgement might be warped by caring.

Companies which resolutely soldier on with the industrial view of their purpose are always vulnerable to the cutters, choppers, and hackers who espouse the first view. It is always easy to improve shareholders' immediate values—but money cannot be conjured from nowhere. Someone pays. In such cases it is tomorrow's shareholders, employees, customers, the country.

The debate about the purpose of companies touches deeper notes because in the end they are not just dessicated profit-making machines. Their success will depend on the total commitment of those who serve them, and the company's profit is not of itself a sufficient motivator. Furthermore, a company is a living organism which touches society at many points. It must serve it, or it will eventually fail. The commitment to colleague, product, company, and society which is to be found in the greatest companies is not wholly compatible with the financial view of purpose. Profit is necessary but not sufficient.

The financial view of the purposes of a company gives a primacy of interest to those who happen to be its current stockholders—many of whom may, given the turnover of shares, have only come aboard in recent weeks. The fluidity of ownership does in a macro-economic sense avoid rigidities in the economy, but in a micro-economic sense it can undermine the future of a company and all who work in it. The present balance in the UK is an inheritance from the nineteenth century when the world was a very different place. It is not clear that it is appropriate for the twenty-first century, when in many industries success will depend on sound medium-

and long-term planning and investment. Writers like Goyder put the point in moral terms, but it can be expressed in other language. One aspect of the question to be addressed, for instance, is whether the optimum economic outcome can be expected unless an organization can invest adequately with the future and, crucially, draw from those it employs all that they have to offer. The UK work-force at any level is as good as any and better than most—if properly led and trained; and there are many examples to prove it. Is the commitment required from all concerned compatible with the financial view of the purpose of companies in the extreme form which obtains in the UK? In industries where success depends heavily upon investment of all kinds, including investment in the commitment of all the employees, is the argument sustainable that a company's future should be seen to be so readily at risk for short-term considerations and at the hands of 'owners' who know little and care less about the company, save that a quick turn can be made from selling it off?

The lack of consensus about the purpose of companies has important consequences. Profits are neither the god the City would make them nor the devil that socialists believe. They are necessary (for survival and progress), but cannot be relentlessly pursued in an anti-social way (e.g. by ignoring damage to health or the environment). To create a sense of harmony between necessarily competing priorities so that everyone feels they should support the principle of profit, within a framework of responsibility, is a major task for the UK in the next century.

This reconciliation requires adjustments on both sides. Management may not pursue its own purposes without regard to the interests of the shareholders; 'jam tomorrow' is not eternally acceptable. The financial world cannot sacrifice tomorrow's prosperity on the altar of 'shareholders' *immediate* values'. The task of reconciliation falls to those to whom management is accountable—the board and shareholders, to which we turn later.

The Heart of Corporate Governance

Introduction

We saw in previous sections that there are two basic principles of corporate governance which apply at all times and in all places. They do not deny the importance either of power or patronage, but require them to be exercised within a framework of accountability. These two principles can be briefly restated:

(i) That management must be able to drive the enterprise forward free from undue constraint caused by government interference, fear of litigation, or fear of displacement.

(ii) That this freedom—to use managerial power and patronage—must be exercised within a framework of effective accountability. Nominal accountability is not enough.

To evaluate the UK system of corporate governance requires us to consider carefully whether or to what extent these principles are followed or breached. The account of the system given above has already touched on some of the issues.

The Freedom of Executive Management

Government. The UK does not have to face some of the worst manifestations of interference by Ministers or Civil Servants: management does not have to seek permission for most things, nor does it need to bribe its way forward.

In most sectors of UK commerce and industry regulation is far more comprehensive than it was—not least because of Brussels. Much regulation is based on the assumption that the modern world has become so complex that citizens, however careful, cannot adequately protect themselves from the dangers of the goods and services they procure. The doctrine of *caveat emptor* is not quite dead, but it is in intensive care. What UK management has to contend with are periodical convulsions by the government of the day which is galvanized into action and then produces a monumental piece of legislation like the Financial Services Act, which imposes great costs in its pursuit of purity.

Fear of litigation. The directors of UK companies are seldom sued and on the whole do not fear litigation. This is partly because there are few causes of action which apply and partly because the machinery is not available (e.g. there are no derivative suits and class actions as there are in the USA, and no contingency fees either). Of course, if directors break the law they may face penalties—for instance, if they are guilty of trading wrongfully within the meaning of the Insolvency Act 1986. My experience at PRO NED suggests, however, that people will accept appointment to the boards of troubled companies, provided they feel they know the facts and that the financial support is adequate to keep them on the right side of the law.

Fear of displacement. As noted earlier the UK can only hope to get the best from its managers if they can operate with sufficient confidence to take care of the enterprise in the medium and long term. It is difficult if not impossible to measure their confidence—so much depends on the firm, the industry, the times, the market, and the individual. An individual must have a suitable standard by which to judge his own attitudes; if managers feel forced constantly to study their stock price it tells us something about the pressures on them which inevitably affect their decision-making. A proper awareness of the market seems in many cases I have encountered to lead insensibly into fear of vulnerability and displacement.

In all countries, displacement will occur eventually for incompetence, though it may mean shunting the culprit sideways rather than outright dismissal. The displacement that is of concern in the UK is the displacement of the competent—following a merger.

The difference between a take-over and a merger is that in the former the board has rejected the first approach (it may agree at a later stage). In most mergers and a very high proportion of take-overs, there are indeed winners and losers: one side is on top and the other loses place and power. We saw earlier that after a contested bid a much higher proportion of the target's top echelon lose their jobs. Even proper mergers seldom produce even-handed treatment for all; but commentators have praised SmithKline Beecham and Coats–Viyella–Tootal as among the better examples. Even 'friendly' mergers present management problems because of differences in culture. That is why so many disappoint or fail.

Take-overs constitute only a small fraction of mergers, but their effects are disproportionate. It is these not the total number of mergers that affect the corporate governance of UK companies.

Many commentators praise, or at least are content, with the elegance of the take-over market, quite unswayed by the argument that many corporate take-overs and mergers turn out badly, and that 2 + 2 turns out to be less than 4 and is sometimes nearly 0. Companies are seldom totally worthless, since any viable parts of a business can be sold on to new management, so for some parts of some businesses there is life after bankruptcy. This may indeed be the inevitable outcome, but if a business has been ruined by a bad take-over, it seems unreasonable to argue that its failure does not matter because something can be salvaged. That is like arguing that one can watch with equanimity a new car being pushed over a cliff as its remains will have scrap value.

A market economy is concerned with wealth creation not the manipulation of assets unless it serves that purpose. There is little evidence that extra wealth creation consistently follows from merger or take-over. The odds are against it for various structural reasons like differing cultures. Even so, their role is sufficiently important for no simplistic condemnation of them to be correct. They can be useful in extending into strange markets, securing economies of scale where it is truly necessary, organizing the run-down of a declining industry, and finally (and rarely), securing a change of poor management when the board and shareholders have failed to do it.

Were it not for the 'fear' effect which many commentators (including me) believe on balance to be distracting, destructive, and inhibiting, it would be right to leave things as they are: we interfere with markets at our peril. It is as well to remember, however, that this market is not like a medieval farmers' market dealing in natural produce. It is highly artificial dealing with products of statute. Without statute there would be no companies. It is entirely appropriate therefore for government to consider whether the law provides for a system and a process for transferring power which works in the national interest.

This does not lead to the conclusion that contested bids should be abolished. The Germans and Japanese may yet regret that their systems lack them as a long-stop, since theirs could easily degenerate into inefficient cosiness. But there are times when the UK has had too much of a good thing.

The weaknesses of the UK's system are manifest. Research shows that in many cases mergers and take-overs do not work out well—that is not itself unreasonable; all economic activity involves taking risks. Far more importantly the system ensures they are likely not to work well because bidders are obliged to act in partial and often significant ignorance. They have to fly blind to a great extent. This is an imperfection in the market for companies which the market itself cannot solve. But the most important issue of all is the one mentioned above—the fear effect.

Of course any attempt to modify the UK's system and process will excite the opposition of those who make their living by it. Those who made fortunes from the creation of conglomerates some years ago are now making second fortunes from dismembering them. Shareholders should remember that it is their pockets whence come the substantial costs of any kind of restructuring. Employees from chairman to canteen hand have to accept that others can settle their livelihoods and prospects, changing at will the implicit contracts on which they entered employment. It is for consideration whether they should have some voice; people are not chattels. To regard competition as the only issue which calls for evaluation in a merger is like judging an elephant by examining its trunk.

So much ink has been spilt about the ugly word 'short-termism' that there seems little else to say. What it means is the willingness of companies to put money into investments that will take a long time to pay off: the allegation is that the UK's system of corporate governance—and in particular market pressures—puts UK industry at a competitive disadvantage against firms from countries in which these pressures are less.

It is wrong to generalize about industries, as the circumstances vary so much. Here is the relevant passage from *Time Horizons and Technology Investments*, a 1992 booklet produced for the National Academy of Engineering of the USA. The accompanying diagram is given as Figure 6.2.

There is no single or standard definition of the term *time horizon* and no agreement on what business functions are affected by time horizons that are too short. What is clear is that time, as an element of planning, decision making, and execution, is a crucial aspect of competitive performance in a number of industry sectors. Examples of the role of time in company activities include.

- The time required to commercialize a new product or service that depends on the development and deployment of new technology
- The planning time frames (operating, business, and strategic) for which a company develops actions it chooses to pursue
- The time needed to build critical skill bases and teams, or to develop or deploy long-lived assets needed to improve company productivity
- The expected time between investment in development of a new technology and payoff
- The time it takes for a new market to develop and become saturated
- The length of time ahead that an organization can plan because of uncertainties affecting forecasts (procurement cycles, legal changes, or regulatory practices) for the industry
- The time it takes for a competitor to copy a product and get that product to the market
- The time scale embedded in the employee incentive and reward system

This list makes clear that every corporation operates with a host of different time horizons for its activities; companies must balance a range of different time-dependent business activities. In addition, companies in different industries obviously face different time horizons as a function of different economic, technological, market characteristics, and competitive conditions. Figure 1 [6.2] shows the variation in company options through the wide dispersion, by industry, of both the development times of new products and the market life of products.

The position of different products in Figure 1 [6.2] shows how two important operational time constants—time to develop and market new products and market life of products—vary by industry. The implication of these variations in industry-specific time cycles is that there will be substantial 'natural' variation among industries in many time-dependent business matters. Industry norms for research and development funding levels, development investment per product cycle, plant and equipment investment life, new product pricing strategies, employee-reward systems, and competitive strategies are all affected by industry-specific timing factors.

Industry-specific variation in time-dependent business matters illustrates an important point about time horizons: that individual company management and governance practices play a fundamental role in determining time horizons. Companies in industries with long product or market development cycle times— pharmaceutical or airframes, for example—must have relatively long investment horizons. Stable, successful companies in longer product cycle businesses—and there are many—are proof that effective management can collect and organize financial, human, and technological resources for competitive commercial activities with payback far in the future. This conclusion is buttressed by the fact that, within a given industry, it is possible to find companies with different time horizons and different levels of success. Companies in a single industry face a similar competitive environment, yet some are able to compete much more effectively than others. Such companies have different methods of managing, different time horizons and, consequently it seems, different levels of performance.

In general, therefore, the possibility of short-termism being a factor is much greater for some industries than others. Furthermore, it is evident looking at the UK that it fares well in some which are quintessentially long-term—oil, pharmaceuticals, and chemicals, for instance—and this against a national ethos in which no particular virtue is ascribed to long-termism.

Why should it be? If X PLC has a choice of investment between project or market A which produces a satisfactory return in four years, it naturally prefers that to project or market B which takes ten. However, in any given market or product range, if X PLC's competitors are willing to wait longer to get a satisfactory return, it has two choices—match them or exit. As long as X PLC has adequate other outlets for profitable investment, it does not matter in the short run to its shareholders if it exits. From the country's point of view, however, it may mean surrendering markets or products, probably for ever. Whether that matters depends on whether there are enough other opportunities for the country as a whole, and how much importance is attached to the nationality of companies.

In his book *Short-Termism on Trial*, Paul Marsh of London Business School demolished the argument that the stock market was short-sighted. But he admitted a 'lingering sense of unease' (Marsh 1990:59), in regard to project appraisal methods. My own concern is more fundamental—and extremely difficult either to dispel or to substantiate because it rests on an assessment of behaviour. Chief executives generally aver that their behaviour is un-affected by fear of market pressures (falling share price; greater risk of take-over); they say that they invest what is optimal for the company's future. I believe this response may well be honest but wrong, simply because the standards by which they are judging themselves have already been affected, subconsciously, by their concern about market reaction. As I noted earlier, I

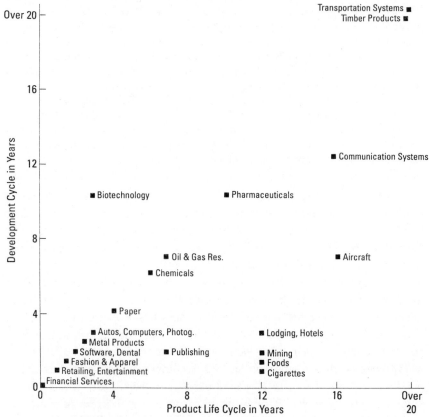

Source: Graph adapted by J. B. Quinn, from a concept introduced in a seminar by W. H. Davidson, University of Southern California, Spring 1986

Fɪɢ. 6.2 Typical time horizons by industry

am fortified in this belief because so many directors have told me of their sense of relief when their company was taken private or of the greater pressure after flotation. The market is not the villain of the piece; it is I believe the fear of take-over which inhibits risk-taking, and since all risk increases with time, a long-term approach to investment.

At every point in a nation's history a price has to be paid for its objectives. Economic contests can no more be won without losses than wars can be won without casualties. The extent to which losses and casualties are acceptable depends upon pressures and upon the appeal of the cause. In a nation addicted to gambling and which does not esteem industry, long-termism is not a cause for which many would pay much of a price. The highest price we pay for short-termism is in relation to people and their development. The best UK companies build people. In this regard there is real merit and intrinsic value in long-termism.

For all the reasons stated above I conclude that there is a powerful case for reconsidering the *public* interest in the effects of the threat of take-over on the long-term international competitiveness of UK industry.

Accountability

'Accountability' has an unpleasant and threatening ring to it; no one really rejoices in being accountable. Its importance however is twofold, both prophylactic and curative. If the system of accountability works well high standards will tend to be set; if management consistently fails to maintain them, accountability leads to remedial action. We have seen in Chapters 2 and 3 that the German and Japanese systems with their combination of informal networks and formal structure seem to be able to achieve these objectives pretty well—not perfectly, since humans are fallible—but generally to a high degree of effectiveness. The UK system has the same objectives, though its methods of achieving them are quite different. It relies mainly on boards and to a limited degree on shareholders.

It would be idle to pretend that any amendment to the system or change to the law could of itself guarantee success or freedom from failure. No type of structure ensures the competence of individuals or effective group dynamics, but some obviously help more than others. In the political sphere the UK has over the centuries successfully avoided most but not all of the bloody schisms that racked others by setting up and adapting effective structures to control the use of power. The accountability of management to the board as a whole is by common consent the bedrock of the system. The plain fact is that in many companies it scarcely works at all; in some companies it works partially; and in some it works poorly most of the time. In short, the UK system works erratically.

The law. It is not surprising that the system is so erratic since the legal framework which defines the governance of companies in the Companies Acts is extraordinarily sketchy. It barely mentions boards at all, let alone ascribing functions to them or requiring them to meet at regular intervals. As there is no need in law for a company to have a board, it follows there can be no requirement for a chairman of the board. In fact, save for a minor reference, the chairman—whether of company or board—is unmentioned. The duties of the directors being are minimal.

Defenders of the Act praise its 'flexibility'. It is open to doubt whether flexibility is double-talk for 'fudge'. 'Flexibility' implies a choice of means towards a given end; 'fudge' means obscuring or not facing the real issue. The intention of the Act is that management should be accountable to the directors and the directors to shareholders. In many cases it is clear beyond doubt that the intention is not met. Furthermore, the whole idea of a board-less chairman-less company being able to discharge its manifold responsibilities to all stakeholders is absurd and quite contrary to all good management practice on both sides of the Atlantic. Reports like Cadbury which are not in any way revolutionary are based on the assumption that all companies need boards and chairmen. It might be said that corporate govenance in the United Kingdom exists despite the Companies Act, not because of it.

George Goyder in his book *The Just Enterprise* (1987), which I read after drafting this chapter, has reached the same conclusion by a different route. 'It is absurd that a law designed for family business a century ago should continue to apply, without substantial change, to the whole of industry today regardless of the size and purpose of the company. This represents the abdication of the state from its responsibility to create responsible institutions.'

There may be a good case now for admitting the existence of the board in the primary legislation and defining in broad terms what its functions are, stipulating at the same time the minimum number of times it should meet. None of this would affect the vast majority of UK companies, but it would catch some whose practices to say the least leave much to be desired.

It is also for consideration whether the position of chairman should be recognized in law and some limited duties formally ascribed to it. It might go further and require that the position should be held by someone who was not chief executive or managing director. Simply by defining what the chairman of the board should do, the Act would go a very long way. It is not labels we need worry about, but the concentration and abuse of power. There is a school of thought which asserts that to insist on a formal division would be to impose too rigid a structure. In real life, however, the natural wish of powerful people to concentrate power in their hands for the sake of it (whilst arguing that it is best for the company) makes one feel that enforced separation would be marginally preferable.

With the definition of the board's duties set down clearly, the way would be clear to ease the present problem described by Davis and Kay (1990) in these terms:

So non-executives have responsibilities as advisers, as decision-makers and as monitors; yet it is apparent that there are serious incompatibilities among these functions. There is a clear distinction between the role of the adviser who provides input into a decision based on specific, if necessarily limited, expertise and perspective, and those who make the decision. It is also obvious that one cannot both make decisions and assess the performance of those who do. It is the inconsistency of these functions which makes the non-executive directorship a weak institution in practice, and explains why many conscientious non-executive directors find the job an unsatisfactory one. . . . The blending of these functions diminishes the ability of the non-executive to perform any of them.

The position of the non-executive director on a unitary board will always be difficult, but the UK need not make it worse than it need be. In the first place there should be a minimum number required by law. The Cadbury recommendations (to which I was a party) require quoted companies to appoint audit committees composed of independent directors. In this it follows at long last the lead set by the New York Stock Exchange in 1978— and they made it mandatory for boards to have independent directors. The Cadbury Committee had no power to ensure its recommendations were enforced. It recommended (para. 3.7) 'that companies should state in the report and accounts whether they comply with the Code and give reasons for any areas of non compliance. The London Stock Exchange intends to require such a statement as one of its continuing listing obligations.' The idea is that shareholders should take up the cudgels where a company does not comply. I subscribed to the Committee's recommendations because they are indeed a step forward. I believe, however, that the issue of accountability is fundamental to the concept of the company and that the mechanism through which it should be ensured should be prescribed by law. The UK is now faced with a further period of evasion and prevarication.

There are those who would go further and place a specific duty on the non-executive director to act as monitor. As noted earlier, this is to misread the Companies Act. All directors have to act as monitors whether or not they have executive powers. If it is desired to put an end to fudge, the logic is to differentiate between the duties of supervisors and the managers, whether they are on a single- or two-tiered board. Such a suggestion arouses deep opposition from those who are happy for the non-executive director to have a dual role as contributor and monitor. A formal differentiation is seen as a step to a two-tier system, which many distrust.

There is no need to take sides—there could be a choice. Even without pressure from EC Directives, there is after all something to be said for the separation of the functions of management and supervision: clarity and an elimination of conflict of interest. On the other side of the scales is the loss of valuable experience to the management board. There is a trade-off. In their pragmatic way the French, as we saw in Chapter 4, offer companies either a single-tier or two-tier board system, and the choice is invariably made not on ideological but on personal grounds. I suggest that the French are correct in principle though, as noted, many of them feel their law is flawed. There is no logical reason why all companies should be best suited at all times by a single structure; much depends on personalities and circumstances. *Why not give shareholders a choice as the French do?*

Recasting the Act in the way suggested would (whether a French solution is adopted or not) go some way to helping companies reach a solution of the dilemma described by W. T. A. Allen, Chancellor of the Delaware Court of Chancery: (quoted more fully in Part 5)

For outside directors to assume a more active role in corporate monitoring may require implementing changes of many kinds, but most basically of all it requires that outside directors understand that their duty requires more of them than simply acting as advisors and requires more than acting once a crisis has arisen. It requires that directors understand and assume the burden of active long-term monitoring.

Effective long-term monitoring requires more of outside directors than an appreciation of the scope of their responsibility. It requires a sympathetic and productive relationship between the outside board members and the CEO and the acknowledgement by the CEO of the legitimacy of the monitoring role and its requisites. More than this, effective sympathetic monitoring requires a commitment of time and resources, especially information, and sometimes independent advice. A few hours a quarter may satisfy the role of passive advisor in good times; it is not sufficient to meet the obligation to act as a monitor. The demands of the position, if properly understood, are inconsistent in my opinion, with service on an impressively long list of boards. (Allen 1992)

There is one diversionary argument which must be settled: that there are not enough non-executive directors to go round. We know this to be false. PRO NED has on its books some hundreds of people, carefully screened, who are well fitted to serve. If the demand were there more would be available; demand would quickly create its own supply.

A real problem exists with the boards of public companies where the executive directors—perhaps even one man—are in effect the controlling shareholders. The Cadbury Report requires all quoted companies to have independent directors (because they are needed for the audit committee). If they are to do the directorial job properly it is unsatisfactory to put them at the mercy of a proprietor who may be ruthless and mercurial. The Maxwell case was but one example of a wider problem. It is not necessary to protect the non-executive directors for all time, since they may prove incompetent or inattentive as in other companies. They do, however, need a safeguard against the domineering and capricious. There is not much point in building splendid-looking formal structures, NEDs' audit committees, and so on, if the whole lot can be blown out of the window by a powerful CEO who effectively has a controlling shareholding. *There is a case for revising company law to give directors better protection on such PLCs.*

The role of shareholders. Probably the weakest link in the UK system of corporate governance is that between board and shareholders. The reality is that many shareholders do not see their interests, or those on whose behalf they hold shares, being best served by their taking any interest in or playing any part in corporate governance. Accountability is like a telephone conversation: it cannot take place properly unless both parties listen, and if one party has taken its phone off the hook it cannot take place at all. Many UK institutions do not want a telephone or feel they need it; they consider their interests adequately served by market operations—even if the counter-party is an institution like themselves, which is almost always the case.

The system is built on the assumption that shareholders will monitor the performance of the companies in which they invest, not in the sense of vetting every move or double-guessing management, but by being concerned about the handful of strategic issues a company faces every decade and above all about the continued competence of its leadership. Consideration needs to be given to the consequences of this assumption now proving unwarranted. Perhaps shareholders' hands need strengthening or their incentives need changing, or both. The earlier analysis raised questions about the effect of 'active' portfolio management and the role of trustees. There are those who consider that the present system cannot survive if one of the basic assumptions on which it rests continues to prove ill founded. The seriousness of this issue cannot be overestimated.

Big private companies. Although this paper is mainly about quoted companies it is demonstrably true that after a company reaches a certain size, whether quoted or not, its potential for doing damage is great enough to warrant public interest in its governance. The damage that may be inflicted on all the stakeholders reaches the point where it becomes a public policy issue. That is what the Germans believe. Chapter 2 described how the German counterpart of a limited company (GmbH) may, if small, be run by one manager (Geschäftsführer), but it must have a supervisory board (Aufsichtsrat), complete with employee representatives if it grows in size and employs between 500 and 2,000 people. *I suggest there is a parallel case for suggesting that big (say 1,000 or 2,000 employees), unquoted companies in the UK should be required to have non-executive directors on the board with some degree of protection of tenure.*

Small private companies. As noted earlier, the Companies Act covers businesses of all sizes. In recent months the feeling has been growing that in particular respects—audit, for instance—too costly a burden is being imposed on very small businesses. A working party of the Institute of Chartered Accountants of Scotland has not only looked at this but also at disincorporation as a means of making life simpler. It is widely agreed that the establishment and success of small businesses is vital for the health of the economy because many of the next generation's majors will emerge from them. There is a case for considering the whole subject afresh, to produce a separate Act much shorter and simpler than the present Companies Act to facilitate the establishment and sound running of small companies: it is good to see that the Department of Trade and Industry has announced that it intends reviewing this area.

The 'other constituencies' debate. In one important respect the law does not need to be changed: namely, the bodies to which the board is accountable. In the 'other constituencies' debate, it is argued that management has a great many interests to consider other than the shareholders, such as employees, customers, suppliers, bankers, and the community. Of course it does; it cannot hope to succeed unless it takes all these interests properly into account. At the end of the day, however, it has to be able to service its debt and attract new capital when it needs it. If it fails in this it will lose control—or the company itself will fail. In today's world the demand for capital is likely to rise (and its price with it if supply does not expand). Shareholders may come at the end of the queue for dividends (and for distribution if the company ceases to trade), but they are the anchormen. If the board's accountability to them is lessened it will be altogether weakened: the distinction between 'taking into account' and 'being responsible to' must be maintained.

Annual general meetings. It was suggested earlier that shareholders might make better use of annual general meetings than they do. A thorough-going review of the Companies Act might examine this subject in depth, and in particular the advantages and disadvantages of:

(1) Requiring a quorum;
(2) Following the ERISA legislation in the USA and requiring trustees to see that their shares are voted (ERISA = Employee Retirement Income Security Act);

(3) Improving procedures, e.g. by introducing the pre-lodging of questions.

The Role of Banks

The banks clearly have an important and continuing role in providing finance for industry; they have made great strides in adding longer-term instruments to the overdraft which was designed primarily for short-term money.

Genuine short-term loans are often needed, but the majority of hard-core lending (from the precedents of Germany and Japan) seems to be managed better both for the sake of borrower and lender if it is accompanied by a relationship which is far deeper than is currently the case. This implies a willingness on the part of banks to incur the costs such a relationship implies, and also considerable experience among those who deal with companies: they must know the right questions and understand the answers and be able to provide sound advice. The firm must be prepared to provide full information—not, for instance, scurrying off to borrow secretly elsewhere; and to bear some of the costs a supportive relationship implies.

Argument has raged for many years about the floating charge. Its proponents praise its flexibility. Its opponents say it makes the banks careless of the interests of those less well secured. In fact, the banks' own security is often less than it appears as assets seem to melt in the heat of a depression. From the point of view of corporate governance the main issue is whether it helps or hinders the relationship which both parties need. What matters is the determination of both parties to reach the right relationship and their preparedness to pay for it.

The advocates of relationship banking for the sake of both parties do not overlook the many cases where local managers get and stay close to their customers. Their fear is that if this is a matter of personal style and not of policy it may endure only as long as a manager's term of office, because his successor may not have the same approach. Occasional shafts of enlightenment are no substitute for a systemic approach—a daunting task given the habits and assumptions of so many years. Sir David Walker, then an Executive Director of the Bank of England, commented as far back as 1988, 'The quality of relationships between industry and its suppliers of loan and risk capital is deficient.' There are signs since then that the UK major banks have embarked on a new course, carrying with them a greater range of services so that the contact costs are not prohibitive: the UK may not yet be ready for a 'universal bank' concept, but it is getting closer to it.

Just as the prosperity of companies so often depends heavily upon their bankers, so the prosperity of banks depends heavily on industrial and commercial corporate performance. The management of banks owes it to their owners and depositors to be knowledgeable and concerned about this performance, as a basis for their lending decisions, both individually and collectively. The mere act of lending to a company, however, does not in the UK's system impose a wider responsibility for the way that company conducts itself, though it is true that in certain circumstances banks may find a more active role essential. Companies deeply resent pressure and interference, and are reluctant to listen until the point is reached when they cannot take their overdraft elsewhere. At the moment in the UK the banks' role in corporate governance is negligible, except in rescue cases where they sometimes require management changes as part of the price for continuing support.

If banks were closer to their clients they might if they chose bring benign influence to bear before the eleventh hour. They would need to tread with some care lest they infringe the provisions of the Insolvency Act 1986 and, in acting as shadow directors, expose themselves to suit should the company ultimately collapse. Normally they see themselves dealing with companies at arms' length. Even so the idea of the banks acting a little earlier has attractions.

Trustees

Like the lay magistracy, trustees are a typically British device—sensible, acceptable, effective, and cheap. In both cases for hundreds of years responsible people were charged with dealing with the familiar in a context which came within their range of knowledge. Both institutions have endured, although the world in which they were called upon to act has become ever more complex and technical. Magistrates have the Clerk of the Court to lean upon; even so, they now receive training. The analogy between trustees and the magistrates cannot be pressed too far, since by and large magistrates have a uniform task (with some specialism, e.g. in respect of juvenile offenders). The object of a trust may vary immensely from a small house or legacy with a single beneficiary, to a monster pension fund with a myriad pensioners.

The role of trustees is much broader than the subject of this book, but in the context of corporate governance it is of real importance because they are in effect the owners of so much of UK industry. What seems to emerge is that in the world of investment most are likely to need training. Whether this means that over time a new profession of trustee should emerge, properly trained and remunerated, is an interesting point: after all, it is not thought wrong to pay the Public Trustee for his trained services. Stockbrokers are paid for their services and so are fund managers. So why not make sure that trustees are properly trained—and then paid?

The Maxwell case has raised questions about the powers and duties of trustees in relation to dishonesty. This aspect lies outside the scope of this book. But it is not enough nowadays for trustees to be honest; they must be skilled—however much they delegate. It is no more pleasing for beneficiaries to see their resources dwindle through honest ineptitude than dishonest depredation. The training of trustees is not, as we have seen, as remote from issues of corporate governance as appears at first blush.

These paragraphs were drafted before I read *On Trust* (1992), the report of a working party under Winifred Tumin on trustee training, set up by NCVO and the Charity Commission. Tumin's report was drafted in the context of charities and voluntary organizations, but its general message about the need for trustees to be properly trained applies, in my view, with especial force to the trustees of pension funds, etc. There is a passage in the report on trustees' financial responsibilities which touches on the need for them to be properly trained in this regard. One could argue with some of the detail but the general thrust is surely in the right direction. It is an area to which too little consideration has been given for far too long. But the more professional they are required to be, the more cogent the case for paying them.

In fact there are already stirrings. The trade union movement has become more aware of the significance of its members' role as trustees and some training courses are already in place. The implications of having more active and informed trustees for corporate governance have not been carefully considered. We saw earlier how small a percentage of equity is now held by private individuals. It is only too easy to forget that they do in fact have a huge interest—at one remove—through collective savings. Perhaps their trustees may prove instrumental in changing the balance back to real ownership.

It is not to be expected of trustees that they should become versed in the details of investment selection and monitoring, if for no other reason than that this is time-consuming and requires considerable experience and skill. On the other hand they need training and experience to evaluate alternative investment policies. How many today would be qualified to set limits to the extent to which their funds should be diversified: 15, or 50, or 500 different shares? By what criteria do they decide on take-over bids? At what point and for what reasons should a fund manager's performance give rise to concern? An unpaid trustee is expected to handle the assets as a prudent man would his own assets. But 'prudence' in today's world surely calls for skills and knowledge of a different order from the days when trustees dealt with the familiar and straightforward.

Like their counterparts on boards, the non-executive directors, trustees of pension funds (or for that matter of other collective savings schemes) must be independent, that is to say, not subject to interests which conflict with those of the beneficiaries as a class. However they are chosen—and the selection process ought to take into account the nature of the duties to be performed and the candidates' skills and character, and not to be distorted by other considerations—they must be clear when they enter office whose interests they serve and what duties they have accepted.

iv. Review

During the last decade I have heard at first hand from countless directors how poorly the UK governance system often works. This is in flat contrast to what one hears at any general meeting of the good and great of industry whose companies are on the whole impeccably run; it seems axiomatic on both sides of the Atlantic that any meeting about the reform of corporate governance is attended only by industrialists whose companies do not need it. Even so, there are 2,000 quoted British companies, and the evidence I have seen has convinced me that nothing less than a major review is now required, with the government at the end of it being ready to put its own shoulder to the wheel of enforcement instead of leaving it to others.

The British machinery for tackling questions of general importance but technical complexity—the Royal Commission—was abused by governments more interested in delay than solution (the 'kicking for touch' technique), and it is not at all surprising that the Thatcher administrations abandoned it. Company law is, however, precisely the type of subject that requires the quasi-judicial process of a Royal Commission which can consider the views of the powerful, the evidence of the commentators, and the interests of the community.

No one who talks to any of the protagonists in the worlds of commerce, politics, unions, or even in its own way academe, has the slightest doubt that beneath the elegant logic and complex arguments, the basic dynamics are those of power. Everyone speaks their own book.

As this is so, government departments are squeezed between contending pressures. They may have doubts about what exists but be concerned about offending those who would be affected by change. There is little political mileage in corporate governance, however important a topic it is. It is not a subject to set the voters' imagination aflame except in relation to scandal and excess.

It is little wonder, therefore, that governments tread gently if they move at all. At present (1992/3), the Parliamentary Under-Secretary of State of the Department of Trade and Industry (under whose aegis the Companies Act lies) has been charged with a consideration of aspects of it. No doubt, as in the past, the Department will, very properly, consult and do so with care and fairness. There must be some doubt, however, about the adequacy of the process of consulting the interested parties.

It is no use asking butchers whether to eat meat or a fiddler to be dispassionate about help for the arts. Power begets lobbying, and enough contending lobbyists can produce gridlock as we see in the USA. Consultations with powerful 'interests' do nothing to protect those affected but not technically 'interested'. The government has a far more difficult task—to consider those whom the interested parties' actions affect, and that includes society as a whole; it is a fallacy to believe that the common good will be served by leaving it solely to the interested parties (as Adam Smith recognized in a famous passage).

The joint stock company is a legal construct, not a product of nature. It is not interventionist or *dirigiste* for governments to ensure that the balance of interests between all parties affected by companies is maintained. The Companies Act now creaks in some fundamental ways.

The framework of the Companies Act, and its operation, are matters of public as well as private concern. The exercise of economic power is as important as the exercise of political power, and may touch individual lives more sharply. This does not mean that the state itself must intervene at every turn, but that it must assure itself that the machine it has created for balancing the various interests is working effectively. At the moment the best one can say on looking at the evidence is that it works in fits and starts; sometimes, as in the Maxwell case, it does not work at all. His case was unique only in degree and intensity. I make no apology, therefore, for suggesting that the time has come for a deep and impartial scrutiny of the law affecting companies with particular regard to the following subjects, in addition to the role and training of trustees, which turns out to be so important.

(1) The division of the Companies Acts to produce:
    (a) A short simple Act for small owner-run businesses;
    (b) A redrafted and simplified Act for quoted and big unquoted companies.
(2) In regard to 1(b), a definition of the basic role of the board; and its composition, including non-executive directors; a definition of the

basic role of the chairman; a definition of the basic role of audit committees and a requirement to have one; the process by which outside directors are chosen and elected.

(3) Consideration of the tenure of non-executive directors in companies which are controlled by members of the board.

(4) Examination of the principle of reciprocity, i.e. take-overs by firms which are themselves inviolable in practice; reconsideration of the role and effects of 'hostile' take-overs; and of the position of employees affected by them.

(5) Examination of the possibility of letting shareholders choose between two alternative types of structure—single- or two-tier.

By far the most difficult area is to make the shareholders' role more significant. In a system with minimal networking the informal pressures on the board as a whole depend almost exclusively on the shareholders; the banks saw others scarcely come into the picture at all. That they do play the limited part assigned to them thoroughly is in the long run essential. If it can never be—then the Companies Act is fundamentally misconceived, for it is built upon a rotten foundation. My own view is that this is not so, but ways have to be found of encouraging, enabling, and conceivably rewarding shareholders for playing their part. These may include revising the procedures for general meetings and establishing bodies to facilitate joint action by spreading the cost of investigation and action itself. This is, I believe, an area the UK will neglect at its peril.

Although a Royal Commission has much to commend it a thorough-going inquiry could take other forms—the Cohen Committee, which preceded the 1948 Act, is an example. Perhaps the work could be done by a somewhat reconstituted Cadbury Committee, but if so its terms of reference should be agreed by government and it should report to the Department of Trade and Industry. In essence, an inquiry needs to be broad and thorough: and to make recommendations to the responsible authority.

v. Envoi

How UK commerce and industry will fare in the twenty-first century against constantly intensifying competition depends very much on how honestly and effectively it faces some of the issues posed in this book about the place of industry in society. There is a part for everyone to play—chairmen, boards, employees, government, the City, academe, shareholders, banks. The UK's interests and indeed those of other nations will be best served by sound corporate governance to ensure that each has its share of competent businesses that do not needlessly fail. But the UK's home market is, like most others, small—far too small to sustain those industries in which heavy investment is necessary, and for these the future lies in some form of collaboration. In other industries, where time horizons are short and invest-ment not so burdensome, there may be a bright future for small and medium-sized enterprises which are competently run, and from some of these tomorrow's giants will emerge—which is why good corporate govern-ance is so important up and down the scale. One of the saddest sights is the company which failed to live up to its early promise, and this is usually because its governance did not match up. In many sectors of the commercial and industrial world companies will be multinational, operating directly or indirectly over much of the world. This is inevitable, but it is not enough. Companies need to be truly *inter*national from top to bottom if the sterility and antagonism of economic nationalism are to be avoided; differences in language and culture should be seen as challenges, not insuperable obstacles. But the UK needs to start at home by putting its corporate governance in order; many, like the members of the Cadbury committee, have contributed. There is still far to go.

Appendix 6A. *The Role of Company Boards*

The Board of NatWest and how it Works

The Board of NatWest consists of 21 Directors. We have a significant number of Non-Executive Directors, or as they are sometimes described, independent Directors. It is from the perspective of a Non-Executive Director that I describe the function of the Board and the role which the Non-Executives play in the governance of the Bank.

The Board is a unitary Board: each and every member is responsible for the decisions it takes. We regard it as extremely important to ensure that the Bank is run with integrity. The Board and Management appreciate that our ethical standards are the foundation of all we do, but our tasks go well beyond this. The Board ultimately determines the strategy of the Bank and monitors performance. The Executives are responsible for the management of the Bank and are accountable to the full Board in the discharging of that duty.

I would like to describe the attitudes we adopt and the way we approach our work so that you may know how seriously we take our obligations.

We all, as a Board, have a primary function to guard the interests of shareholders. We can only discharge this duty by recognizing the wider responsibilities we have to those who can, in broad terms, be described as the stakeholders in the Bank: our employees, our customers, our business partners, and the community at large.

We aim to limit the Board to around 20 members. When appointing new Board members we assess our existing expertise and search for those who can contribute other skills and experience so that our Board remains well balanced. We are fortunate in having Non-Executive Directors who are prepared to participate fully and with enthusiasm in the governance of the Bank.

Board matters are initiated and progressed by the Chairman's Committee, which is made up of selected Non-Executive Directors and Executives. The Committee usually meets twice between Board meetings to prepare agenda items for the Board and to take decisions on matters not requiring full Board approval.

The full Board meets on a monthly basis, except August, and convenes for extra meetings prior to Interim and Final Results. In addition, the Board meets each year for a longer period to discuss and debate the Annual Plan as presented by the Executives.

There are two Board committees made up entirely of Non-Executive Directors. These are the Remuneration Committee and the Audit and Compliance Committee, chaired respectively by Martin Harris and myself.

The Remuneration Committee is responsible for recommending to the Board the total remuneration packages of the Chairman, the Deputy Chairmen and the Group Chief Executive and is closely involved with determining all other executive remuneration. The Committee is assisted by our Group Personnel Division which provides comparative data where appropriate.

The Audit and Compliance Committee reviews accounting procedures, policies and control systems throughout the Group. It also monitors the response of the Executive to the accepted recommendations of the external auditors. It will approve responses to the regulatory authorities such as the Bank of England and the Investment Management Regulatory Organization. The Committee meets three or four times a year, and from time to time is convened at short notice to deal with urgent issues.

Where Non-Executive Directors have specific knowledge and influence they may be consulted informally by Executives; they may also visit Divisions and Regions and make presentations to staff. This is a valuable activity as it helps to deepen the knowledge of the Non-Executive Directors of the activities of the Bank.

The General Manager of Group Personnel reports regularly to the Board to ensure that it is kept fully appraised of significant employee issues. Non-Executive Directors are encouraged to visit staff and customers to get direct feedback on these and other matters. This is, of course, supplementary to the procedures already in place to enable us to learn our customers' views on the service we provide.

In addition, Non-Executive Directors serve in other areas where they can support the Executives, for example on the Boards of subsidiaries and divisions like Coutts, Lombard North Central and NatWest Markets, Non-Executive Directors are also members of the Bank's Public and Social Policy Committee which established guidelines for NatWest's active programme of community involvement.

In summary, Non-Executive Directors are fully, actively and energetically involved in the government of the Bank and provide a valuable independent perspective to debates at Board. From my viewpoint, I believe we are coming through a period of not inconsiderable difficulties as a much more effective and dynamic organization. This change is underlined by the new balance in the Executive and Management of the Bank where the infusion of younger talent is blended with experience.

The Non-Executive Directors will continue to play a leading role in addressing the challenges of the 1990s.

Sir Edwin Nixon
Deputy Chairman

The Board of ICI

As the senior Non-Executive Director on your Company's Board, it is my privilege, on behalf of my colleagues, to address shareholders on our responsibilities to them and to ICI.

All of your Directors are, of course, accountable under law for the proper stewardship of ICI's assets and undertakings. The Non-Executive Directors have a particular responsibility to ensure that the principal operational and financial strategies and policies proposed by our Executive colleagues are examined and discussed fully and objectively. In making decisions, we consider carefully the balance of interests of our shareholders, employees, customers and the many communities in which ICI is represented.

I can confirm that, to enable your Non-Executive Directors to contribute effectively to ICI's affairs and progress, we are given full access to all appropriate information. We engage in open, constructive debate and are involved fully in ICI's strategic plans and in such things as helping to guide the extensive reshaping programme set out in this and last year's Reports. This programme provides an excellent example of a vital strategy which has been considered diligently by the entire Board and which will help us to achieve our primary objective of improving earnings quality and shareholder value.

Since ICI's foundation, the Board has had a significant representation of Non-Executive Directors, and today we have equal numbers of Executive and external Directors. We bring to all the Board's deliberations, and to strategic and financial matters, wide experience from our various business backgrounds. As befits a company with global operations and markets, half of your Non-Executive Directors are from outside the UK.

We participate in the committees of the Board listed below, ensuring high standards of financial integrity and the independent determination of the employment terms and rewards of the Chairman, Executive Directors and senior managers. We are directly concerned in planning the senior management succession, including the Chairman and other Board members.

For each of us, membership of the ICI Board is a challenging and stimulating responsibility. We look forward to continuing to serve the interests of the Company and its shareholders.

Sir Patrick Meaney

Audit Committee

Members:
Mr T H Wyman (Chairman)
Lord Chilver
Sir Antony Pilkington
Terms of reference: To assist the
Board in the discharge of
its responsibilities for corporate
governance, financial reporting and
corporate control.

Remuneration Committee

Members:
Sir Patrick Meaney (Chairman)
The Non-Executive Directors
Terms of reference: To determine
employment terms and retirement
provisions for Executive Directors and
the most senior management in the
company. To exercise the powers of
the Directors under the Senior Staff
Share Option Schemes.

Appeals Committee

Members:
Mr F Whiteley (Chairman)
Mr J D F Barnes
Dr P Doyle
Sir Patrick Meaney
Sir Jeremy Morse
Terms of reference: To determine the
policy and practice for the making of
charitable donations in the UK.

Appendix 6B. *University of Exeter Survey into Audit Committees in Financial Institutions*

Preliminary Findings: Functions

Audit committees carry out a wide range of functions involving external reporting, external auditors and internal auditors and other matters. On average respondents had 20 of the 32 functions listed in the questionnaire under these four categories.

The functions relating to external reporting, which were present in over 75 percent of respondents, were:

(i) Review company accounting principles and practice, and significant changes during the year.

(ii) Review audited annual financial statements.

(iii) Monitor compliance with statutory and Stock Exchange reporting requirements.

The functions related to external auditors, which were present in over 75 percent of respondents were:

(i) Review their evaluation of the company's internal control systems, recommendations to management and management's response.

(ii) Discuss with the auditors their experiences and problems in carrying out the audit.

(iii) Discuss the meaning and significance of audited figures and notes attached thereto.

(iv) Review factors that might impair, or be perceived to impair, the auditor's independence.

Only a third of respondents reported that the AC nominated or approved the auditors.

The functions related to internal auditors, which were present in over 75 percent of respondents were:

(i) Discuss the effectiveness of internal controls.

(ii) Discuss the relationship between internal and external auditors and the coordination of their audit work.

(iii) Review internal audit objectives and plans.

(iv) Review organisation of the department, lines of reporting and independence of the internal audit function.

(v) Discuss with the internal auditors their findings and reports.

(vi) Ascertain whether proper action has been taken on recommendations.

Of the functions under the heading other matters, none were present in the functions of the ACs of over 75 percent of respondents and only the following were present in the functions of the ACs of over 50 percent of respondents:

(i) Enquire into illegal, questionable, or unethical activities.

(ii) Initiate special projects or investigations on any matter within its terms of reference.

7 WHICH SYSTEM IS BEST?

The Multinational Company

The people who have first-hand experience of the question 'Which system of corporate governance is best?' are those who run companies which have incorporated subsidiaries in many countries—the multinationals.

Corporate governance laws apply territorially. A company based in the UK, for instance, is subject to British law, but its subsidiaries in France, Germany, and the United States would be subject to the law prevailing there. As this is so, companies nowadays need to understand not only the laws in the countries in which they have incorporated subsidiaries, but also the background to those laws, and how the system works. To give an example: the managing director of the UK subsidiary of a Japanese company recently raised with me the way in which the Japanese president of the parent company set about appointing a chairman of the UK subsidiary. The process was unfamiliar to the Englishman and appeared threatening. In fact, however, it was just the normal way in which a Japanese president would proceed, totally well intentioned. Misunderstandings may arise because of such differences in culture and behaviour.

The contrast between the differing styles and systems of corporate governance which this book has illustrated may not for the most part matter much for a multinational company: it will simply adapt to local laws and conditions. It may not feel entirely painless. A German company operating a big subsidiary in England, for instance, is not obliged to practice co-determination, though it would be perfectly free to do so under UK law, provided that those designated as directors honoured their formal obligations. A UK company's big subsidiary in Germany, however, would be bound to follow German law and practice and therefore accept the works council and co-determination arrangements.

Because these differences arise there are those who would like to see greater uniformity together with the specification of what they regard as minimum standards—hence the introduction of the European Company Statute (ECS). It is significant that its failure to make progress has been occasioned by the feeling of some countries that the price of uniformity is too high. Although the benefits of common practice are apparent, it would appear that some countries are reluctrat to abandon their own style. Perhaps the introduction to the chapters of this book explain why— corporate governance systems have deep roots.

Within Europe I am not aware of any case where a company has moved from country to country primarily to take advantage of different corporate governance laws, though within the USA it is well known that this has occurred between States. The choice of Delaware as the State of incorpora- tion by numerous companies which have no significant operations there shows that they consider it to be an important factor. Companies may shift their headquarters for political reasons like those which have left Hong Kong rather than risk what may happen after 1997. And there are many examples of companies which shift their seat of operations for tax purposes. Even for tax reasons, however, companies move away from their natural home with reluctance. Many UK companies struggled for years with the burden of unrelieved Advance Corporation Tax because they did not make enough profit from their UK operations to offset against the tax they incurred from profits overseas. Even though large sums of money were involved, no company moved abroad, though this may possibly be due to the fact that notwithstanding the ACT problem, total taxation is not unreasonable. In short, companies seem to accept the corporate govern- ance system they happen to encounter. If they move it is for other reasons.

As companies' operations become more multinational, to the point where they do relatively little business in their country of origin (e.g. Nestlé do only 2 per cent of their turnover in Switzerland), it might be imagined that the board would reflect the international nature of their markets and operations. There does indeed seem to be some evidence that boards in many countries now have more foreigners on them. My impression is that the UK and USA are rather better at this than others, but still not very good, and the Japanese companies have scarcely begun, though this may be partly ascribed to the relatively limited function of Japanese boards, as described in Chapter 3. Germany presents a unique problem. The Vorstand of a German company may, and indeed sometimes does, have foreigners on it. The supervisory board, the Aufsichtsrat, has on it employee representa- tives drawn from the home country. To the extent that German companies increasingly establish manufacturing units abroad, the question of international employee representation on the main Aufsichtsrat will surely grow. I have spoken to many directors who serve on the boards of foreign companies, and superficially at least they seem to adapt well to different systems. This is, however, an area which would bear close scrutiny and more careful research—as the opportunity for it increases.

Shareholders

Multinationals often seek quotations on stock exchanges in several countries, first as a means of widening their shareholders' base, and secondly to demonstrate their commitment to a particular market. Even where they do not, portfolio management has now become so sophisticated that major funds are likely to hold a significant proportion of assets in foreign equities. As it is, an increasingly significant part of shareholders' voting power is controlled from abroad. This poses a series of technical problems because the shareholders need to get the documents in good time to vote and to receive them in a language they understand. It will be a black day for corporate governance internationally if a vote abroad were considered to be a vote lost. With regard to shares held in the USA, however, this is not likely to be the case, especially when the funds that own them come under ERISA rules (see Chapter 5). The trustees of these funds must, as we have seen, ensure that the votes are cast. It may therefore be that foreign companies will find many of their American shareholders using their votes, and these votes will form an increasingly significant proportion of those cast. In principle, international proxy solicitation should over the next decades be a growth industry.

The reason why it is so important that shareholder power is not destroyed—especially by accident, because of the mere mechanics of passing information and voting—is that the boards of multinationals must be accountable and in this regard shareholders stand proxy for their countries. The power of the multinationals is such that governments will neglect this aspect at their peril. If boards were ever to become unaccountable they would in time engender such hostility as to occasion a governmental response. The anti-trust legislation within the USA owes its origin to that kind of reaction.

Take-overs were an area of concern. As we have noted, the markets in Germany and Japan are virtually closed: hostile take-overs there are not at all illegal—just impossible. In many cases they are virtually impossible in France as well. Only the UK and USA have truly open markets, and even the latter has become much less open than it was, thanks to protective State legislation and anti-take-over devices. The fact that the issue has not received more prominenence is, in my estimation, due to the restraint shown by German and Japanese companies in not making hostile bids. Judging by the outcry in the UK when Nestlé bid for Rowntree, any rapid escalation of hostile bids from countries which do not in practice permit them would be likely to produce a strong reaction—which would not be unjustified. Lack of reciprocity should not only be viewed in its international context, however, because it applies within a country as well: an unquoted company, if it is rich enough, can bid in the open market for a quoted company, but not vice versa. It is just conceivable that if there is another huge surge in take-over activity, as there was in the 1980s, pressure may increase for a rule of effective reciprocity, that is, no company would be permitted to make a 'hostile' bid for another unless it was itself open to such a bid in practical and not just theoretical terms—a nice teaser for any court which had to adjudicate! But that is at the moment mere speculation. Within the UK concern has diminished, but could easily be rekindled.

Finally, I turn to the role of the banks. Many multinational companies already raise capital of various sorts in varying denominations in a wide range of markets. They also use the banking facilities in many countries. None of this need necessarily weaken the links between the company and its main bank or banks, especially in countries like Germany or Japan where this is still significant. Elsewhere complications may arise if a company gets into trouble because marshalling the support of literally dozens of foreign banks may prove difficult if not impossible. When Polly Peck ran into trouble, for instance, well over a hundred banks were involved. Boards of multinationals which are careless about the spread and nature of their banking relationships may well find that governance becomes more difficult in choppy waters.

We can conclude therefore that few, if any, companies feel the pull of an alternative governance system to be so irresistible as to want to cross national boundaries to obtain it. Given a common cultural background the US experience demonstrates that companies will see what suits them best. On this analogy, if Scotland developed a system which other UK companies preferred they might incorporate there. Such movement would, however, not prove that the system chosen was better, any more than it necessarily follows that Delaware offers 'the best' system in the USA. Mere popularity does not imply excellence. It is to the criteria of excellence that we now turn.

What do we Mean by Best?

There is a great danger that when we think of the big modern corporation we do so primarily in terms of its products or factories or offices or advertising. The very word 'corporation' sounds impersonal and inanimate. The term 'company' is better because it has about it the ring of the essential truth, that all enterprises are collections of *people* with intelligence, spirit, and emotions. Their performance together will depend heavily on the way they are treated and led.

No matter how perfectly a company is led and how well its staff are motivated, it may have no control over events which have a profound effect on its future. The best firm in Pompeii in AD 79 perished with the incompetent; the twentieth-century wars gave the aircraft industry potential markets and the prospect of growth it would not otherwise have had. What we can observe, however, is that except in cataclysms some firms do survive much better than others; and that over time everything perishes, however difficult this may be to believe today. The *Stock Exchange Year Book* of 1962 already reads like a corporate Valhalla. The 1992 version will doubtless look similar in 2020. *Nos morituri te salutamus.*

The place of systems of corporate governance in the fight for survival and scramble for prosperity is, in human terms, to enable the company to draw on the constructive vitality of its people while containing the effects of their weaknesses. Most people have some talent to some degree, while those who acquire power in business often have many talents to a high degree. What they do not possess, however, is all the talents to the highest degree; and, moreover, no one is capable of sustaining the highest quality of decision-making for ever. To give two examples: we have all seen with regret lopsided talent unable to recognize its shortcomings (for instance in financial or marketing skills) ruin an otherwise promising business by not bringing in, and according power to, others who might have created the necessary balance. Worse still, we have all seen business geniuses inebriated by the applause for their undoubted ability hang on too long, till immodesty led to disaster and the business, successor-less, was in steep decline.

The role of systems of corporate governance is to address such failings steadily, regularly, and with as little drama as possible. Systems cannot produce miracles or arrest secular decline; still less should they try to eliminate risk, without which nothing can be achieved—but even there they can help by stopping impetuous leadership 'betting the business' on an ill-considered and unresearched proposition. Above all, systems of corporate governance are there to help maintain standards of competence, and (as noted earlier) to the extent they succeed in this preventative role, their curative role becomes less important. The test of a good system is not the number of companies from which poor CEOs are removed, but the number of times a CEO is so competent that he or she can reach retiring age in place.

The Test of a System

The test of a system is therefore how well it delivers consistently behaviour which satisfies the two criteria postulated in the introduction to this book and discussed in each of the five country studies, namely:

Dynamism. Does the system permit the management of the enterprise to drive it forward without undue fear of governmental interference, litigation, or displacement?

Accountability. Does the system ensure that in exercising its freedom management is effectively accountable for its decisions and actions so that the necessary standards are maintained and the appropriate remedial action can be taken in a timely way if they are not?

The criteria suggested are economic in nature, that is to say, they relate to the company's economic performance. There are those who add a separate dimension—a firm's social performance, on the grounds that the mere making of money is not from society's point of view enough. A company must contribute to society's well-being, or at the very lowest must not impair it: they imply a third criterion for corporate governance, one which relates to 'social' performance.

Adding a 'social' criterion to the economic ones has attractions but it may turn out to be a case of the best being the enemy of the good. If we consider that a market economy, however imperfect, is the best-known economic system, it must follow that those who, within the law, engage competitively in it are conferring a benefit; their success depends on their supplying satisfactorily the goods and services society needs or can be induced to want, for if they do not do so they will fail. Their success is doubly important since it also ensures employment. In a competitive world it is difficult to sustain success over time, and society is best served when companies concentrate on that and not on other causes, however desirable in themselves, because the social consequences of failure are not costless. Fortunately, social and economic behaviour often run together. Successful employers will in the long run have looked after their people and trained them properly; will have behaved responsibly to suppliers; and will have produced honest goods and reliable services. In some areas it is for government to establish the boundary between acceptable and unacceptable standards (e.g. pollution), hence the requirement for activity to be conducted 'within the law'.

For these reasons I would not add a third criterion by which to judge a system of corporate governance. At the same time it is important to recognize that 'accountability' covers standards of behaviour as well as standards of competence.

Which Systems Meet Best the Criterion of Dynamism?

The issue here is whether management as a whole has the power it needs (free from unnecessary constraints) to drive the enterprise forward, however that power may be distributed. It may be concentrated in the hand of a single individual, such as the role of Directeur General (PDG) in France or CEO in the USA, or held much more collectively, as by a Vorstand in Germany. As noted in the country by country studies, constraints on management fall into three groups: government, litigation, and fear of displacement.

Government

In a general way government may make the task of corporate governance easier or not—for instance, by their policies on:

macro-economic management
infrastructure
education
foreign trade assistance/subsidies
taxation
trade union legislation.

But all these factors are of importance whatever kind of corporate governance system a country employs. Some of these factors may indeed be far more important than the corporate governance system; if a poor macro-economic policy ruins a country it can make life almost impossible for company management whatever system is employed—but even then the best-run firms will last longer.

Taking all this as given, however, the question still arises whether governments interfere with or impose constraints upon management in such a way as to cramp their style or prevent their driving the business forward in the way they think best. It is difficult to get at the whole truth, since in all countries governments prefer secrecy. The ways in which they exert influence or pressure are many and various and often deliberately hidden from view. Governments' views differ, for instance, about how much of their taxpayers' money should be ladled out to companies to help them secure contracts abroad, but this does not have any bearing on the corporate governance system. There are subtle rewards for co-operation—and the opposite. To take another example. When an industry is in secular decline, governments see their responsibilities differently. In general, moreover, policy and practice may vary greatly within a given country dependent on which party is in power.

Whole industries like defence depend on governments for existence, and many contracts cross-subsidize civil ventures (e.g. through the benefits of R&D). Much of the US aviation industry developed in this way. Sometimes governments cajole, threaten, and bribe industries into actions to support social objectives such as locating plants in a particular town, and if the UK be any guide this can be a costly failure if the economics are unsound.

The whole area of government interference is one in which hard facts are and will remain in relatively short supply. I am inclined to believe that it is easier for governments to interfere in networked systems than in high tension ones. In practice the government in Germany interferes very little, but my general impression is that 'influence' is greatest in Japan, though less now than formerly and diminishing. As Chapter 4 suggests, it still counts in France. Since 1979 in the UK the main policy of the Department of Industry seems to have been to have no policy, and there have been relatively few scratchings in the wainscot. In the USA, pork barrel politics endure, as anyone can testify who wonders about the location of Washington's international airport. Every reader of these paragraphs will know of subtle (or not so subtle) influences in this form or that in every country mentioned (and all those which are not). The worlds of business and politics have coexisted for millenia and it is bound to be so: politicians enjoy meddling and businessmen like support. From the evidence I have seen I conclude that management's freedom of action is not generally circumscribed in most of the systems, and that even when it is, this would remain a feature of the landscape even were the system to change. It would not make a scrap of difference to the role of the Japanese government were the country tomorrow to change to the German two-tier system, lock, stock, and barrel.

Proof of this point comes from France where companies may choose between two quite different systems; it does not matter a jot to French governments which system a company uses when it comes to issues connected with the favours of the state.

By and large, none of the systems put government in such a position that management needs to appear as a suppliant (or offer bribes) to move forward. On the other hand, government has been inclined to lean on management in various countries, in various ways and at various times (and of course to help in various ways), but there seems little evidence that it does so anywhere as a part of the system, save possibly in Japan and France, where as far as we can tell the lines of communication between firms and sponsoring departments seem a little shorter. The tendency is for government to get less rather than more deeply involved.

Litigation

Litigation only figures in one of the countries studied—the USA—and that is much more to do with their legal system than their corporate governance regime. The unheavenly trio of derivative suits, class actions, and contingency fees is unique to the USA and affects their society at many points. It undoubtedly adds to the costs of US products and services compared with their competitors, partly from direct legal costs, partly from insurance. There are those who would argue that the threat of litigation keeps US management on its toes; in my observation it does make them acutely conscious of the prospect of suit, hence the ubiquity of lawyers—and that despite the protection of D&O insurance. In fact the Business Judgement Rule keeps the law away from all the decisions that really matter, for if it did not US business would not be able to function. Compared with all other countries there are far more lawyers and far more suits. In recent years many of the cases have related to the events surrounding take-overs and the defences. Much work remains to be done by the USA on the balance-sheet of advantage to them of their legal system, but I would judge that no other country would be remotely interested in following them down a similar path.

The Threat of Displacement: Market Pressure and Take-overs

Some managers would place these issues in the section on 'accountability', arguing that they feel accountable to the market. What is at issue here, however, is something different—the degree to which management feels constrained in its range of options by the market, or more exactly by their fear of what rightly or wrongly the market reaction will be to a given course of action. Should they, for instance, cut back on advertising this year (which feeds straight through to the bottom line) in order to maintain profits, regardless of the danger to market share which will only show up later? It is claimed that if the market is fed enough information about a company's plans and progress it will factor into the price due allowance for tomorrow's expected stream of profits (depending on the coefficient of confidence in the management, itself based on past performance).

This is an area in which it is extraordinarily difficult to get at the truth because we are researching individuals' decisions. Whether or not a given manager at a particular time makes a decision which is affected by the market is something he himself may not even know; even the standards he sets himself may be affected by the market without his knowing it! He may, for instance, consider that £n spent on R&D is lavish—judged by international standards—but he may well be subconsciously influenced by the market in this judgement. Who can tell? Long study of this issue leads me to present the following points.

(1) Many managers in the UK and USA have told me the market does affect their decisions, i.e. they do not always take the course they think is in the best medium-term interests of the company because of short-term interest.

(2) Many managers in the UK and USA have asserted otherwise with, I am sure, total sincerity. But *they may be wrong*, for the reasons given above.

(3) Many managers who have 'gone private' or who have found themselves with a handful of owners and off the market, have talked graphically about their changed sense of perspective and freedom from inhibiting pressure.

(4) Managers of public companies in Germany and Japan do NOT feel subjected to the same pressures as their counterparts in the UK and USA, nor I would judge do most in France. This does not mean they are totally insensitive to the market, but simply that their decisions are far less influenced by it, for the following reason.

In a system in which 'hostile' take-overs do not generally exist, like Germany and Japan, there is a limited pressure the market *can* exert. What matters in other words is not the share price itself but the risk that a fall may lead to a take-over and displacement of the existing management. The reason why this problem is less acute in France is because the pattern of shareholdings in many companies makes a contested bid unlikely to succeed.

Does this matter? UK industry was deteriorating at a time when contested bids were virtually unknown: their absence did not ensure long-term thinking. On the other hand, in certain industries, particularly those with long time-scales, it puts UK and US managers at a disadvantage against their rivals, and this disadvantage is compounded if their rivals' cost of capital is less. An excellent analysis was produced in 1992 by the US National Academy of Engineering, entitled *Time Horizons and Technology Investments*.

What Conclusions can we Draw from All This?

(i) That the threat DOES exist in the UK, US and in some French companies and it is a constraint which in certain industries imposes a competitive disadvantage.

(ii) That the threat of takeover is nevertheless an element of the high tension systems which should not be abandoned because of their other imperfections. That for the networked systems they are unnecessary *provided those systems maintain their efficiency.* If the German and Japanese networks become less efficient, they may need some contested bids too. In the UK and US, however, there is no doubt now that the eighties were times of excess to the long-term disadvantage of those countries. If such excesses reappeared it ought to be a matter of concern for governments.

Which Systems Best Meet the Criterion of Accountability?

Business leaders sometimes dismiss the concept of accountability on the grounds that the market takes care of it; that is, competition is all that is necessary. It is indeed true that unless they satisfy their customers they will have no business, but that is quite a different matter from being accountable for the resources with which they have been entrusted and over which they have considerable power. In reality there is a confusion between 'taking account of' and 'being accountable for'. It is noted above that arguably UK and US management certainly takes account of the market. They do indeed watch their share price carefully, which is important to them both in relation to raising new capital and to the possibility of being taken over against their will. Everyone knows, however, that the market's signals are often ambiguous and that it is prey to all sorts of fashions and rumours. In theory the market is supposed to capture all the latest information; in reality it captures buyers and sellers' evaluation of information, which is not at all the same thing. Indeed, if everyone evaluated information the same way there would be no market. Managers can no more be accountable to the market than swimmers to a hungry shark.

Industrial and commercial management have considerable choice and exercise great power, and ought for that reason alone be accountable for its use: the concept of power without accountability in a political context is regarded as intolerable and it is hard to see why it should be acceptable in the economic sphere. At many points the state has already intervened to limit or guide the use of power—for example, safety, pollution, quality— but the use of resources it properly leaves to the market, having constructed as part of the market a formal mechanism by which accountability should operate, namely, the control of management by the board and the appointment of the board by shareholders.

In formal terms all five systems studied above look remarkably similar, with the important exception that Germany puts the supervisory function into a separate organ (the so-called two-tier board system)—an option French companies possess but seldom use. There is, it seems, a spectrum upon which it is possible to place the various systems:

Co-operative_____	Confrontational
Private_____	Public
Informal_____	Formal
Well informed_____	Poorly informed
Collegiate_____	Individualistic

which I characterize as

Networked	High tension

When placing particular systems on the spectrum we must remember that they are not uniform in every dimension. Germany, for instance, is very much towards the networked end, but its two-tier structure has a strong formal framework; and sometimes the flow of information in the UK and USA is better than others, though in neither case does it reach the levels achieved by the German and Japanese banking system. France seems by itself on the spectrum, hovering somewhere in the middle and uncertain which way to move, if at all.

The country by country analyses showed what the various strengths and weaknesses of each were in their own terms. The time has now come to compare their apparent effectiveness. We must never lose sight of what accountability is for—it is to ensure that power and patronage are exercised competently and properly. That means above all keeping up management's standards and taking remedial action where necessary. But to repeat a point made earlier, the test of a system is not the number of CEOs dismissed, but the number who reach retirement without dismissal being in any way desirable.

For there to be an adequate system of accountability certain elements are essential.

(i) There must be an adequate and timely flow of relevant information from management (I have encountered many examples of its being suppressed, or delayed, or more often overlaid by the irrelevant);

(ii) Those who receive it must be able to understand it (it is no use packing a board with worthies who cannot really see deeply into what they are being told); and

(iii) These people, be they bankers, fellow members of the board, or shareholders, must be in a position and willing to exert influence. (If a CEO over-dominates his board its members will feel powerless to act whatever their legal rights. Shareholders often feel helpless—or prefer to act as if they were.)

These elements are present in Germany and Japan but in rather different ways, as we have seen in Chapters 2 and 3. Chapters 5 and 6 show that in the USA and UK they exist in some companies some of the time. The weakness of their systems is precisely that only too often—

- Information is unsatisfactory;
- Boards are not good enough to do their job;
- Neither boards nor shareholders are willing to exert necessary and timely influence, to ensure that management standards are adequate and the board itself capable of making them so.

Chapter 4 shows that France lies somewhere in the middle.

In postulating that the Germans and Japanese in general make a better fist of accountability, I do not suggest their systems are perfect. Their companies fail too; competition always ensures that some will. There are bound to be accidents and mistakes. Some bankers are dilatory or make poor judgements. Some businessmen set out to deceive—and succeed. Of course, some risks fail; but on the whole their systems do seem to satisfy the criteria most of the time.

Is it a coincidence that their systems appear to be the most collegiate in style? It may prove to be the case that contrary to the old saying 'The best committees are committees of one', in fact a committee is actually a more efficient way of running a large and complex modern corporation than relying on a powerful and charismatic leader. A committee of equals—or a committee with a *primus inter pares*—is more likely to have an in-built process for ensuring accountability and is quite likely to be able to do this without sacrificing much, if any, entrepreneurial drive. The Anglo–US–French cult of the individual may be tolerable for small businesses or for bigger businesses for a short time, but may be rather poor at maintaining standards, avoiding foolish mistakes, or securing continuity in the medium and longer terms. Some of the consistently best European companies, like Shell and Unilever, appear to be governed by a more collegiate process. This may be a coincidence, but the connection between sustained success and collegiality of style is one well worth considering. The trouble with dominant figures is their increased propensity as time goes on to listen less, believe their own hyperbole, and as a consequence to make bad mistakes.

There are, however, inherent weaknesses in these systems which may yet undermine them. There is always a danger when any formal structure is ignored. The Japanese board, huge and ceremonial as it is, serves little useful purpose. The dignity that titular membership confers could be provided in other ways. The absence of outsiders reinforces natural inwardness. As a general principle obsolescent structures and institutions present the greatest difficulties in troubled times.

In both countries the absence of what Americans call 'sunshine' enables the dark corners to escape attention: this is inherently dangerous.

Both systems depend to a large extent on the owners' rights being as it were put into commission, which is all very fine and well whilst they remain undemanding, and whilst their expectations are modest. Owners have indeed tended to remain relatively undemanding, accepting low dividends and growth rates as long as steady solid progress was being made. To other eyes such shareholders are patient and supportive; but then no doubt success has made them so. We have yet to see how difficulty will be surmounted. When the Nikkei index was nearly 40,000 I remarked that the Japanese stock market could only be explained on 'Van Gogh' principles, since it seemed to lack a rational method of valuation based on past, present, and expected earnings (capital values were irrelevant as companies cannot be taken over and the assets put to better use). The point is that a Van Gogh painting has no intrinsic monetary value; its price depends entirely on the subjective interest of art lovers. If the Japanese stock market were rationally valued, shareholders might be a little less happy with miniscule dividends and exert greater pressure on company management.

There is a far greater risk in a networked system—that of systemic risk of two kinds. The risk of systemic failure, however, is not wholly absent from the high tension systems. There are particular reasons for the losses incurred by banks in the USA and UK in respect of poor MBO and property loans, but they show only too clearly how industrial misjudgement can weaken banks even when there is a stand-off between the sectors. Indeed, in Chapter 6 it was argued that the stand-off was a contributory factor, as bad lending was based on inadequate information. German and Japanese banks are not exposed to that particular risk, but the Japanese banks have to handle the problems brought about by the decline in the market value of their industrial holdings. This at least is a risk the UK and US banks do not share. Too much emphasis should not be placed on it. The other kind of systemic risk is the unwholesome concentration of power—as the USA felt after the 1920s. The authorities in Germany and Japan are and it is hoped will remain exceptionally vigilant against what this implies.

And the Winner?

This is the point at which I 'nail my colours to the fence' and leave it to each reader to decide in the light of the evidence which system passes the tests with, so to speak, the highest marks. In surveying the scene we must forget the heroics of a bygone age, the brilliant inventors, engineers, and financiers of Britain who set the modern industrial world on its way; the great American entrepreneurs and buccaneers who created many of the world's great corporations, some of which still bear their name; and the Germans and Japanese of yester-year who did likewise. Every company in its fledgeling state still needs its leader who will carry it clear of its competitors and failures; every company throughout its life needs leadership. But the day has come when in many industries the individual virtues though still essential quite clearly last best and produce most when part of a good system. It is no good harking back to simpler solutions which fitted simpler times; they will not recur.

In sifting the evidence we have to make allowances for two kinds of prejudice or bias, the first in favour of the national institutions with which we are most familiar (and by inference against the unfamiliar—like supervisory boards—if we are British), and the second by contrast in favour of everything foreign:

> The idiot who praises with enthusiastic tone
> All centuries but this and every country but his own.

When we survey the UK scene and its relative decline, and consider the differences that manifestly exist between companies in the quality of their governance, we may well feel it difficult truthfully to award it the palm despite the excellence of its best companies. The system just does not consistently meet the criteria. Nor does that of the USA, though it seems to come closer. The reader may feel that the French system is too short on real accountability for comfort, despite the choice between different types of system that their shareholders uniquely have.

The Japanese system has worked remarkably well considering that what is regarded in most countries as the most important component—the board—scarcely functions at all. The reader may well have some difficulty in deciding whether it works as well or better than the German.

As between the two I am inclined to consider that with all its faults and failings, with its tendency towards rigidity, the Germans make their system work more consistently, though it probably needs attention at the margins—a little more daylight and less defensiveness would not come amiss. The supervisory board clearly does not always work as effectively as it should. The feeling in Germany is that their system is the result of a long process of evolution; it suits them and it has served them well. And most of those outside Germany who criticize it do so from positions of relative weakness. My judgement is not based on Germany's phenomenal rise since 1945 but on its development for more than a century. The two terrible conflicts into which its leaders drew the country conceal the probability that continuous peace might well have shown the relative superiority of their corporate governance system much sooner. The doubt now is not so much that it will collapse under the pressure of difficulty and failure, but that success might damage the balance on which the efficient operation of the system has so long relied.

In refusing to award the palm I am not just exhibiting moral cowardice. We are still too close to events to form a substantive judgement. If the German and Japanese systems hit choppy water during the next few years, weaknesses—which are already there—will become more apparent. It may just be that the weaknesses in the US and UK systems have shown up sooner. As I was completing the paper on Germany the steel firm Klockner filed for protection: but then many major UK and US companies were in trouble too, the stresses were apparent in Japan, and even in France a certain amount of public money was being trowelled about to cover cracks in the brickwork. To praise the apparent effectiveness of a particular system is not to advocate that others should seek to emulate it. There are many paths to the top of the mountain.

The Way Ahead

The emphasis throughout the papers on the distinctive nature of each country's culture, history, and institutions means that it would be impossible for one nation to copy another's arrangements in their entirety. What it would be sensible for each to do is to put its own system under the spotlight, using for guidance the criteria suggested above. In the case of the UK a Royal Commission might be entrusted with the task, as suggested in Chapter 6.

The problem for the USA and UK is not one of diagnosis or prescription but of will and self-interest. Many people are locked into the system and do well from it; others less prosperous nevertheless fear change. Some realize only too well that their skills are limited. To take one example, which was discussed in Chapters 5 and 6 in the context of the limited but important role of shareholders. Why should fund managers risk their futures when they have scraped by with 'active investing' for twenty years? What's in it for them in the near future if they start taking an interest in corporate governance, when at best the benefits may take time to show through? True, that if they had been in value investing a decade ago they would probably have shown better results than at present. Their problem is making the change. There is little incentive at present to change since their employers do not require it and their competitors are like them. Furthermore, like their competitors, they operate in a social environment not in solitary confinement, and the world in which they work is full of agreeable salesmen and analysts offering guidance, information, tips (and perhaps hospitality). But if their advice were infallible could they not make fortunes for themselves? One is reminded of the down-at-heel sellers of lucky white heather at race meetings—if it truly brought one luck, why are they so poor and miserable?

In the short term, therefore, many of the players see their interests in different, sometimes conflicting terms. Only in the long term is there a coincidence of interest for shareholder, fund manager, board, a company, and its employees and country; it is in the prosperity of the enterprise. This machine has many parts, and as these papers have shown, they can be made to work effectively together in more than one way. In the short term anything goes. What they will not do is work properly over time if one or more parts are malfunctioning. The analysis in these papers has shown where attention needs to be directed. In the US/UK systems (and to a large extent in France), the passivity of shareholders is not a virtue for it leaves all the running to boards, and that, over time, is to accept the vice of unnecessary risk, in a system in which necessary risk is a virtue. For these countries there are two issues which lie at the heart of the matter: first, the more consistent functioning of boards; and second, a more active role for shareholders (whose hands may need strengthening). And these issues need to be considered in an increasingly international context in which all the world's leading companies will trade and have both establishments and shareholders over much of the globe.

The five studies that form this book of course only cover a part of the industrial and developing world. Many other countries already have sophisticated systems of their own which differ in some respects from those here described. Others will gradually decide what best suits their own history and culture. It would be a vast task to chronicle each and the changes occurring within them. It would, moreover, not seem to be necessary, since the underlying basic principles appear to be universal, however they are applied. Of course, it is one thing to diagnose, another to prescribe, and a third to ensure the patient actually accepts the prescriptions. We must never ever forget that what is here discussed is power, and that in every country someone already enjoys it however well the corporate governance system works as a whole. Reformers beware, therefore, and bear in mind Machiavelli's observation that no popularity awaits you:

It must be remembered there is nothing more difficult to plan, more doubtful of success, nor more dangerous to manage than the creation of a new system. For the initiator has the enmity of all who will profit by preservation of the old institutions and merely lukewarm defenders in those who would gain by the new one.

It is, nevertheless, vital to keep a system of corporate governance under review. It is as important to a nation as any other crucial part of its institutional framework, because on it depends a good portion of the nation's prosperity; it contributes to its social cohesion in a way too little recognized. A proper framework for the exercise of power is an economic necessity, a political requirement, and a moral imperative. So those who recognize this should not be deterred: in the words of the poet, 'Say not the struggle naught availeth.'

Appendix. *The Cadbury Code*
i. The Code of Best Practice

1   *The Board of Directors*

1.1 The board should meet regularly, retain full and effective control over the company and monitor the executive management.

1.2 There should be a clearly accepted division of responsibilities at the head of a company, which will ensure a balance of power and authority, such that no one individual has unfettered powers of decision. Where the chairman is also the chief executive, it is essential that there should be a strong and independent element on the board, with a recognized senior member

1.3 The board should include non-executive directors of sufficient calibre and number for their views to carry significant weight in the board's decisions. (Note 1)

1.4 The board should have a formal schedule of matters specifically reserved to it for decision to ensure that the direction and control of the company is firmly in its hands. (Note 2)

1.5 There should be an agreed procedure for directors in the furtherance of their duties to take independent professional advice if necessary, at the company's expense. (Note 3)

1.6 All directors should have access to the advice and services of the company secretary, who is responsible to the board for ensuring that board procedures are followed and that applicable rules and regulations are complied with. Any question of the removal of the company secretary should be a matter for the board as a whole.

2   *Non-Executive Directors*

2.1 Non-executive directors should bring an independent judgement to bear on issues of strategy, performance, resources, including key appointments, and standards of conduct.

2.2 The majority should be independent of management and free from any business or other relationship which could materially interfere with the exercise of their independent judgement, apart from their fees and shareholding. Their fees should reflect the time which they commit to the company. (Notes 4 and 5)

2.3 Non-executive directors should be appointed for specified terms and reappointment should not be automatic. (Note 6)

2.4 Non-executive directors should be selected through a formal process and both this process and their appointment should be a matter for the board as a whole. (Note 7)

3   *Executive Directors*

3.1 Directors' service contracts should not exceed three years without shareholders' approval. (Note 8)

3.2 There should be full and clear disclosure of directors' total emoluments and those of the chairman and highest-paid UK director, including pension contributions and stock options. Separate figures should be given for salary and performance-related elements and the basis on which performance is measured should be explained.

3.3 Executive directors' pay should be subject to the recommendations of a remuneration committee made up wholly or mainly of non-executive directors. (Note 9)

4   *Reporting and Controls*

4.1 It is the board's duty to present a balanced and understandable assessment of the company's position. (Note 10)

4.2 The board should ensure that an objective and professional relationship is maintained with the auditors.

4.3 The board should establish an audit committee of at least 3 non-executive directors with written terms of reference which deal clearly with its authority and duties. (Note 11)

4.4 The directors should explain their responsibility for preparing the accounts next to a statement by the auditors about their reporting responsibilities. (Note 12)

4.5 The directors should report on the effectiveness of the company's system of internal control. (Note 13)

4.6 The directors should report that the business is a going concern, with supporting assumptions or qualifications as necessary. (Note 13)

Notes

These notes include further recommendations on good practice. They do not form part of the Code.

1 To meet the Committee's recommendations on the composition of sub-committees of the board, boards will require a minimum of three non-executive directors, one of whom may be the chairman of the company provided he or she is not also its executive head. Additionally, two of the three non-executive directors should be independent in the terms set out in paragraph 2.2 of the Code.

2 A schedule of matters specifically reserved for decision by the full board should be given to directors on appointment and should be kept up to date. The Committee envisages that the schedule would at least include:

(a) acquisition and disposal of assets of the company or its subsidiaries that are material to the company;

(b) investments, capital projects, authority levels, treasury policies and risk management policies.

The board should lay down rules to determine materiality for any transaction, and should establish clearly which transactions require multiple board signatures. The board should also agree the procedures to be followed when, exceptionally, decisions are required between board meetings.

3 The agreed procedure should be laid down formally, for example in a Board Resolution, in the Articles, or in the Letter of Appointment.

4 It is for the board to decide in particular cases whether this definition of independence is met. Information about the relevant interests of directors should be disclosed in the Directors' Report.

5 The Committee regards it as good practice for non-executive directors not to participate in share option schemes and for their service as non-executive directors not to be pensionable by the company, in order to safeguard their independent position.

6 The Letter of Appointment for non-executive directors should set out their duties, term of office, remuneration, and its review.

7 The committee regards it as good practice for a nomination committee to carry out the selection process and to make proposals to the board. A nomination committee should have a majority of non-executive directors on it and be chaired either by the chairman or a non-executive director.

8 The Committee does not intend that this provision should apply to existing contracts before they become due for renewal.

9 Membership of the remuneration committee should be set out in the Directors' Report and its chairman should be available to answer questions on remuneration principles and practice at the Annual General Meeting. Best practice is set out in PRO NED's Remuneration Committee guidelines, published in 1992. (Available at the price of £5 from PRO NED, 1 Kingsway, London WC2B 6XF, telephone 071-240 8305.)

10 The report and accounts should contain a coherent narrative, supported by the figures, of the company's performance and prospects. Balance requires that setbacks should be dealt with as well as successes. The need for the report to be readily understood emphasizes that words are as important as figures.

11 The Committee's recommendations on audit committees are as follows:

(a) They should be formally constituted as sub-committees of the main board to whom they are answerable and to whom they should report regularly; they should be given written terms of reference which deal adequately with their membership, authority and duties; and they should normally meet at least twice a year.

(b) There should be a minimum of three members. Membership should be confined to the non-executive directors of the company and a majority of the non-executives serving on the committee should be independent of the company, as defined in paragraph 2.2 of the Code.

(c) The external auditor and, where an internal audit function exists, the head of internal audit should normally attend committee meetings, as should the finance director. Other members should also have the right to attend.

(d) The audit committee should have a discussion with the auditors at least once a year, without executive board members present, to ensure that there are no unresolved issues of concern.

   (e) The audit committee should have explicit authority to investigate any matters within its terms of reference, the resources which it needs to do so, and full access to information. The committee should be able to obtain outside professional advice and if necessary to invite outsiders with relevant experience to attend meetings.

   (f) Membership of the committee should be disclosed in the annual report and the chairman of the committee should be available to answer questions about its work at the Annual General Meeting.

Specimen terms of reference for an audit committee, including a list of the most commonly performed duties, are set out in the Committee's full report

12 The statement of directors' responsibilities should cover the following points:

- The legal requirement for directors to prepare financial statements for each financial year which give a true and fair view of the state of affairs of the company (or group) as at the end of the financial year and of the profit and loss for that period;

- the responsibility of the directors for maintaining adequate accounting records, for safeguarding the assets of the company (or group), and for preventing and detecting fraud and other irregularities;

- confirmation that suitable accounting policies, consistently applied and supported by reasonable and prudent judgements and estimates, have been used in the preparation of the financial statements;

- confirmation that applicable accounting standards have been followed, subject to any material departures disclosed and explained in the notes to the accounts. (This does not obviate the need for a formal statement in the notes to the accounts disclosing whether the accounts have been prepared in accordance with applicable accounting standards.)

The statement should be placed immediately before the auditors' report which in future will include a separate statement (currently being developed by the Auditing Practices Board) on the responsibility of the auditors for expressing an opinion on the accounts.

13 The Committee notes that companies will not be able to comply with paragraphs 4.5 and 4.6 of the Code until the necessary guidance for companies has been developed as recommended in the Committee's report.

14 The company's statement of compliance should be reviewed by the auditors in so far as it relates to paragraphs 1.4, 1.5, 2.3, 2.4, 3.1 to 3.3, and 4.3 to 4.6 of the Code.

Appendix. *ii. Audit Committees*

1 In the main body of the report the Committee recommends that all listed companies which have not already done so should establish an audit committee, and places great emphasis on the importance of properly constituted audit committees in raising standards of corporate governance.

2 Many UK companies already have an audit committee, and a recent research study ('Audit Committees in the United Kingdom', published by the ICAEW, April 1992) has found a steady growth in their number. Audit Committees are now established in 53% of the top 250 industrial firms in the Times 1000, and the figures rises to 66% if unlisted companies and foreign subsidiaries are excluded from the calculation. Most major UK listed financial institutions have also formed an audit committee.

3 Audit Committees are well established in the United States, where they have been a listing requirement of the New York Stock Exchange since 1978. A 1989 study revealed that 97% of major corporations had them. In Canada, they are a legal requirement.

4 If they operate effectively, audit committees can bring significant benefits. In particular, they have the potential to:

(a) improve the quality of financial reporting, by reviewing the financial statements on behalf of the Board;

(b) create a climate of discipline and control which will reduce the opportunity for fraud;

(c) enable the non-executive directors to contribute an independent judgement and play a positive role;

(d) help the finance director, by providing a forum in which he can raise issues of concern, and which he can use to get things done which might otherwise be difficult;

(e) strengthen the position of the external auditor, by providing a channel of communication and forum for issues of concern;

(f) provide a framework within which the external auditor can assert his independence in the event of a dispute with management;

(g) strengthen the position of the internal audit function, by providing a greater degree of independence from management;

(h) increase public confidence in the credibility and objectivity of financial statements.

The effectiveness of audit committees will be reduced, however, if they act as a barrier between the auditors and the executive directors on the main board, or if they encourage the main board to abdicate its responsibilities in the audit area, so weakening the board's collective responsibility for reviewing and approving the financial statements. They will also fall short of their potential if they lack the understanding to deal adequately with the auditing or accounting matters that they are likely to face, if they remain under the influence of any dominant personality on the main board, or if they simply get in the way and obstruct executive management, and stifle entrepreneurial skills.

Audit committees will be as good as the people on them: effectiveness depends crucially on a strong, independent chairman who has the confidence of the board and of the auditors, and on the quality of the non-executive directors. Structure is also important, however, and adherence to the following recommendations, repeated here from the main part of the report, will ensure that audit committees are soundly based.

(a) Audit committees should be formally constituted as sub-committees of the main board to whom they are answerable and to whom they should report regularly; they should be given written terms of reference which deal adequately with their membership, authority and duties; and they should normally meet at least twice a year.

(b) There should be a minimum of three members. Membership should be confined to the non-executive directors of the company and a majority of the non-executives serving on the committee should be independent of the company. This means that apart from their directors' fees and shareholdings, they should be independent of management and free from any business or other relationship which could materially interfere with the exercise of their independent judgement as a committee member. It is for the board to decide in individual cases whether this definition is met.

(c) The external auditor and, where an internal audit function exists, the head of internal audit should normally attend audit committee meetings, as should the finance director. Other board members should also have the right to attend.

(d) The committee should have a discussion with the auditors, at least once a year, without executive board members present, to ensure that there are no unresolved issues of concern.

(e) The audit committee should have explicit authority to investigate any matters within its terms of reference, the resources which it needs to do so, and full access to information. The committee should be able to obtain outside professional advice and if necessary to invite outsiders with relevant experience to attend meetings.

(f) Membership of the committee should be disclosed in the annual report and the chairman of the committee should be available to answer questions about its work at the Annual General Meeting.

7 Specimen terms of reference for an audit committee, compiled from the many examples that are available, are annexed. They are intended simply as a guide for companies who will wish to adapt and build on them to suit their own circum-

stances. They will particularly need tailoring for group rather than single company audit committees. The list of duties in the annex reflects the most commonly performed duties in the UK and the US but no single set of duties has emerged as standard practice.

8 There are many excellent publications on audit committees. The Committee's objective is not to rewrite them but to secure the widespread adoption of best practice. For further discussion of the duties and functioning of audit committees, readers are referred in particular to:

- Chapter 3 of the Report by the Institute of Chartered Accountants of Scotland entitled 'Corporate Governance—Directors' Responsibilities for Financial Statements', February 1992
- Guidance booklets produced by individual firms of accountants
- Chapter 2, section IV of the Report of the National Commission on Fraudulent Financial Reporting (the Treadway Commission), USA, October 1987
- 'Audit Committees in the United Kingdom' by P. Collier, published by the Institute of Chartered Accountants of England and Wales, April 1992.

List of References and Further Reading

ABEGGLEN, JAMES C., and STALK, GEORGE, jun. (1985), *Kaisha: The Japanese Corporation* (Basic Books: Hobart, Ind.).

ALLEN, W. T. (1992), 'Defining the Role of Outside Directors in an age of Global Competition', *Directors' Monthly* (Nov.), 16/11. 1–6.

AOKI, MASAHIKO (1990) (Stamford University and Kyoto University): 'Toward an Economic Model of the Japanese Firm', *Journal of Economic Literature*, 28: 1–27 (Mar.).

AUERBACH, A. J. (1988), *Mergers and Acquisitions, 1988* (University of Chicago Press: Chicago).

——(ed.) (1988), *Corporate Takeovers: Causes and Consequences* (National Bureau of Economic Research; University of Chicago Press: Chicago).

BACON, JEREMY (1979), *Corporate Directorship Practices: The Audit Committee* (Conference Board Report 766; The Conference Board: New York).

——and BROWN, JAMES K. (1977), *The Board of Directors: Perspectives and Practices in Nine Countries* (Conference Board, Report 728: New York).

——and—— *Corporate Directorship Practices: Role, Selection and Legal Status of the Board* (Conference Board, Report 646: New York).

Bank of England Quarterly Bulletin (May 1988) (issued by Economics Division).

BARNETT, CORELLI (1986), *The Audit of War* (Macmillan: London).

BAUMS, THEODOR (1992), 'Takeovers vs Institutions in Corporate Governance in Germany' (Oxford Law Colloquium).

BERLE, A. A., and MEANS, G. C. (1932), *The Modern Corporation and Private Property* (rev. edn. 1967).

BIERSACH, JEFFREY W. (IRRC) (1990) 'Voting by Institutional Investors on Corporate Governance Issues in the 1990 Proxy Season' (Investor Responsibility Research Center) (Oct.).

BLACK, BERNARD S. (1990) 'Shareholder Passivity Re-examined', *Michigan Law Review* (Dec.).

——(1992), 'Agents Watching Agents', *UCLA Law Review*, 39.

——(forthcoming), *The Value of Institutional Investor Monitoring: The Empirical Evidence*.

BLAIR, MARGARET M. (1991), 'Who's in Charge Here? How Changes in Corporate Finance Shape Corporate Governance', *Brookings Review* (Fall).

BREALEY, RICHARD A., and MYERS, STEWART C. (1991), *Principles of Corporate Finance* 4th edn. (McGraw-Hill: New York).

BRUCK, CONNIE (1988), *The Predators' Ball* (Simon & Schuster: New York).

BURROUGH, BRYAN, and HELYAR, JOHN (1990), *Barbarians at the Gate: the Fall of J. R. J. Nabisco* (Harper & Row: New York).

BUSHKIN, ARTHUR A. (President, Telemation Associates Inc.) (n.d.), *Breaking the Language Barrier: How to do Business with the Japanese* (Telemation Associates: Washington, DC).

BUXBAUM, RICHARD M. (1991), *Institutional Owners and Corporate Managers: A Comparative Perspective* (Working paper series; School of Law, Center for Study of Law & Society, California).

CADBURY, SIR ADRIAN (1990), *The Company Chairman* (FitzWilliam Publishing: Cambridge).

The Cadbury Committee Report: Financial Aspects of Corporate Governance (1992) (Burgess Science Press: UK).

CARMOY, HERVÉ DE (1990), *Global Banking Strategy* (Blackwell North America: Blackwood, NJ).

CARY, W. L. (1974), 'Federalism and Corporate Law: Reflections upon Delaware', *Yale Law Journal*, 83.

Central Statistical Office (1989), Share Register Survey.

CHARKHAM, J. P. (1989), 'Corporate Governance and the Market for Control of Companies' (Bank of England Panel Paper, 25; Mar. 1989).

CLARK, RODNEY (1979), *The Japanese Company* (Charles E. Tuttle: Tokyo).

COFFEE, JOHN C., jun. (1991), 'Liquidity versus Control: The Institutional Investor as Corporate Monitor', *Columbia Law Review*, 91/6 (Oct.).

Competitiveness Policy Council (1993), Reports of the Sub-Councils; Report of the Sub-Council on Corporate Governances and Competitiveness Policy Council.

COLLIER, P. A. (1992), *Audit Committees in large UK Companies* (Research Board of ICAEW: London).

CORBETT, JENNY (1987), 'International Perspectives on Financing: Evidence from Japan', *Oxford Review of Economic Policy*, 3/4.

CRYSTAL, GRAEF S. (1991), *In Search of Excess: The Overcompensation of American Executives* (W. W. Norton & Co.: New York).

DAVIS, EVAN, and KAY, JOHN (1990), 'Corporate Governance, Takeovers and the Role of the Non-executive Director', *Business Strategy Review* (Autumn 1990).

DAVIS, STEPHEN M. (IRCC) (1989), 'Shareholder Rights Abroad: A Handbook for the Global Investor' (Investor Responsibility Research Center: Washington, DC).

Deutsche Bundesbank (n.d.), 'The New Principles 1 and 1a Concerning the Capital of Banks' (Special Series (2a).

DIXON, NORMAN F. (1988), *Our Own Worst Enemy* (Futura: London).

DORE, RONALD (1988), *Flexible Rigidities: Industrial Policy and Structural Adjustment in the Japanese Economy, 1970–80* (Athlone Press: London).

DRUCKER, PETER F. (1968), *The Practice of Management* (William Heinemann: London).

EISENBERG, M. A. (1989), 'The Structure of Corporation Law', *Columbia Law Review* (Nov.), 89/7.

EPSTEIN, EDWARD JAY (1986), *Who Owns the Corporation? Management vs Shareholders* (Priority Press Publications: New York).

ETZIONI, AMITAI (1988), *The Moral Dimension: Towards New Economics* (The Free Press: New York).

Federal Securities Law Reports, 1117 (20 Mar. 1985), pt. ii, 'Responsibilities of Corporate Officers & Directors under Federal Securities Laws' (Commerce Clearing House: Chicago).

FLEISCHER, ARTHUR, jun.; HAZARD, GEOFFREY C., jun; and KLIPPER, MICHAEL Z. (1988), *Board Games: The Changing Shape of Corporate Power* (Little, Brown & Co.: Boston).

FRANKS, J., and MAYER, C. (1990), 'European Capital Markets and Corporate Control', *Economic Policy* (Winter).

FRIEDMANN, W. (1984), 'Business Finance in the United Kingdom and Germany', *Bank of England Quarterly Bulletin*, 368–75 (Sept).

FUKUDO, HARUKO (1992), 'A New World Order and Japan' (Speech to American Chamber of Commerce in London, 21 May).

'The Future Development of Auditing: A Paper to Promote Public Debate' (1992) (a paper by the Auditing Practices Board; 16 Nov.).

GALBRAITH, J. K. (1967), *The New Industrial State*.

—— (1975), *The Great Crash, 1929* (Penguin Books: Harmondsworth).

German Monopolies Commission (1973–83), summaries of the first five *Biennial Reports* (Nomos Verlagsgesellschaft: Baden-Baden).

GIARDINA, JAMES A., and TILGHMAN, THOMAS S. (1988), *Organization and Compensation of Boards of Directors* (Arthur Young: New York).

GIBSON, R. J., and ROE, M. J. (1992), 'Understanding the Japanese Keiretsu; Overlaps between Corporate Governance and Industrial Organization' (Stamford Law School Working Paper, Aug.) (Stamford, Calif.).

GOOLD, MICHAEL; CAMPBELL, NIGEL; and KASE, KIMEO (1990), 'The Role of the Centre in Managing Large Diversified Companies in Japan' (Manchester Business School) (Sept.).

GOYDER, GEORGE (1987), *The Just Enterprise* (André Deutsch: London).

GRAHAM, B., and DODD, D. L. (1934), *Security Analysis* (McGraw-Hill: New York).

HALBERSTAM, DAVID (1986), *The Reckoning* (William Morrow & Co.: New York).

HEARD, JAMES E., and SHERMAN, HOWARD D. (1987), *Conflicts of Interest in the Proxy Voting System* (Investor Responsibility Research Center: Washington, DC).

HERZEL, LEO, and SHEPRO, RICHARD (1990), *Bidders and Targets: Mergers and Acquisitions in the US* (Basil Blackwell: Cambridge, Mass.).

HOUSTON, WILLIAM, and LEWIS, NIGEL (1992), *The Independent Director: Handbook and Guide to Corporate Governance* (Butterworth-Heinemann: Oxford).

HUTTON, WILL (1990), 'Takeover Legacy has Touched us all at Great Cost', *Financial Times* (3 Sept.).

Industrial Groupings in Japan, 1982/83 (1982) (Dodwell Marketing Consultants: Tokyo; Sept.).

INSEE (n.d.), *Rapport sur les comptes de la nation*.

The Institute of Chartered Accountants of Scotland (1988), *Making Corporate Reports Valuable* (Kogan Page: London).

Investor's Chronicle (1992), 'Management Buy-out' (Survey; 3 Apr.).

IPPOLITO, RICHARD A. (1986), *Pensions, Economics and Public Policy* (Pension Research Council of the Wharton School, University of Pennsylvania).

IRRC (1990), *Writing Proxy Voting Guidelines* (Feb.) (*Investor Responsibility Research Center: Washington, DC*).

JACOBS, MICHAEL T. (1990), 'Corporate Boards and Competitiveness' (A paper presented to the Conference on Fiduciary Responsibilities of Institutional Investors, New York University, June).

——(1991), *Short-Term America: The Causes and Cures of our Business Myopia* (Harvard Business School Press: Boston, Mass.).

JOHNSTON, ALEXANDER (1980), 'The Panel and Code' in *The City Take-over Code* (Oxford University Press).

JOHNSTON, KRISTA M. (IRRC) (1990), 'How Institutions Voted on Social Policy Shareholder Resolutions in the `1990 Proxy Season' (Investor Responsibility Research Center: Washington, DC) (Sept.).

KAKU, RYUZABURO (1991), Speech to Caux Round Table, Caux, Switzerland on 20 Aug. 1991 (Mr Kaku is the Chairman of Canon Inc.).

KEELEY, MICHAEL C. (n.d.), 'Deposit Insurance, Risk, and Market Power in Banking' (Mr Keeley is Vice-President, Cornerstone Research, 1000 El Camino Real, Menlo Park, CA 94025, USA).

Korn Ferry International Survey, 1990.

KUROKAWA, M. (1988), Chairman of Nomura Securities, Inc., Speech.

KYNASTON, DAVID (1990), 'The City and Industry, 1880–1990: An Uneasy Relationship' (paper to the LSE Business History Unit, 15 Oct.).

LAMY, RENÉ (1992), 'Narration Authentique d'une OPA'.

LINDEN-TRAVERS, KEN (1990), *Non-Executive Directors: A Guide to their Role, Responsibilities and Appointment* (Director Books: Cambridge).

LIPTON, MARTIN (1992), 'Takeover Bids and United States Corporate Governance' (speech given to the Oxford Law Colloquium).

——and ROSENBLUM, STEVEN A. (1991), 'A New System of Corporate Governance: The Quinquennial Election of Directors', *University of Chicago Law Review*, 58/1 (Winter).

London Stock Exchange (1992), *A History of the London Stock Exchange.*

LONGSTRETH, BEVIS (1991), *Modern Investment Management and the Prudent Man Rule* (Oxford University Press: New York).

——and KANE, NANCY (1992), 'Executive compensation: A Current Issue of Corporate Governance' (paper given to University of California, San Diego, Nineteenth Annual Convention of Securities Regulation Institute, 22 Jan.).

LORSCH, JAY, W., with MCIVER, ELIZABETH (1989), *Pawns and Potentates: The Reality of America's Corporate Boards* (Harvard Business School Press: Boston, Mass.).

——with——(1993), *Corporate Governance and Investment Time Horizons* (Harvard Business School Press: Boston, Mass.).

LOWENSTEIN, LOUIS (1991a), 'The Changing Role of the Stockmarket in the United States', *Rutgers Law Review* (Spring), 43/3.

——(1988), *What's Wrong with Wall St.: Short-Term Gain and the Absentee Shareholder*, (Addison-Wesley: Reading, Mass.).

——(1991), *Sense and Nonsense in Corporate Finance* (Addison-Wesley: Reading, Mass.).

MACE, MYLES L. (1971), *Directors: Myth and Reality* (Harvard Business School Classics, Harvard Business School Press: Boston).

MAIN, B. G. M., and JOHNSTON, J. (1992), 'The Remuneration Committee as an Instrument of Corporate Governance' (University of Edinburgh).

McLagan, Patricia, and Krembs, Peter (1988), *On-the-Level: Performance Communication that Works* (McLagan International: Minnesota).

Marsh, Paul (London Business School) (1990), *Short-Termism on Trial* (Institutional Fund Managers Association, London).

Marston, C. (1993), *Investor Relations Project* (University of Northumbria at Newcastle: Newcastle Business School, and University of Glasgow: Glasgow Business School, Dept. of Accounting and Finance).

Meyer, Brown, and Platt (1991), 'American Depositary Receipts', *Cross-Border Newsletter* (25 Sept.).

Monks, Robert A. G., and Minnow, Nell (1991), *Power and Accountability* (Harper Collins: USA).

Morgan, E. V. and A. D. (1990), *The Stockmarket and Mergers in the UK* (The David Hume Institute: Edinburgh).

Nash, John M., and Lajoux, Alexandra R. (1988), *A Corporate Director's Guide to Responsibility and Liability under Current State Law and Federal Securities Laws* (rev. edn.) (Publications Inc.: Washington, DC).

National Academy of Engineering (1992), *Time Horizons and Technology Investments* (National Academy Press: Washington, DC).

Neuberger, Doris, and Neumann, Manfred (1991), 'Banking and Antitrust: Limiting Industrial Ownership by Banks?', *Journal of Institutional and Theoretical Economics*, 147.

Nippon Steel Corporation (1984), *Nippon: The Land and its People* (Nippon Steel Corporation: Japan).

O'Barr, William M., and Conley, John M. (1992), *Fortune and Folly: The Wealth and Power of Institutional Investing* (Business One Irwin: Homewood, Ill.).

Ohmae, Kenichi (1987), *Beyond National Borders: Reflections on Japan and the World* (Dow Jones-Irwin: Homewood, Ill.).

On Trust (1992), Report of the NCVO/Charity Commission Working Party on Trustee training, Chair: Winifred Tumin (NCVO Publications).

Paribas Conjoncture, [André Lévy-Lang], *Japan: Waiting for Confidence.* (Compagnie Financière de Paribas, Paris.)

PE-International Survey, Summer 1991.

Pemberton, Louis W. (1989), *The Enigma of Japanese Power* (Bear Stearns & Co.; Fortune Book Excerpt, 8 May 1989).

Porter, Michael (1992), *Capital Choices* (report to Council of Competitiveness).

Price Waterhouse, *Doing Business in France* (London).

PRO NED 1990 Survey.

Pugh, Peter (1991), *A Clear and Simple Vision* (Cambridge Business Publishing).

Robertson, Sir L. (1993), Speech to the National Association of Pension Funds (25 Feb.).

Rock, Edward B. (1991), 'The Logic and (Uncertain) Significance of Institutional Shareholder Activism, *Georgetown Law Journal*, 79/3: 399–590 (Feb).

Roe, Mark (1991), *Political Elements in the Creation of a Mutual Fund Industry*.

Sametz, Arnold W., in collaboration with Bickster, James L. (1991), *Institutional Investing: The Challenges and Responsibilities of the Twenty-first Century* (Business One Irwin: Homewood, Ill.).

Schrager, Ronald E. (1986), *Corporate Conflicts: Proxy Fights in the 1980s* (Investor Responsibility Research Center: Washington, DC).

Seiroren (1992), *Eiri Kigyo no shushoku no shonin ni kan-suru nenji hokokusho*.

Shearson Lehman Hutton Securities, 'The Secret Restructuring of European Financial Services'.

SHLEIFER, A., and SUMMERS, L. H. (1988), *Corporate Takeovers: Causes and Consequences* (University of Chicago Press).

SINGH, AJIT (1992), 'Regulation of Mergers'.

SMITH, ADAM (1986), *The Wealth of Nations*, i–iii (Penguin Classics: Harmondsworth).

SMITH, TERRY (1992) *Accounting for Growth* (Business Books: London).

SODERQUIST, LARRY D., and SOMMER, A. A. (1990), *Understanding Corporation Law* (Practising Law Institute: New York).

TAKEUCHI, HIROTAKA (1991), 'The Japanese System of Corporate Governance: Will Stakeholders Remain Silent?' (prepared for UK/Japan 2,000 Group 8th annual conference, Brocket Hall, 6–9 March 1992; Hitotsubashi University, Dec.).

Toyo Keizai Shinposha (1991), *Toyo keizai tokei geppo*.

—— (1992), *Kigyo keiretsu soran*.

TRICKER, R. I. (1984), *Corporate Governance* (Corporate Policy Group, Oxford; Gower Publishing: Aldershot).

WAGNER W. H., and LAU, S. C. (1971), 'The Effect of Diversification on Risks', *Financial Analysts' Journal*, 27 (Nov.–Dec.), 48–53.

WALTER, INGO, and SMITH, ROY C. (1990), *Investment Banking in Europe* (Blackwell: Oxford).

WHITING, ROBERT (1990), *You Gotta Have Wa'* (Vintage Books: Random House, New York).

WIENER, MARTIN (1981), *English Culture and the Decline of the Industrial Spirit, 1850–1980* (CUP).

WOLFEREN, KAREN VAN (1990), *The Enigma of Japanese Power* (Macmillan: London).

WRIGHT, RICHARD W., and PAULI, GUNTER A. (1987), *The Second Wave: Japan's Global Assault on Financial Services* (Waterlow Publishers: London).

YAMAMOTO, ISAO (1992), 'Corporate Governance in Japan' (paper given at Namura Equity Seminar).

YATES, IVAN (1992), *Innovation, Investment and Survival of the UK Economy* (Royal Academy of Engineering: London).

YOSHINO, M. Y. (1968), *Japan's Managerial System: Tradition and Innovation*.

Index